HOME AFTER FASCISM

THE MODERN JEWISH EXPERIENCE

Deborah Dash Moore and Marsha L. Rozenblit, editors
Paula Hyman, founding coeditor

HOME
AFTER FASCISM

Italian and German Jews after the Holocaust

Anna Koch

INDIANA UNIVERSITY PRESS

This book is a publication of

Indiana University Press
Office of Scholarly Publishing
Herman B Wells Library 350
1320 East 10th Street
Bloomington, Indiana 47405 USA

iupress.org

© 2023 by Anna Koch

All rights reserved
No part of this book may be reproduced or utilized in any form or by any
means, electronic or mechanical, including photocopying and recording, or by
any information storage and retrieval system, without permission in writing
from the publisher. The paper used in this publication meets the minimum
requirements of the American National Standard for Information Sciences—
Permanence of Paper for Printed Library Materials, ANSI Z39.48-1992.

Manufactured in the United States of America

First Printing 2023

Cataloging information is available from the Library of Congress.

ISBN 978-0-253-06695-4 (hardcover)
ISBN 978-0-253-06696-1 (paperback)
ISBN 978-0-253-06697-8 (e-book)

CONTENTS

Acknowledgments   vii

List of Abbreviations   xi

Introduction   *1*

1. Returning Home?   *20*

2. Entangled Memories   *56*

3. Reclaiming Home   *102*

4. Belonging   *141*

    Conclusion: The Old House and Its Shadows   *181*

Notes   *191*

Bibliography   *243*

Index   *285*

ACKNOWLEDGMENTS

I BEGAN THINKING ABOUT THIS PROJECT WHEN I wrote my MA thesis on the German Jewish writer Hermann Kesten and poured over the many letters he wrote after the war. Michael Brenner first gave me the idea to look at Kesten's letters in Munich's literary archive, and he has been a source of advice since these early days. I would like to thank him for his continuous support. More than a decade has passed since then, and there are numerous people who have generously helped this project in various ways. I had the great fortune to work with several brilliant women when I began this research project as a graduate student at New York University (NYU). Foremost, I would like to thank my *Doktormutter*, Marion Kaplan, who has been a role model both as a scholar and mentor. Marion has shown endless energy and willingness to help in all matters small or big. Our discussions about gender, emotions, and Jewishness were crucially important for this work, and her own scholarship continuous to inspire me. I am immensely grateful for her support and encouragement. Next to Marion, Mary Nolan has been a crucial source of advice, carefully reading my work and making sure I do not lose sight of the bigger questions. I would like to thank Ruth Ben-Ghiat for sharing her insights on Italian memory culture and Fascism and Maura Hametz for encouraging me to think deeper about home and belonging. These scholars have offered the rare combination of brilliance and kindness in their feedback, and I cannot thank them enough for the time and effort they invested in me and my work.

While many archivists helped facilitate my research in Germany, Italy, the United States, and Israel, I would especially like to acknowledge Laura Brazzo from the Archivio Centro di Documentazione Ebraica Contemporanea, Gisèle Lévy from the Archivio Unione delle Comunità Ebraiche Italiane, Silvia Haia Antonucci from the Archivio Storico della Comunità Ebraica di Roma, Cristina Cangi from the Archivio Diaristico Nazionale, Misha Mitsel from the JDC Archives, Alon Tauber from the Zentralarchiv zur Erforschung der Geschichte der Juden in Deutschland, and Frank Mecklenburg from the Leo Baeck Institute; they helped me find materials I would have otherwise overlooked.

vii

viii | *Acknowledgments*

This study would not have been possible without generous fellowships from the Memorial Foundation of Jewish Culture, the Studienstiftung des Deutschen Volkes, the Center for Jewish History, the NYU Tikvah Center for Law & Jewish Civilization, the German Historical Institute in Rome, the European Holocaust Research Infrastructure, and the Fondation pour la Mémoire de la Shoah. I am also deeply grateful for the travel and research grants I received from the Social Science Research Council, the Graduate School of Arts and Science, and the Taub Center for Israel Studies at NYU, as well as for NYU's Mellon Dissertation Fellowship.

Beyond financial support, a number of these fellowships have also provided me with a scholarly community. During two workshops, the Leo Baeck fellows, Raphael Gross, Miriam Rürup, and Daniel Wildmann, have provided valuable comments as well as a warm environment of constructive criticism. The fellows at the Center for Jewish History, Judy Siegel, Donna Frieze, and Francesca Bregoli, have offered crucial feedback during my time there. The German Historical Institute in Rome has offered me a scholarly home during my months of research in the city, and I would like to especially thank Lutz Klinkhammer and Ruth Nattermann for sharing their expertise on Italian history. I am also grateful for the opportunity to present this work at numerous workshops. In the early stages, the participants of NYU's Modern Europe Dissertation Writers' Workshop have provided crucial feedback; more recently, colleagues at the University of Southampton, the University of Leeds, and the Dubnow Institute have asked important questions and provided helpful comments.

I truly enjoyed being a part of the community of graduate students at NYU, and I am grateful for the friendship and support of Allan Amanik, Franco Baldasso, Tom Fleischman, Felicitas Jaima, Laura Honsberger, Shira Klein, Larissa Kopytoff, Dan Tsahor, Sarah Zarrow, and many others. Silvano Longhi has shared his knowledge and research findings, and I am very grateful for our many stimulating exchanges over coffee at the Stabi. Numerous people have read drafts, shared ideas, and provided thoughtful comments on this work in the past decade. I am grateful to Leora Auslander, Martin Baumeister, Deborah Cohen, Daniel Cohen, Federico Finchelstein, Ben Frommer, Atina Grossmann, Emiliano Perra, Lidia Santarelli, Michele Sarfatti, Anne Clara Schenderlein, Joachim Schloer, Guri Schwarz, and Stephan Stach for generously sharing ideas and providing feedback at different stages of this project. I am sorry that David Shneer will not see this book in print. Our many conversations on Jews in the GDR and antifascism

Acknowledgments | *ix*

helped me tremendously, and he is greatly missed. Shirli Gilbert, Joachim Schloer, Mark Hewitson, Mererid Puw-Davis, Eva Frojmovic, Griselda Pollock, and Diane Koenker all welcomed me into their respective scholarly communities. I am grateful for their support. During my time at the University of Leeds, our weekly writing group proved crucial in keeping me going, especially during those lockdown months, when the group became virtual but not distanced. The sound of my colleagues typing accompanied the writing of the book's final draft. Diane Otosaka and Helen Finch helped me see beyond a historian's perspective during our stimulating conversations in our memory study group.

I would like to thank the editorial team at Indiana University Press and, in particular, Dee Mortensen, Gary Dunham, Nancy Lightfoot, Anna Francis, and Pete Feely, for providing helpful guidance and editorial input. Deborah Dash Moore and Marsha Rozenblit, the series editors, were enthusiastic and extremely helpful, and I cannot thank them enough for their constructive comments and support in this process. I would like to thank Rachel Kantrowitz for her careful reading of this manuscript and correcting many misplaced commas. Special thanks are due to the two anonymous reviewers for their careful reading of the manuscript and their thoughtful comments.

I would like to thank Yifat and Thomas Geve for talking with me about Thomas's experiences during and after the war and for generously making his artwork available. Federico Benadì, Giulia Cohen, Emanuele Cohenca, Sandro Lopez Nunes, and Fabrizio Roccas all invited me into their homes and answered my many questions about their lives under and after Fascism. I am very grateful for their patience and generosity.

I would like to thank my brothers and my parents for supporting me, always, and offering comfort and an immensely cozy home whenever I needed it. My parents instilled in me a love for books and reading, fed my thirst for historical stories, travelled with me to visit some of the more depressing corners of Germany's capital, and years later provided much needed childcare. I am grateful for all of it. This book has been a constant companion in my children's life, and I am grateful to Ben and Ella for always cheering me on. Ben, you often asked why I am writing such a sad book. Admittedly the stories this work tells are often sad, sometimes shatteringly so. They are stories of disappointments, of indifference, cruelty, and betrayal. But there are also stories of immense courage, rebuilding, and believing the world could be better. The joy and happiness you and Ella give *x* | *Acknowledgments*

me made it easier to write the sad stories, and when I look at the two of you, I think the optimism of those who believed in a kinder world, against all odds, may be justified. Most of all, I would like to thank Shaul Mitelpunkt for his constant support and unfaltering belief. Always a song on his lips, and another brilliant idea to share, endlessly encouraging and never lost for a joke, Shaul has been my "portable home" in the numerous cities we have lived in these last ten years. I dedicate this book to you.

ABBREVIATIONS

AJC	American Jewish Committee
AJDC	American Jewish Joint Distribution Committee, also Joint
ANED	Associazione nazionale ex deportati (National Association of Ex-Deportees)
CRDE	Comitato ricerche deportati ebrei (Committee for the Search for Jewish Deportees)
CRSDE	Comitato ricerche soccorsi deportati ebrei (Committee for the Search and Rescue of Jewish Deportees)
DELASEM	Delegazione per l'assistenza agli emigranti ebrei (Aid Committee for Jewish Emigrants)
DPs	displaced persons
EGELI	Ente di Gestione e Liquidazione Immobiliare (Office for the Management and Liquidation of Property)
FRG	Federal Republic of Germany
GDR	German Democratic Republic
IMT	International Military Tribunal
KdAW	Komitee der Antifaschistischen Widerstandskämpfer (Committee of Antifascist Resistance Fighters)
NSDAP	Nationalsozialistische Deutsche Arbeiterpartei (National Socialist German Workers' Party)
OdF	Opfer des Faschismus (Victims of Fascism)
PCI	Partito Comunista Italiano (Italian Communist Party)
PNF	Partito Nazionale Fascista (National Fascist Party)
RSI	Repubblica Sociale Italiana (Italian Social Republic)
SA	Sturmabteilung (Stormtroopers, the Nazi paramilitary group)
SED	Sozialistische Einheitspartei Deutschlands (Socialist Unity Party of Germany)
SMAD	Soviet Military Administration
SBZ	Sowjetische Besatzungszone (Soviet Occupation Zone)
SS	Schutzstaffel (Protective Squad)
UCII	Unione delle Comunità israelitiche italiane, also Unione (Union of Italian Jewish Communities)

xi

xii | Abbreviations

VSJF   Verband Schweizerischer Jüdischer Fürsorgen/Flüchtlingshilfen (Association of Swiss Jewish Welfare/Refugee Aid)

VVN   Vereinigung der Verfolgten des Naziregimes (Association of Persecutees of the Nazi Regime)

WJC   World Jewish Congress

HOME AFTER FASCISM

INTRODUCTION

IN APRIL 1945, THOMAS GEVE, A FIFTEEN-YEAR-OLD FORMER inmate of Buchenwald concentration camp, drew a picture book depicting his experiences. On the last page of the booklet, we see a car with two signs that read "we are free" and "we are going home." Several people head toward the vehicle, suitcases nearby. Below the picture Geve wrote again, "we are going home!" In June 1945 Thomas left Buchenwald, spending the summer at a Red Cross home for teenage refugees in Zug, Switzerland. At the end of August 1945, he reconnected with his father, who had managed to immigrate to England in 1939, and a few months later, Geve left Switzerland to reunite with him. He did not return to Beuthen, the Silesian border town where he grew up, or to Berlin, where he had lived with his mother before their deportation.[1] I asked him what he thought about when he wrote about returning home and if he considered living in Germany. He wrote to me, "After the liberation I first of all wanted to find out about my mother. I would have joined her anywhere, even in Berlin."[2] Home for him was not a place. It was his family. Without his mother, there was no reason to remain. Like Geve, many Jewish survivors desperately wanted to go home after the war. Yet they grappled with the questions of what and where *home* was.[3]

Hans Winterfeldt, a Berlin Jew and Auschwitz survivor, asked himself, "Home? Did I still have a home?"[4] Goti Bauer, an Italian Jew who, like Winterfeldt, had been deported to Auschwitz, felt similarly: "We were liberated," she wrote, "but the emotions of this moment were overshadowed by an incredible sadness and by fear of a future full of uncertainties: The return home? But which home? With whom?"[5] Bauer returned to her hometown of Fiume (Rijeka) in the hope of finding her brother, but he had not survived the war. She soon left what was now a Yugoslavian city, eventually settling in Milan. Similarly, Winterfeldt went to his hometown to search for relatives; luckier than Bauer, he soon reunited with his parents. Three years later, Winterfeldt left Berlin and emigrated to New York.

Like Bauer and Winterfeldt, other Italian and German Jews depicted the difficulties they faced when trying to return home after the war. *Home*

Figure 0.1. Drawing by Thomas Geve, titled *Wir fahren heim* (We are going home). © Thomas Geve. (From the collection held at Yad Vashem, Jerusalem.)

after Fascism tells their stories and explores the meanings of home for people whose home had been violently destroyed. They faced the challenge of renegotiating their place in national communities that had targeted them for persecution and extermination. This book focuses on Italian and German Jews' complex and often changing feelings toward their home and highlights the ways in which three distinct national contexts—East Germany, West Germany, and Italy—shaped the parameters in which they could formulate their responses to the question *what is home*? in the immediate aftermath of the war.

The Destruction of Home

The destruction of German Jews' homes began when the Nationalist Socialist German Workers' Party (Nationalsozialistische Deutsche Arbeiterpartei, or NSDAP) came to power in 1933. The creation and protection of a nation based on blood and race and the elimination of those labelled racially unfit formed the basis of Nazi ideology and excluded Jews from the national community. Two months after Adolf Hitler's appointment as chancellor, he demanded a boycott of Jewish businesses and issued the Law for the Restoration of the Professional Civil Service that excluded Jewish civil servants from their professions. In 1935 the Reichstag passed the infamous Nuremberg laws, which prohibited Jews from marrying or having sexual relations with whom the Nazis termed Aryans and stripped them of their political rights, turning them into second-class citizens.

Most German Jews reacted with shock to these attacks on their rights.[6] As the situation gradually deteriorated, many considered emigration. But they had always lived in Germany and spoken German, and they felt they belonged there. While in hindsight the trajectory of Nazi persecution may seem clear, mixed messages and temporary lulls in persecution made it difficult for contemporaries to foretell what was coming.[7] Some tried to adapt to the situation and cope with the hostilities they faced in the hope that the antisemitic persecution would abate or the regime would fall. Others emigrated early on, leaving behind families and friends, homes, properties, and jobs.

Those who remained witnessed the Nazis appropriating their homes, businesses, and belongings. Nazi laws and regulations increasingly restricted Jews' access to public space and turned their environment into a hostile space.[8] On November 9 and 10, 1938, Nazi leaders unleashed a pogrom against the Jewish population that has become known as Kristallnacht or Reichskristallnacht. The SA (Sturmabteilung, the Nazi paramilitary group) and the Hitler Youth looted and destroyed Jewish businesses, homes, and synagogues. The SS (Schutzstaffel, protective squad) and Gestapo arrested about thirty thousand Jewish men. A few days later the Nazi state legalized forced Aryanization, and Jewish businesses not yet sold were confiscated, closed, or transferred to non-Jewish owners. By this point most Jews desperately tried to flee the country. About 278,000 managed to emigrate, leaving a little over 200,000 Jews in Germany on the eve of the Second World War.

Following the outbreak of war on September 1, 1939, the government imposed new restrictions on Jews such as a strict curfew and banning Jewish individuals from public spaces and public transportation. Starting in September 1941, the Nazis evicted Jews from their homes and resettled them in designated areas and houses, the so-called Jewish houses (*Judenhäuser*), and forced Jews over the age of six to wear a yellow Star of David on their clothing. Jews faced desperate living conditions, received reduced rations, and were subjected to forced labor. Most Germans remained indifferent as the fate of their Jewish compatriots deteriorated, some became hostile, and many profited as the Nazis robbed Jews of their businesses and possessions and fired them from their professions. The social death of German Jews preceded their physical murder in the Nazi death camps.[9] Systematic deportations to camps and ghettos in occupied Poland, the Baltic states, and Belorussia began in the fall of 1941. Some Jews escaped deportations because of their marriages with non-Jews, others were able to pass as Aryan under a fake name, and some went into hiding. The Nazis murdered about 165,000 German Jews.

In Italy, the Fascists coming into power in 1922 did not immediately threaten the country's Jewish population. Like National Socialism, Fascism aimed at the recreation of society, yet initially Fascist ideology promoted assimilating Italian Jews rather than excluding them. In fact, a significant number of Jews became members of the National Fascist Party (Partito Nazionale Fascista, or PNF).[10] Others joined the antifascist opposition. After 1922, antisemitic as well as anti-Jewish polemics in newspapers and magazines increased, and some members of the PNF were outspoken antisemites. Yet few Italian Jews picked up on this latent antisemitism in the regime's attitudes toward Jews.[11]

The open persecution of Italian Jews began in July 1938 when a group of Fascist scholars published the *Manifesto della razza* (Manifesto of race).[12] The manifesto constituted the theoretical foundation for the enactment of the racial laws the following fall. On October 6, 1938, the Grand Council of Fascism issued a *Dichiarazione sulla razza* (declaration on race), and on November 17, 1938, the regime imposed the Laws for the Defense of the Race, which outlawed intermarriages between what they termed Aryans and non-Aryans.[13] The Fascist regime adopted racial legislation without pressure from its German ally.[14] Over the following years, more restrictions followed, pushing Italian Jews to the margins of society. Like Germans, non-Jewish Italians appeared largely indifferent to the plight of their Jewish compatriots, and many turned away from Jewish friends and neighbors.[15] By and large the non-Jewish population approved of the racial legislation. Shopkeepers, academics, liberal professionals, and many others benefitted from the restrictions placed on their Jewish colleagues.[16]

For most Italian Jews, the enactment of the racial laws in 1938 was a radical turning point in their lives, and they suffered emotionally, economically, and socially.[17] Yet only about 3,000 of around 46,500 Jews who were living in Italy in 1938 fled the country after the issuing of racial legislation.[18]

Economic difficulties and bureaucratic obstacles prevented some from leaving, and few had families abroad that could help in procuring visas. Deeply attached to their home country, the majority of Italian Jews judged leaving the country an exaggerated response.[19]

Fascist Italy's racist policies further radicalized with the outbreak of war. The Fascist state subjected foreign as well as some Italian Jews to internment and forced labor. In the fall of 1941, Fascist squads attacked a number of synagogues, yet physical violence remained sporadic before the German occupation.[20] In July 1943 military defeats and fear of mass mobilization and strikes in northern Italy led the Grand Council of Fascism to issue a vote of no confidence, and King Victor Emanuel asked Il Duce to resign. Mussolini was arrested and replaced by Marshal Pietro Badoglio, who soon entered into negotiations with the Allies. The two parties signed an armistice on September 3, 1943, made public on September 8. Italy surrendered unconditionally. At the same time, German troops started taking over the Italian peninsula and quickly occupied northern and central Italy. By mid-September the country was divided between territories under the control of the Allied Military Government in the South—the king, and Badoglio had limited influence, and the German forces in the North. German troops freed Mussolini from prison, and he subsequently established the Repubblica Sociale Italiana (Italian Social Republic, RSI), also known as the Republic of Salò.

Six weeks after Mussolini's fall, the Allies freed about two thousand mostly foreign Jewish internees from the Ferramonti di Tarsia internment camp in Calabria.[21] Yet the vast majority of Italian Jews resided in the northern part of the country, and their fate deteriorated rapidly. After Mussolini's fall the RSI needed to provide explanations for Fascism's failure. The Salò Fascists pointed to the betrayal of an inner enemy and named the Jews prominently among the traitors.[22] In September 1943 the RSI issued *Il Manifesto di Verona* (the manifesto of Verona), which under point seven declared: "That those belonging to the Jewish race be considered foreigners. During the war, they belong to an enemy nation."[23] Two weeks later the minister of the interior, Guido Buffarini Guidi, ordered the arrest and internment of all Jews, as well as the seizure of their property.

September 1943 marked the beginning of systematic deportations of Jews to the concentration and extermination camps in central and eastern Europe. While the Germans planned and executed the murder of Italy's Jews, the Italian authorities in the Republic of Salò assisted them. Without

6 | Home after Fascism

the collaboration of the Italian police and militia and access to their resources and information, the deportation of Italy's Jews would have proven difficult.[24] Many ordinary Italians also participated in the anti-Jewish persecution, informed Germans, and looted Jewish property.[25] Others, however, mounted significant resistance against the Republican Fascists and the German occupiers. Numerous young Italian Jews joined this resistance movement. Other Jews found shelter in the countryside, assumed false names, or hid in church dormitories, convents, and medical institutions.[26] Many Italians were willing to hide Jews, sometimes as an act of resistance, sometimes for monetary compensation, and sometimes out of sheer humanity. Several thousand Italian Jews managed to cross the border to Switzerland illegally. The majority of the about thirty-nine thousand Jews who lived in the RSI in 1943 survived the war. The Nazis and their collaborators killed about seven to eight thousand Italian Jews.[27]

Liberation and Its Aftermath

In Italy, Fascist and German forces surrendered in late April 1945. Germany's capitulation followed on May 8, and one month later, the four Allied powers formally assumed authority. In both countries Jewish communities found themselves in a disastrous situation: impoverished, traumatized by persecution, and—to differing degrees—decreased in number. German Jews faced a significantly more dramatic population loss. In January 1933 around 500,000 Jews had lived in Germany; about 278,000 of them managed to flee. About 15,000 Jews survived the war in Germany, the majority of them protected by a non-Jewish partner in a so-called mixed marriage. About 9,000 returned from camps in Poland and Czechoslovakia. Many of the survivors left, while a small number of Jews, about 4 to 5 percent of those who had emigrated, returned. By 1948 about 20,000 members were registered in the reestablished Jewish communities.[28] In addition to German Jews, a much larger number of Jewish refugees from eastern Europe, over 250,000, lived in Germany temporarily as displaced persons (DPs). Most of them left the war-torn country as soon as possible, though a small fraction, about 15,000, remained in Germany after 1950. In particular in the South, the DPs formed the majority in a number of Jewish communities. Relations between DPs and German Jews proved difficult as cultural, linguistic, and religious differences divided the two groups.[29]

The Italian Jewish community also faced significant loss. Prewar Italy counted about 48,000 Jews. About 6,500 Italian Jews emigrated, while others crossed the border illegally to Switzerland after 1943. Almost all the latter returned at the end of the war, and others came back from Palestine, South America, and the United States.[30] Only about 800 Italian Jewish deportees returned from the camps. Italy also hosted Jewish refugees; about 13,000–15,000 mainly eastern European Jewish DPs sojourned in Italian camps after the war, but only an insignificantly small number of them decided to remain.[31] After the war the Jewish communities counted about 26,000 members.[32] In Italy as in Germany, some Jews preferred not to join the official communities, making it challenging to establish exact numbers.

Italian and German Jews rebuilt their lives in countries marked by the war; struggling with shortages of food, fuel, and housing; and soon shaped by the beginnings of a new international conflict. Particularly in Germany, the divisions that would lead to the Cold War impacted the country's postwar trajectory. In 1945 the Allies had divided Germany into four zones that soon merged into two spheres. In 1947 Britain and the United States formed an administrative state for its territories called Bizonia, which became Trizonia once France joined in 1948. In June of the same year, the western Allies announced a currency reform linked to the US Marshall Plan. Shortly thereafter, in May 1949, came the formation of the Federal Republic of Germany (FRG), created from the occupation zones formerly administered by the United States, Britain, and France. The German Democratic Republic (GDR) was founded on the territory occupied by the Soviets in October of the same year. In 1949 the occupying powers in both East and West Germany replaced their military governors with civilian leaders; in the West the occupation formally ended in May 1955 and in the East in September of the same year.

The division of Germany affected the reconstruction of Jewish life. Like others, Jews could not easily move from one occupation zone to the other, and regulations as well as the social makeup of the Jewish communities (*Jüdische Gemeinden*) differed from zone to zone. Most DPs settled in the zones administered by the United States and more remigrants returned to the western zones, though several prominent, mostly leftist Jewish intellectuals and politicians chose to settle in the Soviet occupied zone. The Jewish communities in West Germany counted about 20,000–30,000 members in the first postwar decade. The East German communities had some 3,500 members in 1945, and that number decreased further in the following years.

8 | *Home after Fascism*

However, a significant number of persons of Jewish origin did not register with the official community.

Some returnees, like the writer Alfred Kantorowicz, who established a journal titled *Ost und West* (East and West), hoped to form a bridge between the two sides, and initially there seemed room to collaborate across the zones. Jews of all four occupation zones attended the constituent meeting of the Jewish postwar organization, the Zentralrat der Juden in Deutschland (Central Council of Jews in Germany), in Frankfurt on July 19, 1950. The Zentralrat represented Jews living in both German states until 1961, and the Berlin Jewish community remained united until 1953.[33] The division into East and West happened gradually, and Jews in the four zones shared experiences and concerns.

The Cold War also shaped Italy's reconstruction. Both the United States and Britain underestimated Fascist violence and considered Germany as the real threat, leading to a comparatively mild peace treaty, signed in Paris in February 1947. Fear of the strength of the Italian Communist Party, and a perception of Italians as gentle, naive, and malleable, led the Americans to heavily influence the political development in Italy and aim to prevent a Communist victory in postwar elections.[34] The first general elections took place in 1946, resulting in a narrow win for the Christian Democrats and a coalition government under Alcide De Gasperi. Together with the election, a constitutional referendum took place that abrogated the monarchy. Most Italian Jews, disappointed in the king, supported the move to a republic. The 1948 constitution established a parliamentary democracy, and elections were held in April of the same year. The Christian Democrats received 48 percent of the vote and continued to dominate Italian politics in the following decades. Italy, like West Germany, benefitted economically from US aid, though the country remained deeply divided, with a much poorer South. Most Italian Jews continued to live in the North and increasingly in larger cities. The Jewish communities in both Milan and Rome grew significantly in the postwar period. By the mid-1950s, Rome counted twelve thousand Jewish residents and the Milan community six thousand.[35] Many smaller Jewish communities struggled, and some eventually vanished entirely.[36]

After the war, Jewish survivors in both Italy and Germany quickly reestablished communities, reopened synagogues, founded newspapers, and organized assistance for their neediest members. Often homeless, and in many cases unable to work, numerous Italian and German Jews had to rely on relief from international aid organizations as well as social welfare and support from reestablished Jewish communities. Most of their property and belongings had been looted, and many found their homes destroyed or occupied by strangers. In particular for Germany, and increasingly also for Italy, there is significant literature dedicated to the institutional reorganization and material recovery of the Jewish communities as well as to the restitution process.[37] Material rebuilding, however, was only a part of the reconstruction process. In both countries Jews tried to come to terms emotionally with their losses, make sense of their persecution, and reclaim their homes.

Meanings of Home

Scholars across various disciplines have examined the meanings of home, yet the term remains elusive.[38] We often think of *home* as a place, a country, a city, a neighborhood, a house, or an apartment. Indeed, a spatial perspective plays an important role in investigating Jews' relationships to their homes after the Holocaust.[39] But for returning Jews, home was not necessarily, or not merely, territorial. Home could be people and memories, food and smells, language and culture. One's childhood home as well as its language and culture play a crucial role in one's life, and in the formation of the self. As Eva Hoffman writes, "It is because these things go so deep, because they are not only passed on to us but are us, that one's original home is a potent structure and force and that being uprooted from it is so painful."[40]

Home conveys feelings of belonging, attachment, and safety. In his essay "How Much Home Does a Person Need?" the Austrian-born writer and Holocaust survivor Jean Améry likewise emphasizes the linkages between home and self. For him, *Heimat* entails our use of language, the ability to understand the world around us, our sense of belonging, our status as citizens, and the connection between us and a collective. In short, he defines home as "security."[41] He continues, "At home we are in full command of the dialectics of knowledge and recognition, of trust and confidence."[42] The place we call home provides us with a surrounding that is familiar and readable. At home we move easily, freely, and safely.

This book explores these different aspects of *feeling at home*. Emotions play a crucial role in humans' relationships to their homes. And indeed emotions shape the human world: they influence decision-making processes, human behavior, and social relations. In recent decades, historians have paid increasing attention to the importance of emotions.[43] While this

10 | *Home after Fascism*

study is not a history of emotions per se, we cannot understand Jews' post-war relationships to their home without considering emotions.[44]

Italian and German Jews' sensual and emotional relationships to their homes were highly individual. And yet, as historians of emotions have pointed out, emotional relations are influenced by our environment. Relying on Barbara Rosenwein's concept of *emotional communities*, I suggest that returning Jews formed such communities and expected their members to depict their feelings toward home in specific ways.[45] German and Italian Jews used expressions of emotion to highlight their belonging to or distance from various groups. Emphasizing detachment was one way in which Jews in West Germany justified their living in what many now considered the country of murderers. Communists of Jewish origin in East Germany stressed an emotional connection to their comrades, while Italian Jews' emphasis on attachment to their homeland highlighted their belonging within the national community. I explore these performative aspects of emotions to analyze how they functioned as signifiers of distance or attachment.

This book contributes to the discussion of what constitutes home by focusing on people who had particularly difficult, fractured relationships to their homes, and it portrays a moment when these relationships were in flux. The Nazis and Fascists had attacked Jews' sense of feeling at home—they had appropriated the language, taken over the public space, and violently excluded them from the national community. They had robbed them of the feeling of safety and poisoned their recollections. They stole houses and apartments in which Jews had often lived for decades—places full of memories and small things with great emotional value. And they appropriated the home countries that had provided them with a sense of belonging and shaped their self-understanding. Some Jews turned away, identifying the rise of Fascist regimes as a sign that their home had been destroyed. Some decided that they must have been mistaken to imagine that a place that created these regimes could have ever been their home in the first place.

Not all Jews who lived in Germany and Italy could feel at home there after the war. They had returned to their physical homes, but they no longer felt they were in their affective homes. Their former homes no longer provided them with a feeling of safety, and many perceived them as hostile and often scary environments. Others, however, insisted that their homes were still their homes, that they could not be taken from them. After the war, they faced the challenge of reclaiming their homes and renegotiating their places in their national communities. Those who managed to do so either reconstructed the homes of their past or envisioned radical new beginnings that would allow them to shape the future. This book reveals Jews' often changing and at times contradictory feelings toward their homes and suggests that we need to understand home as a constantly negotiated and renegotiated concept rather than as a fixed entity. Those who stayed found different ways to reconstruct their senses of home. Distinct national contexts played a crucial role in how they considered the possibilities of regaining a sense of home.

Most Italian Jews remained deeply attached to their home country and aimed to return to what they considered a briefly interrupted path of integration. Fascist racism had excluded them as not truly Italian; after the war they declared the Fascist *ventennio* (1922–1945) not part of their country's history. Italian Jews tended to emphasize a return to normalcy and their wish to resume the lives that war and persecution had violently interrupted. In contrast, few German Jews perceived the Nazi past as a temporary lapse. Rather, most understood these years as an irreparable break that had transformed or destroyed their home. Some held onto smaller parts of home. They found a sense of belonging in the culture or language or felt attached to a specific region or city. They retrieved parts of their home from the Nazi past and thus created what I term *niches of belonging*. They developed a fractured sense of home: one that allowed them to remain distant from their home country but still gain some sense of belonging.

Others looked to the future. Some German Jews, especially those with strong political convictions, often Socialist or Communist, planned to build a new and better Germany. Many of them settled in the eastern part of the country where radical change seemed to be occurring. Rather than returning home, they wished to build a new home. Yet in many ways the postwar realities fell short of the future they had imagined, leading to disillusionment. Some Jews in West Germany likewise hoped to contribute to building a different postwar society. But the farce of denazification, the resumption of important political posts by former Nazis, and a widespread refusal to face the past deeply troubled and disappointed them and made regaining a sense of home difficult.

Remembering Home

Feeling at home depends on memories. Recollections of creaking stairs, recognizing every stone in a street, remembering the smell of a favorite

12 | *Home after Fascism*

dish, being able to navigate streets blindly, or recollecting the myriad times of having walked the same path—all provide a sense of home. At times returning Jews could hold onto these memories and upon their return recognized the same streets, trees, paths, smells, and sounds. But, in particular for German Jews, these memories were often tainted; they had become cues for loss and suffering rather than feelings of home and safety.

A return forced a confrontation with the past. By showing Jews' earliest efforts to mourn and commemorate their loss, this book joins recent works that have upended the notion that Jews remained silent about the Holocaust after the war.[46] Geve's picture book, which he drew "as a memento [*Andenken*]" of his time in Auschwitz and Birkenau, offers just one example of the myriad ways German and Italian Jews recounted their experiences in the immediate aftermath of the war.[47] Geve made the book in the hope of sharing his experiences with his father. He drew, rather than wrote, because he was struggling to find the right language. Survivors often found it difficult to communicate their experiences, and while some felt the urgent need to recount what happened, others were unable to do so.

These individual memories of persecution did not exist in a vacuum. Rather, Jews communicated their experiences within a broader collective framework. Following Maurice Halbwachs's work, this study approaches memory as a social process and highlights the intertwined relationships between individual memories and collective narratives. While most works on Holocaust memory examine public representations of the past, this book focuses on the individuals who mourned, commemorated, and narrated their experiences.[48] It unearths how individual Jews were informed by and contributed to memory narratives within the Jewish communities as well as how individuals and communities reacted to and influenced the emerging national representations of the past. It also considers how these, in turn, shaped personal and communal recollections.[49] I examine the often painful intersection between states' efforts to use the past as a means to shape the present and the memories of victims trying to come to terms with their traumatic experiences.

This interplay between private and public recollections of the past crucially affected Jews' sense of belonging after the war. Others have pointed to the importance of the construction of a shared past, suffering, and achievements in shaping individuals' sense of belonging to a larger collective.[50] Jews' postwar understanding of the most recent past did not depend merely on their war experiences but also on how they interpreted these experiences—whether they considered themselves as part of a larger community of Jewish victims, as members of a community of antifascists who fought against Nazism, or primarily as citizens of an occupied country. Looking at three different contexts (West Germany, East Germany, and Italy), this book allows us to see how Jews made different choices in situating their recollections vis-à-vis the emerging narratives. Their narration of the past placed them either within or without particular "communities of experience," to borrow a term from Mary Fulbrook.[51]

In Italy, even though Jews and non-Jews had different experiences under Fascism and under the German occupation, the dominant postwar narratives, both within the Jewish community and among most individual Jews, emphasized a shared past. After the war Italian Jewish leadership contributed to the narrative that described Italians as *brava gente* (good people) who had acted honorably during the war, opposed antisemitism, and protected their Jewish neighbors from the Germans. Few challenged this dominant discourse. Historians have looked at Italian Jews' willingness to accept the myth of the good Italian with astonishment. "How can we explain that among the persecuted there was an equal will to forget as among the persecutors?" asks Carla Forti in her fascinating history of Pisan Jews' memory of the murder of Pardo Roques, president of their community.[52] Guri Schwarz emphasizes pragmatic reasons and shows that the Jewish leadership supported the myth to facilitate reintegration, while Shira Klein's recent study looks at the longer trajectory and argues that the roots of Italian Jews' attachment reach back to the nineteenth century.[53] Undoubtedly both postwar pragmatism as well as Italian Jews' comparatively strong integration into Italian society before the racial legislation and their long-held patriotism set the stage for their persistent wish to reintegrate after 1945.

If we understand Italian Jews' longing for their Italian homeland as a starting point, their acceptance of and even contribution to memory narratives that free Italy from guilt become less surprising. They needed this narrative that placed Jews and non-Jews on the same side (in opposition to Nazi Germans) in order to regain a feeling of belonging. Italian Jews' wish to reclaim their home also explains their efforts to subsume Jewish war experiences under the postwar narrative around the Resistenza (resistance). The notion of a unified Italian resistance against the German occupier, which depicted the years of 1943–1945 as a war of liberation and obscured popular support of Fascism, played a crucial role in the reconstruction of Italian

Home after Fascism

society.[54] Italian Jews, who had been violently excluded from the national community under Fascism, now emphasized Jewish contributions to the resistance and thus constructed their experiences as part of a larger Italian narrative.

Like in Italy, postwar Germany also promoted a narrative that claimed innocence. But since Germans had not mounted any substantial resistance to the Nazis, German Jews could neither accept nor adopt this narrative. Neither could they be part of a conception of home that "meant forgiving, and also a measure of forgetting."[55] Rather than narrating a shared past, they highlighted the radical difference of their experiences. Both the public and private voices of most German Jews disputed emerging and soon widespread conceptions of German innocence, pointing to the population's responsibility for Jewish suffering.

While a narrative that highlighted German innocence did not allow for the construction of a shared past, the public memory focusing on antifascist resistance that emerged in the Soviet occupation zone enabled some, in particular, though not only, Communists of Jewish origin, to create such a narrative. Similar to the Italian case, this emphasis on antifascism enabled Jews to link their recollections with a larger community of memory, in this case of antifascist resisters. Some employed the state's narrative in order to integrate particular Jewish memories of the war into the public antifascist culture, while others highlighted the common, universal experiences of all antifascists. However, others struggled with and against a narrative that created a hierarchy between Communists and other victims of the Nazi regime.

In all three national contexts, individual Jews narrated their pasts in varied ways, and not all subscribed to larger communal memories. Some, if few, individual German Jews depicted the German people as misguided and innocent, both in the East and in the West. Some Jews in Italy opposed the narrative of the good Italian and pushed for a public acknowledgment of Italian antisemitic persecution and collaboration. Memories in both countries were fractured, fluid, and at times contradictory. Different narratives competed and frequently dominant voices marginalized those with differing perspectives.[56]

Home beyond Borders

Narratives about the past are not confined to the borders of the nation-state. As Stefan Berger and Bill Niven point out in the introduction to *Writing the*

History of Memory, there is "a need not only to look 'below' the level of the national when seeking to understand collective memory in its full variety, but also 'above' it towards transnational memory frameworks which transcend 'national containers.'"[57] Jewish memory narratives in all three postwar states were influenced by broader transnational perspectives. Jews from all over—German and Italian Jews who remained in exile, international and American Jewish relief organizations, Jewish DPs, representatives of Palestinian and later Israeli Zionist organizations, and Jewish soldiers from occupying armies—all commented on and shaped Italian and German Jews' understandings of the past.

Transnational Communist understandings of the past that linked the experiences of Jews during the Second World War and resistance to Fascist violence with other fights against racial oppression and colonialism influenced the discourse among Communists of Jewish origin in the Soviet occupation zone and later the GDR. By contrast, most West German Jews constructed their memories within a larger framework of Jewish suffering. More so than before the war, Jews in West Germany considered themselves part of a broader, transnational Jewish community that had shared the same experiences. Most non-German Jews, whether in Palestine or the United States, however, vehemently rejected German Jews' choice to remain in what they now could only perceive of as the country of murderers. This rejection of a future for Jews in Germany led to a widespread sense of guilt about living in the wrong place—in particular, though not only, in West Germany. The negative discourse around the rebuilding of Jewish life in postwar Germany had less impact on Communist and Socialist Jews since they often had few ties to the broader Jewish community.

Individual German Jews often felt deeply conflicted. They found themselves caught between their love for certain aspects of their home country and the knowledge of Germany's horrific crimes and its condemnation in the eyes of most Jews. Italian Jews did not face this challenge, even though they also by and large also considered themselves part of a larger Jewish collective. While the international Jewish community fiercely condemned Germany and Germans after the war, it supported Italians' self-portrayal as brava gente.

By examining the impact of discourses and people who crossed borders and by shedding light on Jews' negotiation of a sense of home in three distinct national contexts—East Germany, West Germany and Italy—this study "break[s] the confines of traditional national history."[58] Jews who returned to other places across Europe faced many similar challenges, and there are numerous parallels as well as important differences to Jewish postwar histories in Poland, Czechoslovakia, Hungary, Poland, or France. However, integrating further examples would have rendered this undertaking unfeasible.[59] Italy and Germany make for particularly fruitful case studies to examine Jews' return home after Fascism, as these countries arguably brought about the two most dominant Fascist regimes.[60]

Both countries experienced violent regimes, and—to differing degrees—both states persecuted their Jewish minorities. Jews in both countries faced persecution not by the hands of a foreign occupier but by their own state, their police, and their neighbors. Most Italian and German Jews had been deeply patriotic, and the exclusion hit them hard. Despite the great variety of German and Italian Jews' individual experiences during the war, they all shared the loss of home. Both countries lost their sovereignty after the war—Germany fully, Italy partially—and both West Germany and Italy then became parliamentary democracies with strong Christian Democratic parties. More than in other Western European countries, the Communist Party remained strong in Italy after 1945, and the country shared East Germany's emphasis on antifascism in its public memory. All three states demonstrated a wish to leave the past behind, proved reluctant to admit their responsibility for war and genocide, and aimed to refashion themselves as welcoming to Jews.

There are few histories that look at postwar Jewish lives comparatively, and none that focus on Germany and Italy.[61] Reluctance to compare the histories of Jews in Italy and Germany may stem from the notion that the Fascist and National Socialist regimes are incomparable in terms of racial ideology and policy.[62] This assumption can be partially ascribed to a historiography that for a long time contributed to the myth of the good Italians. Historian Renzo de Felice, for example, denied that National Socialism and Italian Fascism constituted similar systems, pointing to the lack of antisemitism in Mussolini's state.[63] Even scholars who venture a comparison of the two regimes often emphasize differences in regard to racism.[64] In an article comparing the origins of the two Fascist regimes, Adrian Lyttleton states that "Italian Fascism was decidedly the exception—even in western Europe—so far as the marginal role of anti-Semitism is concerned."[65]

It is true that Italians never committed mass war crimes on a scale comparable to the Germans. Yet scholarship on the antisemitic legislation of the fall of 1938; the collaboration in the deportation of Italian Jews;

Italian concentration camps; and Italian war crimes in the Balkans, Greece, Libya, and Ethiopia has challenged the notion that Mussolini's Italy had been a Fascist regime free of racist politics.[66] While this book does not compare Nazi and Fascist racism or antisemitism, it shows how both Italian and German Jews struggled with the aftereffects of vicious and violent racial exclusion and reveals commonalities and overarching experiences of surviving Jews, such as the search for relatives, the loss of property, and mourning for the dead.

Comparing the two cases does not mean equating the countries' histories. Rather, a comparative viewpoint shows crucial differences in terms of racism and genocidal violence: Fascist Italy, in contrast to Nazi Germany, never crossed the line to systematically killing its Jewish population. Antisemitism played a far more dominant role in Nazi ideology, and the German Jewish community underwent a far more dramatic decrease in its numbers and membership. This study underlines the consequences of the different roles the two countries played in the Holocaust for Jews' postwar relationships with their home countries. It acknowledges these differences as a starting point for distinct narrative strategies in the Jewish communities. That is, while German Jews could not evade Germany's responsibility and struggled with their own choice to live in the country of murderers, Italian Jews could more easily obfuscate racial laws and collaboration.

A third point of comparison arises as the stories of Jews in East and West Germany diverged during the Cold War. Jews on the two sides of the Iron Curtain shared experiences and sentiments about their lives in Germany, and the histories of East and West remained intertwined rather than separating into two clearly divided trajectories.[67] Yet faced with the decision of whether to return, different motives drove Communists of Jewish origin. The distinct developments of the two German states influenced their Jewish inhabitants' lives. The shared beliefs of Italian and East German Jews in antifascist narratives point to similarities not merely across national boundaries but also across the East-West divide. In the existing literature on Jews in postwar Germany, West Germany often stands for the entire country, but this book highlights postwar experiences on both sides of the Iron Curtain, and contributes to several recent studies that have used transnational and comparative perspectives to unravel the legacies of war and violence in postwar Europe.[68]

To reconstruct Italian and German Jews' expressions of feelings and perceptions of their home, my research relies heavily on letters, memoirs,

18 | *Home after Fascism*

diaries, and oral testimonies. Some of these were published; many others I found in archives in Italy, Germany, Israel, and the United States. These sources, like all other sources, have shortcomings. Memory is fallible, and memoirs, sometimes written decades later, are shaped by the author's present. Writers aim to create a linear narrative from their memories, and memoirs, letters, and diaries are often distorted by self-fashioning. Writers also shape their narration with a particular audience in mind. Still, these sources allowed me to analyze how surviving Jews told their story after the war and foreground the views and feelings of individuals rather than looking at the reconstruction of Jewish communities or organizations.[69]

Such documents also make it possible to include people the Nazis persecuted as Jewish but who did not actively associate with an official Jewish community. Neither the German nor the Italian Jewish community was internally homogenous. While this book attempts to highlight trends and frictions within Italian and German Jews' relations to their home, it cannot claim to provide a complete picture of the myriad voices. However, it includes people who stood at the margins of Jewish life and whose stories are often excluded from the historiography. Acknowledging that individual as well as collective understandings of what constituted Jewishness were in flux after the Holocaust, this work examines individuals' changing relationships with their Jewish origin rather than postulating a fixed definition of Jewishness.

The book is organized thematically, with each chapter focusing on a different aspect of Italian and German Jews' postwar relationships with their homes. Chapter 1 depicts German and Italian Jews' initial consideration of whether or not to return to their home countries and traces their return journey and their emotions upon arrival. Focusing on returnees' efforts to make sense of their traumatic experiences, chapter 2 illustrates how Jews' understanding of the past was shaped by and in turn influenced emerging postwar narratives. Chapter 3 examines Jews' efforts to reclaim their homes by bringing perpetrators to justice, reeducating the non-Jewish population, battling latent antisemitism, and demanding a return of their homes and assets. Chapter 4 examines how experiences of persecution changed Italian and German Jews' self-understandings and depicts their efforts to recreate a sense of belonging. While not strictly chronological, the order of the chapters contains a chronological element, as they depict people's frequently unsuccessful journeys home, in the spatial as well as the emotional sense.

Home after Fascism begins with Italian and German Jews' reflections about their returns to their homes after their liberation, which in some cases predated the end of the war. The book's stories end in the mid-1950s. At this point most memoirs and diaries turn from the struggles of rebuilding that dominated accounts of the first postwar years to narratives of more settled lives. By then, most Italian and German Jews had either managed to reclaim their houses or apartments and jobs or had found substitutes. Their economic conditions had significantly improved. In Italy, the American Jewish Joint Distribution Committee, the main Jewish aid organization, decided to end its assistance in October 1948, and after 1951, it halted food packages for German Jews.[70] In 1953 the West German government issued its indemnification law, which provided some compensation for surviving Jews. By that time the flux of emigration and remigration of German and Italian Jews had not come to a full stop, but most of those who urgently wanted to get out had left by the mid-1950s.

While this is a story about a particular time and people, the challenges Jews faced during and after the war remain pressing. They, like so many refugees today, did not leave home of their own volition. They were forced to run for their lives, and they felt tremendous loss. This book shows the deep affection and persistent love people felt for their home and the suffering that comes with losing it. The attachment to home explains, along with other more mundane reasons, why, against all odds, some returned and why some decided to forgive and forget. It explains why some tried to build something new out of the rubble, why they searched for something small— a tree, a song, a piece of bread that still looked, sounded, and smelled like home—even if it no longer could be the home it once was.

1

RETURNING HOME?

IN 1939, GIORGINA LEVI, A JEWISH SCHOOLTEACHER FROM Turin, left Italy for Bolivia. Born in 1910 into a family with strong Socialist leanings, Levi felt strongly attached to her home country and struggled with the decision to leave. But living conditions for her and her partner, Heinz Arian, a German-born Jew, had become increasingly difficult after the Italian Fascists issued the racial laws in 1938. Once in Bolivia, the couple faced taxing material conditions. Despite the news of atrocities, they idealized not merely Italy but Europe at large from afar.[1] In December 1940 Levi wrote to a former teacher who had become a friend and frequent correspondent, "[My husband and I] tried to imagine our excitement at the moment of return, when you can see Genoa looming from afar: it seemed too much to both of us. Homesickness truly is a disease."[2] Levi never felt at home in her Bolivian exile, and like many other Italian Jews who had left Italy due to antisemitic persecution, she planned to go back as soon as possible. She returned in 1946.

The German writer and literary critic Alfred Kantorowicz fled his home country in 1933, living first in Paris and later in the United States. Like Levi, he returned after the war. They shared not only the experiences of persecution, exile, and return but also a strong belief in communism. The ways they imagined the return to their homelands, however, could hardly have been more different. In his diary Kantorowicz wrote of his "black fears" and doubts about a future in Germany, and in a letter to a friend, the writer Heinrich Mann, he related that the "decision to return to the materially devastated, morally depraved land of conflict, which after all is the country of our origin and our language, was not easy."[3] People around him tried to discourage him from returning, and he expected to "find there hunger and hatred, open and hidden Nazism, material and moral destruction."[4] But, he explained, he felt too old to adjust to life in the United States, growing anticommunism made living there increasingly difficult, and as he wrote to Mann, he still felt "that my place and my task lie there [in Germany]."[5] He returned to East Berlin in 1946.

Like Kantorowicz and Levi, thousands of German and Italian Jews returned to their homes after the war. They set out from various places: some returned from exile, others had survived in their home countries in hiding, and a small number embarked on the journey back from the camps. This chapter traces their returns, from pondering what life would be like in their home countries, through their journeys back, to their arrivals. It depicts the distinct ways German and Italian Jews narrated their returns and pays close attention to the emotions they described. For some the return to the original site of trauma triggered horrific memories, their homeland now only serving as a constant reminder of what they had lost, while others seemingly effortlessly picked up their lives where they had been interrupted. Age, gender, political outlooks, and national context all impacted how Jews perceived the possibility of a return and experienced their arrival. While most Italian Jews believed in an unproblematic return, many German Jews were anxious about the future. Most of the surviving German Jews chose not to live in Germany after the war; those who did resettle there needed to justify their choice to themselves and those around them in the face of a frequently hostile attitude toward rebuilding Jewish life in postwar Germany.

Pondering the Return

The end of the war opened options. Return became possible for Jews who had survived the war in exile, and those who had survived in Europe could now consider leaving. Neither remigration nor emigration was easy; borders remained closed, visas were difficult to obtain, and journeys were long and uncertain. Still, many had spent the war years living from day to day, focused on survival, and now faced the question of how to spend the rest of their lives: Should they try to immigrate to Palestine and establish a Jewish state there or remain in their place of exile? Should they stay in Germany or leave? Could they return home?

Most German Jews who chose to return pondered their decision at length. They devoted much time and space to rationalizing their choice, providing multiple reasons for why they wound up rebuilding their lives

Home after Fascism

in Germany. Others maintained that their postwar return to Germany had not been a choice at all but rather a matter of contingencies or simply due to the absence of any other options.[6] Letters from exiles to newly reestablished communities inquiring about conditions in postwar Germany show how survivors tried to evaluate the situation and what factors played a role in their decision. Viktor Karfunkel, a doctor who had immigrated to Shanghai in 1936, planned to return with his family in 1946. He asked the Frankfurt Jewish community about antisemitism in postwar Germany, his chance of being able to open a medical practice, and the housing and food situation.[7]

Professional opportunities played an important role in the decision-making process. In particular, older survivors feared not being able to adapt to and find positions in a new environment.[8] Concerns about their own or their partner's health likewise influenced their choices. German Jews also frequently mentioned their wish to be reunited with family members when explaining why they chose to return. Persecution had broken families apart. Children fled without their parents, mothers were deported without their children, and husbands and wives separated to have better chances of survival. The hope of finding another surviving family member prompted many to set out on the return journey as soon as possible, even if they did not necessarily plan to stay in Germany.[9] In 1949 the painter Lea Grundig returned from Palestine to Dresden to be reunited with her husband, whom she had not seen for a decade.[10] Charlotte Holzer, a member of the Jewish resistance group Herbert Baum, survived the war in Germany but was separated from her daughter and partner. Her decision, she explained, depended on whether or not any of her loved ones had survived: "If I don't find anyone, I will go to France and not stay in Germany."[11] She found both her partner and her daughter, and while the latter soon immigrated to Israel, Holzer and her partner stayed. Others remained because their relatives did not wish to leave. Many of the fifteen thousand Jews living in Germany at liberation had survived because their non-Jewish partners had protected them. With their partners, they had retained a connection to Germany, and often non-Jewish partners remained close to their families and therefore wanted to stay.

Conditions in returnees' places of exile likewise crucially mattered. People were more likely to return from Shanghai, Turkey, or South America than from England or the United States. Those who had rebuilt their lives in the UK or North America may have felt nostalgic for their former lives in Germany, but few seriously considered a postwar return to the economically devastated, occupied country.[12] Yet while many European Jews succeeded in building a life in the United States, the small number of Jewish members of the Communist Party who had immigrated to the United States faced an increasingly hostile atmosphere that pushed some to return to their former homes.[13] The pediatrician Inge Rapoport left the United States after the House Un-American Activities Committee launched an investigation into her and her husband for engaging in Communist activities. Rapoport feared a return to Germany, and the couple tried to find a home in several other places after they were forced to leave the United States. Yet the Cold War reality made it difficult for the two members of Communist organizations to find a new home. When her husband was offered the position of chair of biochemistry at Humboldt University in East Berlin, Inge Rapoport felt it was their only option.[14]

Gerhart Eisler, a prominent member of the Communist Party who later became the head of East German radio, was sentenced to jail in the United States for misrepresenting his party affiliation on his immigration application. When released on bail, he managed to flee the country on a Polish ship.[15] A few months later, the United States deported his wife, the journalist Hilde Eisler. She later explained that the decision to return was out of her hands: "I had no choice. I had no choice because, first, I was married and my husband wanted to return—he was a politician."[16] Beyond the pressures put on them by the United States, Eisler depicted a conflict of interests between herself and her husband—he wished to go back for his career even though she did not want to live in Germany. Yet there is little that points to this conflict in the letters she sent to her husband while he was imprisoned as an alien enemy. In March 1947 Hilde wrote, "It is a month today that they put you in jail—for no reason at all, just taking away a man's freedom under a flimsy pretext, and all this in the name of democracy. A fine democracy." She continued, "You had your share of Nazi persecution in Europe, it is time for you now to go home and do something constructive."[17] In June 1949, after Gerhart's flight from the United States, Hilde, detained on Ellis Island, expressed joy about her husband's return to a friend: "You cannot imagine how happy I am for Gerhart that he finally won this heartbreaking battle for his return home. And it is very gratifying for me to see how wonderfully he was received everywhere."[18] At this point, she stated that she was "very anxious as you can imagine, to join my husband and to see all old friends again."[19] Did the decision appear worse in hindsight when she was explicitly asked about it in an interview decades later? Or had she wanted

24 | *Home after Fascism*

to appear content about the return to her husband and friends, not sharing her fears? Her letters clearly show her disdain for the United States, and she seemed certain that her husband's place was in the GDR. Reading through her letters, we can see, however, that while she mentions her husband's excitement and wish to return, she only relates her wish to be with him and her friends; she does not mention any personal longing for Germany.

Like Eisler, Arnold Zweig was drawn to East Germany because of his political convictions. He explained that he decided to remigrate "in order to use German literature once again as an antifascist weapon in the spiritual fight of humankind."[20] As an author he had found it difficult to make a living in Palestine, where he and his family had survived the war, and he became increasingly critical of the Zionist *Yishuv* (the Jewish settlers' community in Mandate Palestine).[21] He kept his wish to return a secret from his wife, Beatrice Zweig, for a long time. When he eventually told her, she had a nervous breakdown, and her friend remembered that she cried when she left Palestine in 1948.[22]

Gender affected decisions about where to live. Like Hilde Eisler and Beatrice Zweig, other Jewish women did not want to return to Germany while their husbands pushed for going back. Professional concerns influenced men more than women. Women, who often had less illustrious or lower-paying careers, tended to be less concerned about the loss of social status, and prioritized their families' safety.[23] In many families it had been the women who had pushed for emigration in the first place, while their husbands frequently wanted to stay in Germany, disregarding the warning signs their wives heeded more readily. Also, women often more easily adapted to their new situation in exile and thus would have preferred to stay.[24]

Even in cases where their professional opportunities likewise improved with a return, women tended to be more cautious. As an actress, Camilla Spira had better chances to resume her career in Germany. But she did not want to go back, although her husband pushed for their return. Camilla explained, "After 1945 I did not really want to return to Germany. But my husband wanted to go to Berlin. . . . Actually, I wanted nothing to do with those Germans—but was there an alternative? Really, there wasn't any. We both were totally dependent on the German language: my husband as a lawyer and I as an actress. So, we, in spite of concerns—particularly on my part—went to Germany."[25] While Camilla saw some advantages to living in Germany—mainly the German language, which would allow them to develop their careers—she ultimately felt it was not her decision to return from Amsterdam in 1947. Camilla's sister Steffie Spira likewise returned to Germany after the war, and she also felt reluctant: "I did not mean to return to Germany, to Berlin, after the Second World War. It didn't necessarily have to be Germany for me. But for my husband it had to be Germany. He did not wish to move again to a foreign country, and I understood."[26] While Steffie framed her disagreement with her husband differently from her sister, emphasizing that she understood his difficulties rather than him dominating the decision-making process, both sisters returned to Berlin despite their own misgivings, Steffie to the East and Camilla to the West.

Upon their return, they seemed to have kept their doubts to themselves. In 1948 a Berlin paper published an article with the title "Berlin Is Still Wonderful: Steffie and Camilla Spira Have Returned Home." While the article quotes Camilla explaining that many of her friends and acquaintances had been killed by the Nazis, it had overall a surprisingly positive tone. The author wrote, "But [Steffie and Camilla] did not want to stay [in exile]. And they were not afraid of the ruins in Berlin. . . . Berlin was still wonderful, said Camilla Spira, and she was glad to be able to perform there again."[27] The different ways the sisters reflected upon their return in these sources perhaps point to the fact that in the late 1940s, Jewish returnees did not feel they could openly discuss their fears in face of a German public, whereas in interviews conducted decades later, people expected Jewish returnees to feel discomfort about their return. Their different statements also highlight the complexities of thinking about a return. The sisters' memories of persecution and the knowledge of the murder of friends and family stood in conflict with their familiarity with the German theater scene and the draw of Berlin. For Steffie, who was a member of the Communist Party, the wish to build an antifascist and Socialist country also played into her decision-making.[28]

The pull of the German language, which Camilla highlighted, affected the decision-making of many German Jews, especially authors, lawyers, and actors who depended on it. The writer Ralph Giordano, who had survived the Nazi years in hiding, maintained that he had been convinced he would leave as soon as Germany was liberated.[29] He stayed, however, because he could not imagine writing in any other language; because, in spite of it all, he felt some connection to the country; and because he did not want to give way to those who still believed in Nazi ideology.[30]

Other German Jews shared the notion that a "liquidation" of the Jewish community would be a victory for Nazism. They decided to stay or return because they did not want Hitler's aim of a Germany "free of Jews" to become reality.[31] Heinz Galinski, a survivor of Auschwitz and chairman of the Jewish community of Berlin from 1949, emphasized that "the Wannsee Conference cannot be the last word in the life of the Jewish community in Germany."[32] In a letter to all Jewish communities from November 1946, Leo Loewenstein, who like Galinski had survived the camps and returned to Berlin, emphasized the need to rebuild Jewish life in Germany. Failing to do so would "also be a triumph for Hitler, his only triumph, if he would have succeeded in eradicating Judaism in Germany. . . . He is not supposed to have this triumph, and on this soil, fertilized with Jewish blood, but also with Jewish work and Jewish vocation, a new Judaism, which is worthy of the old tradition and continues it, will rise."[33] Loewenstein stressed the history of Jews in Germany, and he called for a resurrection.

Some surviving Jews wished to contribute to the reconstruction process. They hoped to strengthen democracy, fight antisemitism, create a Socialist state, or build a better, more democratic Germany.[34] After several years in England, where she had never felt at home, thirty-three-year-old Inge Deutschkron returned to Germany to help rebuild the state and create a "new Germany."[35] Looking back at his decision to return from exile in Denmark in 1949, the judge and prosecutor Fritz Bauer, a Social Democrat who later played an essential role in the Frankfurt Auschwitz trials, explained, "I returned because I hoped to be able to bring with me some of the optimism and the belief of the young democrats of the Weimar Republic, some of the emigrant's resistance spirit and will to resist state injustice."[36] Emigrants like Bauer who had been involved in politics before they left were more likely to return.[37]

Alfred Dreifuss, a member of the Communist Party since 1925, was arrested for illegal political activities in 1935. After several years in prison and then in the Dachau concentration camp, his mother managed to get him released under the condition of his immediate departure from Germany. Dreifuss left in 1939 for Shanghai, where he continued his political work. At the end of the war, he agitated for the return of German exiles.[38] In a Shanghai immigrant newspaper, he argued that returning was a political question and that those who chose to go back needed to "have the will and the strength to help with the reshaping of Germany."[39] Political motivations dominated the accounts of other Communist returnees to East Germany. Jewish members of the Communist Party tended to see their flight from Germany as a result of their politics, not their Jewish origin. They had fled, and they returned primarily as antifascists.[40]

In the first years after leaving Germany, most of these Jewish (like non-Jewish) German Communists and Socialists had embraced the notion of the other Germany, the better Germany that would rebel and persist against Nazism and form a foundation for rebuilding.[41] This belief in the other Germany had become increasingly difficult to uphold as news of German genocidal violence spread and the German population not only failed to resist but also supported the regime until its very end. Still, a significant number of German Jewish Socialists and Communists decided to return, hoping to build a different and better Germany after the war.[42] While more people returned to West Germany, the East German zone drew a number of prominent returnees such as the writers Anna Seghers and Arnold Zweig, the composer Hanns Eisler, and the literary scholars Hans Mayer and Alfred Kantorowicz, to name but a few. Others, like the photographer Abraham Pisarek, had survived the war in Germany. In 1943 the Gestapo had arrested Pisarek and other Jewish forced laborers who had previously been protected because they were married to "Aryans." After their non-Jewish spouses staged a public protest, a unique event in the Nazi period, most of them were released. After the war, Pisarek, who was close to the Communist Party, worked for the *Tägliche Rundschau*, the daily newspaper run by the Soviet Military Administration (SMAD).[43]

Recha Rothschild succeeded in escaping to France in 1937, after the Nazis had already arrested her once for her political activities. She survived there in hiding. In 1946, then sixty-six years old, she was eager to return to "be present when the foundation for a new and better Germany was laid."[44] Similarly, Heinz Brandt, like Rothschild a member of the Communist Party, explained his reasoning for rebuilding his life in Germany after his liberation from the Buchenwald concentration camp: "You are a concentration camp prisoner [*KZler*], you are a Berliner, there is great need, every one of us belongs there—that was our opinion. There will be a new Berlin, a new Germany, the times of inhumanities are over."[45] Their sense of purpose separated these Communist Jews from others who returned to Germany. The dream of a better future allowed them to envision a place where they would belong, and the East German zone's antifascist ideology seemed to offer a desired contrast to National Socialist terror.[46]

Some Jews simply stated their wish to return *home* when explaining their decision. Beyond referencing climate and economic opportunities, respondents to a questionnaire from the Central Welfare Board of Jews in Germany frequently listed "return to the old home [*alte Heimat*]" or "to

28 | *Home after Fascism*

live at home [*in der Heimat*]" as the reason for their return.[47] Wolfgang Fischer, a journalist who had escaped to Shanghai, stressed the refugees' yearning for home in an article about the return of about 470 Shanghai immigrants published in the German paper *Nacht-Express*. He even titled his piece "Return out of Homesickness." Fischer explained that they came back because of the unbearable climate in China, because they had experienced persecution there, because they hoped to be reunited with surviving family members, and because of their "longing for their country of birth."[48] He continued, "These 470 believed in the civilized, decent Germany. They wanted to forget and help to rebuild. They wanted to again have a home." Fischer emphasized that these Jewish refugees regained their "citizenship with all their rights and duties" once they returned, and by highlighting the remigrants' *wish* to belong, he thus also reclaimed returning Jews' *right* to belong. He connected the returnees' wish for a home to their willingness to forget and rebuild. Fischer published this article with a non-Jewish German audience in mind, and perhaps he sensed that a willingness to forget might be a precondition for belonging. Most German Jews, even if they hoped to regain a sense of belonging and wished to help in the reconstruction, did not want to forget, and their memories of past persecutions made it difficult for them to express an unequivocal longing for their home.

While the wish to return home contributed to the decision-making process of some returnees, many struggled with their feelings of longing for a place that had violently excluded them. In their work on refugees and migrants who return to their home country, anthropologists Lynellyn Long and Ellen Oxfeld point to returnees' contradictory feelings; returnees may "simultaneously identify with and be estranged from former homelands."[49] For German Jews who had been violently excluded, their remaining feelings of attachment to their home country could be unsettling. As an Austrian Jew, the writer Jean Améry shared such sentiments. In his essay "How Much Home Does a Person Need?," he described surviving Jews' complicated emotions toward their homeland: "What we urgently wished, and were socially bound, to hate, suddenly stood before us and demanded our longing."[50]

Overall, few German Jews expressed homesickness, and most instead depicted pragmatic reasons for returning to Germany. If they referred to homesickness at all in their writing, they often also alluded to the years of persecution or qualified the sentiment.[51] Hans Winterfeldt explained that he wanted "to return to the place, where he had spent several relatively good years, which then were suddenly interrupted,"[52] and an article in *Der Weg*, which aimed to explain the motives of returnees, stated that "the people here in Germany have become strangers to them, but they simply feel homesick for their country of birth, for the familiar places of their youth."[53]

In 1933, the writer Grete Weil left her hometown of Munich for Amsterdam. There she survived in the underground while her husband, Edgar Weil, was murdered in Mauthausen. In 1946 she wrote in a letter to her friend and soon to be second husband, "I would much rather be in Germany [than in Amsterdam] . . . and take walks with you. Not in the rubble of the cities, but in the countryside, after all it is still my country."[54] While her letters repeatedly expressed her wish to be back in a place where she belonged, Weil hesitated to leave Amsterdam: Germany remained her country, but it could be her country only "still" and "after all."[55] Her past experiences of persecution and the murder of her first husband shaped her relationship with Germany, yet she nonetheless returned in 1947.

Making the "Natural Choice"

Italian Jews frequently recalled homesickness, longing, and love for their home country when explaining their choice to go back after the war. In their accounts, feelings, more than pragmatic considerations, drove their decision-making.[56] Giorgina Levi, in her Bolivian exile, not only dreamed about returning to Italy but idealized the European continent and its culture.[57] Like her, other Italian Jews wrote about their longing for the culture, the language, and the food—in short, the home—they missed so dearly. In 1938, seventeen-year-old Bruno di Cori left Rome with his family for Palestine. The family, particularly his parents but also Bruno, struggled with adapting to life there. Remembering his time in Palestine, he reflected: "I felt such homesickness for Italy that when I heard a record with Neapolitan songs that we had at home, I was moved to tears."[58] Fulvia di Segni Jesi, who had emigrated with her husband and two small sons, recalled how a word in Italian heard in the street or an Italian song brought her to tears, so great was her longing for Italy in her Brazilian exile. Similar to Levi, who depicted homesickness as a disease, Fulvia wrote of the "microbe of nostalgia" that "was deeply attacking my whole being."[59] In their writings, homesickness became a force that overcame them. More than merely missing the comforts of their former lives or the coziness of their homes, they expressed more abstract longings for Italian culture or even the Italian nation.

30 | *Home after Fascism*

Lea Ottolenghi, a young Jewish girl from Livorno who had found refuge in Switzerland, filled her diary in the weeks following Italy's liberation with her longing to return. At one point, she decided to take a boat to the middle of a nearby lake and swim so she could "bathe . . . in Italy!"[60]

While longing for home dominated Italian Jews' accounts of return, some provided other reasons as well. A returnee from Argentina explained he went back to Italy because of political motives, and another Italian Jew referred to the "atmosphere of anxiety" in Palestine.[61] Age also played a role; older people struggled to adapt as émigrés, which strengthened their wish to return to Italy. Some Italian Jews emphasized their wish to contribute to the postwar reconstruction of their homeland. Tullia Calabi Zevi, a journalist who returned to Italy from New York in 1946, explained: "The horrors of war, the mass extermination of Jews, Gypsies, and political opponents and the devastation of Jewish communities had recently been uncovered. It seemed right, having had the good fortune to survive, to come back and participate in the reconstruction of the traumatized, unsettled communities and also to participate, after the defeat of Fascism, in the rebirth of democracy in Italy."[62] Yet in contrast to Jews in East or West Germany who hoped to build a new and different country, Zevi aimed for the "rebirth" of the country that had existed before the rise of Fascism.

German and Italian Jews' accounts most strikingly differ in the absence of a discussion of motivations for return in most Italian Jewish memoirs, letters, and diaries. While German Jews felt pressed to justify why they chose to live in "the country of perpetrators," Italian Jews felt no need to explain their wish to live in Italy. Arrigo Levi and his family escaped Fascist persecution and moved to Argentina in 1942. They returned four years later without seriously considering the option of staying in Buenos Aires. As he put it, returning was just the "natural choice."[63] Piero Terracina, a Roman Jew and the sole survivor of his family, pondered the question, "Why did I not emigrate, why did I stay, I, who had lost my entire family and returned alone and desperate" when asked in an interview years after the war. He seemed unsure why he stayed but mentioned that he immediately found work in Italy and that he had been afraid to move to an entirely unfamiliar place.[64] But the way Terracina responds also gives the sense that he simply may not have considered going elsewhere.

When Swiss authorities conducted a survey regarding Jewish refugees' plans after the war, almost every Italian respondent replied that they wished to go "back to Italy."[65] Lelio Vittorio Valobra, chairman of the Delegation for the Assistance of Jewish Emigrants (Delegazione per l'assistenza agli ebrei emigranti, DELASEM), confirmed this in an announcement from June 1945 stating that almost all Italian Jews "had long ago decided to return to Italy."[66] Many of those who had fled the country perceived their exile as temporary. Andrea Bises, for instance, recalled that his father made it difficult for him to adapt to life in Argentina because his father "lived always with the idea of the return to Italy, and so he always said that in Italy everything was better."[67]

Yet not all Italian Jews wanted to return to or stay in Italy. Umberto Beer, born in Ancona in September 1896, volunteered in the First World War and subsequently made his career in the military. In 1937 he was promoted to lieutenant colonel but was forced to leave the army soon after due to the 1938 racial laws. He subsequently left for Brazil with his wife and son. After the war Beer decided to remain in exile. "The punch I had received," he explained, "still hurt and continues to hurt."[68] Beer could not forget the persecution, and these memories made it impossible for him to consider Italy home. Like Beer, Fernanda di Segni Sermoneta, who owned a small shop in Rome where she and her husband survived in hiding, felt she could no longer live in Italy. In the fall of 1944, she wrote a letter to her son Benedetto, who had left Italy after the racial laws were issued. She described what they had experienced over the years and explained their wish to leave: "We feel that this is not our homeland. . . . We feel different, we see among these people, these Italians, many of those . . . who have contributed to our downfall in that fateful period."[69] She and her husband decided to move to Palestine in 1945. However, critical voices like those of di Segni Sermoneta did not shape the discourse about Jewish life in Italy after the Holocaust. They remained decisions of individuals, rather than expressions of a general mood. Indeed, Italian Jewish newspapers, Jewish communities, and international Jewish organizations never debated whether Jews should and could continue to live on the Italian peninsula.[70] The reconstruction of the Jewish community was perceived as a given.

International Jewish and non-Jewish media likewise positively portrayed the rebuilding of Jewish life in Italy. British and American news outlets depicted Italy as led astray by the Germans and Italians as naturally opposed to antisemitism, contributing to a discourse that made return a comparatively easy choice for Italian Jewish remigrants.[71] International

32 | *Home after Fascism*

Jewish organizations likewise supported and welcomed the efforts to reconstruct Jewish life in Italy.[72] Reuben Resnik, the American Jewish Joint Distribution Committee (JDC, also Joint) representative in Italy, pointed "to the admirable spirit of goodwill and brotherhood which existed among the people of Italy,"[73] and the World Jewish Congress (WJC) described Italy "as one of the few countries where after the war those Jews who could not immigrate to Eretz Israel would find a safe haven."[74]

A Future for Jews in Germany?

Three years later, in 1948, the WJC stated that Jews should never again live on the "blood-stained German soil."[75] Most international Jewish organizations vigorously opposed the reconstruction of Jewish life in the "country of perpetrators."[76] During a conference in Heidelberg in 1949 on "The Future of the Jews in Germany," the participants expressed pessimism. For example, Peisach Piekatsch from the Central Committee-US Zone, opined: "there is no place for Jews in Germany. . . . Neither the political, economic, nor the moral atmosphere prevailing in Germany is conducive to the development of a Jewish community here. To remain here is to die."[77] Other organizations—like the Jewish Relief Unit, a British relief agency, and the Jewish Agency, the primary organization responsible for the immigration to Palestine/Israel—likewise put pressure on Jews to leave.[78] Rabbi Leo Baeck, one of the most prominent German rabbis, relocated to the UK after the war. He declared during a visit to Germany in 1948 that the history of Jews in Germany had ended.[79] Jews who had survived in Germany likewise expressed uncertainty about the reconstruction of Jewish life. The Committee Representing the Interests of the Jewish Communities debated this question at a June 1947 meeting. One participant maintained, "German Jewry has ceased to exist."[80] The German Jewish paper *Der Weg* frequently discussed surviving Jews' options. An article in the first edition warned those who stayed that they should carefully consider the risks of a life in Germany.[81]

German Jews who decided to rebuild their lives in Germany knew that their choice would appear surprising, if not shocking, to other Jews. A letter by a returnee from Portugal sent to the WJC in September 1946 exemplifies this:

> As you may see—and I am sure it will surprise you—I returned to Germany even as a religious Jew and though the Nazis killed my whole family. . . . You may believe me, I returned quite voluntarily. . . . It may be strange: a German-born

Jew going back to these people who tortured his own family and killed six million Jews! . . . I returned together with my wife, the first voluntarily repatriated from Portugal! And being now about one month in Berlin, I have to state: At least until now I do not regret [my choice]![82]

Friends and family confronted those who chose to resettle in Germany, accusing them of stupidity, naivete, or even betrayal.[83] A fellow German Jewish émigré to England called the writer Inge Deutschkron "not quite normal" when she spoke about her plan to go back.[84] Alfred Döblin, who had returned to Germany in 1945, warned fellow writer Hermann Kesten of the deeply rooted antisemitism when the latter pondered returning from the United States in 1948.[85] Hans Frankenthal recalled that he and his brother received looks of disbelief when they declared they wished to go back to Schmallenberg, the village where they had lived before their deportation to Auschwitz.[86]

The repeated condemnations caused some to feel defensive and others outright guilty about living in what was perceived to be the wrong place.[87] Grete Weil, who wished to return from the Netherlands, wrote about the difficulty of standing by her unpopular choice: "I live against the world's opinion, which understandably finds it nonsensical that I want to go to Germany, and sometimes I lose breath swimming against the current."[88] Fellow writer Wolfgang Hildesheimer returned to Germany in 1946, at age thirty, to work as a translator at the International Military Tribunal in Nuremberg. His correspondence with his parents, who remained in Palestine, reveals their disapproval of their son's plans. In December 1947 Hildesheimer wrote to them, "Mother says that she would not like it if I stayed in Germany. . . . But it is not as if I would 'return' to Germany. I would just work for an organization concerned with the education and rehabilitation of Germans."[89] In his letters to his parents, Hildesheimer emphasized the temporary nature of his sojourn in Germany, though he wound up living there for a decade before he moved to Switzerland. To his parents, and perhaps to himself, admitting a return to Germany was not possible.

Jews who left Palestine or (after 1948) Israel to resettle in Germany faced particular condemnation.[90] Some explained that due to health reasons a return was unfortunate but necessary; others, like Erna Proskauer, a lawyer who had never felt at home in Palestine and returned to Berlin in the early 1950s, kept their decision as quiet as possible.[91] The artist Lea Grundig, who wished to leave Tel Aviv for her hometown of Dresden, commented that "back then it was impossible to openly organize a return to Germany."[92]

34 | *Home after Fascism*

The Israeli authorities aimed to restrict a return to Germany by stamping Israeli passports with "not valid for Germany" and declaring that people who settled permanently in Germany would be barred from reentering Israel. When the president of Regensburg's Jewish community informed the Israeli consul that a few families had returned from Israel to Germany, the latter advised him to let the families know that they would not receive any support from the community or from Jewish aid organizations. This, the consul hoped, would discourage others from returning.[93]

The atmosphere of disapproval explains why German Jews, in contrast to Italian Jews, felt the need to explain and defend their wish to return to Germany. Articles in Jewish newspapers as well as statements by Jewish organizations and public figures created an emotional regime that influenced how surviving Jews discussed their choice to resettle in Germany.[94] This discourse that strongly condemned living in Germany after the Holocaust made it more difficult to publicly discuss homesickness. A few German Jews, however, pushed back against this view. Replying to the many articles published in *Der Weg* that questioned a future for Jews in Germany, one author argued that Jews should feel no shame because in their hearts Germany remained their "fatherland."[95] Heinz Ganther, a journalist who returned from Shanghai, published an edited volume, titled *The Jews in Germany*, in 1953. In the introduction he pointed out his disagreement with the many voices who doubted that Jews should live there: "For it had to be said that there are Jews who also in the future want to live in this country."[96]

The extent to which the negative discourse around a future for Jews in Germany affected surviving Jews depended also on how much they perceived themselves as part of a Jewish community. The German-Jewish dancer and cabaret artist Valeska Gert did not seem to consider her wish to return to Berlin, her hometown, as problematic. She had not come to North America, Gert writes, "with the intention to stay. I needed a connection to Berlin, and I suffered terribly because I could not yet return. I was born in Berlin and wanted to die in Berlin."[97] People like Gert who moved within an artistic milieu, or communists of Jewish origin who mainly associated with other political émigrés, did not give much thought to the opinions of the World Jewish Congress, though they also faced friends and family who warned them of a return. Italian Jews did not face similar disapproval and tended to return with less weight on their shoulders.

The Journey Home

Yet even after they made their decisions, the majority of German and Italian Jews faced considerable difficulties on their homeward journeys. Many had to wait months and some even years before they could reenter their homes. The start of their return journey depended on the time of liberation, which varied drastically: the Allies liberated the Italian internment camp of Ferramonti di Tarsia in Southern Italy in September 1943; the US Fifth Army made it to Rome the following June; the Soviet Army entered Auschwitz in January 1945; Berlin's city garrison surrendered on May 2 of the same year; and the Jewish ghetto in Shanghai was liberated in September.

Surviving Jews faced numerous hurdles: destroyed infrastructure, need for visas and travel permits, closed borders, and overcrowded trains. Some had to cross countries and continents, but even Jews who survived inside Germany and Italy faced difficulties when trying to return to their hometowns. Italian Jews who had fled to the South or hid in the countryside needed to wait months before their hometowns were liberated, and even after the end of the war, the lack of infrastructure prevented an immediate return. Emma de Rossi Castelli, who had been hiding with her husband in the countryside, hoped to return to Livorno after her liberation in July 1944. At the end of May 1945, she noted in her diary that finally civilians were allowed to move about the entire peninsula, but transportation remained poor. In September 1945 she still remained far from her home, and she expressed her frustration in her diary, "Days, weeks, months, and even the Jewish New Year and the fast have passed, and we are still here, without a home . . . ! I thought I could go back to Livorno at the end of '44 and now very soon 1945 will end and we have not yet been able to get a small place to finally settle down in our home."[98] She finally returned to Livorno in October 1945. German Jews likewise faced lack of transportation and destroyed infrastructure. Moreover, crossing the borders between the different occupation zones proved difficult. Victor Klemperer, a linguist whose diaries of the Nazi years made him famous, had survived the last months of the war with his wife in Bavaria. As soon as they had been liberated in May 1945, he wished to return to his home in Dresden.[99] He managed to return about a month later.[100]

Many camp survivors found themselves in camps on German soil at the end of the war as the Nazis had forced them to march westward when the Allied troops progressed. When the Soviets entered Auschwitz, they encountered a mere seven thousand prisoners, many of whom died shortly after liberation. Some survivors remained in the camps for weeks after their liberation. Most were too weak to face the long journey home and lacked papers and documentation, which made it extremely difficult to cross borders. Josef Warscher, who grew up in Stuttgart, survived Buchenwald and managed to return to Stuttgart in May 1945, about a month after his liberation. He remembered, "You couldn't go wherever you wanted. . . . Until May 25, I stayed in Buchenwald, over a month in the same barracks. . . . Then two or three inmates from the local area went to Stuttgart on a military pass, brought back a bus and relatives, and took us—inmates from Stuttgart—to Stuttgart."[101]

In some camps, like Theresienstadt, survivors had to apply to the camp committee and ask for their names to be added to a list for transport. But they still had to wait until their hometowns, aid organizations, or Jewish communities organized means of transportation, which could take a long time.[102] The Italian state faced immense difficulties in repatriating the mass of displaced Italian citizens of whom Jewish deportees formed only a small percentage. While governmental and nongovernmental institutions invested energy and effort, they proved largely unable to effectively organize repatriation.[103]

Some survivors tried to find their way on their own. Far from home and in poor physical condition, they often traveled for months. In his *La tregua*, Primo Levi described his arduous journey from Auschwitz to Turin, which brought him through large parts of eastern and central Europe. Liberated in January 1945, Levi finally reached his home in October of the same year.[104] Like Levi, then sixteen-year-old Piero Terracina was liberated in Auschwitz, but he was too weak to travel home. He was brought to a Russian military hospital and later to a sanatorium at the Black Sea.[105] While in the sanatorium in Sochi, he wrote to Pietro Quaroni, the Italian ambassador in Moscow, asking for assistance. The letter, written in April 1945, reveals the boy's grief and loneliness. Piero explained that he had been deported with his siblings and parents and that his parents had been murdered in the camp. He continued, "I haven't spoken a word in Italian for about 40 days. I still don't speak Russian, so all I do is stay in bed all day and a thousand thoughts are going through my head. I think a lot about my family, I cry, but then I console myself, hoping to be able to see at least my brothers and my sister again. It would bring me much comfort, ambassador, if you answered. Remember that it's a boy who writes to you."[106] Quaroni replied, and a correspondence between Piero and the ambassador ensued. While Quaroni, who intervened with Soviet authorities on the Piero's behalf, could ultimately do little to speed up his return home (Piero was one of the last returnees and only arrived in Rome in December 1945), the young survivor felt grateful for the ambassador's attention and encouragement.[107]

It took Anna Di Gioacchino Cassuto about three months to return from Auschwitz to Italy. Anna was born on January 21, 1911, in Ancona to a wealthy Jewish family. She trained as a teacher and married Nathan Cassuto, an ophthalmologist, in 1934. The racial laws forced Nathan to leave the Faculty of Medicine in Florence, and he begun to work as a rabbi, first in Milan and then, from 1943, as the chief rabbi of Florence. In November 1943, Nathan, Anna, and their brother-in-law, Shaul Campagnano, were arrested while working for DELASEM. They were deported to Auschwitz on January 30, 1944. Anna survived the internment and the transfer to Theresienstadt, where she was liberated in May 1945.[108]

Together with other survivors, Anna set out on the long journey home. They went to Prague, where they were hosted by the Italian consulate and promised a speedy return. However, their train, heading originally to Linz, was redirected to Vienna. Anna and the others in her group were told to wait in the Wiener Neustadt camp for their repatriation. After five weeks they were transported to Hungary. Anna and three others decided to try reaching Graz. Following the advice of a chance acquaintance, they headed to the Hungarian-Yugoslavian border and then took a train to Ljubljana. In Ljubljana they were supposed to head to another refugee camp, but they decided to leave and took a train to Postojna and then to Trieste, crossing the border without any documents. For once gender bias worked in the women's favor, as Anna wrote in a letter in August 1945: "Another night spent in a station, taking the train in the morning for Trieste: I cannot tell you the excitement in crossing the border: an American got on to check documents but only the men's, so we entered with no difficulty. It was like a dream! It was the 1st of August!"[109]

At some point on their journey, probably when they were at the Wiener Neustadt camp, Anna and her friend had their picture taken.[110] The photograph shows Anna, Amalia Navarro, and Enrica Zarfati, standing arm in arm; possibly their fourth travel companion took the picture. The photograph differs from the pictures of weak, emaciated survivors, unaware of the camera, that were widespread in the press at the time. The women

Figure 1.1. Anna Di Gioacchino Cassuto, Amalia Navarro, and Enrica Zarfati at the Wiener Neustadt camp in Austria, spring 1945. © Fondazione CDEC Archive, Milano.

appear in charge. They stand united, strong, and smiling. They look directly into the camera. If not for the destroyed houses in the background, it could be a vacation photograph. The women could have stood in front of a tree or a house that did not have its roof blown off, but they chose to have their picture taken surrounded by ruins, their white clothing contrasting against the dark background. Photographs, as Roland Barthes writes, "establish . . . an awareness of [the object of the picture] *having-been-there*."[111] Just weeks after their liberation, this simple proof of existence takes on extraordinary meaning. They had survived, against all odds. They were still there, standing, while around them the world had collapsed.

Hans Winterfeldt had also been in Auschwitz, but he was forced to move toward the end of the war. He was liberated in a small camp in Austria where SS guards left the inmates behind. No one organized food or transport for the survivors. Winterfeldt, initially unaware of the general chaos in the postwar world, hoped his uncle, who had been protected from deportation because of his non-Jewish wife, would come and pick him up. But he soon realized that without a working mail service, he had no way of

Returning Home? | 39

contacting his uncle and informing him of his survival and whereabouts. He also understood that no one would provide transportation for the former inmates. Eventually he set out on his own, and after several weeks in a hospital in Linz, he made it through Germany and crossed the border into the Soviet occupied zone and to his hometown, Berlin.[112]

For those who had survived in immigration, the return home proved likewise difficult. They had to overcome numerous bureaucratic hurdles, often waiting months for visas and entry permissions.[113] Cold War tensions soon made it difficult for Communists and Socialists to receive permission to enter the western zones. After leaving the United States in February 1947, the writer Walther Victor was sent back when he arrived at the German border; he had not been able to obtain the necessary signature from the British occupying authorities. According to Victor, the British refused his entry because of his political activism. As they told him, they "had enough radical German patriots."[114] A few months later, he managed to cross illegally and made it back to Germany.[115] The writer Anna Seghers had initially hoped to return to her hometown of Mainz in the American sector, but the occupying administration refused her entry because she was a Communist.[116] Recha Rothschild grew increasingly frustrated with the paperwork that impeded her return. She had to provide various papers, including an official proof that she held German nationality. In 1947 she finally managed to return to East Berlin.[117] Alexander Abusch, later a leading member of the Socialist Unity Party of Germany (Sozialistische Einheitspartei Deutschlands, SED), berated the United States for preventing his return from Mexico, explaining that in 1945, "we literally sat on packed bags, for many months, because, after Roosevelt's death, the 'free democracy' of the US had denied German antifascists the simplest human right for returning refugees, that is transit visas."[118] Abusch arrived in Berlin in July 1946, after traveling for three months. People like Alfred Dreifuss who had immigrated to Shanghai needed to wait until September to celebrate the end of the war and many months more until they could return. Dreifuss maintained that Jewish aid organizations such as the Joint and HICEM (an acronym of HIAS, ICA, and Emigdirect), assisted Jews who wished to immigrate to a new country but did not assist those who wanted to go back to Germany.[119]

Lotte Winter returned to Soviet-occupied Germany from her exile in Sweden in October 1945. Her husband had left with a group of comrades months earlier, leaving her behind with a newborn and a four-year-old. Beyond plans for the future, cleaning diapers, providing food, and making sure her children did not freeze preoccupied her on the long and difficult journey.[120] Like the choice to return, gender affected the experience of the journey, as women faced the added threat of sexual assault when traveling through a destroyed Europe.[121]

Jewish communities in Italy and Germany received letters from all over the world, asking for assistance with repatriation.[122] In April 1949 Moritz Eisenstaedt, a Jew from Danzig who had survived the war in Shanghai with his non-Jewish wife, wrote to the head of the Frankfurt community. After spending ten weeks at sea, they had arrived in Napoli. At the time of his letter, they were living in a DP camp in Southern Italy that he described as "rather primitive." They did not receive sufficient food and "longed for the day on which they could leave Trani." However, to move back to Germany, they needed official approval to settle in Frankfurt, which he hoped the community would be able to organize for them.[123]

Fritz Bauer, who had spent the war years in Sweden, turned to fellow Social Democrats in the hope that they would be able to facilitate his return. Despite the demand for judges in postwar Germany, Bauer struggled to secure a position. He faced barriers because of both his SPD membership and his Jewishness. In May 1946 he wrote in a letter to Kurt Schumacher, chairman of the Social Democratic Party: "Of course, I have a great desire to see how things are in Germany. I had already negotiated with the Americans regarding a trip to Stuttgart in May–June last year. They asked me to complete a dozen questionnaires (they were interested in the lawyer). But I have never received a positive response. The reason is unknown to me. I presume, however, that . . . they did not want Jews or, more correctly formulated, that they hold their more or less public work inopportune."[124]

Italian Jews who had survived the war in Switzerland could rely on the Association of Swiss Jewish Refugee Aid and Welfare Organizations (Verband Schweizerischer Jüdischer Fürsorgen/Flüchtlingshilfen, VSJF). The VSJF aimed to help all Jewish returnees with the "exception of the return to Germany," indicating their disapproval of Jews returning to Germany.[125] Despite the eagerness of the VSJF to help and the desire of the Swiss government to get rid of refugees, Italian Jews in Swiss camps often waited months until they could leave. When the war ended, Lea Ottolenghi was convinced that her departure was a matter of a few days, but the borders remained closed. Rumors of their opening gave her new hope and then even greater disappointment. At one point, Ottolenghi considered crossing the border illegally. In a diary entry in July 1945, she expressed her frustration: "And

I am still here in Brissago and still the order to leave has not come! It's crazy. I am furious, we will probably be the last ones."[126] But a short time later, she received notice that they would be able to leave on July 31. Full of joy, she wrote, "Hurray, hurray, we leave!!!"[127] While Ottolenghi's diary entries speak of her impatience and great longing to return, the account of Alfred Kantorowicz from the same time reads differently. Rather than as filled with happy anticipation, he described the period before his return as a "long brooding waiting time."[128]

Arrival

These different depictions of waiting foreshadow the ways Italian and German Jews tended to describe their emotions upon arrival. Depicting the moment when they crossed the border back to Italy, Italian Jews conveyed strong, positive emotions. Franco Levi, who returned from exile in Switzerland to his home in Milan, remembered that "the Simplon tunnel was interminable, especially when one's heart was beating anxiously in the hope of finding some remnants of a home. . . . We left the tunnel in a cloud of acrid black smoke: the trees that I saw along the railroad were Italian trees, Italian grass and stones, which moved me deeply."[129] Clara Levi Coen, who likewise returned from Switzerland with her husband and young son, described the "wonderful feeling, when the train . . . arrived at the border with Italy. We returned to our homeland, so painfully loved and remembered during the time of exile, and we returned there as free people!"[130] Italian Jews' outpourings of emotions upon arrival marked the connection they still felt to Italy.

The border becomes a focal point in German and Italian Jews' accounts of their flight as well as their homecoming, not only because crossing the border could be stressful due to fears of lacking the right papers; the border also took on a symbolic meaning. When they had first crossed, in some cases several years ago, they had lost their homes and begun their lives as refugees.[131] Now, crossing once again, they left exile behind. The border could also bring back memories of traumatic experiences of a narrow escape. For most surviving Jews, borders had become sites with heightened emotional meaning—part of what geographers term "personal geographies" or "geographies of emotional life."[132]

For many German Jews, the second crossing did not trigger the welcoming sense of return that they had anticipated. Indeed, the following

Home after Fascism

recollections of arrival home highlight the absence of emotions, which they knew contrasted with their readers' expectations. Emphasizing this absence, the writers point to the incompleteness and impossibility of "return." In his memoirs, Hans Sahl wrote about his return from New York: "What does a man feel, who returns after 15 years to his country of birth? He has no emotions. He does not feel anything. He does not know what he feels."[133] Fellow writer Ludwig Marcuse, who, like Sahl, returned in the late 1940s, used similar words in a letter written to friends in the United States in 1949: "What I felt? That I had slept only 4 hours that night, that I had a cold, that I wished the border was behind us. . . . That, after 16 years of anticipation of this hour, I felt nothing."[134] By emphasizing their numbness, these German Jewish men underlined their emotional distance from their former home.[135] A few days later, Marcuse sent another letter, and this time he depicted emotions, though not a sense of safety and homecoming. Rather, the letter reveals his fear, which momentarily overwhelmed him: "Friday, after I wrote the letter to you, I broke down. Begged Sascha [his partner] to leave Germany immediately. Sascha did not take me seriously, ordered a taxi—and we found good accommodations."[136]

The writer Walther Victor published a short essay about his return in the early 1950s. He shared the sense of anxiety but ultimately depicted his experience at the border positively. When he first tried to cross the border via train, a German border guard asked Victor for his passport: "I held my papers convulsively. How long did I not have a real passport? The man leaned forward. Then he looked at me and repeated my name. 'The writer?' . . . His face became human. I was shaking now. Was this really home [*die Heimat*]? 'Yes! Back from exile!' He shook my hand. . . . 'I have hidden your book throughout the whole Nazi period!' he said." In Victor's account the moment of fear and tension is replaced with a sense of arriving home, a moment of welcoming. Yet Victor had to attempt to cross a second time since the British authorities did not allow him to enter their zone. This time he met a Soviet soldier: "I am sending this greeting to the young Soviet officer who served in the summer of 1947 at the Lübeck-Schönberg border. I was not allowed to ask his name. But without knowing it, he has done much for me. . . . When I saw him like this, calm and self-assured, concise, clean and neat, . . . , in every movement the representative of a new power that would transform the world into a peaceful place, I knew, that with this man I was on the right path."[137] Victor's story of his border crossing fashions his arrival in sync with GDR propaganda, praising the Soviet occupying power in contrast to the British, who did not let him enter. He also narrates two sides of his homecoming: His encounter with the German guard symbolizes the old life to which he hopes to return, like the book hidden during the years of Nazi rule. His meeting with the Soviet soldier holds promise for the future.

Like the accounts of their experiences at the border, Italian and German Jews' depictions of their emotionally charged first meetings with non-Jewish Italians and Germans vary. Roberta di Camerino had fled with her husband and two young children to Switzerland in 1943. There, to make a living, she began designing handbags, which later, once she returned and opened her company in Venice, became widely coveted fashion items. Roberta remembered that she had "a lump in her throat" when she stood in front of her destroyed home: "But people come. Some cry, 'they are back,' and in no time we are surrounded by people. They greet us, they laugh, they hug us. An old woman cries, and says, 'You are alive! You are alive!'"[138] Frequently Italian Jews told stories in which non-Jewish Italians not only welcomed them but mirrored their own excitement and emotional upheaval, highlighting their belonging to the national community.

Lotte Paepcke, a German Jewish writer, painted a darker picture of her first encounter. She left the monastery where she had been in hiding since the spring of 1945. Happy to experience the outside world, she described how her emotions changed on her way to nearby Freiburg: "The first human face in my new freedom: the enemy. . . . Fear fell from the open sky and froze me before this face. He was there; the living enemy."[139] Paepcke had been surrounded by non-Jewish Germans throughout the war as she had been hiding in a monastery with non-Jewish refugees. But her first encounter outside the monastery made her understand that she would need to live among people she now considered enemies. Whereas Paepcke highlights an overwhelming sense of fear, Eva Noack-Mosse, who, like Paepcke, was married to a non-Jew, describes warm emotions. In July 1945 Noack-Mosse returned to the small Bavarian village where she had lived with her husband and daughters. Her marriage to a non-Jew had protected her until February 1945, when the Nazis deported her, at age forty-five, to Theresienstadt. In contrast to many others, she had family and friends to whom she could return. In her diary she described the warm welcome she received when staying with a non-Jewish acquaintance on her return journey: "The friend with whom I had spent the night on my journey [to Theresienstadt] was waiting for me. Again, I slept at her home. This woman whom I had only seen twice

44 | *Home after Fascism*

in my entire life greeted me like a mother greets a child whom she thought lost and who finally returns."[140]

Others likewise highlighted the emotional relief of encountering trusted friends or reentering a familiar environment.[141] In reply to a letter from a Catholic friend with whom he had lost touch, Rabbi Neuhaus wrote in the fall of 1945, "Your letter moved me to tears, as I returned to Frankfurt Main after three years in a concentration camp. I am happy about any human sign of life especially—as I had only gotten to know brutes [*Unmenschen*]."[142] Alexander Abusch wrote that he felt truly at home only "when Paul Merker and I took the subway to the House of the Central Committee in order to report back to Comrade Wilhelm Pieck. . . . I felt finally, finally, at last, home again. . . . One took his place here for the party—in the old home country. . . . We were overwhelmed by the feeling: Yes, we had arrived."[143] A strong expression of emotions—"overwhelmed"—marked Abusch's sense of arriving at home.

Some Italian Jews emphasized their disappointment about the unfriendly reception they received. In particular, camp survivors recounted indifference and even hostility. Some remember being asked to leave a train or tram on the final part of their journey, either because people feared they had a contagious disease or because they did not have a ticket and no means to purchase one. The Roman Jewish survivor Eugenio Sermoneta contrasted his expectations of a "better world" with a reality in which "the Italians had abandoned us."[144] Camp survivors were in greater need of physical and emotional assistance when they arrived and consequently suffered most under the lack of support.[145] The trauma they had endured, and in most cases the loss of family members, made it more difficult to reconnect with their home upon their arrival.

A Home Regained, a Home Transformed

In order to feel at home upon arrival, Italian and German Jews needed the landscape, the people, the city, and the house or apartment to trigger feelings of safety and warmth. Whether such feelings were possible depended on the extent of the rupture they had experienced and the possibility of recognizing and remembering the home they had lost. Senses, smells, touch, and sight played crucial roles in awakening this feeling of being at home. Roberta di Camerino's depiction of her return illustrates this. Impatient to go back, the Di Camerino family chose to cross the border illegally. "It is strange," Roberta wrote, "in the years after the war I tried to find these places: those of the flight and those of the return. I could not identify them. Yet, I have them fixed in my memory. I mean, I still smell the scent of the grass, as I crawled under the first fence, on the day of my return from Switzerland. A smell that gave me confidence, as if nature was on my side. An unexplained feeling." In her depiction even the landscape appears welcoming and supportive of her return. They meet border guards who suspect they are Fascists trying to escape Italy, but they manage to explain that they are Jews who wish to return. Once they make it across, they pass a small house with two women who ask them if they needed assistance and offer them coffee. "Real coffee also this time. Like in the other hut, before we had passed the border. It is since then, that every time, the smell of coffee makes me happy."[146] The coffee consumed before her departure and now again at her arrival neatly frames her sojourn in Switzerland, suggesting the possibility of resuming life just where it had been interrupted. Symbolizing her Italian home, the coffee triggered happiness. Coffee, in particular—though also Italian food, smelling pine trees, and hearing the familiar language—features strongly in Italian Jews' accounts of their returns.[147] Their narratives frequently highlight feeling welcomed by their physical environment. Fulvia di Segni Jesi, who returned from Brazil shortly after the end of the war, filled her memoir with images that encapsulated a strong sense of familiarity. Describing the night of her arrival, she wrote that "the small polar star once again greeted me from the skies."[148] Another Italian Jewish returnee from South America, Alma Morpurgo, addressed her hometown, Trieste, directly, underlining her attachment: "Every stone is familiar to me. There is a real bond of affection, of belonging between you and me."[149]

After the 1938 racial laws went into effect, the Di Cori family left Italy for Palestine. They returned after the war, first the parents and later the children. Bruno di Cori, the son, recalled the letters he received from his parents after their return to Italy in 1946. His father who had experienced great difficulty adjusting to life in Palestine, so Bruno "re-entered his world."[150] Cori described how his father resumed his old habits as a Roman Jew, eating foods prohibited by Jewish religious law and impossible to get in Palestine. Di Cori's father did not merely move back to Italy, he returned *home*—to the food, the language, and the family and friends he knew and loved. Culture, as Eva Hoffman writes, "does not exist independently of us but within us."[151] For Bruno's father, the food, the language, and his daily habits were ingrained parts of his self to which he could now return.[152]

46 | *Home after Fascism*

Upon his arrival, life resumed: "As if he picked up a conversation left in the middle, he renewed a ritual interrupted eight years earlier, and invited some old friends to feast with him."[153]

In their recollections Italian Jews tended to highlight the absence of any kind of change or rupture in their social relationships. Lia Levi, for instance, remembers the reappearance of their service woman: "But now, when the war was over, the woman Maria had reappeared as if nothing had happened, and without saying a word she had again occupied the dark little room that had only a little window in the corridor that looked like a gleaming eye."[154] In the end, however, Levi's family could no longer afford to employ a domestic servant, as they had lost most of their property during the war. When Italian Jews depicted their lives after the war, most described an effortless return to how things had been before, though of course years of persecution left their marks.

While Italian Jews returned to the habits that made Italy home and emphasized familiarity in their accounts, most German Jews struggled upon arrival. With their friends, relatives, and colleagues expelled or murdered and their cities destroyed, the postwar country had little in common with the place where they had grown up.[155] While the Italian Jewish community did shrink in numbers, the numerical loss was much more drastic for the German Jewish community. Josef Warscher, who later became the head of the Stuttgart community, explained that he no longer knew anyone in Stuttgart: "I came home and there was no more home."[156] Rabbi Neuhaus, who returned from Theresienstadt in the summer of 1945 and refounded the Frankfurt community, emphasized that "the old Frankfurt no longer exists."[157] A year later, when he was sixty-seven years old, Neuhaus immigrated to the United States. Even those who stayed struggled to find the home to which they thought they would return. Hans Mayer, who returned from Switzerland to the Soviet occupied zone, exclaimed, "And what is Germany? None of this exists anymore."[158] Cultural life as they had known it in the Weimar Republic likewise had ceased to exist.[159]

The writer Anna Seghers, who returned from Mexico to Berlin in 1947, described the distance between emigrants' longing for home in exile and the reality of their arrival: "We had longed for our language—it had become a hard, cold language. . . . The home had flourished in our memory, and now in reality it was rough and grey."[160] Seghers described her disappointment— the discrepancy between an idealized home and the unwelcoming reality returnees faced. While Italian Jews relished hearing their mother tongue,

Seghers emphasizes how even the language had changed. In contrast to Italian Jews, most German Jews did not write about arriving *home* when depicting their returns.

Alfred Kantorowicz noted in his diary that he wished he had a few weeks before starting to work to get adjusted in this foreign place.[161] He underlined how unfamiliar Berlin had become to him; the names of the subway stations had changed, and he could no longer orient himself. For these German Jews, home was lost or transformed in ways that made it unrecognizable. The once familiar environment had become, just like the subway maps, unreadable. Geographers of the Holocaust have emphasized how "the Holocaust transformed the meaning as well as the materiality of every place and space it touched."[162] After the war the destructive power of the Nazi war and genocide showed its lasting impact. While Italian Jews tended to connect their postwar experiences with their memories of life in Italy before the racial laws, German Jews emphasized that the place to which they returned did not resemble the Germany in which they had felt at home. They expressed a feeling of familiarity only with caution. Still, some things remained the same, just enough to remind them of what had once been. Hans Mayer expressed the eerie feeling of returning to this unfamiliar place where they once had been home: "Whatever I now saw or would see: it was completely foreign, of course, but it was also, in a strange, disturbing way, something like a homecoming. A return home to the unfamiliar."[163]

Lothar Orbach, who later called himself Larry Orbach, grew up in Berlin. In 1942 he went underground, but he was caught and sent to Auschwitz. After his liberation Orbach briefly returned to his hometown. He wrote down his impressions upon return and published these in *Der Weg*. "I was walking slowly, still I could not grasp it, no, still I could not believe it, I am alive, I am really alive," Orbach recalled. "A cold wind was rising, and it seemed to me as if it asked me in its unfriendly tone—Where to? Stranger. Where to? I listened—did I hear correctly—stranger? Was I a stranger here in this grey, destroyed city? I began to cry and only had one wish, to once again have friends, to once again be home." Orbach expresses both a desperate wish to feel at home and estrangement from the place where he used to belong. He recounts how he wandered the streets and stumbled upon the destroyed Jewish cemetery, where he found a stone with the word *ben* (Hebrew for son), and exclaimed, "Yes, I was a son of this . . . people [*Volk*]!"[164] He writes about the joy he felt at this moment in which he regained a sense of belonging, not within his former hometown but as a Jew. The destroyed cemetery symbolized the destroyed Jewish past and thus the impossibility of feeling at home in his former hometown. In September of the same year, Orbach left Germany for the United States.

The contrasting ways Italian and German Jews narrated their returns extended to their depictions of the weather. Adriana Luzzati, a young girl who survived the war with her family in Switzerland, recalled that the day she returned to Turin was a beautiful, warm day in July.[165] Max Donati, who, like Luzzati, returned from Switzerland, wrote, "Italy waited for us with its blue sky."[166] Fulvia di Segni Jesi remembered that it was snowing when her ship arrived in Italy but claimed she did not feel the cold.[167] Livio Steindler wrote about his first winter in Italy, after years in Israel, that "the snow covered the city like a blanket," evoking an image of warmth and safety.[168] In contrast, German Jews wrote of suffering under the cold temperatures, and Ludwig Marcuse, who arrived in the summer, described the climate as oppressive.[169]

Italian and German Jews also depicted the destruction of their hometowns differently. Italian Jews emphasized their pain at seeing their hometowns in ruins. One Italian Jew wrote in April 1946, "My God, what have they done to my beautiful Milan?" and another exclaimed four months later, "How many ruins, in what state was my poor fatherland!"[170] Di Segni Jesi, who emphasizes her emotional attachment to Trieste throughout her memoir, writes of the "martyrdom" of the city.[171] All three women personified their city or country in their writings and, by so doing, expressed their sense of connection.

German Jews, on the other hand, often associated the devastation around them with a sense of distance. The ruined streets, churches, and housing blocks rendered unfamiliar the city they had known so well, adding to the already widespread feelings of estrangement. Kantorowicz described his loss of orientation: "Even the victory column, which as if mocking itself still towered among rubble and ruins, was, so it seemed to me, no longer standing at the same place. I didn't know that it had been moved under Hitler."[172] Nazi engineering of public space, and then the bombings, had changed the cityscape and turned it unrecognizable, in particular for remigrants like Kantorowicz who had fled in the early 1930s.[173]

Peter Reiche had left Berlin in 1939 as part of the Kindertransport.[174] He returned from London in 1945 as a civil employee of the US Army. Hearing a rumor that his parents had survived their deportation, Reiche went to his hometown of Berlin to find them. Returning to the city, he and his friend, also a former resident of Berlin, felt disoriented: "From there I got my first glimpse of the destruction which is just beyond description. We got out at Charlottenburg station, and although we both had stood in the same spot hundreds of times before, we just didn't know where we are."[175] In his memoirs Larry Orbach recalled his first day in his hometown, "it was already late morning, when the freight train arrived at *Schlesischer Bahnhof* (train station) in Berlin. I had no idea where to go—the city was in ruins, and nothing recalled earlier times."[176] Beyond his disorientation, Orbach emphasized how his postwar experience remained disconnected from his memories of life before Nazism.

Lotte Winter unveiled a different way in which encounters with the destroyed country reinforced feelings of estrangement. In her memoir she described her shock at the destruction she encountered after her return from Sweden in 1946. She continued, "Yet, as it would soon become clear, a city of ruins was horrifying, but much, much more horrifying were the morally ruined and demoralized people."[177] Other German Jews likewise associated the devastated cities with the moral decay of the non-Jewish population.[178] "Destroyed the city outside—destroyed the inner world of its inhabitants," commented Anna Seghers in the spring of 1947.[179] For them the destruction symbolized the damage Nazi propaganda had caused in people's minds.

A Home That Recalls Suffering

Rather than remembering the time before Nazism, German Jews were frequently reminded of the traumatic years of persecution upon their returns. Their former hometowns became "a lasting reminder of loss," and the familiar streets, sights, and smells confronted them with the past.[180] An article in *Der Weg* referred to the "emotional burden" of being Jewish in Germany, "because every house and every stone reminds them of the sufferings of the past and of the dear ones they have lost."[181]

The journalist Karl Marx had left Germany in 1933. He emigrated first to France, then Italy, and later to England via North Africa. After the war, then in his fifties, he decided to return to help the surviving German Jews.[182] He moved back in 1947 but at least initially did not regain a sense of home: "The majority of us do not feel at home in Germany and we do not know if we can ever feel at home again. All too often we are reminded of the horrific years by a house that we connect with past times, or by the sight of a square on which a synagogue used to stand."[183] In a letter written in the fall of 1947, Anna Seghers explained, "The landscape is no longer connected to my youth, it is too much connected to the cruelties, the destruction of the most beloved people of my youth."[184] In her account even the landscape has become tainted.

For some, their memories made it too painful to resettle in their home-towns, even if they decided to live in Germany. One German Jew, for in-stance, asked the Frankfurt community for help to move from Berlin to Frankfurt because he "did not want to stay in Berlin, as this city reminded [him] too strongly of the past."[185] Lotte Winter chose to return to the Soviet Occupation Zone (Sowjetische Besatzungszone, SBZ) in 1946. Beyond pre-ferring the SBZ for political reasons, she expressed her dislike of returning to the town where she had lived before her emigration and where her family had owned a store in the city center: "When I think of meeting school-mates, clients of my mother, neighbors of our street and house, and old acquaintances, I would see them all as murderers of my relatives."[186]

In another case, a physician wrote to the head of the Berlin Jewish com-munity on behalf of his patient, who since 1946 had lived again in Greiz, her hometown. He asked for assistance in getting her moved to Berlin, ex-plaining that upon returning to Greiz, she had immediately become sick. He suspected that she had suffered a serious mental breakdown. After she spent some time at a friend's house, she recovered, but he feared "that she will surely fall back into her earlier state if she continued living in Greiz"; hence, he advised that they should try to find a place for her in Berlin.[187] The doctor assumed that her illness was connected to her return. In contrast to ascribing healing effects to a landscape, as we often do, this physician per-ceived the environment as literally making his patient sick.[188]

Not all Italian Jews could simply compartmentalize their experiences of persecution, and for some, their returns likewise triggered traumatic memories. Eugenia Servi, who returned with her family from their hid-ing place to Pitigliano, a small Tuscan town, felt she no longer belonged. She had suffered severely under the social ostracism after the racial laws of 1938, and the place functioned as a lasting reminder of her trauma. She considered moving to Palestine, but her parents did not approve. Servi re-membered the postwar years as the most difficult time in her life. She began to feel better only after she moved away to Milan. Later, when she visited her family from time to time, she wrote that she "no longer felt the usual fear when I saw the panorama of Pitigliano, which now appeared to me like any place, with the beauties of a medieval town, and I watched it with the eyes of a tourist who comes back: no love, no hate, it no longer brought back my past, I had liberated myself from it!"[189] Looking back, Servi emphasized the emotional distance she had created between herself and the place where she had grown up and the trauma it had caused her.

Servi had been seventeen when she returned with her family to Pitigliano. Like other young Jews, she had not been able to study due to the racial laws, and she struggled with creating a life for herself after years of persecution.[190] Her generation had suffered particularly under the exclusion, and in contrast to older Jews, they had few memories of the years before the persecution. Still, while Servi contemplated emigration, she eventually settled in Milan. Thus, even though she no longer wanted to live in Pitigliano, the memories of persecution ultimately could be contained in that specific place and she could still feel at home in Italy.

Like Servi, Goti Bauer moved to Milan rather than rebuilding her life in her hometown. Bauer went back to her family home in Fiume, now Rijeka, in hopes of being reunited with her brother. But she could not find him, and her home no longer existed. Bauer explained, "The impact of reality was very hard, the house robbed of everything, occupied by others, the sense of loneliness, pain without end."[191] Upon her arrival in Fiume, Bauer faced the extent of her loss. With her home destroyed and her family murdered, reconnecting with her prewar life proved impossible. Her hometown was now a Yugoslav city. Similarly, Jews who returned to Abbazia and Istria came home to places that were now Yugoslav, and many were forced to leave, while Königsberg and Breslau were no longer German cities, thus adding additional difficulties to the possibility of returning home.[192]

Empty Homes

Like the return to cities, towns, and villages, the first encounters with family homes triggered overwhelming emotions, like for Goti Bauer. Hans Frankenthal recalled his and his brother's reaction when they arrived at their home in a small village in North Rhine–Westphalia: "It was only a few meters from the Schmallenberg train station to our parents' house. . . . We slowly went up this path, dressed in civilian clothes, but still with prisoners' jackets. On the stairs to our front door, I stopped my brother and asked him to take off his jacket, in order to avoid taking bugs with us. In this manner we entered our parents' house after six years. In the last years I had not cried, but now I was overcome by crying fits—I needed hours to calm down."[193]

Taking his prisoner jacket off to avoid contaminating the still-safe space of his home, Frankenthal was overwhelmed by his loss and trauma. He and his brother, in that sense, had been luckier than Bauer, who, like many others, found a destroyed home upon her return. The dancer Valeska Gert returned to Berlin in 1949. She remembers looking for the house in which she had grown up but, "there was nothing left, not even ruins, just a pile of stones." A return to her childhood home proved impossible.[194] Claudio Gallico, an Italian Jew who had survived the war in hiding, described his experience of returning to his house in Mantova: "It was a terrible thing, the house was really in a sorry state; it was no longer a home, it was just another container. There was nothing, and it was cold."[195] Like Gallico, many others found their homes destroyed or occupied by strangers and their possessions gone.[196]

The damage done by the looting of cherished possessions went beyond the material loss. Scholars from a variety of disciplines have examined how dwellings and the objects they contain become central to our political, social, and psychological existence. Psychologist Marc Fried explains that a "sense of spatial identity is fundamental to human functioning," and displacement and loss of home disrupt an "individual's conception of [her or] his own body in space."[197] Similarly, Clare Cooper Marcus asserts in her work on the psychological and sociological meanings of home that, when "faced with an unintentional loss of treasured possessions, most people experience a profound sense of diminishing of the self."[198] Carefully selecting the pieces we put into our homes is a way to express ourselves. By decorating and furnishing a place, we make it into a home. Without these objects, home, in the words of Gallico, becomes a meaningless container. The loss of home, and the loss of cherished objects, brings immense grief.[199]

Jews who returned reacted with shock to the state in which they found their homes and belongings.[200] Albert Meyer, who returned as an American GI, explained in a letter to his relatives his unsuccessful attempt to retrieve some of his family's belongings: "I went to Lützowstrasse 10 [his family's home]. My uniform was my invitation. Someone from upstairs had the key, otherwise I would have broken the door open. . . . The ground floor is empty, the people who lived in it fled from the city. I went through all the rooms but did not see one piece of our old furniture."[201] Samuele "Sami" Varsano, a chemist, escaped the round-ups and survived the war living in Rome with his family. When he returned to his house in Magliana, a neighborhood in southwest Rome, he found "the door to our house . . . wide open. It had been ransacked, turned upside down. . . . . I found my 'good' trousers with the back pocket ripped. I had left my wallet there with my last pay-check, and naturally it wasn't there. . . . On the floor, half smashed-up, was Graziella's doll. . . . I cried for a long time."[202] While the missing wallet points to the material damage, the destruction of his daughter's doll symbolizes the invasion of the family's home, the violation of a space that once promised to provide safety and security.

Eugenia Bassa, then a young woman in her early twenties, recalled her disappointment when she arrived at her home in Ferrara in the spring of 1945: "Our house was still there. But inside, what a disaster. Only the walls were left! All the furniture and of course all the rest was missing."[203] Similar to Claudio Gallico, she invokes the image of an empty space that no longer resembled the place she had left behind. With their furniture, photographs, jewelry, toys, and paintings gone, the personal items that had made their apartment or house *a home* were missing or destroyed.[204] Many surviving Jews experienced a sense of total loss when returning to their homes. Enrica Vitale, a young Jewish woman who had survived the war in hiding, wrote, "About two years passed since our forced departure, and now, at the return, there is nothing anymore that relates to the past, no things and no people. In such short time, the work of a life and the lives of so many dear ones have been destroyed."[205]

Along with the loss of their homes, surviving Jews had lost some of their most valuable mementos, objects that had belonged to or reminded them of people murdered during the Holocaust. Cherished objects like jewelry, books, and photographs play a crucial role in the construction and transmission of family stories.[206] The loss of such objects that embedded precious memories disrupted processes of remembering.[207] Miranda Avigdor, who survived Auschwitz but lost her parents in the camps, wrote in a letter to her cousin in the fall of 1945, "Another sad surprise awaited me; the Germans and Fascists had completely robbed my home, even the jewels of my poor mother."[208] Massimo della Pergola explained that "due to the Nazi looting at my home and that of my mother I have only one photograph of my father. . . . My brother, deported to Auschwitz in 1943, was gassed at that camp in 1944. Of him, too, I have only one photograph."[209] Sonia Oberdorfer, an Italian Jewish teacher who had survived the war hiding in the countryside, described her grief over the loss of family pictures: "Unfortunately, for the most part even the family photographs, which I immediately started

Figure 1.2. Hans Erich Fabian in the destroyed Berlin Jewish cemetery, September 1948.
© Bildarchiv Pisarek / akg-images.

to search for in order to find the beloved faces of those who were no longer there, were gone."[210] Much has been written on the crucial role photographs play within Holocaust memory as memory cues and last remnants of the past. Without even such "fragmentary remnants," reconstructing the destroyed world became even more difficult, and their loss weighed heavy.[211]

Alongside the loss of private mementos, Jews faced the destruction of cemeteries, synagogues, and community archives. Sara Corcos reported on the first postliberation meeting of Jews in Florence. They "gathered in Via delle Oche to say the [the evening prayer.] It was however in a very sad state: the Great Temple had been severely damaged; the offices and the hospital had been totally sacked; the archives lost.... As is well known, the sacred furnishings had been stolen by the Germans."[212] Like the looting of photographs and jewels, the destruction of synagogues, cemeteries, archives, and libraries goes beyond material value. Such public places are a spatial reminder of people's history in and belonging to a city, town, or village. Their loss ruptured the connection to the past. Abraham Pisarek's photograph of Hans Erich Fabian, chairman of the Berlin Jewish community, carefully reading the inscriptions on a pile of partially destroyed stones removed from their graves in the Berlin Jewish cemetery allows the viewer to glimpse this tremendous loss. The stones were supposed to mark the graves for an eternity, but now they were reminders of destruction.

Conclusion

Age, gender, political convictions, and individuals' experiences during the war all influenced how German and Italian Jews perceived their returns. Different discourses about the possibility of rebuilding Jewish life in Germany and Italy likewise shaped their accounts. The constant reminders of Germany's crimes made it more difficult for German Jews to feel or express attachment, and the general discourse of disapproval of Jewish life in Germany colored the way they could perceive and narrate their postwar relationship.[213] Among surviving German Jews, love for their homeland remained outside of their emotional community's "norms of emotional expression and value," to borrow Barbara Rosenwein's terms.[214] Those who mainly identified as and associated with other political emigrants proved less affected by the general condemnation of Jewish life in Germany.

Italian Jews never confronted a negative discourse, as the Italian and international Jewish communities supported their choice to live in Italy. They focused on positive recollections of their preemigration lives in Italy. The symbolic meanings of place mattered—had their home country become a symbol of violence and persecution, or was it still a place with good coffee? While most Italian Jews highlighted attachment in their depictions of return, many German Jews emphasized that the years of persecution, war, and violence had transformed their home beyond recognition.

2

ENTANGLED MEMORIES

IN NOVEMBER 1945 VITTORIO FANO, THE HEAD OF the Venetian Jewish community, sent out invitations to a ceremony in honor of the deported Jews: "In memory of our fellow citizens whose fate remains a dark mystery, the Jewish community has called for . . . a solemn ceremony at the Temple to implore God's return of those . . . for whom not all hope is lost and peace to all the millions of unhappy Jews in Europe who have disappeared, innocent victims of Nazi-fascist cruelty."[1] Fano's words place the ceremony on the threshold of commemoration: it is held "in memory" of the victims, but he still hoped for some to return. In the immediate aftermath of the war, the fate of many deportees remained uncertain.

In the months and weeks following their liberation, German and Italian Jews did not yet refer to the wartime genocide as "the Holocaust."[2] They did not have an overarching term for the horrors they had lived through, and indeed many had a fractured picture of the extent of Fascist and Nazi persecution. Surviving Jews looked back at their individual experiences and searched for words for what had happened; they aimed to gather more information and tried to understand. This chapter explores how Jews in Italy and East and West Germany collected traces of the lives of those murdered to mourn and eventually commemorate those who could not return.

There is an ample and ever-expanding literature on Holocaust memory.[3] Much of the existing scholarship examines political manipulations of the past, focusing on speeches, memorials, museums, historical sites, education, and legislation.[4] This chapter focuses largely on how individual Jews in Germany and Italy recounted their experiences.[5] It centers around people who *remembered* Nazi persecution and genocide, in the literal sense of the word.

These individuals, however, did not and could not communicate their memories in isolation.[6] When individuals turn their recollections into a story, they rely on and draw from existing narratives, knowledge, and belief systems.[7] In his seminal work on collective memory, Maurice Halbwachs emphasizes the social dimensions of remembering. "Our memories remain collective . . . ," Halbwachs writes, "and are recalled to us through others even though only we were participants in the events or saw the things concerned. In reality, we are never alone."[8] He continues, "Our most personal feelings and thoughts originate in definite social milieus and circumstances."[9] Individuals' representations of the past depend on their specific environments and social contexts. Building on scholarship that has highlighted how, starting even before the end of the war, political and cultural elites constructed myths and narratives, this chapter examines how Jews in East and West Germany and Italy responded to and influenced these narratives. I suggest that we should understand the process of creating such narratives about the past as circular. Existing discourses shaped individuals' perceptions of their past while, at the same time, these individuals contributed to or aimed to change these narratives.

The German and Italian Jews at the center of this chapter came from various backgrounds and looked back at diverse experiences. They all belonged to the broadly defined group of survivors, meaning here that they had survived the war and racial persecution, though only few of them had survived the camps. They all, in this sense, belonged to one "community of experience."[10] Yet not all of them chose to frame their particular memories as part of this community of Jewish victims of racist persecution. By positioning their personal recollection within a specific community, individuals emphasized their belonging to this group. Many Italian Jews preferred to see their experiences as part of a broader Italian story, while many Communist Jews in East Germany perceived themselves foremost as antifascist resisters. Foregrounding some experiences and silencing others, surviving Jews actively shaped and constructed a narrative that supported their place within a specific community of memory. We tend to think mainly about how communities shape the construction of memory, but we can see here also that with the ways Italian and German Jews told their stories they marked themselves as part of a distinct group. In other words, by turning memories into narratives, they signaled their belonging to or distance from specific communities of memory. At the same time, individuals' retellings

58 | *Home after Fascism*

of their experiences were informed and shaped by the community of which they felt themselves to be a part.

Historians of memory have rejected the notion of a singular collective memory. Indeed, while dominant narratives emerged in East Germany, West German, and Italy, other perspectives of the past existed alongside these. The national frame was neither the only nor necessarily even the most meaningful one. As the prior chapter showed, the way the international Jewish community understood the past influenced returning Jews' perspectives. How the local Jewish community framed the past likewise played a role. These smaller communal memories also contained fractures. Highlighting this fractured nature of memory, this chapter shows how Jews in Germany and Italy positioned themselves vis-à-vis these various narratives. It begins with the hesitant and careful beginnings of narrating and traces how individuals started to communicate their recollections and give meaning to their experiences.

Gathering Information

Today most people have a clear idea of what happened to deported European Jews. This was not so for surviving German and Italian Jews in the days following their liberation. They had not yet formed the language to describe their experiences, and they usually were not able to place their individual experiences within a larger framework. Many did not grasp the extent of the destruction. Those who had survived in hiding or protected by a non-Jewish partner started to gather information about the most recent past in the hope of finding out what had happened to their loved ones.

A short time after the city's liberation in June 1944, the Roman Jewish community formed a search organization, the Committee for the Search and Support of Deported Jews (Comitato ricerche soccorsi deportati ebrei, CRSDE), which aimed to compile information and search for Jewish deportees as well as prepare for their return. The committee's papers reveal their lack of knowledge. One report states that the "elderly, women, and children, who left bereft of the necessary clothing, are in German concentration camps for almost a year, including winter time, and one can therefore assume that they are in a miserable physical and moral condition."[11] While the Vatican and the Allies possessed information about the death camps, most Italian Jews only knew that their loved ones had been put on trains and transported to an unknown destination.[12] Lia Levi, a young

Pisan Jew who survived in hiding, remembered that after their liberation, her family discussed the fate of her deported cousins: "I knew only that the Germans had brought them who knows where, together with their parents. In my family we believed that the cousins would return and tell us."[13]

By and large, German Jews for whom systematic deportations had begun already in the fall of 1941 had a better idea of what had happened to their deported relatives. By the summer of 1942, many suspected that deportation would mean death, though others still held onto the belief that the authorities merely "evacuated"—the Nazi term for the deportations—Jews to work camps. Over time more and more German Jews started to take rumors seriously, and in early 1943, suspicion had become certainty for most.[14] But their knowledge about the camps remained fractured as they lacked basic information, such as where exactly their relatives had been deported.

In the aftermath of the war, Italian and German Jews used similar language to describe how their loved ones had seemingly disappeared into nothingness. Expressions such as "and never a word again," "and then there was no trace," and "since then we know nothing" run through many diaries, letters, and testimonies.[15] Maria Simonetta Sacerdoti, a Roman Jew, tried to find information about her cousins, of whom "she knows nothing since August 1943," and Kurt Grote, who sent a letter to the reestablished Jewish community in Frankfurt on behalf of friends, explained that their relatives had been "sent away in November 1941 and since then no trace."[16] In many cases German Jews wrote that their relatives had been deported "nach dem Osten," to the East, while Italian Jews imagined "per la Germania," to Germany, as the destination.[17] While they named different locations, both referred to a vague place.

Nazi euphemisms that obfuscated reality continued to shape the discourse in the immediate aftermath of the war. Both German and Italian Jews used *deported* (*deportiert* in German, *deportati* in Italian), a term that fails to describe what happened to those sent to the death camps. To deport means to send off, to expel, but it does not convey that those deported would be murdered. Others used *evacuated*, the term used by the Nazis, which even more so than *deported* misrepresented events as people are usually evacuated for their own safety.[18] Others used *verschickt*, sent away, which, like evacuated, rings positive.[19] The usage of such words made it more difficult to get a clearer understanding of the most recent past. Some German Jews used *verschleppt* (abducted), which in contrast conveys the violent nature of the deportations.[20] Italian Jews used *catturati* (caught) or

60 | *Home after Fascism*

presi (taken), in addition to *deported,* terms focusing on the moment of arrest rather than on what happened after, which remained obscure.[21]

In the first weeks and months after liberation, Jews often did not yet know whether the Nazis had murdered their loved ones or whether they had survived the camps. But the Roman Jews' belief that the deported would return did not last. With the liberation of the camps, more news began to reach those who had survived. In its first postliberation edition from December 1944, the journal *Israel* published an article, translated from Russian, that described Majdanek. The Soviet journalist, who had visited the camp, estimated that the Nazis had murdered several hundred thousand people there.[22]

Within days after the end of the war, pictures and news of the camps began to circulate in the postwar societies.[23] This, however, did not mean that surviving Jews could understand and process what had happened; the murder of millions was incredibly hard to grasp. On April 28, 1945, Elena Morpurgo, who had fled to Switzerland while her non-Jewish husband remained in Italy, noted in her diary, "Before going to bed, I also glanced at the newspapers, and I read—with horror—what journalists returning from a trip to Germany wrote about the Buchenwald camp for deportees, near Weimar. Instinctively, you would want to believe that this is exaggeration. . . . They estimated the Jewish victims of Nazism at six or seven million. One could go crazy with the revelation of such atrocities!"[24]

In the spring of 1945, Italian and German Jews saw the first survivors returning and hoped that their loved ones would be among them. With most lacking concrete information about the whereabouts and fate of deported family members, a desperate search began.[25] Some traveled extensively while others returned to their hometown in the hope of reuniting with family members.[26] When Hans Winterfeldt returned to Berlin after his liberation from Auschwitz to search for his mother and father, he found a note on the apartment door of the woman who had last hidden them with his parents' current address.[27] Peter Reiche, who came from London to Berlin in 1945, likewise managed to find his parents, who had survived Theresienstadt. But most were not so lucky. After his liberation from Bergen-Belsen in mid-April 1945, Heinz Galinski made his way back to Berlin with the hope of finding relatives there, but "the hope was not fulfilled."[28] In their search, many contacted the newly reestablished Jewish communities, consulted lists in newspapers, placed ads asking for information, got in touch with Jewish and non-Jewish relief organizations, and turned to survivors in the hope that they may have sighted their relatives in the camps.[29] With time passing, the return of deportees became more and more unlikely, though some surviving Jews continued to search for years or even decades.[30] Others concluded that their loved ones had been killed.

Keeping Memories Alive

When Anna Di Gioacchino Cassuto returned from Auschwitz in July 1945, she hoped to reunite with her family. She learned that her youngest daughter had died but that her other children had survived in hiding. Anna tried desperately to gather information about her husband, Nathan Cassuto, from whom she had been separated upon arrival in Auschwitz.[31] But with time the purpose of her letters to community officials changed. She no longer hoped that Nathan would return.[32] In September 1947, at which point Anna had emigrated to Palestine, she turned to Raffaele Cantoni, the president of the Union of Italian Jewish Communities, (Unione delle Comunità Israelitiche Italiane: UCII), asking if they would support her efforts to commemorate Nathan. Anna's sister Sara appealed to the committee for the celebration of the resistance in "the hope that this noble figure of Italian Judaism will finally be remembered as he deserves in the next celebration."[33]

Like the Cassutos, other Italian and German Jews hoped to keep their murdered relatives alive in memory. Their loved ones had died "without leaving a trace," and no grave marked their life and death. In their work on memorial books of Polish Jewry, anthropologists Jack Kugelmass and Jonathan Boyarin argue that these books "came to be seen by them [the survivors] as substitute gravestones."[34] Most Italian and German Jews did not publish memorial books, but by writing about their murdered friends and family members and adding their names to plaques and monuments, they likewise ensured that their loved ones would not disappear.[35] In the preface to her autobiographical novel, Marta Ottolenghi Minerbi, whose husband was murdered in Auschwitz, expresses this wish to eternalize the victims, "the millions of creatures, innocent victims, swept away by this hellish storm, lost forever, without a stone to remember their name, dissolved into nothing. . . . I would like them to be eternalized in these poor pages of mine."[36]

In most cases memories were all that remained. Not only had their fathers, mothers, children, or friends disappeared but also the belongings of deported relatives were no longer there. Not having any material remains exacerbated the sense of loss and made dealing with death even more difficult.[37] Psychologist Isaac Tylim argues that "the material world, be it bones, stones, or wrecked metal, assists mourners in the process of working through depressive affects. In this manner, the psyche may symbolically restore that which was damaged or destroyed."[38] In the case of the Holocaust, most of the objects the deceased had cherished were destroyed or stolen; there was no body to bury and no grave to visit.[39]

Italian and German Jews, as Jewish survivors elsewhere, bemoaned the lack of graves: "38 members of the family died. No gravestone tells of their life, of their death," wrote Fritz Selbiger, a Berlin Jew who lost most of his family.[40] The sisters Luisa and Silvia Zaban escaped to the South of Italy just as Trieste, their hometown, came under Nazi control. They survived the war, but their parents were murdered. Like Selbiger, they expressed sorrow about the absence of a grave: "There is not even a tomb for them [their parents], only a name carved on a stone in the cemetery of Trieste."[41] Ellen Rathé, whose mother had been deported in 1942, decided to spend some of the money she received from the restitution payments on a gravestone for her, which she had placed next to her father's stone in the Jewish cemetery in Berlin Weissensee. The stone read: "To my beloved mama, who was murdered by Hitler."[42] Thus she marked not only her mother's life and death but also the brutal way she had died.

Giorgio Bassani's most famous novel, *The Garden of the Finzi-Continis*, begins with the narrator's visit to an Etruscan cemetery. He reflects on the meanings of the tombs for those whose relatives were buried there, describing them as a "second *home*." There, "at least," Bassani writes, "nothing would ever change." The visit reminds the narrator of Ferrara's Jewish cemetery, and he thinks back to the Finzi-Continis, who had built a "monumental tomb" there. Like the Etruscan tombs, the Finzi-Continis' tomb was meant to mark their importance and belonging within their hometown and allow them to remain there for an "eternity." Grasping the discrepancy between the wish and the reality, the narrator is pained by his memories:

> And my heart ached as never before at the thought that in that tomb, erected, it seemed, to guarantee the perpetual repose of the man who commissioned it—his and his descendants'—only one, among all the Finzi-Continis I had known and loved, had managed to gain that repose. In fact the only one buried there is Alberto, the older son, who died in 1942 of a lymphogranulona. Whereas for Micòl, the second child, the daughter, and for her father, Professor Ermanno, and her mother, Signora Olga, and Signora Regina, Signora Olga's ancient, paralytic mother, all deported to Germany in the autumn of '43, who could say if they found any sort of burial at all?[43]

The novel's prologue thus marks the violent rupture in Italian Jewish history and highlights the pain that stemmed from the inability to bury and visit the graves of those murdered. More than a resting place for the dead, graves provide spatial links to the past for the living and strengthen their sense of belonging to the village, town, or city where their ancestors were buried.

Confronting their loss, surviving Italian and German Jews aimed to create spaces that allowed them to commemorate and remember their loved ones. For the Jews of Rome, the Ardeatine Caves, the site of a mass killing during which the SS killed 335 Italians, became a place of mourning. The massacre's victims included prisoners serving jail sentences, most of them for political offenses, along with members of the resistance, male civilians randomly rounded up in the streets of Rome, and seventy-five Jews. The eldest victim was in his seventies, the youngest fifteen. After the war, Italians who had a relative murdered in the massacre went to identify the bodies, and some were able to bury their loved ones. But the caves gained significance not only for the victims' relatives. In Roman Jewish memory, the massacre of the Fosse Ardeatine was intertwined with the deportations and death camps, all part of their sufferings and loss.[44] The caves became a place for pilgrimage. Families brought flowers, and the community organized visits.[45]

Others searched for a space that could connect them with their murdered loved ones. One German Jew decided to visit the French transit camp, Gurs, where his parents had been sent. "All I could do was to visit the place where they were held," he explained.[46] An Italian Jew suggested to the head of the Committee for Searching Jewish Deportees (Comitato ricerche deportati ebrei, CRDE), the renamed CRSDE, that the Jewish community should undertake a pilgrimage to the camps, arguing that "many survivors (including myself) are eager to gather at the place where their relatives were tortured."[47] His idea, initially rejected as costly and impractical, highlights the need of survivors to find a place where they could mourn and commemorate.[48]

Giving Meaning

Communities created sites of mourning by erecting monuments or plaques that listed the names of the deported. These monuments, stones, or plaques carried a ritual significance for surviving Jews.[49] They offered a substitute for a grave, a place they could frequent to mourn and feel connected with

64 | Home after Fascism

their loved ones.[50] "Other faces which we did not see again we met on the tombstone in the garden of the Synagogue, where we read the names of students, schoolmates, acquaintances, who had been deported and did not return," wrote Sonia Oberdorfer about the plaque in the Jewish cemetery in Florence.[51] The monument at the Jewish cemetery in Mannheim, shaped like a big urn, carries the inscription "To those who found no grave."[52] The inauguration ceremonies for such memorials, in an albeit imperfect way, substituted for funerals as they provided an occasion to name and remember the dead.[53]

With the erection of plaques and monuments, the personal mourning of loved ones entered a public space and became part of a larger communal Jewish memory as well as of broader national narratives. During inauguration ceremonies Jewish leaders and often state officials as well held speeches that framed the persecution and murder of European Jews within a particular context, such as, depending on place and background, Zionism or antifascism.

The inauguration ceremony for the Monumento al Sacrificio Ebraico in Milan in April 1947 exemplifies this. The architect, Manfredo D'Urbino, who had survived the war with his wife and children in Switzerland, designed the monument under the direction of Raffaele Cantoni. The monument, consisting of a large menorah and a crypt containing twelve tombs, was erected in the Cimitero Monumentale in Milan. It holds ashes from Dachau as well as ashes from twelve Jews who died in Italy under different circumstances— one died a natural death, one committed suicide to avoid deportation, the others were killed in massacres or fighting as partisans. It also contains the ashes of Israel Epstein, a member of the Irgun, a Zionist paramilitary group. Epstein had arrived in Italy only after the war and, having been accused of participating in a terrorist attack on the British embassy in Rome, was arrested by Italian police. When trying to escape prison, Epstein was shot by a guard and died.[54] Commemorating members of the resistance, Zionist fighters, and victims of the Holocaust, the monument presented the notion that all were part of the same fight and had died for similar reasons.

In his speech at the Monument's inauguration, Cantoni emphasized this idea: "The ashes," he declared, "symbolize the contribution that the Jewish people gave in this war for the establishment of an ideal of justice and freedom." He then reminded his audience "that thousands of refugees, the rest of this immanent tragedy, still run without a home and should find some understanding among those who control the Palestinian mandate today."[55]

Figure 2.1. Monumento al Sacrificio Ebraico, Milan. © Fondazione CDEC Archive, Milano.

With his speech, Cantoni placed the Jewish memory of persecution in a Zionist as well as an Italian national frame. Similarly, the monument that commemorated the Fosse Ardeatine massacre, inaugurated in 1949, emphasized national unity. Its inscription suggests that all the victims had been partisans and had been killed because of their resistance to the Nazi occupation, neither mentioning the Jewish origin of some of the victims nor alluding to the randomness by which the victims had been picked.[56]

The Jewish community in Fürth, a small town in West Germany, erected a memorial stone within the local cemetery in 1949. Here the victims are also depicted as martyrs who gave their lives for a cause, in this case for the Jewish people and their belief. The text on the stone reads:

> Our loyal brothers and sisters
> Gave their life as martyrs in the dark years 1933–1945
> For our people and our belief.
> In silent memory erected by
> The Jewish community in Fürth.[57]

66 | Home after Fascism

In the inauguration ceremony, Jean Mandel, the head of the community who had survived the war hiding in Poland, described the immense losses the community had suffered: "The once proud Jewish community of Fürth counted only 1,003 members in the end of 1939, and except for nine returnees, their destinies were sealed by the deportations which commenced on November 27, 1941." He continued: "All of these Jews from Fürth, along with 6 million of our brothers and sisters, gave their lives for our people and our faith. And so today we have come together here to erect a memorial stone in grief and profound sorrow." Referring to "our people and our faith," Mandel, as well as the inscription on the stone, placed the loss within a Jewish frame. Like Cantoni, he also linked Nazi persecution with Zionist aspirations: "For us few survivors, however, this stone is now a reminder, never to forget that our Jewish people can only live and be happy in their homeland."[58] This stone, while physically in Germany, functioned, in Mandel's perspective, as a memento that their true home was Israel. While Cantoni's references to the Italian resistance merged Zionist and Italian national narratives, Mandel separated the surviving German Jews from Germany, even though they remained there. Rabbi David Spiro, who also spoke at the inauguration ceremony in Fürth, likewise placed the memories within a Zionist frame, emphasizing that the murdered died with the wish that Jews should never again live under foreign rule. Now the survivors had a duty to build a home in Israel.

The non-Jewish district president, Hans Schregle, placed the stone in a different context. He emphasized that the murdered "were fellow citizens who, like all of us, loved their home, and as the monument in the background [referring to a First World War monument] shows, also were willing to sacrifice their lives for the honor of this home."[59] In his speech, *home* meant Germany, and he did not see the most recent persecution as a break in the connection between Jews and Germany and its history. The Jewish and non-Jewish participants at the inauguration ceremony perceived not merely the past differently but imagined different homelands for the victims. While perhaps vague enough for non-Jewish contemporaries to overlook this, the stone refers clearly to Jews as separate; "our people" does not mean Germans, but Jews.

While Jewish survivors across Germany struggled with similar difficulties of commemorating the victims in the country of the perpetrators, the antifascist narrative that emerged in the East provided a different framework that posed both possibilities for the construction of a shared past as well as challenges. In November 1948 the Jewish communities and the Association of Those Persecuted by the Nazi Regime (Vereinigung der Verfolgten des Naziregimes, VVN), the largest postwar organization for survivors of Nazi persecution, organized an event at the Deutsches Theater in Berlin to commemorate the November pogrom. In his speech, Wolfgang Langhoff, the theater's director, stressed the need to establish a society that punishes racial fanaticism and a false sense of superiority among the upper classes, or *Herrendünkel*. Naming both racism and classism in connection to the November pogrom, he cast the persecution of German Jews within a Socialist reading of the past. Walther Bartel, one of the two heads of the VVN, did the same by linking November 9, 1938, to November 9, 1918—the day both Philipp Scheidemann, deputy chairman of the Social Democrats, and Karl Liebknecht, leader of the left-wing Socialist organization Spartakusbund, proclaimed the end of monarchy. Bartel explained that the pogroms would not have been possible if the German working class had managed to get rid of the old economic and military elites in the 1918 revolution. The other head of the VVN and the only Jewish speaker, Heinz Galinksi, provided a different emphasis in his speech, stating that "this night should never be forgotten, and it is discouraging for Jews in Germany that in the past three years neither in word nor act could they sense any sign of regret."[60] Such pushback against a German memory culture that failed to acknowledge its own guilt played an important role in German Jewish postwar discourse, both in East and West Germany.

The aftermath of the war saw many similar events in which stones were erected, and victims remembered, across Europe. Those mentioned here provide just a glimpse into the construction of monuments that began before the end of the war and continues today.[61] These three examples allow us to see the different frameworks that emerged. People do not simply chronicle past events but rather construct a commemorative narrative that ascribes meaning to these events.[62] Individuals' personal experiences as well as their *Weltanschauung*, and the national and regional contexts, influenced the construction of a meaningful narrative. The participants in the commemorative ceremonies in Milan, Fürth, and Berlin all remembered the victims of Nazi persecution, but they interpreted the past differently.

Distinct and at times competing memories and narratives emerged, not only between Jews and non-Jews but also between Fascists and antifascists, Nazis and Communists, East and West, old and young. Even within the

68 | *Home after Fascism*

Jewish communities, people perceived the past differently. Depending on their war experiences, ideological outlook, and self-understanding, surviving Jews in Italy and East and West Germany became part of distinct communities of memory. Beyond narratives emerging on a national level, the perspectives of the local Jewish communities as well as the international Jewish community mattered. Jews in Italy and East and West Germany negotiated and situated themselves within different intersecting but also frequently competing strands of memory while also aiming to shape broader narratives. Placed between antagonistic or at least contradictory narratives, Jews could either aim to adapt them to make them fit their own perception of the past or remain outside a particular community of memory.

A Shared Past

Two interlinked narratives, one portraying Italians as brava gente and the other as united in antifascist resistance, dominated the Italian postwar discourse. The image of the good Italian emerged before the end of the war, supported by people like the philosopher Benedetto Croce. Croce differentiated between Italian and German national character, designating the former as essentially good and honorable. Fascism, in his depiction, remained foreign to Italian history.[63] After the war, Italy's postwar government and political elites more broadly, including both the Communist Party and the Christian Democrats, aimed to portray Italians as rescuers of Jews while obfuscating war crimes to strengthen Italy's position in the peace negotiations. The Italian press widely propagated the myth of the Italian people as innocent victims who had been horrified by antisemitic persecution, and most Italians across the political spectrum embraced this version of the past. As historians such as Filippo Focardi and Angelo Del Boca have shown, the myth of the brava gente played a crucial role in forming the Italian postwar national identity.[64]

Many Italians regarded themselves as victims of both the Fascist regime and the Nazi occupation.[65] Their experiences under the Germans after Mussolini's downfall overshadowed the two decades of Fascism, the war in Ethiopia, the antisemitic legislation of 1938, and the Italian occupation of Greece and the Balkans. Rejecting responsibility for the twenty years of dictatorship and the violence it brought, Italians refashioned themselves as victims of Nazism and fighters against Fascism and mostly chose to forget that they had also been perpetrators.

From the end of the war onward, the myth of mass resistance against the Germans likewise played a powerful cultural and political role.[66] Communists, Socialists, and Christian Democrats aimed to spread the narrative of an Italy unified in a national and patriotic war of liberation in order to boost their legitimacy and define themselves in opposition to the Fascist regime.[67] The notion of Italians as resisters and the understanding of the last two war years as a fight for liberation against the Germans stood in contrast to the personal memories of a large contingent of Italians who had supported the Fascist RSI. Still, the perception of Italians as united in resistance soon dominated public memory.[68] The particular experiences of Jewish as well as non-Jewish deportees found little resonance within this postwar narrative, which focused on the victorious and armed resistance. Thus, Italy's foremost deportee organization, the National Association of Ex-Political Deportees (Associazione Nazionale Ex Deportati, ANED), aiming to integrate its members' pasts into the national frame, highlighted links to the resistance and, while including Jewish victims, privileged political deportees.[69] The persecution of Jews remained marginal and submerged into a national, antifascist narrative within ANED.[70]

Italian Jews by and large also depicted their past within this framework of antifascist resistance and showed little interest in highlighting the particularity of their experiences. Rather than contradicting the dominant postwar narratives, Italian Jewish leadership and cultural elites contributed to the emergence and popularization of these myths.[71] They promoted the view that antisemitism did not exist among Italians and emphasized benevolent and humane behavior. For instance, in March 1945 the Italian Zionist convention declared: "The convention of Italian Zionists, reunited in Rome for the first time after the liberation, remembers with a grateful heart the work of the silent, often heroic solidarity that so many of the oppressed Italian people—following the humanitarian example of the Catholic Church—offered to the persecuted Italians."[72] The statement highlights the experiences of the—comparatively to Germany, many—Italian Jews who were hidden by individual Italians or within institutions of the Catholic Church. Such experiences colored the postwar narrative and as here are often portrayed without reflection on widespread antisemitism, the Italian state's conduct, or the Catholic Church's implication.[73] Writing about help "offered to the persecuted *Italians*" rather than to Italian *Jews*, the Italian Zionist convention underlined Jews' belonging to Italy and avoided highlighting the particularity of the Jewish experience during the war. Moreover, the declaration emphasized not only Jewish but also Italian victimhood ("oppressed Italian people"), alluding to the German occupation and ignoring Italian collaboration. It created a narrative that united Jewish and non-Jewish Italians in a community of shared experience. In her seminal work *Reckonings*, Mary Fulbrook writes that "those who were persecuted formed, ultimately, a distinctive wider community of experience, separating them from those on the other side of the chasms by Nazi policies."[74] However, the dominant narrative among Italian Jews defied this chasm created by racial policies and instead insisted on a version of the past in which Italian Jews and non-Jews had shared the same experiences.

Many Italian Jews promoted the notion that all Italians had suffered and pointed to similarities between their own fate and the majority population's experiences.[75] "Their shoulders were also burdened with stories of poverty, separations, and loss," wrote Sonia Oberdorfer, an Italian Jewish teacher who had lost her job in 1938 due to the racial legislation, about her non-Jewish coworkers.[76] The editorial of the first postwar edition of *Israel*, an Italian Jewish journal that resumed publication in Rome in 1944 under the direction of Carlo Alberto Viterbo, similarly emphasized that both Italians and Jews had suffered horribly.[77] Rather than pointing to the particularity of their fate, many Italian Jews wished to integrate their individual experiences into a larger frame of a unified Italian memory.

Giacomo Debenedetti, one of Italy's most influential literary critics, wrote two short essays shortly before the end of the war in which he addressed the persecution of Roman Jews. He rejects seeing the Jewish fate as unique and rather maintains that "what Jews would prefer is that the suffering of those of them presently liberated and of those still being persecuted, be poured into, mixed, mingled with the long collective, the common levy of tears and pleas that all humans worthy of the name have sacrificed, and are still sacrificing, to assure the world its longest period of civilized centuries."[78] Italian Jewish postwar discourse aimed to merge the persecution of Jews with the narrative of Italian resistance against the German occupiers.[79] In April 1945 Raffaele Cantoni, who a year later would become the president of the Union of Italian Jewish Communities, gave a speech that celebrated the end of the war in Italy. He maintained that Jews could be especially happy "as they played an active role in the last phase of the war, which led to an expulsion of the enemies. Also because they know that their participation in the resistance and among the partisans has been significant and effective in every aspect. In the resistance and among the partisans, many felt finally again equal to other citizens."[80] Cantoni's speech promotes a narrative in which Italians liberated their home country from foreign enemies, and by taking part in in this war of liberation, Italian Jews marked their belonging to the nation, as they had in the Risorgimento a century earlier. The resistance, constructed as a "Second Risorgimento," allowed for narrating a shared past.[81]

In a letter to a Joint representative from January 1945, Lelio Vittorio Valobra, a lawyer from Genoa and chairman of DELASEM, described his interactions with the resistance movement. More pragmatically than Cantoni, he emphasized the importance of connecting Italian Jews with the resistance to ensure reintegration:

> Recently I contacted the heads of the Italian national liberation committee. . . .
> I am of the opinion that it would be useful to make gestures that prove our sincere recognition of the committee's duties. I am thinking of the donation of a small amount. One should also ascribe political value to this gesture, for it is of greatest importance already at this time that connections are fostered between Italian Jewry and the circles that will lead the future Italy. On the other hand, one would underline that Jews do not remain passive, but rather actively, with the means available, support the Italian resistance movement.[82]

Valobra, considering the political gain Italian Jews would receive from supporting the resistance movement, remained deeply invested in the position of Italian Jews within Italian postwar society.

A Dividing Past

Germans never mounted a significant resistance during the war and consequently lacked, at least in the West, a similar narrative that would have allowed Jews to fashion a shared past. Looking at the non-Jews around them, surviving German Jews saw experiences opposed to Jewish suffering. Lotte Paepcke described the past as an insurmountable gap that separated her from the non-Jewish population: "The hatred, the rifle butt, and the gas had severed their and our lives, our eyes would no longer find each other."[83] Most surviving Jews perceived the population as implicated in their persecution. Hans Jacobus, who had escaped Nazi Germany as part of the *Kindertransport*, returned from London to the Soviet occupied zone in 1947. He remembered that upon his return, he could not cease to think about what the Germans he encountered had done in the war; he kept asking himself, "And him? Had he also been a part of it?"[84] Many Jews lived

72 | *Home after Fascism*

with the suspicion that any stranger they encountered could have taken part in murdering their friends and family.[85]

Alfred Meyer, who had left in 1939 and returned as an Allied soldier, carefully considered the Germans' conduct, and when reporting to friends and family back in the United States, he pointed to the complexities in evaluating German behavior under the Nazis: "Dr. Beudel [the principal of his school] joined the party in 1937. Does that make him a Nazi? I don't think it does. On the other hand he was always for German glory, expansion, colonies, imperialism. So, I am sure, was our father."[86] It proved difficult to differentiate between the guilty and the innocent.[87]

While surviving Jews wondered and worried about what the Germans had done in the past decade, most Germans, at least publicly, did not.[88] Rather than considering their guilt, they perceived themselves as victims of the war. Historians Michael Geyer and Konrad Jarausch refer to a "selective perception," pointing out that Germans concentrated solely on their experiences as victims and helpless bystanders of the Nazi regime, overlooking their own participation in the Second World War's mass killing, genocide, and slave labor.[89] Similarly, Robert Moeller, focusing on public memoirs in West Germany, notes, "German victims . . . lived, breathed, organized, demanded recognition, and delivered speeches from the floor of parliament. What Germans had inflicted on others remained abstract and remote; what Germans had suffered was described in vivid detail and granted a place of prominence in the public sphere." [90] The emerging East German state, as Moeller indicates, restricted such public declarations of German victimhood and promoted a different narrative, though in private accounts stories of personal suffering overshadowed the suffering inflicted on others.

Jewish and non-Jewish Germans did not merely remember different experiences during the war, they also interpreted these experiences differently. Perhaps, if Germans had owned up to their past as perpetrators and implicated bystanders, it may have, in some ways, made living among them easier for returning Jews. Germans' insistence on their victimhood and innocence came as a shock to the victims. They reacted with surprise and anger to this discourse, which diametrically opposed their memories of suffering at the hands of those who now claimed ignorance. After emigrating to Palestine in 1935, the architect Julius Posener joined the British Army in 1941 and returned to Germany a month before the end of the war. Two years later he published his impressions in a short book titled *In Germany*, where he comments sarcastically on the denial of guilt: "It is well known that no one had been a Nazi, and that especially no one had favored the persecution of Jews."[91] Similarly, an article published in *Der Weg* in July 1946 criticized the German attempts to shift responsibility to the regime's leadership, observing ironically that "by the way, from Nuremberg word got out to all of Germany that Hitler and Himmler were the only really active party members."[92] Victor Klemperer's diary is filled with his annoyance about the general denial of guilt;[93] Hannah Arendt complained about the "deep-rooted, stubborn, and at times vicious refusal to face and come to terms with what really happened;"[94] and an article in the *Aufbau* commented, "The situation reminds one of the story of a guy who slaps another and then graciously remarks that 'for the sake of peace, let's write the whole thing off.'"[95]

After all they had endured, Jews wanted Germans to admit their guilt. An editorial in the *Jüdisches Gemeindeblatt für die britische Zone* published in December 1946 described the author's search for Germans who owned up to their past: "I came to Germany and was bitterly disappointed. In the first months I found not a single National Socialist in spite of hundreds of conversations." The author explained that Germans' refusal to deal with the past had made him regret his decision to return.[96] Others likewise saw this as reason to leave. The architect Julius Posener, for instance, had considered a return to Germany, but Germans' conviction that they had been the main victims of Nazism drove him away.[97] "The fact that the German people feel no compulsion to make amends for the crimes of Nazism is the most important reason why a substantial part of the few remaining German Jews have decided to emigrate," reports Moses Moskowitz for *Commentary* magazine in January 1946.[98] Germans' discourse of innocence stood in stark contrast to Jewish loss and suffering, and surviving Jews experienced the lack of remorse as painful and infuriating.

German Jews responded specifically to a widespread self-depiction as innocent bystanders who had been ignorant of the regime's crimes. In an article in *Der Weg*, Nelly Cohn-Leschzer, a survivor of Auschwitz who settled in Berlin after the war, emphasized collective responsibility and stressed that people were guilty of crimes that happened in their environment, even if they themselves were just witnesses.[99] Others likewise insisted that Germans had been guilty, even if they had not played an active role. In November 1946 another article in *Der Weg* stated: "Neither indifference to crimes that were committed in Germany's name, nor complicity through cowardly silence can be excused."[100] For these surviving Jews, Germans

74 | *Home after Fascism*

were guilty because they had failed to act and because they had passively stood by as their Jewish neighbors' fate deteriorated.[101]

Ralph Giordano and his family—his father was a non-Jewish Italian, his mother a German Jew—went into hiding toward the end of the war. In his book *Die zweite Schuld* (The Second Guilt), published in 1987, Giordano depicted the non-Jewish populations' reluctance to own up to their crimes.[102] In an earlier text, published in 1948, he called it the "personal cowardliness of the Germans" and perceived this as their main fault: "Cowardliness was not only *a* form of German complicity, it was *the* form. The main guilt of these millions was their great silence over the wrongs they encountered everywhere, daily, hourly. This silence sanctioned murder. This silence was therefore indirect murder."[103] Looking back at the most recent past, these German Jews did not claim that all Germans had been violent, and to some extent, they allowed Germans' insistence that they had not actively participated in the crimes. Some even accepted the notion that the Nazi leadership had led the people to war and violence. An article in *Der Weg* published in July 1946 argued that citizens had duties and that the "German people, as a whole, neglected their duty when they delivered themselves to a clique of desperados and let themselves *be instrumentalized*."[104] But German Jews did not accept that German citizens, as bystanders, were innocent. They called them out for following blindly and for their silence and passivity.

Recent scholarship has criticized the term *bystanders*, which presumes the possibility that those on the sidelines remained innocent.[105] The discourse among the German Jews in the immediate aftermath of the war foreshadows this discussion. In their understanding of the recent past, there were no innocent bystanders, there were the very few who helped, those who killed, and the many who were guilty because they failed to act. This understanding and the wish and need to point to non-Jews' responsibility for their suffering placed German Jews outside the national discourse. They lived among people whose interpretation of past events they rejected and indeed found offensive. German Jews expected apologies, remorse, and an acknowledgment of guilt, which most Germans wished to avoid by all means. Indeed, while German Jews' ability to regain a sense of home depended on a confrontation with the past, Germans' postwar conception of *Heimat* hinged on a denial of guilt and detachment from their most recent history.[106]

Consequently, Jewish voices that pointed to Jewish suffering and German responsibility found little attention in the immediate aftermath of the war. Wishing to forget their own responsibility, the non-Jewish majority belittled Jewish suffering. Victor Klemperer frequently heard, "It probably was not so bad,"[107] and someone told Inge Deutschkron, who had survived with her mother in hiding, that a concentration camp was nothing more than a prison and that Germans had suffered just as much as Jews.[108] In the spring of 1948, Moritz Goldschmidt heard the mayor of Bergisch-Gladbach exclaim, "One should finally stop making such a big deal because a few Jews were beaten to death."[109] Goldschmidt did not tolerate the mayor's hostile, antisemitic attitude to Jewish memory and filed a complaint with the state attorney. Most German Jews reacted with anger and frustration to the disinterest in their experiences. They did not wish to forget or forgive, but they voiced much of their critique of the German discourse internally, in exchanges with other Jews or published in Jewish journals and newspapers. Declaring their frustrations with Germans' inability to admit guilt to a Jewish audience, German Jews created a distinct Jewish community of memory.

The Other Germany

German Jews who wished to remain part of the broader German community, which soon took different shapes in East and West, had to adopt a different perspective. As Aleida Assmann states, "To be part of a collective group such as the nation one has to share and adopt the group's history," though more accurately here the group's *narration* of their history.[110] Historian Hans Rothfels, the son of a solicitor in Kassel with no strong ties to his Jewish roots, he had converted to Christianity in 1910, returned from emigration shortly after the war. A German nationalist, he remained deeply attached to his home country, and his work placed him within the West German discourse. In his book *The German Opposition to Hitler*, published in 1948, Rothfels portrayed Germany as "an occupied country" after 1933. He depicted Germans as innocent and Germany as distinct from Nazism. Asserting the existence of a true or other Germany that had resisted Hitler, he connected the time before 1933 with the postwar years, bridging over the Nazi period.[111] While the understanding of Germans as guilty made most Jews wait for an apology they did not receive and thus impeded any sense of belonging, the notion of the other or true Germany allowed Rothfels to conceive of a shared past with "good Germans," which placed him within the German discourse.

76 | *Home after Fascism*

Initially, when they had fled the country in the early 1930s, many politically engaged German Jews had embraced the idea of the other Germany, the better Germany that would rebel and persist against Nazism and form a foundation for rebuilding, and in discussions about Germany's future among emigrants, this notion had played an important role.[112] In his correspondence with Heinrich Mann, Alfred Kantorowicz expressed his hopes for a future Germany, and he saw his friend as the "voice of this better, the other Germany."[113] Kantorowicz lost his optimism as the years passed and toward the end of the war he conceded, "We know that we won't return to the other Germany with flying colors. The other Germany, that we talked about, that we hoped for, is buried under the rubble."[114] Believing in this other Germany proved increasingly difficult with the news about atrocities, destruction, and violence steadily growing.

Jews who had remained in Germany rarely depicted the other Germany, untouched by Nazism. Yet some had received help during the war and owed their lives to non-Jewish Germans, which shaped their perceptions. Siegmund Weltlinger, a Berlin Jew who had survived the war in hiding together with his wife, maintained that "many brave Germans . . . had opposed the government."[115] Experiences while in hiding also shaped Hans Rosenthal's understanding of Germany's past. The women who had risked their lives to save him, Rosenthal explained, made it possible for him to live in Germany without hatred.[116] Rosenthal, who survived as a teenager in a small garden allotment in Berlin-Lichtenberg, had barely known the three German women who hid him, but for many others it was their husband or wife who had stuck with them throughout the years of persecution. In most cases non-Jews in a "mixed marriage" did not leave their partner, even though the regime pressured them to do so.[117] Reflecting on this, Kurt Hirschfeld concluded, "Where would we have been, had no one helped us? That I, for instance, am now in charge of the orthopedic department in the Virchow hospital, I owe . . . to the luck of having found people, who truly risked their lives for me, above all my wife."[118]

Often, however, German Jews perceived these "good Germans" as an exception that contrasted to the majority's guilt.[119] While they acknowledged that a few Germans had behaved decently, they did not see them as representative of a "better Germany." An article in *Der Weg* from July 1946 argued, for instance, that the "heroic fight" of a minority remained irrelevant when evaluating Germans' guilt.[120] Hans Erich Fabian, who returned from Theresienstadt in 1945, explained in *Der Weg* that the number of those who had tried to help was "unfortunately very small compared with those who only thought of their own advantage."[121] Not long after writing these words, Fabian left with his family for the United States.

Few Germans resisted Nazism, and public memory in what would become West Germany did not, at least initially, focus on them. Persistent anti-Communist resentment among conservative elites, hardened by emerging Cold War tensions, impeded celebrations of Communist resistance against Nazism. In the immediate aftermath of the war, few embraced even the conservative resistance around Claus von Stauffenberg. In the first postwar years, public discourse still colored resistance with a hint of treason. Public memory focused on the Germans' sacrifice and resisters remained outside of this narrative.[122]

Most Germans viewed emigrants with suspicion and believed they had "watched the German tragedy from the box seats and stalls of foreign lands [*aus den Logen und Parterreplätzen des Auslandes*]."[123] Author Frank Thiess coined this dictum as part of a dispute that followed the letter of another conservative German writer, Walter von Molo, to Thomas Mann in which Molo asked the famous German to return to his home country. Mann explained that he, for several reasons, had no intentions to return, and a heated debate ensued in which a number of German intellectuals expressed their disdain for emigrants. When the Americans conducted a survey in 1947 among people who had not been NSDAP members, chosen for positions in the postwar bureaucracy, most expressed that they had little interest in the return of Thomas Mann or other emigrants. Thus, rather than aggrandizing the small potential for a narrative of the other Germany, public discourse in the Western zones excluded such stories from the postwar discourse. Thomas Mann had initially published his damning response in the German Jewish exile journal *Aufbau*, and as the journal states in a later edition, its readership had followed the debate closely.[124] Jews in Germany likewise paid attention to the Molo-Mann controversy.[125] The public's disdain for emigrants and resisters further distanced Jews' interpretation of the past from the dominant public discourse.

The Antifascist Germany

Even during the war, believing in the existence of the other Germany had become increasingly difficult, including for Communist Jews; Kantorowicz's disillusionment is but one example here. Still, some remained hopeful that after the war a Socialist and antifascist Germany could become reality. In contrast to West Germany, the GDR employed the notion of the other Germany within its foundational myth.[126] The Communists and Socialists who formed the political and cultural elite of the Soviet occupied zone and later the GDR fashioned a narrative of the most recent German past that differed from the West German version. Communists became the main heroes in this depiction that centered on the myth of antifascist resistance against Nazism. This narrative held its share of challenges for surviving Jews but at least initially enabled some to place their memories within this larger framework of antifascism. Surviving Jews could find or construct similarities between their own fate and the experiences of Communist emigrants, resisters, and camp survivors who also had been victims of Nazism.

The Association of Those Persecuted by the Nazi Regime, founded in Berlin in 1947, advocated on behalf of both Jewish victims and those persecuted for political reasons. Jews in the Soviet occupied zone hoped the VVN would support them in their compensation claims as well as in commemoration efforts. The inclusion of Jews in leading positions within the organization as well as initiatives of the VVN that commemorated the persecution of Jews seemed to justify the repeated expressions of confidence in the organization.[127]

Scholarship on eastern European memory often depicts the states' ideology of antifascism as impeding the memory of the Holocaust, and historians of the GDR have criticized the marginalization of the Holocaust under the Communist regime.[128] However, antifascism was more than just state doctrine. It provided a discursive framework that enabled a discussion of the murder of European Jews, if from a viewpoint that differed from the western understanding. Moving beyond the "marginalization thesis," more recently scholars have pointed to the multiple actors who played a role in the construction of official memory as well as to voices who criticized public memory in eastern Europe and the GDR.[129] Even in East Germany, memory was neither homogenous nor static.[130]

Communist and leftist Jews who returned to the SBZ and later the GDR considered discussing Nazi antisemitism and its roots as a crucial part of their efforts to construct a Socialist state. Numerous Jewish authors with Communist sympathies addressed the genocide against the Jews in the immediate aftermath of the war.[131] The writer Arnold Zweig, one of the most prominent Jewish intellectuals to return to the Soviet occupied zone after the war, aimed to bring attention to the persecution of Jews. He worked with the survivor Hilde Huppert on her memoirs, which were published in 1951 with the VVN's publishing house, and later wrote the preface for *Im Feuer Vergangen*, a collection of victim diaries from Poland.[132]

Three years earlier, in 1948, Buchenwald survivor Stefan Heymann published a book titled *Marxismus und Rassenfrage* (Marxism and racial question). Far from underestimating Nazi racist crimes, Heymann emphasized that "the racial ideology of the Nazis was undoubtedly the centerpiece of the fascist worldview, was the pole around which the Nazi 'world view' turned." And he further argued that eradicating racism would be crucial in the future: "That is why an important part of our moral reparation is the annihilation of the racial ideology with its roots here, where it is far from extinct. Through our fight against racial barbarism, we make a significant contribution to strengthening democratic forces in our own people and among all peoples."[133]

While Jews in West Germany tended to frame their experiences as part of a broader Jewish suffering and Italian Jews placed their past within the framework of Italian antifascist resistance, Heymann here perceives antisemitism and the persecution of Jews as part of racist discourses and practices that, while especially radical in Nazi Germany, existed elsewhere as well. Rather than highlighting the uniqueness of Jewish suffering, Heymann as well as other Jewish intellectuals in the emerging East German state perceived the fight against racism as an international struggle. Their analysis mirrored, in some ways, W. E. B. Du Bois's reflections on the persecution of Jews and Blacks that the African American intellectual and political leader published in the magazine *Jewish Life* after his 1949 visit to the Warsaw ghetto. Du Bois writes,

> The result of these three visits, and particularly of my view of the Warsaw ghetto, was not so much a clearer understanding of the Jewish problem in the world as it was a real and more complete understanding of the Negro problem. In the first place, the problem of slavery, emancipation, and caste in the United States was no longer in my mind a separate and unique thing as I had so long conceived it. . . . No, the race problem in which I was interested cut across lines of color and physique and belief and status and was a matter of cultural patterns, perverted teaching and human hate and prejudice, which reached all sorts of people and caused endless evil to all men.[134]

East German Jewish intellectuals' discussion around Nazi racial persecution synced with this broader leftist discourse around racist injustice.[135] They opposed the oppression of any group on racist grounds and tended to universalize the persecution of Jews under Nazism. Articles in

Kantorowicz's journal *Ost und West* (East and West), Siegbert Kahn's *Antisemitismus und Rassenhetze* (antisemitism and racial hatred), and Alexander Abusch's *Der Irrweg einer Nation* (A nation's wrong path) examined Nazi racial hatred, perceiving it as central to their analysis of National Socialism and as leaving a lasting mark on German society. In his *Der Irrweg einer Nation*, published in 1946, Abusch, a leading figure within the Cultural League for the Democratic Renewal of Germany (Kulturbund zur demokratischen Erneuerung Deutschlands), wrote, "Maidanek, Oswiecim, Mauthausen, Buchenwald, Belsen-Bergen, Dachau, and the other extermination camps merge to one image, undeletable from Germany's history." And he pushes Germans to face "the truth about yesterday, the truth about today."[136] While Abusch lists Jews among other victims—he writes about "murdered Jews, Russians, Ukrainians, Poles, French, and German Antifascists"—the economist Siegbert Kahn highlights anti-Jewish persecution in his *Antisemitismus und Rassenhetze*: "The world followed with growing disgust the gruesome drama that had played out in Germany since 1933—and in almost all of Europe since 1939—the oppression and bloody extermination of Jews. There was a straight line from the political, economic and social boycott of the Jews to the Nuremberg Laws and finally to the extermination camps, where six million people were exterminated just because they were Jews."[137] Kahn, as other Communists of Jewish origin, overemphasized economics in his analysis of antisemitism, but he did not marginalize Jewish suffering.

In the immediate aftermath of the war, Jews in the Soviet occupied zone reflected publicly on their experiences of persecution. The Auschwitz survivor Julius Meyer, who had joined the Communist Party in 1930, became an important advocate on behalf of Jewish victims after the war. He led the department for Victims of the Nuremberg Laws within the Berlin Office for the Victims of Fascism and in 1946 became the leader of the Jewish community in East Berlin. Meyer spoke openly about his and his family's persecution. In reply to a letter he received from a student asking about his political engagement, Meyer wrote about his experiences under Nazism: "83 of my family members were killed in Nazi Germany's concentration camps. My wife and my son were gassed in Auschwitz and burned.... I had to watch once, how thousands of children were gassed and burned. I will do all in my power to make sure that such a thing can never happen again in Germany."[138] In his letter Meyer connected Jewish experiences during the war with the need to build a better future and thus narrated his personal experiences within the larger framework of the newly founded state.

Figure 2.2. Julius Meyer speaks at a memorial event in Berlin, 1946. © Abraham Pisarek; SLUB / Deutsche Fotothek.

Initially an acknowledgment of Jewish suffering also played a part in public commemoration of the war. Abraham Pisarek's photograph of a memorial event at the Funkhaus Berlin shows Julius Meyer delivering a speech on a podium decorated with the inscription "Honor to the victims of Fascism" and the red triangle. Above him, suspended in the air, is the Star of David (Magen David). At other memorial events, the flag of the state of Israel was flown.[139]

In the immediate aftermath of the war, the Soviet occupying powers as well as the party leadership publicly condemned Nazi perpetrators and admitted German guilt. In June 1945 Walter Ulbricht, soon to be named general secretary of the Sociality Unity Party (Sozialistische Einheitspartei,

SED) Central Committee, declared to party functionaries, "It would be to the shame of our own nation if we did not have the courage to recognize that the German working class and the productive classes have failed historically," and in 1947 an article in *Neues Deutschland*, the official organ of the SED, declared that with the "silent toleration of the pogroms, the German people became complicit in the deaths of six million innocent people."[140] Such words must have comforted surviving Jews and raised hopes that an admission of guilt would lead to a genuine new beginning and a continued willingness to face the most recent past.

Yet the official interpretation of the Nazi past, while acknowledging Jews as victims, did not depict their persecution as central but rather as a by-product of the Nazi state's capitalist interests.[141] A hierarchy of victimhood emerged. The SED leadership provided assistance for health, housing, and employment as well as pensions to those persecuted under Nazism, including Jewish victims of racial persecution. However, the interests of those considered "fighters" were privileged over those of the mere victims of Fascism, and the former also received higher material support.[142] Jewish survivors criticized the injustice of this hierarchy among victims of Fascism.[143] Fritz Selbiger remembered that shortly after the war, he received a position in the newly founded cultural office that he lost after six weeks because "I was not a resistance fighter against National Socialism, but only its victim."[144] This renewed official declaration that marked them as "less worthy" angered some Jewish survivors, though others did not perceive the hierarchy as problematic.

Many Communists of Jewish origin did not view their past through the lens of racial persecution but rather perceived themselves as part of a Communist community of memory and as fighters against rather than victims of Fascism. Born to a Jewish merchant family in Dortmund in 1914, Kurt Goldstein joined the Communist youth movement as a fourteen-year-old. Five years later, after the Nazis took power, he emigrated to Palestine, but he returned to Europe soon after to fight in the Spanish Civil War. From Spain he fled to France, where he was caught and held in the French internment camp Gurs. From there Goldstein was deported to Auschwitz. In his account he emphasized that the inmates had resisted every day and depicted his experience in the camp as part of a Communist history. Remembering his experiences as those of a "Communist fighter," Goldstein constructed his narrative in a way that placed him within a Communist "community of experience."[145] Other accounts likewise concentrated on Nazis' persecution of Communists, and some even shared the official contempt for Jews' supposed "passivity."[146]

Application forms to the Organization of Victims of the Nazi Regime show both the value system ingrained in the official narrative and surviving Jews' efforts to fit their stories within this framework. The particular way the form asked about the applicant's history dictated how respondents could narrate their experiences. It contained questions about personal details, time of imprisonment, life in hiding, and emigration but none about religious belonging, ethnicity, or persecution on racial grounds. The only category that reflects Jewishness was *Sternträger*, which referred to whether the Nazis had marked someone as Jewish by forcing them to wear the yellow star. On the other hand, the questionnaire asked about party and union membership before 1933, whether one had fought in the Spanish Civil War, and illegal membership in political parties or resistance groups.[147] The requirement to depict their experiences in this particular framework may well have shaped Jews' subsequent narrations as well as their perceptions of the most recent past. Some Jewish applicants left the fields regarding political belonging blank while others emphasized their belonging to the Communist Party before 1933, and again others mentioned that they had joined the SED immediately after the war. One applicant explained in a longer report that he regretted his former apolitical life. Another ended with, "If Germany finds the way to socialism, our suffering and our struggle will have not been in vain," strongly framing his experiences during the war within the narrative of antifascist resistance leading to a Socialist state.[148]

In response to questions concerning resistance, some Jewish applicants remarked that as Jews they had not been able to resist. Others described their survival under Nazism as a form of resistance. Redefining resistance to include their own lived experiences, these Jewish survivors aimed to reshape the discursive structure in which they were asked to narrate their past.[149] Some specifically asked to be included as fighters against Fascism, rather than victims. One of them explained: "We heard prohibited broadcasts and propaganda every night. We collected leaflets and re-distributed them to like-minded people. . . . I believe that although I am considered a victim of fascism, I can confidently count myself as a fighter against fascism and I am asking for your opinion."[150] There were economic benefits to being acknowledged as a fighter that may have spurred Jews to shape their stories this way, but other reasons—a wish to belong, pride in their past, and a need to be acknowledged—may have played a role as well. For instance, Arnold

84 | *Home after Fascism*

Munter, whose father was Jewish and who was interned in Theresienstadt, emphasized in his report that while he was recognized as a "victim of fascism," he insisted on being acknowledged as a "fighter against fascism," not for material but for idealistic reasons.[151]

In the first years after the end of the war, the climate in the emerging East German state changed. While the SED leadership showed initial willingness to acknowledge Germans' guilt, the narrative soon shifted to a story of good people seduced by an evil leadership. Aiming for widespread reintegration, the party leadership blamed the Nazi crimes on a few exceptions and exculpated the German people.[152] East German authorities emphasized that most former Nazis had fled from the Soviet zone to the western zones of occupation. While indeed many had left East Germany, assuming correctly that they would be less likely to be punished for their crimes in the West, many others remained and either stayed silent about their past or constructed stories of their conversion from Nazism to Communism.[153]

Most Jews in the Soviet occupied zone remained well aware that not all Nazis had fled and that this part of the country "had also belonged to Nazi Germany," as Hilde Eisler commented in an interview in the 1980s.[154] Picking up on the widespread conversion stories, Anna Seghers voiced her distress over a baker who used to have a Nazi sign in his window before changing it to one stating, "long live Bolshevism."[155] In another letter to her cousin Sally David Cramer in the United States, she commented on the widespread denial of guilt: "They are all doing so damn badly, they are so very responsible for that, they don't understand that in the least, and the few decent ones are so damn decent that everything else appears tepid and blurred."[156] Seghers emphasized how the few "good Germans" merely highlighted the moral shortcomings of the majority. Like Jews in the western zones, most Jews in the East perceived the majority population as guilty and antifascist resisters as an important but small exception.

Still, some Communist Jews supported the official narrative. In her memoirs Lotte Winter commented, "I also know that numerous [Nazis] left the Soviet occupied zone, later the GDR, and played an active role as Neofascists."[157] Charlotte Holzer, who had survived the war in Germany, explained that no Nazis lived in her street in Prenzlau, "they had all run away."[158] Both women wrote these memoirs after the end of the war, Winter presumably in the early 1980s, Holzer in the 1960s, at a time when the repeated propagation of this narrative may well have shaped their accounts. Both criticized the SED regime in other parts of their memoirs, and Holzer specifically mentioned that her writings needed to remain secret. Presumably, then, they did not adhere to the official version to avoid censorship or worse. In interviews the writer Wolfgang Herzberg conducted in the late 1980s and published just after the fall of the wall, such fears may have shaped the interviewees' responses. Three of them reflected on the question of guilt. Kurt Goldstein, a survivor of Auschwitz and an SED member, maintained that the Nazis left because the Communists reminded them of their crimes, and Ilse Lewin, who had joined the Communist youth organization in 1927, differentiated strongly between the Nazi leadership and the German people, whom she did not perceive as guilty.[159] Ruth Gützlaff, who joined the Communist Party after the war, maintained, "The Germans, who committed crimes against the Jews, were caught, or fled. They were not there anymore."[160] As with most myths, there was a grain of truth in the East German states' story of the Nazis who had fled to the West, which may have made it easier for Jews in East Germany to accept this version of the past. Moreover, believing that the Nazis were no longer there must have been a more comforting thought than living with the knowledge that their neighbors may have played a part in the murder of friends and relatives.

The Brava Gente

Myths that contained a grain of truth played a crucial role in how most Italian Jews depicted the recent past. Italian Jews had varied experiences during the war, some confirming and others contradicting the myth of the brava gente. When telling their experiences, most framed their past in support of this dominant narrative; however, rather than silencing memories that did not neatly fit, they found a way to reconcile the contradictory elements. Indeed, Jewish newspapers, as well as letters, diaries, and memoirs, frequently mentioned the role Fascist denouncers and collaborators had played in anti-Jewish persecution.[161] A Roman Jew invoked the atmosphere of fear and mistrust during the last year of the war, when "one could discover that someone you knew or a close acquaintance was actually a denouncer."[162] Another exclaimed in an interview: "The Fascists took us, not the Germans! The Fascists!"[163] Luigi Carmi, a Pisan Jew, argued in a letter to the community in Pisa a few months later that "there is no doubt that the Italian population— either because of active collaboration with the Fascist regime, or by guilty abstinence—was directly involved in the sad events of the war."[164]

86 | *Home after Fascism*

In 1944 then sixteen-year-old Davide Schiffer had witnessed Italian policemen arrest his father, who was subsequently murdered in Auschwitz. In his memoirs, published decades later, he criticized the Italian population: "The attitude of the government and institutions against the Jews had no exceptions and found no opposition; people had accepted antisemitism as the dominant ideology without protest." He maintained that while individual Italians had helped, Fascist ideology and propaganda had been fundamental in isolating, persecuting, and eventually murdering Italian Jews.[165]

The different voices, some emphasizing Italian heroism and others pointing to betrayal, reflect in part the varied experiences of Italian Jews during the war. Whether Jews described the behavior of the population as benevolent or hostile depended undoubtedly on their personal experiences. It also mattered whether one wrote in a public newspaper or in a private letter, as Jews appear to have been more comfortable voicing critique in private. Generally speaking, younger Jews tended to be more critical when looking at the most recent past. Class influenced how Italian Jews had experienced persecution during the war and may also have affected how they remembered the Fascist period. Poorer Jews, like many of the inhabitants of the Roman ghetto, had faced greater obstacles trying to emigrate, hide, or flee. They also more often pointed to Italian responsibility when recounting their experiences.[166] However, they wrote little, and their voices hardly affected the public discourse. Intellectuals who supported the myth of the brava gente, such as the literary critic Giacomo Debenedetti and the journalist Eucardio Momigliano, had greater influence in shaping public Jewish memory.[167]

Yet an explanation that looks at two competing narratives fails to fully portray Italian Jewish recollections of war, persecution, and Fascism. Scholars of memory frequently point to the existence of multiple and contradictory narratives that can exist within a community. A close look at Italian Jews' narration of Italians' role in their persecution reveals seemingly contradictory versions of the past that exist not only within one community but within single accounts. The contradiction between the notion of Italians' essential humanity and the Fascist perpetrators seeps through Italian Jewish memory. In Jewish journals, articles about perpetrators stand next to others depicting Italians as brava gente. Frequently the same people spoke of the goodness of the Italian people while recalling how an Italian had denounced or arrested them. Goti Bauer, for instance, remembered the solidarity of Italians with Jews and later described how Italian police arrested her and her family.[168] Liana Millu, a Pisan Jew who survived Auschwitz, recounts a conversation she had with a French survivor who claimed that Italian bombers had destroyed his home in her memoir *I ponti di Schwerin*. In her reply she expresses her belief in the goodness of the Italian people: "I intervened, saying that Italians did not do such things. The Germans shot refugees from airplanes, *we* were not like them."[169] In spite of her own criticism of Italians—Millu had been denounced—she included herself among the Italians: "*we* were not like them." Yet Millu also voiced her distress at having to take the side of those who had shunned her: "They hunted and imprisoned me in a camp saying that I was not Italian. That I contaminated Italy with my presence and that this was a crime punishable by Birkenau and its agonies. Now what? Birkenau was a week in the past, and apparently they began making me responsible for the sins committed by those who had convicted me."[170]

In their depiction of the role of their compatriots, most Italian Jews took a perspective diametrically opposed to German Jews. While many German Jews, both in the East and the West, saw those who helped them as an exception that only attested to the majority's guilt, Italian Jews tended to portray rescuers as representative of the Italian people and depicted perpetrators as an exception. Going even further, much of the Jewish postwar discourse marked perpetrators as essentially not Italian. Differentiating between Nazi-Fascists and Italians, they stripped those who had persecuted them of their *Italianness*.[171] In postwar Italian discourse, "the Nazi-fascist," in the words of historian Lutz Klinkhammer, "is not a person of flesh and blood, he is a symbol of absolute evil, the image of an enemy, who has no resemblance to a human being."[172] While Klinkhammer does not focus on the Jewish population, his observations hold true here as well. Like the majority population, Italian Jews distinguished between Italians and Nazi-Fascists, seeing the latter as not being part of the true Italy. The memoir of Dan Vittorio Segre, who had emigrated to Israel but whose family had stayed behind, provides an example of this externalization of Fascist perpetrators. Segre differentiated between the Germans and the Fascist Republicans—that is, those who remained Fascists under the RSI on the one hand and the Italian people on the other: "This grotesque situation . . . combined a deep sense of human solidarity with an equally deep hate for the Germans and the Fascist Republicans. It also gave an idea of the links between my family and the seven hundred or so villagers."[173]

88 | Home after Fascism

The enemies were not German Nazis and Italian Fascists but "Germans and the Fascist Republicans." When referring to perpetrators as Fascist Republicans or Nazi-Fascists, Italian Jews marked those Italians who had collaborated with the German occupiers as marginal. Only antifascists were "real" Italians. Italian perpetrators had to be externalized or simply deleted from memory. An article published in *Israel* in December 1944 about Roberto Farinacci, one of the leading figures in Italian Fascism and an outspoken antisemite, articulates the wish to do the latter. The author, writing about Jews' reaction to Farinacci's death, explained that "we will not remember his name with hatred, because we will not remember it at all," promoting the willful forgetting of his existence.[174]

Like the rest of the population, Italian Jews tended to differentiate between the twenty years of Fascist dictatorship and the foreign-tinged Nazi-Fascism of Salò, which they considered the real evil.[175] Undoubtedly the deportations and massacres of the last two war years overshadowed their experiences under Fascist racial laws. Emphasizing suffering under the German occupation and German persecutors also enabled Italian Jews to look at past experiences they shared with other Italians. The racial laws, on the other hand, had marked them as outsiders. Moreover, numerous Italian Jews had supported the PNF before 1938, which contributed to their wish to push the early years aside.[176] While some individual Jews called for an internal reckoning with Jews who had supported Fascism, the postwar Jewish leadership preferred to move on.[177] After the war the Jewish community, aiming to emphasize the belonging of Jews to the "nation united in resistance," had no interest in bringing attention to the high numbers of Jews who had originally joined the Fascist party. Individual Jews who had been members of the PNF tried their best to explain their membership as a matter of necessity rather than conviction or to obfuscate this part of their past.[178]

Marta Ottolenghi Minerbi, a Jewish teacher, had been an active member of the Fasci Femminili, the women's section of the PNF, since 1926. Like many others, she and her husband wrote to Mussolini after the issuing of the racial legislation in 1938 in the hopes of being exempt, but to no avail. While Minerbi survived in hiding, her husband was captured, deported, and murdered in Auschwitz.[179] Immediately after the war, Minerbi wrote an autobiographical novel, focusing on the years 1943–1945. While she writes about the racial legislation, which led to her losing her job, Minerbi does not mention her and her husband's Fascist past and the subsequent betrayal. The text promotes the notion of the brava gente, portrays Fascist persecutors as an evil exception not representative of Italians or Italian Fascism, and avoids a reflection on systemic repression and the continuities between the two phases of Fascist rule.[180]

By focusing on the period of German occupation, public narratives shifted the responsibility for antisemitic persecution to the Germans. Surviving Jews frequently stripped Italian perpetrators of their agency and perceived them as directed by the Germans. One Italian Jew, for instance, described the "violence produced by the Germans and misguided Fascists."[181] Frequently, Italian Jews depicted the racial laws, issued years before the German occupation, as a German product. They shared the then widespread misconception that Mussolini had issued the racial laws due to German pressure.[182] Adriana Luzzati, a Jew from Asti who had survived the war in exile in Switzerland, declared: "The Germans had influenced Mussolini; making him enact the racial laws and making him do whatever Hitler wanted."[183]

Raffaele Cantoni declared in a radio program in April 1945, "The testimony of human solidarity, which the sane part of the Italian people has provided, awakens the secure confidence that in Italy the weeds of the theories *imposed upon us by the Nazis* will be eradicated."[184] As Cantoni did in this statement, Jewish postwar elites supported contemporary Italian politicians and intellectuals in promoting the idea of racism as foreign to Italian national character and propagated an image of Italians as *in essence* immune to racism. In a letter from May 1944, Lelio Vittorio Valobra described Italy as a country that "never knew antisemitism."[185] Two years later Luciano Morpurgo, a Roman Jew, published his diary of the war years, in which he sang Italy's praise, "beautiful Italy, dear Italy," in which "race and racism [are] distant and useless words."[186] A newsletter published by the Italian representatives of the WJC in June 1945 claimed that the Italian people had "never shown antisemitism."[187]

Building on older stereotypes, Italian postwar discourse promoted an antithesis between the good Italian and the evil German, emphasizing the difference in the nature of the two people as well as in the character of the two regimes.[188] The fanatical, racist Germans following their *Führer* willingly into war were juxtaposed with the image of the peaceful and good-natured Italians who opposed Fascism, war, and racial persecution. In their effort to shape Italy's image, obtain a favorable peace accord, and improve the country's prospects, political elites, among them the Italian Ministry

90 | *Home after Fascism*

of Foreign Affairs and the War Ministry, propagated the notion of Italian soldiers as simple men with a good heart who were forced into the war against their will and who tried to save Jews from the disciplined and cold Germans.[189]

Italian politicians believed that Jews would play an important role in the international acceptance of this narrative. A memo from the foreign ministry, dated October 24, 1944, shows how they, still believing in the myth of Jewish power, depicted the importance of Jews in shaping public opinion abroad. The memo concluded, "Although the antisemitic measures in Italy have been generally mild and have not found favor in the country as a whole, it would seem to be no easy matter to regain this trust [of the Jews] unconditionally, but this is undoubtedly the goal to be pursued."[190] In 1946, in its efforts to create a favorable image of Italian treatment of Jews, the foreign ministry published a volume entitled *Relazione sull'opera svolta dal Ministero degli Affari Esteri per la tutela delle comunità ebraiche (1938–1943)* (Report on the work carried out by the Ministry of Foreign Affairs for the protection of the Jewish communities). Emphasizing Italian resistance to Nazi racial measures and Italian moral superiority when compared with Germans, the Italian government presented the volume to the Allies to inform their drafting of the peace treaty.[191] The narrative of the good Italian and the evil German, promoted by political and cultural elites and spread via magazines, books, and films, shaped the image of Italians at home as well as abroad for decades to come.[192]

Italian Jews contributed to the effort to sharply differentiate between Italians and their former allies. They used strong words when it came to judging German perpetrators and emphasized the perceived difference in German and Italian national character.[193] A leaflet distributed among Italian Jewish refugees in Switzerland in June 1945 argued: "As far as relations with Germany go, it is our sacred duty to the millions of deported, tortured, murdered brothers—and Italian Jews have unfortunately made their contribution to blood and sacrifice!—that any relationship to the perpetrators will be terminated."[194] An article on Italy published in the *American Jewish Year Book* in 1944 quotes the chief rabbi of Rome, Israel Zolli, who contrasted "the good hearts of the Italians" with the cruelty of the Germans.[195] Leone Maestro, a Jewish doctor from Florence, wrote in his diary in March 1944: "I do not think that Hitler holds onto power longer than Capone [Mussolini] because he is more intelligent, but because he followed for better or for worse the historical line of imperial and bellicose Germany while

Mussolini in all regards went against the nature, the character of Italy, from the black uniforms to the total militarization, from the goose-stepping to the racism."[196] Apparently Maestro did not consider that Mussolini gained power in 1922, using his marching Blackshirts, and had ruled Italy for over two decades before he was ousted in 1943.[197]

While it seems self-explanatory why Italian elites pushed the myth of the good Italian and why Italians across the political spectrum found it attractive, it seems more puzzling that Italian Jews likewise supported and spread this narrative. There are different factors that contributed to this. The transnational discourse about Italy's role in the war surely played a role, and it helped that representatives of international Jewish organizations supported the myth. A report from the AJDC from May 1946, for instance, states that "very often indeed it was found that the Italians had been very helpful in saving Jews from deportation,"[198] and a memorandum from the American Jewish Committee concluded, "Italian non-Jews are traditionally cordial to their fellow Italians of the Jewish faith, and even during the period of Hitler-inspired racial legislation they demonstrated their friendship and loyalty."[199] Clearly the Italian Jewish leadership's reports on the conduct of Italians during the war influenced foreign Jewish institutions; at the same time, the latter's affirmation of the myth of the brava gente strengthened and disseminated this narrative further.

Political considerations played a role for the Jewish leadership, which defended Italians' conduct especially fervently. Struggling with a diminished and impoverished community, the Union of Italian Jewish Communities focused on facilitating the reintegration of Italian Jews. Moreover, mediating between Zionist organizations and the Italian government, the Jewish leadership hoped the latter would continue to support the illegal immigration of the many foreign Jews sojourning in Italy before their departure to Palestine.[200] In his analysis Guri Schwarz points to these practical and diplomatic concerns, adding astutely that "there is no doubt that the leaders of Italian Judaism shared the ideas and feelings typical of their age."[201]

By supporting the myth of the good Italian and emphasizing shared suffering under the Nazi-Fascists and shared achievements in the resistance, Italian Jews merged their own past with the dominant, national memory and thus reclaimed their belonging to the nation. Those who had excluded them in the first place—that is, the Fascists—could not be part of this common past and were thus now depicted as outside the national narrative. Italian Jews did not so much forget or silence their experiences under

92 | *Home after Fascism*

the Fascist regime but rather told their stories in a way that fit the larger national narrative.

The voices of those who pointed more strongly to Italian collaboration and responsibility garnered less attention, and there was little interest in a closer investigation of Italy's role in their persecution—as those who tried soon came to realize. Forced by the racial legislation to resign his commission as an army colonel in 1938, Massimo Adolfo Vitale had immigrated to London, Paris, and finally Tangier. Upon his return to Rome in 1944, Giuseppe Nathan, then commissioner of the Union of Italian Jewish Communities, appointed Vitale to direct the CRDE. Vitale pushed for a greater effort to investigate the past and tirelessly collected information. He also encouraged other Italian Jews to document and testify, thus gathering materials for a different and more complete history. In his writings, Vitale emphasized that they "must not forget!"[202] In 1947 Vitale presented a report on "the persecutions against Jews in Italy 1938–1945" at a European conference on Holocaust documentation in Paris.[203] Vitale, rather than shying away from discussing Italian involvement, emphasizes in his report that the persecution of Italian Jews had begun already before the war with legislation issued by the Italian government. He furthermore argues that the roots of Fascist antisemitism can be traced back to the early years of the regime.[204] However, Vitale's view stood at odds with the dominant discourse, and he soon ran into problems with the Jewish communities. In November 1949 he complained to Cantoni about his difficulty gathering information about the Fascist period.[205]

When he tried to gather information about the murder of Pardo Roques, the former head of the Pisan Jewish community, Vitale soon hit a brick wall.[206] In March 1946 an Italian court tried a local man named Enrico Giordano who probably led the Germans to Roques's house. The defendant admitted to having given Roques's address away but claimed he had not known the Germans' intentions. The court found him not guilty. After the war the Pisan community commemorated the tragic death of its leader but remained silent about the trial and kept its opinion about Giordano's guilt concealed.[207] In their response to Vitale, the Pisan community leaders gave scant and often inaccurate information. They did not mention the Giordano trial, and their reports depicted the Italian population and even the Fascists in the best possible light. Vitale reacted with anger to the omissions but failed to get a more complete picture.[208]

Other Italian Jews likewise voiced frustrations about the gaps in the public representation of the past. One of them remarked, "Italy, as always, forgets too soon."[209] A Roman Jew, Aldo de Benedetti, wrote a letter to the Roman Jewish community in June 1946 complaining about the inscription of a memorial stone that he had passed on a recent walk. He explained that it lacked an acknowledgment of "the indispensable complicity of the Italian Fascists" in the persecution of Jews.[210] But the Jewish and even more so the non-Jewish community of memory did not want to highlight Italian involvement in war crimes. Outside the Jewish communities, there was little interest in the particularity of Jewish suffering.[211] Some Italian Jews commented on the widespread indifference to their experiences. "In my school," remembered schoolteacher Eugenia Servi, "my past was rarely talked about—no one was interested,"[212] and Auschwitz survivor Jenny Ravenna explained that she thought there was "little interest" in the "things we lived through in these tragic years of Nazi dominance."[213] Goti Bauer's recollections emphasized not only the lack of interest but also the ignorance and insensitivity among Italians when it came to the fate of Jewish citizens: "I had a number tattooed on my arm, A5273, no 5372. I arrived in Milan in the summer, and when I moved from one part of the tram to the other and clung to the handle, one could read this number and I heard comments around me of people who wanted to be funny, 'look she has the phone number of her boyfriend tattooed on her arm' and things like that."[214] Testimonies of Holocaust survivors published in Italy in the first postwar decade received hardly any attention. Famously, several publishing houses rejected Primo Levi's *Se questo è un uomo* (If this is a man, published in the United States as *Survival in Auschwitz*) until 1947, when Da Silva published the first edition.[215]

The memories of deportees—Jewish as well as non-Jewish—did not fit with an Italian public discourse that aimed to bury its Fascist past and recast the nation as victorious against rather than implicated by Fascism.[216] Italy wanted to move on. As Frank Biess notes, the "forward-looking, optimistic 'emotional regimes'" propagated by postwar states stood at odds with individuals' "massive losses, deprivation, and suffering."[217] Both in Germany and Italy, Jews faced immense loss and traumatic memories. While the public discourse within the Italian Jewish community highlighted a shared past, some, often younger, Italian Jews expressed the feeling that their experiences separated them from non-Jewish Italians.[218] For instance, Luisa Franchetti, a young Jew from Florence, explained that her schoolmates did not understand "what we had gone through."[219] Aldo Zargani, a journalist and writer from Turin, remembered encountering resentment when

94 | *Home after Fascism*

speaking about the past: "We were seen as petulant whiners in a world of courageous, stoic folk full of Christian forgiveness." He felt that they, as Jews, had become bothersome in their mourning and that the society around them expected them to forgive and forget.[220]

Others seemed to have seen little to fault in Italians' indifference to their particular past. Levi, when explaining the initial lack of interest in his work, seemed understanding, rather than judgmental. Reflecting on the initial rejection, he concluded that his book did not fit Italians' interests at the time: "People did not want that, they wanted something else, for example, to dance, to party, to bring children into the world."[221] Bruno di Cori found his neighbors' amnesia amusing rather than troubling. He and his family had immigrated to Palestine because of the 1938 racial laws. After their return, their neighbors, "confusing Palestine with Africa and recalling the Ethiopian campaign," referred to them as "the Abyssinians."[222]

Some wished to leave the past behind them. Lelia Foa, a Turinese Jew, survived the war in Italy. Her son Vittorio joined the antifascist resistance and was arrested in 1935. He spent eight years in prison before the Allies freed him in 1943.[223] Lelia's daughter Anna fled to the United States with her husband and young children.[224] Writing to her daughter in May 1946, Lelia described "a great need to forget: one feels an enormous desire to live, to breathe . . . and great need also to forgive—although this last thought has generated much protest from friends. . . . So be it: I need to feel at peace."[225] With her son spending years in prison and her family broken apart by Fascist racial laws, Lelia Foa had little reason to be forgiving. Still, she preferred not to dwell on the past.

Silence?

For a long time, scholars believed that survivors silenced the Holocaust in the postwar years. In her work on Jewish identities, Stephanie Tauchert claims, for instance, that German Jews began to deal with the Holocaust only in the 1960s; in the earlier decades, she maintains, "dealing with the collective and individual experiences of persecution was marked by taboo-ization and repression."[226] Scholars of Italian Jewish history likewise point to silence among the victims.[227] Yet in the past decade, historians have challenged the long-held assumption that survivors were unable or unwilling to speak about their experiences. We now have ample documentation showing that, starting even before the end of the war, survivors gathered evidence, gave testimonies, established archives, and recounted and wrote down what had happened to them and their loved ones.[228] Yet survivors who wished to recount their experiences often struggled with finding an audience inclined to listen. While a significant number of survivors' diaries, reports, and memoirs were published in eastern and western Europe in the immediate aftermath of the war, publishing houses lost interest in publishing such testimonies by the late 1940s.[229]

Italian and German Jews wrote memoirs, testified, and collected information about the Holocaust right after the war.[230] Still, while some chose to talk, others preferred to remain silent, finding the past too painful, struggling to find words, or fearing no one would believe them. Some, like Lelia Foa, wished to leave the past behind. Some wanted to forget and return to a normal life as soon as possible.[231] Hans Frankenthal explained that he did not speak with his wife or children about Auschwitz.[232] His brother likewise remained silent and pretended he had forgotten their time in the camps.[233] The writer Natalia Ginzburg stated that she did not want to write about the murder of her husband, Leone Ginzburg, as memories of his death were too painful.[234]

Survivors struggled to create a safe space, separate from their horrific experiences, and some feared that telling could mean reliving their trauma.[235] Some survivors commented on the immense difficulty they faced when narrating their experiences. For instance, Max Jacobson, who wrote about his time in Theresienstadt immediately after his liberation, explained, "I had to take a break in my writing, because the images that appear in these memories bring agitation with them to which I am no longer equal."[236] Even listening to accounts of the camps could shake surviving Jews. After receiving a letter from Nelly Cohn-Leschzer, a survivor of Auschwitz, the writer Jonas Lesser wrote of his struggle to come to terms with the past: "I am well advised to hold onto the joyous surprise occasioned by your letter, because everything else in there is too horrible for tears or laments. One has to somehow continue living with all the horrific experiences, through which the world went and still goes through, one has to try to cope, however difficult it might be—and for me it is immensely difficult, my nerves suffered very much."[237] A short time later, he received a second letter from Cohn-Leschzer, to which he replied: "Now I also received your letter from November 25 of last year, which alludes to your experiences in Auschwitz, and which upset me terribly. There is no consolation that I know

96 | *Home after Fascism*

for me or for you."[238] Lesser suffered reading about his friend's traumatic experiences even though he himself had managed to emigrate.

Jews who survived the war found myriad different ways to approach their trauma. Some published their accounts but chose not to talk about the past with family members, while others spoke only within circles of people who shared similar experiences. Some connected with other survivors who could grasp their experiences and were willing to listen to their accounts. In an environment that left little room for their grief, survivors created networks in which they could express their feelings. Such exchanges allowed both sides to express their pain and created a sense of community in mourning. Victoria Schoenmaker, for instance, received news about the deportation of her sister from Fritz Selbiger, a glazier from Berlin whose wife and sisters had been murdered in the camps. She replied to Selbiger's letter, in which he had detailed his own loss: "Believe me that I wholeheartedly feel for you. I had to experience the same with my sister."[239] H. Hartogson learned about his brother from a woman who had spent time before his deportation in the same house with him. She explained that the only thing she could tell him "about this sad time" was that his brother, his brother's wife, and his in-laws were taken away suddenly and that "they never received another sign of life from the people who were part of that transport." She assumed they were murdered on the train. Comparing the fate of Hartogson's brother with that of her mother, she tried to lighten the sad news: "Even if it is no consolation, I would like to say that these people have at least been spared from a long time of suffering. My mother of 80 years endured a year and a half ordeal in KZ Ravensbrück, until she was still gassed at the end."[240] Siegmund Weltlinger detailed his experiences in a letter to his cousin: "My sister Resi and my brother-in-law were battered to death near Riga, my daughter, on the other hand, lived in London, has now gone via India to Australia, is married and has two children. We did not see her for twelve years. Our son lives in England. We survived the difficult time illegally hidden after I had spent some time in the concentration camp.... I heard of your fate with great interest."[241]

Eugenio Ravenna was deported to Auschwitz with his entire family and was the only one to return after the war. Shortly after his return, he received a letter from Luciana Nissim, who wrote him about the few other survivors she knew and informed him of the death of his mother and other relatives who had been with her in Auschwitz. She asked him to keep in touch, and a lasting correspondence ensued between them. Both also wrote with other survivors who shared their pain. In December 1945 Primo Levi wrote to Ravenna, "I can very well understand the terrible feelings of emptiness that surrounds you: only now we realize exactly how much we have lost."[242] Sofia Schafranov, who was deported to Auschwitz in 1944, replied to a letter from Enrico Rosenholz, who was hoping to gather information about his mother and siblings, that while she recognized the writer's mother, brother, and sisters in the included picture, she unfortunately had no information about their fate. Yet, she emphasized, she felt with him: "Your pain is my pain."[243] Having shared similar experiences, survivors formed a community of memory and mourning. In an environment that failed to recognize the needs of survivors, such exchanges constituted an emotional refuge.[244]

Sometimes such exchanges crossed national borders. Anna Di Gioacchino Cassuto received—via the secretary of the Milan community—a message from Erich Cohn regarding her husband, Nathan Cassuto. They had been in Auschwitz together, but Cohn had lost sight of Cassuto and hoped to get information about Nathan's fate. He writes of the latter, "I can say that I have rarely or perhaps never met such a good and noble person. His trust in God was limitless."[245] Anna herself was searching for her husband at the time but with little success. Indeed, the response to Cohn's request states that "unfortunately we heard nothing regarding Nathan Cassuto. Your news, may be the last that was heard of him."[246] These exchanges also point to a crucial function of survivor accounts in the first months after the war had ended. Often returnees from the camps were asked to talk about their experiences because others who were searching for deported relatives and friends were desperate for information.[247] Alberto Sed, a Roman Jew who survived Auschwitz, identified the role camp survivors played in helping others to begin grasping the situation: "Those who had not been deported did nothing but ask for information about their mother, father, son, daughter, and so on. Some continued to hope for years, but with our return for the first time they felt what had happened."[248] Spreading information was a crucial part of survivors' accounts in the immediate aftermath of the war.

Survivors bore witness because they wanted the world to know what had happened. For some, the hope that they would one day be able to tell their story kept them going during the worst moments. Some felt a sense of duty to the murdered; they had survived, so they needed to speak on behalf of those who could not. Eva Noack-Mosse, a Berlin Jew, kept a secret diary of her experiences in Theresienstadt that she completed after her liberation.

98 | *Home after Fascism*

In the preface to her account, dated July–August 1945, she explained her motivation: "We cannot wake the dead, our friends, our relatives. We, the survivors, are connected to them in mysterious ways. By telling about them, I pay my debt to them."[249] Other survivors shared this sense of duty to play the role of witnesses, and they often did so despite reluctant, hostile, or fearful listeners.

Giorgio Bassani depicts a survivor who cannot stop recounting his experiences in his short story "A Plaque in Via Mazzini," first published in the periodical *Botteghe Oscure* in 1952.[250] With this story Bassani reminds his readers of a past marked by moral compromise, collaboration, and complicity that most did not wish to remember. Geo Josz, the protagonist of the story, unexpectedly returns to Ferrara from Buchenwald. His return unsettles his environment, as it reminds people of a past they would rather forget. Even the Jews in Ferrara feel discomfort: "Even Signor Cohen, the engineer, the President of the Jewish Community, who had insisted on dedicating, in memory of the victims, a large marble plaque the moment he got back from Switzerland, which now stood out, rigid, enormous, brand-new, on the red brick façade of the Temple . . . even he, at first, had raised a host of objections; in short he wanted nothing to do with it [Josz's wish to retell the past]."[251] In the story the memorial plaque, which erroneously included Josz's name among the dead, constitutes a way to move on from the past rather than grapple with what happened. Tellingly, the workman who puts the plaque in place avoids reading what it says, and the narrator comments that "in a few years no one will notice it [the plaque] anymore."[252] Josz's need to recount his stories of the camp becomes a nuisance and irritant to the people of Ferrara. At the end of the story, Josz leaves his hometown a second time. The memories he could not forget had created a rift between him and the citizens of Ferrara, and their refusal to grapple with the traumatic past made it impossible to bridge this rift.

While most Jews experienced persecution, displacement, fear, and loss, they had survived the war in different circumstances. Those who had survived by fleeing the country, hiding, or being protected by a non-Jewish partner looked back to different experiences than those who survived the camps. The latter felt that their experiences stood out. They lacked a shared language or framework in which to communicate their past. "We have memories that are so brutal that they appear unlikely even to fellow Jews," explained Nelly Cohn-Leschzer in an article published in *Der Weg* in 1950.

She marked the distance between camp survivors and their environment. The survivors, she contends, "have the feeling of coming from a different world into a new one that escaped the general destruction that surrounded us."[253] Franco Schönheit similarly felt that it was impossible to recount what had happened because "no one will believe us." He regarded his experiences as neither representable nor understandable: "Buchenwald was outside the normal sphere of life," he explained. His memories of the camp belonged to a world outside the "sphere of ordinary humanity."[254] At several points in his *Survival in Auschwitz*, Primo Levi refers to the limitations of language that impeded sharing their experiences. "Then for the first time we became aware," he observes, "that our language lacks words to express this offense, the demolition of a man." And later he continues:

> Just as our hunger is not the feeling of missing a meal, so our way of being cold has need of a new word. We say "hunger," we say "tiredness," "fear," "pain," we say "winter," and they are different things. They are free words, created and used by free men who lived in comfort and without suffering in their homes. If the [camps] had lasted longer, a new, harsh language would have been born; and only this language could express what it means to toil the whole day in the wind with the temperature below freezing, and wearing only a shirt, underpants, cloth jacket and trousers, hunger, and knowledge of the end drawing near.[255]

Much like historians in the decades to follow, survivors faced the question of how to find words for the ineffable.[256] They emphasized both the necessity and the impossibility of recounting what had happened.[257] As much as they believed they had to speak up in place of those who had been murdered, they could not actually provide testimony on their behalf. The few survivors constituted the exception, and as Levi writes, they "speak in their [the dead's] stead, by proxy," but they were not "the true witness."[258]

Conclusion

The divergent experiences of Italian and German Jews and the different roles their home countries played during the war as well as the specific memory cultures that emerged in Italy and West and East Germany affected how they narrated the past. In Italy, Jews contributed to a public discourse that emphasized Italian rescuers and obfuscated Italian antisemitic persecution and collaboration. Sidelining both Fascists and Fascism as not part of the true Italy helped legitimize Jews' continuous attachment to their home country. Moreover, marking Jewish suffering as part of Italy's fight for liberation, stressing that all Italians had suffered during the war, and marginalizing any particularity of Jewish experiences created a unifying representation of the past that inserted Jews into the national community.

Jews in Germany responded to a widespread emphasis on German innocence by pointing to Germans' responsibility for their suffering. They picked up on a discourse that framed Germans as innocent bystanders and confronted it with the guilt that resulted from silence and passivity. But their voices found little hearing within a society that would not confront its crimes. While the discourse of innocence played a part in both Germanies, the emphasis on antifascism in the Soviet occupied zone created a distinct narrative that had no counterpart in the West. In contrast to the depiction of innocent German bystanders, the glorification of Communist resisters and fighters against Fascism opened space for Jews, especially though not only for those who were Communists, to place their memories within this framework. The hierarchy that placed fighters above victims of Fascism caused some to emphasize their self-understanding as fighters while others protested against the marginalization of their experiences of persecution.

"Communities of experience" did not have clear boundaries. A close look at Italian and East and West German Jews' particular ways of approaching their recent past shows that a shared understanding of the past did not merely depend on lived experiences but also on the creation of "communities of memory." Jews who rebuilt their lives in their former home countries used the representation of the past as a signifier for belonging. Asking "how memory *forms* social relations," we can see that divergent understandings of the most recent past sharpened the rift between Jewish and non-Jewish Germans, while, on the other hand, widespread efforts among Italian Jews to fit their memories within a narrative of Italian resistance helped in their reintegration after the war.[259]

Individual Jews positioned themselves in myriad ways toward the interpretations of the past that emerged in the national Jewish communities, on a broader public national level, and within the international Jewish community. Some isolated voices among Jews in West Germany supported a view that exculpated Germans from guilt, while some Italian Jews aimed for a more complex understanding of Italian collaboration. Jews in the aftermath of genocide did not silence their experiences. But a wish to commemorate was not total; not everyone wanted to remember, and many did not wish to remember everything. Silences, like memories, were partial and fractured. Individual Jews found different ways to negotiate between their personal recollections, communal understandings of the past, and broader public narratives. How surviving Jews made sense of these different overlapping and sometimes contrasting discourses shaped their choices, hopes, and expectations for the future.

3

RECLAIMING HOME

IN HER MEMOIR, LOTTE WINTER RECOUNTS HER THOUGHTS on the days before she returned from Sweden: "How will I deal with the hatred of the Germans, of the murderers of my loved ones? . . . How will I suppress my thoughts of vengeance?"[1] Other German Jews voiced similar concerns and also Italian Jews shared such sentiments, even if the dominant discourse portrayed perpetrators as the exception. Elena Morpurgo, an Italian Jew who had fled to Switzerland, expressed similar thoughts if less vehement feelings: "What will our return be like? And what sort of contact will we have with those who we know behaved badly towards us?"[2] After the war, Jews dealt with living alongside perpetrators, denouncers, and people who— as Dora Venezia, a survivor of Auschwitz, wrote—had "pretended as if they did not see or hear anything."[3] Aware of the widespread complicity in their persecution, returning Jews grappled with the idea of living among perpetrators. Many surviving Jews refused to passively accept the status quo in their home countries, and in all three postwar states, Jews played an active role in bringing perpetrators to justice.[4]

Bringing the guilty to justice and reeducating the population were crucial for Jewish returnees who hoped to play a role in rebuilding their country. Battling latent antisemitism and fending off anti-Jewish stereotypes likewise constituted important parts of these efforts. Other scholars have written on antisemitism in postwar Italy and Germany, but where much of the existing literature focuses on the non-Jewish population, Jews' reactions to persistent antisemitism are central here.[5] Hostilities flared in particular when surviving Jews demanded the return of their belongings.[6] By demanding justice and restitution, battling antisemitism, and aiming to restore or change their social and political environment, returning Jews reclaimed their home. After experiencing immense injustice, they nurtured hopes that they would be able to see their perpetrators punished and either return to their former lives or radically change society. Often these hopes ended in disappointment.

Putting Perpetrators on Trial

The knowledge that they lived among perpetrators deeply troubled Jews in East as well as West Germany. How could they live among people who had murdered their relatives? Hans Frankenthal remembered that soon after his return from Auschwitz, he was stopped by a police officer for a minor offence. Frankenthal yelled at him, called him a Nazi, and threatened to kill him. He saw in the policeman the murderer of his parents.[7] Frankenthal did not know the policeman or whether he had played a role in the persecution of Jews. In other cases, Jews encountered someone whom they knew to be guilty. Larry Orbach recounted that after the end of the war, he went to the apartment of a Jew catcher, beat him up, and delivered him to a Russian officer.[8]

Such acts, however, were uncommon. Most surviving German Jews refrained from physically assaulting known Nazis. Tracking down Nazis and beating them up would not have been possible for many of the survivors, who were often elderly, ill, or emaciated. Most did not have the opportunity, strength, or power to act upon their anger. But more than just unfeasible, such direct acts of revenge also stood at odds with the emotional norms postulated in the Jewish press and among Jewish intellectuals in the aftermath of the war. Indeed, Jews in Germany invested considerable effort to counter a depiction of Jews as vindictive. The Nazis had repeatedly propagated the stereotype of the vengeful Jew, an image that survived into the postwar years. Rebuking this notion, German Jews stressed the difference between the Nazi stereotype and the reality, in which the victims refrained from revenge.[9] In a report published in *Commentary* magazine in January 1946, Moses Moskowitz, secretary general of the Consultative Council of Jewish Organizations, stressed the absence of vengeful thoughts among the surviving Jews in Germany, emphasizing instead the humanity and goodness of the victims:

> The great majority of the surviving Jews feel no particular vindictiveness towards the German people. . . . If the Jews had been given to vindictiveness, they would have had many opportunities to avenge themselves. But there has been no recorded incident of Jews who took the law into their own hands, unprovoked. . . . To be sure, they deeply resent the freedom enjoyed by those

104 | *Home after Fascism*

> Germans whose rightful place is behind bars, and the comfortable quarters of others who belong in dungeons. But they are careful to distinguish between innocent and guilty, and to think clearly about the Germans as a political and human problem. The attitude of the Jews towards Germans seems to be guided by an unshaken belief in humanity, a deep sense of justice, plus incurable optimism. . . . Like the Rabbi of Berdichev, the Jews in Germany, native or foreign, bend over backwards to find some goodness in the German so as to justify his existence on this earth.[10]

Moskowitz responds to the Nazi depiction of the vengeful Jew by emphasizing surviving Jews' decency and "belief in humanity," which he describes as rooted in Jewish tradition. Similarly, Richard May emphasized in *Der Weg* that vengeance did not fit the Jewish tradition.[11] The writer Ralph Giordano pointed out that the fear of retaliation among the non-Jewish population "existed mainly in their own imagination."[12]

Survivors may have eliminated thoughts of revenge from public testimonies in order to be heard in an environment that required them not to voice any resentment. As Mark Roseman suggests, surviving Jews needed to self-censor their accounts to get their stories published in front of a German public that rejected accusatory accounts.[13] Yet much of the discussion about the absence of revenge took place within the Jewish community and was published in Jewish papers, addressing mostly Jewish readers. German Jews may have been less interested in responding to the expectations of a German audience than in shaping their own stories according to their self-image. Writing about her first visit to Germany in 1949, Hannah Arendt discussed Germans' obsession with vengeance: "The insistence that there must be a careful scheme of revenge serves as a consoling argument, demonstrating the equal sinfulness of all men."[14] Arendt was commenting on Germans' view of the Allies, but her analysis could be applied to their position vis-à-vis Jews as well. Jewish revenge would have allowed non-Jews to claim that everyone acted immorally. By insisting that they did not seek vengeance, German Jews rebuked this notion even as Germans obsessed over it. By stressing that revenge played no role in their own wishes and stood in contrast to their tradition, Jews challenged Nazi stereotypes and aimed to reclaim and shape the public image of "the Jew."

Beyond pointing to Jewish tradition, Jews mentioned multiple other reasons why they rejected revenge. Ernest Landau, a concentration camp survivor, explained that their hatred left no room for vengeance, while Rabbi Max Eschelbacher, who had immigrated to England but remained vocal in the German Jewish world, conceded that what Jews had experienced was too horrible to allow for revenge.[15] In an article in *Der Weg*, Wilhelm Meier similarly argued that "most bloody retaliations appear worthless when measured with the magnitude of our sacrifice."[16] The enormity of the crimes and violence the Germans had unleashed hindered acting upon a thirst for vengeance and made it difficult to pin down individual responsibility.

Meier concluded his article by stating that remembering the victims meant more than revenge. Bearing witness could function as "displaced revenge," as could playing an active role in enacting justice.[17] Not wanting vengeance did not mean that German Jews wished to forgive, and many emphasized the need for meting out justice.[18] As Moskowitz wrote, "They deeply resent the freedom enjoyed by those Germans whose rightful place is behind bars."[19] In an article on the Nuremberg trials, Julius Meyer, who later became the president of the Association of Jewish Communities in the GDR, emphasized how justice differed from vengeance. He maintained that it was not vengeance "when we demand the death of all war criminals, but rather the understanding that clemency and consideration mean encouragement for all Fascists and antisemitic forces."[20] Similarly, an article in *Der Weg* insisted that "the borders between justice and vengeance can be clearly drawn. Vengeance is always the concern of the individual. . . . Justice, however, is an expression of national coexistence [*staatliches Zusammenleben*]." The author, Richard May, concluded, "Especially after twelve years of despotism, one must decidedly demand that these ethical foundations be resurrected and secured against any violation."[21] In contrast to vengeance, which he asserted depends on the individual's conviction that he or she had been harmed, justice entailed a public understanding of wrongdoing, which could prevent a recurrence of the crimes. May then pointed to justice as a means of regaining a feeling of safety. He showed a strong reliance on the *Rechtsstaat* (the law-based state) and a perhaps surprisingly optimistic belief, given the German Jewish experience, in its restoration. Other German Jews raised the question of whether justice was possible, given the severity of the crimes. Wilhelm Meier maintained that "the magnitude of our loss lets us recognize that it would be impossible to see even the hardest punishment as atonement." Still, he considered it necessary to put the perpetrators behind bars: "For us, only the fact that those inhuman beasts will be eradicated can be reassuring."[22] How else could they regain a feeling of security?

The prosecution of perpetrators played a role in German Jews' decisions about where to live after the war. Rumors that the Soviets were more

106 | *Home after Fascism*

serious about punishing former Nazis convinced some German Jews to settle in the East rather than in one of the Western zones.[23] Helmut Eschwege had left Germany in 1934 and eventually settled in Palestine where he joined the local Communist Party. At the end of the war Eschwege, who wanted to return to Germany, was able to obtain a visa for Czechoslovakia. While in Prague he read that in the Soviet occupied zone denazification was taken seriously and thus decided to go there.[24] This notion was not only shared among party members. In a letter to the Jewish community, Kurt Grobe, son of a baptized Jew and Christian mother, exclaimed, "The Russians are said to handle things differently."[25] Victor Klemperer contemplated joining the Communist Party in November 1945—and did eventually join—as he believed they were the only ones who really wanted to get rid of the Nazis.[26]

In both east and west Germany, most of the proceedings regarding National Socialist crimes took place in the immediate postwar period. German courts reopened in the fall of 1945, operating under the rules of the German Code of Criminal Procedures in effect since 1877. Whereas prosecution of most Nazi crimes remained reserved for Allied courts until the establishment of the two postwar states, Allied Control Council Law No. 10 authorized German courts to pass sentences on crimes committed by German citizens against other German nationals or against stateless persons.[27] This meant that those charged with murdering Jews in eastern Europe outside of Germany, such as members of the Einsatzgruppen or camp guards, were tried in Allied courts, whereas people charged with committing crimes against German Jews in Germany, such as denunciations, blackmail, or violence in the course of the November pogroms, had to be tried in German courts.[28] After the foundation of the two new states in 1949, German courts could prosecute perpetrators for crimes committed against foreign nationals. Most of the cases put to trial in the first postwar decade focused on crimes against resisters, violence committed due to internal divisions in the Nazi state, crimes committed in concentration camps, the so-called Röhm-Putsch (the purge of part of the Nazi Party in 1934), and the November pogroms. German courts barely touched the murder of Jews in extermination camps.[29]

Neither was the genocide central to the most prominent Allied trial—the Nuremberg International Military Tribunal (IMT), held between October 18, 1945, and October 1, 1946. Still, the trial investigated the murder of European Jews and showed the footage the Allied armies shot during the liberation of the camps and thus brought awareness to the immensity of Nazi crimes.[30] Wolfgang Hildesheimer, who worked as a translator with the IMT after his return to Germany, expressed his impressions in a letter to his parents in February 1947: "The material that one receives [at his work] and also the testimonies you hear at the Doctors' Trials exceed everything imaginable. While I had earlier scruples and was not sure if I wanted to participate in the whole Nuremberg-machine, I am now quite sure that all judgments made and those that will be made are just."[31] Tullia Zevi, an Italian Jew who had immigrated to New York City after the racial laws went into effect, accepted an invitation from the Religious News Service to report from the IMT. In an interview with her granddaughter decades later, she recollected her impressions. "I was there for three months," Zevi remembered, "and this is how I understood the magnitude of the horror. . . . It was a traumatic experience facing Nazi criminals and seeing the impassivity of their faces. . . . Some of the things I have seen and heard in Nuremberg I have never been able to leave behind."[32]

While the Nuremberg trials displayed Nazi crimes against Jews, Jewish witnesses played a minor role. For Jewish survivors, the murder of European Jews constituted *the* major Nazi crime, whereas the Allies focused mainly on the launching of an aggressive war.[33] The DP (mainly eastern European Jewish) population in Germany voiced frustration over the marginalization of their voices.[34] German Jews, however, did not formulate a similar critique and reported mostly positively about the trial. They perceived it as an important opportunity to spread awareness about Nazi crimes. Writing in *Der Weg*, Hans Erich Fabian argued that one of its main benefits was "discussing the charges in public and thus also to show the German people the degree of guilt of the defendants, whom they had tolerated for years as their government."[35]

While they merely observed the Nuremberg trials, several German Jews played an active role in other trials. They denounced perpetrators and served as witnesses, plaintiffs, attorneys, and judges.[36] German courts asked the Jewish community to assist in finding witnesses, and Jewish institutions spurred their members to play an active role in the prosecutions.[37] Beginning in the summer of 1947, *Der Weg* published lists of camp guards' names in the hopes that witnesses would step forward.[38] For Jewish witnesses, facing their perpetrators in court could prove traumatic, and the hostile climate they encountered further exacerbated the challenges of providing testimony. German judges showed little sympathy toward Jewish witnesses, cross-examining and probing the deeply traumatized survivors.

108 | Home after Fascism

German Jews also faced threats when testifying. One witness, for instance, asked the court for protection because the defendant had persuaded former members of the Hitler Youth to break into his apartment and demolish it.[39]

German Jews denounced Nazis on a number of occasions, and most of the early trials against Nazi criminals resulted from the charge of a witness, camp survivor, or relative who turned to the state attorney's office.[40] In May 1946 *Der Weg* recounted how a group of former Auschwitz prisoners recognized a female SS guard in a theater audience. The guard was delivered to the police, and at the time of publication, she awaited trial. The writer concluded with the optimistic note that "still, many of our tormentors from the camps stay hidden, but sooner or later they too will be recognized and held accountable for their nefarious deeds."[41]

Some made the prosecution of Nazi criminals their life's work. Fritz Bauer had begun considering the question of prosecuting war criminals during his exile in Denmark.[42] Upon his return to West Germany in 1949, he actively worked on prosecuting Nazi criminals and obtaining justice and compensation for the victims, first as presiding judge of the Brunswick regional court, and from 1959 as Hessian state attorney general.[43] Lawyer Henry Ormond, born as Hans Ludwig Jacobson, like Bauer returned to Germany determined to make sure perpetrators would be punished.[44] And not only professional jurists worked to bring Nazi criminals to justice. After spending a few months in Berlin, Florence Singewald moved to Erfurt, where she began working for the municipality. She put her efforts into denazification as she wanted to "extirpate fascism." She helped bring two persons to trial who had been involved in her friends' deportation to Treblinka, and a merchant who had refused to sell to her lost his business.[45]

The denazification process by which former members of Nazi organizations were to be barred from government administration and other leading positions in society depended on Jews as witnesses. The Americans established civilian tribunals (Spruchkammern) to investigate party members' past deeds. The Frankfurt Spruchkammer sent several requests to the local Jewish community asking for witnesses against former Nazis. In December 1948 the Spruchkammer requested that a picture of a policeman who had served as a guard in the Warsaw ghetto be posted in the Jewish community center.[46] Apparently the denazification courts struggled to find witnesses for the prosecution while defendants provided a number of witnesses in their defense. An article in *Der Weg* from May 1946 called on German Jews to play close attention to district office announcements listing people undergoing denazification trials.[47] Following such requests, a Frankfurt Jew wrote to the *Spruchkammer* in regard to the denazification trial of a Gestapo officer. He attested that the latter was responsible for the deportation of an elderly Jewish acquaintance and suspected that the officer had played a role in the deportation of at least one other person.[48]

But Jews also helped clear German acquaintances called before the denazification courts.[49] Victor Klemperer commented in his diary on the frequent requests for *Persilscheine* (denazification certificates):[50] "A constant demand of the influential Jew. I am supposed to help the whole world."[51] But despite voicing his disapproval of the Germans' "whining," he wrote many such letters in support of individuals.[52] Considering that the German Jewish postwar discourse emphasized German guilt, German Jews' willingness, both in the East and the West, to provide *Persilscheine* is striking.[53] Jews testifying for former Nazis greatly upset Jewish institutions. In the summer of 1946, the council of Jewish communities in the British zone prohibited its members from providing former members of the NSDAP with such *Persilscheine*.[54] *Der Weg* addressed the matter in March of the same year. After suggesting that almost every former party member seemed to have a letter from a Jew testifying to their friendliness, the article examined what might cause a German Jew to supply such a certificate. Rejecting greed as a motive, the author suggested that such evaluations tended to be subjective and reminded readers that the same person who treated them well might have "driven other Jews into their death"; indeed, just "by his being a member in the party, he [the party member] contributed to the murder of almost six million of our brothers and sisters." The author concluded with a warning: "We need to ensure purity among ourselves if we demand respect and if we do not want to betray our dead brothers and sisters. Whoever as a Jew acts against this in the future, whoever issues certificates for party members without knowing all the facts, whoever takes on legal representation of a party member without examination of all the circumstances, puts himself outside our Jewish community and must be publicly denounced. To monitor this is the task of the Jewish community, the religious aid agencies, and the Committee for Victims of Fascism."[55] Beyond seeing *Persilscheine* as an insult to the victims' memory, the article makes clear that the Jewish leadership worried about Jews' reputation. How would they be judged if it became widely known that German Jews exculpated numerous individual Germans? Although Jewish institutions continued to issue similar warnings, they seemed to have had little effect.[56]

110 | *Home after Fascism*

The article does not provide a final answer as to why Jews might have been willing to provide positive testimonies. There are a few possible explanations: while the article's author dismissed the notion of financial gain as a motivation, it is not inconceivable, given the often-desperate material situation of surviving Jews, that some were tempted to certify an ex-Nazi's *Judenfreundlichkeit* (friendliness to Jews) for pay. Others may have acted generously toward people who behaved decently to them. In an increasingly hostile environment, small gestures meant a lot and may have been interpreted in an especially positive light after the war. Some favorable testimonies came from emigrants who had left before the war and had not personally witnessed the worst horrors. Those who survived in hiding or in what the Nazis had termed a "privileged mixed-marriage" may have been more likely to supply supportive testimonies, and in some cases, Jews owed their survival to people who were members of the NSDAP.

Gray zones of guilt and rescue efforts color the story of Margarete Landé, an anthropologist who worked closely with Ludwig Ferdinand Clauss, a race scientist. After the war Landé wrote to the Jewish community to ask for support to resume her scientific work. In her letter she depicted how she had survived the Nazi years, hidden by her colleague. However, she omitted that this colleague, Clauss, had joined the NSDAP in 1933.[57] Decades later, in 1979, Landé filed an official request with Yad Vashem, Israel's Holocaust Remembrance Center, asking them to include Ludwig Ferdinand Clauss as one of the Righteous Among the Nations. Initially the institution accepted the request, though later they withdrew the honor. Landé owed her life to Clauss, who had hidden her for several years and had built her an underground hiding place in his garden. She did not see him as implicated but knew not to disclose the information about his NSDAP membership to the Jewish community.[58]

While some surviving Jews chose to assist individual Germans, the Jewish communities grew increasingly weary of the flood of letters from Germans who had abandoned their Jewish friends, colleagues, and acquaintances but turned to them with no shame after the war, when they hoped for help in clearing their names.[59] Julius Dreifuss, the head of the Jewish community in Düsseldorf, voiced this frustration in an exchange with Adolf Caspari, a non-Jewish state official. Caspari wrote to the community in January 1948, asking for the current addresses of several Jewish merchants. Rather than providing the addresses or explaining that he did not know their whereabouts, the more common reaction of Jewish community heads, Dreifuss asked Caspari why he wanted this information. The latter replied that he needed it in order "to once again enter a friendly correspondence and also to ask them for an opinion on our conduct towards them during the Nazi period." He continued describing how he and his wife had "helped" Jews under the Nazis, including an episode in which he still greeted a Jewish family he knew on the street in 1937. Perhaps the trigger was Caspari's pride in what amounted to halfway-decent behavior toward people with whom he claimed to have a "hearty relationship," or maybe it was his use of terms like "Jew-families" (*Judenfamilien*), which sounded like Nazi terminology, but in Dreifuss's reply we can sense his anger and resentment:

> We understand from your letter . . . , that you want an opinion from the specified persons about your behavior towards them during the Nazi era. From this we deduce that you are in need of such a testimony. Consequently you must have been a Nazi, otherwise you would not need a denazification certificate. We are convinced that the persons to whom you refer showed a more dignified behavior than you during the Nazi period and would certainly never have asked you to issue them a certificate of exoneration. We therefore regret that we cannot meet your wish and will not be able to provide the addresses.[60]

There are many similar examples of Germans approaching Jewish communities. For instance, Peter Hartmann, formerly the chauffeur for Karl Mayer, a German Jew who had been a consular officer before 1933, explained in a letter to the Jewish community of Mainz that he had worked for Karl Mayer for fourteen years, between 1914 and 1933. Hartmann wrote that "the trust that Mr. Mayer invested in me was unfortunately interrupted by the unfortunate circumstances (*unseligen Verhaeltnissen*) of 1933."[61] The use of the passive voice and the vagueness of his language—"unfortunate circumstances"—are telling. Hartmann reconstructed the break with Mayer as if he had had no agency in the matter. But no one had forced him to cut all ties with his Jewish employer as early as 1933. The head of the Mainz community replied briefly that he did not have Mayer's current address. Such exchanges show surviving Jews' growing frustration with the complete unwillingness among Germans to confront their guilt.

In Italy, defascistization began after the coup against Mussolini in 1943, though these initial purges yielded few results.[62] Italy's self-liberation both stimulated and hindered the purging. While the coup against Mussolini in 1943 encouraged antifascist forces, it also assured that many of those involved in the sanctioning had themselves been deeply implicated with

112 | *Home after Fascism*

Fascism. After Ivanoe Bonomi replaced Badoglio as prime minister in June 1944, the Bonomi government issued a new purge law. With the liberation the purging received new impetus from partisan forces. Hans Woller estimates that in spontaneous acts of vengeance, members of the resistance killed about fifteen thousand people.[63]

Numerous Italian Jews had joined the resistance, and they may have taken part in the retaliation at the end of the war, though I did not come across any mention of this in Jewish memoirs or diaries. However, some commented on these wild purges. Emilio Canarutto, secretary of the Italian Committee of the Association of Swiss Jewish Refugee Aid and Welfare, described the last days of the war in a letter written in April 1945: "The only events worthy of note are those concerning the war, with its radical cleansing of the city and the countryside of wild beasts who have persecuted us and who now are atoning."[64] Others, like Elena Morpurgo, disapproved of the violence. In April 1945 she noted in her diary, "last night the radio gave news of arrests, suicides, shootings . . . I cannot exult like so many people around me. . . . Rather, I feel a sense of nausea and horror."[65] Benito Mussolini faced popular justice when partisans captured and shot him along with his mistress, Clara Petacci, in April 1945. His body was publicly displayed in Piazzale Loreto in Milan.[66] Marcello Pacifici, who had survived the war in Switzerland, wrote in his diary upon receiving this news, "Justice is done! Mussolini, la Petacci, and their other worthy consorts have been arrested in Dogno and were executed, after a summary judgment."[67]

Fascist collaborators who escaped these wild purges were to be tried at the extraordinary assize courts, which the Bonomi government established in the spring of 1945. The defendants were tried according to the guidelines of the decreto legislativo luogotenenziale no. 159, article 5 (collaborationism) and articles 51, 54, and 58 of the military war code. These courts, like the sanctions against Fascists in general, focused on the Salò regime and collaboration with the Nazi occupiers after 1943 and not on the *ventennio*—that is, Mussolini's regime between 1922 and 1943.[68] Thus, crimes committed against Jews under cover of the racial laws between 1938 and 1943 played no role in these trials. The Jewish community did not protest. The discourse among Italian Jews focused strongly on the persecution under the Salò regime, and because many had initially joined the PNF, an investigation of early Fascist crimes might have incriminated some Jews as well.

Italian Jews followed these trials closely and participated in a number of ways—as witnesses, attorneys, and plaintiffs.[69] In several cases Jews brought the defendants to the attention of the courts. Vittorio Cremisini went to police headquarters to denounce the person responsible for arresting him, his father, and a friend, which had led to their deportation and his father's murder in Auschwitz.[70] Lea Pincherle, who had fled to Switzerland, reported her sister's son-in-law, a member of the militia, who had betrayed her mother and brother. She wrote her memorandum before the end of the war in order to ensure his prosecution "in case she did not survive."[71]

After the war, Jews in Italy, as across Europe, sought to bring Jews who had collaborated with the regime to justice.[72] Teresa Pescatori pressed charges at the Venice police headquarters against Mauro Grin (also referred to as Mauro Grün and Mauro Grini), who had informed on her husband and brother-in-law, causing their subsequent arrest. Grin had been an informant for the SS and had tracked and denounced numerous Jews in Trieste, Venice, and Milan. Grin's postwar fate remains somewhat unclear. Toward the end of the war, in February 1945, Emilio Canarutto, who was a member of DELASEM, received a letter from his cousin about Grin, "the terror of the Jews in Venice." In his reply Canarutto assured his cousin that he knew about the informant and confirmed that they "had reported him to the proper authorities."[73] Less than two weeks later, he added in a postscript that he had received "the news that Mauro Grün (Grini) aka Dr. Manzoni, terror of the Jews in Venice and Milan, was liquidated. RIP."[74] Grin was most likely killed at San Sabba, the transit and extermination camp in Trieste.[75] Perhaps unaware of this, after the war Vittorio Fano, head of the Venice community, wrote to the president of the Unione and the heads of the communities of Trieste and Milan, suggesting that they would join together as plaintiffs in a trial against Grin; Paolo Sereni, a Venetian Jew who had been deported with his family but later returned, would serve as witness.[76] The Milan assize courts sentenced Grin to death, possibly posthumously, in the spring of 1947.[77]

At times Italian Jews participated in trials beyond their country's borders. The Polish government invited representatives from several other countries to participate as witnesses in the trial against Rudolf Höss, the commandant of Auschwitz, which took place in Warsaw in March 1947.[78] Massimo Adolfo Vitale, head of the CRDE, acted as the Italian representative. Besides reporting from the trial, he chose two Italian witnesses. Vitale sent letters to several Auschwitz survivors asking them whether they would be willing to go to Warsaw to testify. Most replied favorably and seemed eager to have the opportunity to give testimony, though some felt too sick

114 | *Home after Fascism*

to face the journey to Poland.[79] Eugenio Ravenna struggled with a different challenge. Vitale had specified that witnesses should be able to provide the court with new, precise facts.[80] Ravenna replied that he had considered the request at length but concluded that he would not be able to "bring this new light that the tribunal aims to collect with the aim of justice. . . . I am not able to specify individual, concrete facts, precisely because I am not able to provide the names of persons who were in charge in the camps."[81] The structure of the Nazi extermination camps made it difficult for the victims to provide testimony. Cut off from the outside world, physically and mentally abused, traumatized, constantly lied to, and without means to take any notes or even keep track of time, how could they be expected to provide a precise account? Like Ravenna, other survivors also struggled with the courts' request for detailed information.

Facing perpetrators and narrating their horrific experiences while the information they provided was questioned and their testimony scrutinized proved difficult for survivors, in Italy as elsewhere.[82] In 1948 Ferdinando Altmann, a survivor of Auschwitz who lost his family in the camps, charged the guides at the Swiss border who had denounced him and his family. The community helped him hire Pia Levi Ravenna, a Jewish lawyer who represented a number of Jewish plaintiffs in trials against Italian collaborators after the war.[83] During the trial Ravenna described the inhumane treatment of children and women in the Nazi camps. According to a court reporter, at that moment one could hear the "long and desperate cry of poor Altmann, who lost his children in the camps."[84] Listening to the description of violence must have been traumatic for him as a survivor.

A year later, Altmann wrote to the president of the Union of Italian Jewish Communities to inform him that the trial against the guides had been referred to the appeals court. He explained that he had no financial means and asked for support to again hire Pia Levi Ravenna for the case. He did not want these criminals to be "free tomorrow" just because he could not afford a lawyer to "ascertain their full responsibility in the massacre of more than 70 of our coreligionists who must be avenged, and who are asking to be avenged."[85] In contrast to the German Jewish discourse that marked the difference between justice and revenge, Altmann perceived revenge and justice as intertwined—he could avenge his family by putting the guides who betrayed them into prison.

While revenge was widely discussed but rejected in the German Jewish press, Italian Jews did not refrain from calling for revenge against perpetrators. The creation of a postwar narrative in which good Italians and Italian Jews had fought against a minority of traitors made a search for vengeance acceptable. The language of postwar trials in Italy stressed that the perpetrators' treachery had been against Italy and thus it was not the Jews who sought vengeance but rather the Italian nation. One verdict against two Italians who had assisted in the arrest of a large number of Italian Jews, for instance, charged the defendants for "betraying their country with their greed and throwing dozens of families into mourning and misery."[86] A few years after an Italian government had declared Jews enemies of the state, the trial whitewashed the state's implication in these crimes and obscured the victims' particularity—the Jewishness of the families that were thrown into "mourning and misery" was not mentioned. The idea of the brava gente was pervasive in postwar trials, while the Italian state's mistreatment of Jews remained absent. During another trial against a group of guides at the Swiss border who had betrayed Jews to the Germans, Pia Levi Ravenna pointed to the goodness of the Italian people at large: "Almost all Italians have understood the injustice and have often tried to help, but unfortunately there were many obstacles in their way."[87] It seems that part of her strategy was to contrast the guilt of the accused with the goodness of the Italian people, thus marking their crimes not merely as against Jews but as a betrayal of Italy.

Fighting Antisemitism

The effort to bring known perpetrators to justice constituted only one part of the many ways surviving Jews tried to shape postwar societies and rid them of the worst aspects of the past. Though no longer officially condoned by the postwar governments, antisemitism did not disappear in 1945, and Jews in both Germany and Italy found a variety of strategies to deal with and combat persistent hostility and prejudices.

There are numerous examples that show the continuity of antisemitic prejudice and even policies from Fascism to the postwar period. Renzo Levi, vice president of the Union of Italian Jewish Communities, complained to the head of the Italian police that some people were under police surveillance simply because of their Jewish origin.[88] As late as 1948, the police arrested people because of their Jewish "race," pursuing warrants that had been issued by the Fascist Italian Social Republic.[89] In the spring of the same year, a neo-Fascist group attacked the former ghetto of Rome and threatened Roman Jews with shouts, insults, and truncheons.[90]

116 | *Home after Fascism*

While such violent attacks remained rare, hostilities such as offensive writings on the walls of Jewish neighborhoods and threatening phone calls to community offices occurred more often. Italian Jews depicted encounters with antisemitism at school and in the workplace. Liliana Spizzichino—a Roman Jew—remembered that her fellow students "spoke ill of the Jews, they said they were stingy, unreliable, and they knew that they would recognize them from afar." She consequently preferred to remain among Jews and keep her Jewishness to herself when she was "in an environment that is not mine."[91] While Liliana kept her Jewishness quiet to escape antisemitism, others took a more defiant route. Lia Levi, a teenage girl who had survived the war hidden in a Catholic convent near Rome, likewise remembered troubles with a teacher who made nasty remarks about Jews when she returned to school after liberation. However, her family did not let it pass. Her mother visited the principal several times to demand that the teacher stop insulting her.[92]

In contradiction to the widespread discourse around antisemitism as "un-Italian" and nonexistent in Italy, Italian Jews publicly documented antisemitic incidents. Italian Jews wrote to journals, radio stations, and other media outlets in order to call out antisemitic discourse. The newsletter of the Milan community, for instance, contained a rubric detailing antisemitic actions by officials.[93] Massimo Adolfo Vitale, who pushed for an acknowledgment of Italian guilt, also pointed out subliminal antisemitism. In October 1947 he wrote to Massimo Mercurio, editor of the journal *Il Mattino d'Italia*, criticizing an article that emphasized a swindler's Jewish origin. Vitale asked why the author showed such interest in the criminal's Jewish background when the paper never mentioned the religious backgrounds of non-Jews. Referring to the journalist Telesio Interlandi, one of the most fervent advocates of antisemitism in Fascist Italy, he concluded, "There are already too many . . . 'Interlandi' in Italian journalism; do you also, dear Dr. Mercurio, want to proceed in such low company?"[94]

Like Vitale, other Italian Jews did their best to combat prejudice. In June 1948 the president of the community of Parma, Giacomo Camerini, wrote to Raffaele Cantoni to report that during a conference of the Missione Paolina, he got into a dispute with one of the speakers over the latter's wrong presumptions about Jews and their faith. Apparently, the argument got so heated that the police had to come and quell the fight. Camerini added that he also frequently came across anti-Jewish articles in the Catholic press.[95] After the war, Italian Jews still faced the centuries-old anti-Judaism of the Catholic Church. Articles in Catholic periodicals and priests in Sunday sermons continued to accuse Jews of deicide, blame them for not acknowledging the "true faith," and even defame them for the ritual murder of Christian children.[96] Publications such as Giovanni Papini's *Lettere agli uomini di Papa Celestino VI* (1946), which argued that Jews' rejection of Christ was the reason for anti-Jewish discrimination, as well as the *Enciclopedia Cattolica*, which made similar arguments, legitimized Christian antisemitism.[97]

Italian Jews protested against Catholic antisemitism. Elena Foa, a Jew from Ancona, complained in a letter to the Italian Radio Auditions Authority, the national radio network, about a broadcast to which she had listened the previous night. Foa wrote that she had hoped the religious conversation "would lift my spirits, instead after a few sentences . . . the speaker started to speak with such bitterness of the Jewish people that I had the impression of listening to a fascist or Hitler propagandist rather than a religious person. This Father Ricardo Lombardi . . . explained that the chosen people, the Jewish people had become the cursed people."[98] At times Catholic anti-Jewish sentiments went beyond talk. In July 1945 Vitale Milano, president of the Roman community, complained to the management of a local hospital. A midwife had baptized the infant of a Jewish patient against the latter's outspoken will. The child died a few hours later. Milano asked the hospital leadership to take action against their employee.[99]

In June 1947 an American Jewish Committee (AJC) representative reported that "from time to time the Vatican circles attack the Jews, mostly based on religious grounds. Many books and pamphlets written by religious authorities at the time repeated the age-old charges against the Jews as enemies of Christianity and partly justifying their suffering because of it."[100] In their efforts to improve the situation, AJC officials managed to convince a publisher to change the title on a postcard depicting a fresco in a church in Padua from "Christ tortured by Jews" to "Christ tortured." A book about the church depicted the same image. The AJC contacted Massimo Adolfo Vitale, but the latter did not believe "that there is very much that can be done." Vitale wrote, "Until the edition is sold out, I see no possibility of modifying the inscription which is bothering us. . . . God only knows how many cases similar to this are met with here and there."[101] Vitale's resigned attitude points to the difficulty of combatting Catholic antisemitism given the church's dominant position within Italian society. A negative image of Jews and Judaism continued to be prevalent in pre–*Nostra Aetate* Catholic

Home after Fascism

teaching.[102] While preaching clemency toward Nazi war criminals, Pope Pius XII refused to condemn antisemitism and advised changing rather than abolishing Fascist racial legislation.[103]

The church, with its centuries- old anti-Judaism, was not the only sphere in which Jews faced prejudice. Antisemitic attitudes also existed in liberal, secular circles. In the immediate aftermath of the war, Cesare Merzagora, who had joined the resistance and later made a political career in the liberal party, published an article on the reintegration of Italy's Jews into society, asking Jews not to complain and instead to try harder to adapt to Italian society. Merzagora concluded by advising Italy's Jews to be careful not to leave the right path; after all, two thousand years of persecution could only be explained by the "genetic defects" of the Jewish people.[104] Merzagora's article made it into a pamphlet entitled *I pavidi* (The Cowards), published in January 1946 with a preface by the famous philosopher Benedetto Croce. In contrast to most Italian intellectuals, Croce had taken a firm stand against racial laws during the Fascist period. In this preface, he highlights his opposition to the Fascist persecution of Jews and, promoting the narrative of the good Italian, suggests that Italians, in contrast to Germans, "comforted and protected the persecuted in every encounter." Yet he reveals his prejudice, asking Jews to "blend in more with other Italians, in order to do away with the distinction and separation they have kept up for centuries and which in the past has been used as an opportunity and apology for persecutions—there is reason to fear this might happen again in the future."[105] Statements that asked Jews to change and blamed the victims for persecution were common, echoing a centuries-old discourse that blamed Jews for their difference from "real" Italians.[106]

Croce's statements met with disapproval among Italian Jews. Dante Lattes, a scholar, journalist, and promoter of Jewish culture—together with Alfonso Pacifici he had founded the Zionist weekly *Israel* in 1916, and later on the scholarly monthly *La Rassegna Mensile di Israel*—replied angrily. In an article in *Israel*, he commented that "what is most surprising is the advice given to the Jews to decide to disappear and to put an end to their existence, their idea, their faith, their history after so many centuries of resistance and martyrdom."[107] The famous historian Arnaldo Momigliano, who admired Croce, asserted that the statement "stems from his [Croce's] affection and sympathy for the Jews." He explained Croce's attitude with his "complete lack of contact with Jewish culture[, which] can explain that not even Benedetto Croce managed to understand that Italian Jews have the right . . . to remain Jewish." Momigliano understood this as a general deficiency of non-Jewish Italian intellectuals who proved unable to "acknowledge the Hebrew tradition, which has been a component of Italian culture since the beginning of Christianity."[108] While asserting the right to Jewish difference, Momigliano depicted lack of knowledge rather than a hostile attitude as the cause of Croce's attack.

Responses to antisemitism frequently stopped short of blaming Italians for their prejudiced attitude, steeped in the notion that Italians *in their nature* were not racist. A January 1945 article in the journal *Israel*, for instance, after expressing how little antisemitism had influenced Italians during the war, discussed the awkward behavior of non-Jews when they realized that the author was Jewish and described their ignorant and often antisemitic remarks. The author ascribed such behavior to misinformation and lack of knowledge and asked for greater understanding from Italians, "as the good-natured teasing of a friend can become, with the complicity of the bad faith of others, a dangerous weapon in the hands of those who hate us."[109] It remains opaque whom the author envisions when he mentions "those who hate us," further separating antisemites from Italians. The discourse within the Italian Jewish press frequently portrayed antisemitic prejudice as based on a lack of understanding and carefully asked Italians to try to educate themselves. The editorial in the first edition of *Israel* also voiced such a need: "We want them to understand us and in order to understand us they must not only devote a quick look . . . when something unusual happens but benevolent and constant attention that achieves an exact assessment of our soul. Misapprehensions are at the root of so many bad things that have happened and we would like to put a lid on these so that they do not rise again."[110] The contemporary discourse portrayed Italians as good natured but naive, without much agency when it came to their attitude toward Jews and thus easily lured into antisemitic behavior. Still, Italian Jews pushed back against the notion that they had to change, asserting rather that non-Jewish Italians should educate themselves in order to eradicate their prejudices.

German Jews, likewise and often more forcefully, expressed the need for the majority population to change. In its first edition, *Der Weg* explained that it wanted to "encourage understanding for the specific problems of Judaism."[111] Some German Jews hoped to play an active role in eradicating antisemitic prejudice among Germans and explained their decision to resettle in their home country by pointing to their intention to work for

120 | *Home after Fascism*

political reeducation. Wilhelm Meier argued in *Der Weg* that those who stayed in Germany wanted to "take on the fight for the re-education of the German people."[112] Jeanette Wolff, who lost her husband and two of her daughters, wrote down her experiences in the concentration camp immediately after her return in order to educate the German youth.[113] Others, such as Alfred Döblin, Stefan Heym, and Hans Habe in the West and Alfred Kantorowicz in the East, aimed to take an active role in shaping postwar German culture, establishing journals and other media outlets.

While Jews in West Germany wished to build democracy and foster understanding of Judaism, Communists of Jewish origin hoped to teach Socialism and weed out racism.[114] Recha Rothschild, a Jewish Communist who survived in exile, decided to write about her experiences at the end of the war in order to "help today's youth to come to terms with their own doubts and inner struggles more quickly, and to strengthen their belief in the forces of progress and peaceful development."[115] Similar to Jeanette Wolff, Rothschild hoped that reading about her persecution would help young people see the destructive nature of the regime and would thus foster change.

Like Italian Jews, German Jews both in the West and the East reported and spoke out against antisemitic incidents.[116] They complained to the Jewish community and Allied or German authorities and published articles revealing and condemning antisemitism. The *Jüdisches Gemeindeblatt für die britische Zone* published a weekly series ironically entitled "Es gibt keinen Antisemitismus mehr in Deutschland" (There is no antisemitism in Germany anymore), in which it reported on antisemitic incidents. Articles in other Jewish publications likewise focused on the issue.

While the occupying powers had hoped to see antisemitism decrease, they found that anti-Jewish attitudes grew in the immediate postwar years. Bureaucrats continued to stamp food cards with *Jew* or addressed Jewish people with the Nazi-assigned names Sarah or Israel.[117] Like the Italian Roman Catholic Church, Protestant and Catholic German churches took decades to consider their own role in the persecution of the Jews, and church leaders continued to spread prejudice.[118] For instance, in June 1947, K. S., a Protestant of Jewish origin, complained to a victims of fascism (Opfer des Faschismus [OdF]) committee about the latent antisemitism in a sermon at his church.[119] Jews also reported being verbally and physically assaulted. G. N., a Berlin Jew, reported in the spring of 1949 that he had been attacked and called a "Jewish communist" and "Jewish pig." He stated that the police held him in custody, supposedly for his own protection, but did not arrest the attacker. In his letter to the Jewish community, he also asserted a general growth of antisemitism.[120] Yet, as in Italy, physical attacks remained the exception, while the marking of synagogues with swastikas and the destruction of gravestones in cemeteries occurred more often.[121] During a conference of the VVN, Leo Löwenkopf, head of the Dresden community, spoke about such antisemitic assaults, highlighting the community's role to actively combat antisemitism: "Meanwhile cemetery desecrations are again frequently reported. . . . It is our sacred duty to uncover the sick core and warn again and again."[122]

In contrast to the mostly eastern European DP population in Germany, German Jews did not organize demonstrations against antisemitism.[123] But they did speak out and push back when confronted with antisemitic prejudice. Julius Dreifuss, the leader of the Jewish community in Düsseldorf, did not hide his frustration about a letter from a German insurance agency that expected payments from a community member who had been murdered in Auschwitz. In his reply from November 1947, he wrote, "We recommend that for the collection of the premium for Mr. Kurt Israel Frank you turn to Auschwitz concentration camp, where Mr. Frank was gassed."[124] The insurance company's request, as well as their usage of the name Israel, which the Nazis had forced upon German Jewish men, angered Dreyfuss. By writing "gassed," he emphasized the Nazis' crimes as well as German guilt. His direct message stood in contrast to the circumscribed language of the insurance company, which obscured the recent past and denied responsibility. In their defensive reply, they stated that they had many clients with the name Israel and "anyhow the defamation intended by certain circles back then—to which we demonstrably never belonged—can hardly be effective today, apart from the fact that decent people, who also existed back then, never saw a defamation of Jews in these childish acts."[125] The letter focuses on defending their conduct, separating themselves from a past constructed as distant just two years after the war and from Nazism, which they fail to name, minimizing it as "certain circles." There is no acknowledgment of Frank's murder, let alone a word of condolence. The gulf between Dreyfuss's "gassed in Auschwitz" and the insurance company's "childish acts" seems insurmountable.

The radically different ways Jewish and non-Jewish Germans perceived both the past and the present fueled feelings of hostility, anger, and resentment. Jews became increasingly frustrated with the denial of guilt,

Home after Fascism

while Germans continued to blame Jews for their persecution, rejecting any responsibility. For instance, an article published in the *Tagesspiegel* in December 1945, entitled "Jews in Germany: Emigration or Assimilation," maintained that Jews needed to emigrate or assimilate, making Jews responsible for preventing further persecution. Nowhere in the article does the author refer to German racism or make Germans responsible for the attempt to murder Europe's entire Jewish population.[126] Many Germans reacted with jealousy to any real or imagined assistance Jews received after the war, while the latter rightfully complained that they still found themselves in a much-worse situation than the non-Jewish population.[127]

Beyond being outraged and angry at persistent antisemitism, German Jews were afraid. In a diary entry from August 1948, Victor Klemperer credited the absence of antisemitic violence to the Allied presence, and he feared that once the Soviets left, he and his wife would be murdered.[128] Others shared this concern that the Allies' departure would lead to renewed persecution.[129] Klemperer also worried that the benefits Jews received and the relatively high proportion of people of Jewish descent in the emerging East German state's elite would lead to a desire for vengeance in the general population and ultimately to new pogroms. He noted in his diary that "there will be another antisemitic wave, and this time it will really come spontaneously from the people."[130] German Jews in both Germanies frequently wrote of their fear of the non-Jewish population and new attacks.[131]

Postwar relations between German Jews and non-Jews were complicated, fraught, and loaded, and while preferable over hostile comments, even expressions of supposed sympathy could be unsettling for surviving Jews. The niceties of many Germans repulsed Victor Klemperer, as he could not trust their motives.[132] Like Klemperer, others, in Germany as in Italy, perceived self-interest as the main motivator of such philosemitic sentiments. In his *Eight Jews* (1944), Giacomo Debenedetti described witnessing a sudden change in attitude among Italians:

> We [Italian Fascists] have to provide instant, convincing, incontrovertible, palpable, yet indirect evidence that while evil people were collaborating with the "Nazi-Fascists," we, on the other hand, were among the good.... What was black yesterday has become white today, and vice versa. What was the most conspicuous feature of Fascism? Its calling card, so to speak? Its fingerprint? There you go! Persecution of Jews. Therefore, what is the most characteristic indication of anti-Fascism? Protection of Jews. When the Fascists were in charge of things, they condemned, worse, punished any benevolence toward

Jews. Let's show ourselves sympathetic, having had such courage, and we'll immediately be admitted, officially admitted, without the slightest challenge, into the ranks of anti-Fascists.[133]

Flaunting love for Jews became a simple way for Italians and Germans to prove their antifascism. In Italy and even more so in West Germany, pronouncements of philosemitic attitudes functioned as a way to distance the postwar states from their Fascist past. During a conference on the future of Jews in Germany in Heidelberg in 1949, John McCloy, the high commissioner of the US zone, proclaimed that the world would carefully watch Germany's attitude toward the Jews in order to understand if there was indeed "sufficient humanity, sufficient tolerance, sufficient breadth of view and enlightenment" in the emerging state. McCloy further asserted that the Jewish community would be the "real touchstone and the test of Germany's progress toward the light."[134] Similarly, in his report for *Commentary*, Moses Moskowitz stated that "if the German Jews decide to remain and start life anew, their treatment by their neighbors will be the true measure of the German people's progress towards decency, progress, and democracy."[135] Aware of the importance of their behavior toward Jews, West German political leaders wanted to prove that German society had overcome antisemitism. As a consequence, according to Frank Stern, "philosemitism assumed a pivotal function: to serve as the moral legitimizer of the democratic character of the second German Republic during the period of its establishment and the attainment of sovereignty."[136]

Historians examining philosemitic attitudes in postwar Germany have emphasized continuities between antisemitic and philosemitic attitudes. Stern and others highlight that a philosemitic attitude continued to essentialize Jews—to see them as an as abstracted "other" rather than as individuals.[137] Such thinking changed negative stereotypes into positive ones. For instance, rather than fearing Jews' economic power, some Germans, still perceiving "the Jew" as wealthy, hoped for Jewish assistance in the reconstruction efforts. Similarly, still believing in Jewish political influence, politicians now perceived Jews as potential middlemen to represent Germans before foreign powers.[138] Daniel Cohen, looking beyond Germany at broader Western European postwar attitudes toward Jews, evaluates philosemitic attitudes more positively, arguing that "while 'philosemitism' never hindered the persistence or renewal of antisemitism . . . the positive reevaluation of Jewishness in Western Europe since 1945 marks a profound caesura in the course of both Jewish and European history."[139]

Jews in Germany and Italy perceived the emerging state's wish to portray themselves as "pro-Jewish," as a shift that had a deep impact on their lives. In particular, in Germany, both East and West, antisemitism turned from state ideology to a taboo: an attitude to which many still adhered but few would openly admit. While they had been powerless in the face of Nazism's antisemitic attacks, Jews could now, at least at times, rely on the official opposition to antisemitism to defend their interests. In August 1945, Dr. Neuhaus from the Frankfurt community sent a letter to a real estate company on behalf of Max Stock, a member of the community. Apparently, the real estate company refused to expel the Nazi who officially lived in the apartment that was now assigned to Stock. Neuhaus argued that if this proved to be the case, it meant that "you defend the rights and interests of an active National Socialist against a Jew who innocently suffered in a concentration camp. I cannot imagine that such tactics are in line with your true tendencies. Should this be the case against my expectations, I will know how to take the required countermeasure."[140] Neuhaus's letter asserts his expectation that the real estate company would not want to be perceived as antisemitic and that open discrimination against Jews was no longer publicly accepted.

Defying their environment's latent antisemitism, German Jews strongly defended their rights after the war, even if they were often unsuccessful. The power balance had not turned, but it had shifted. Despite the persistence of antisemitism among the German population, Germans could no longer, or at least not always, mistreat Jews and their property without consequences. Little occurrences signaled this change. In 1947 a non-Jewish German, Frau Lied, sent a letter to the Jewish community of Mainz, apologizing on behalf of her son, who had broken a branch on one of the trees at the community's cemetery. The community leader replied that they accepted the apology this time and would not insist on a punishment but would not refrain from consequences the next time.[141] Still, German Jews understood that the new rejection of antisemitism arose more from opportunism than from a change of sentiments. The writer Jurek Becker remembered that his father enjoyed the fact that antisemites now had to deny their antisemitism.[142]

While Jews in Germany and Italy mistrusted the sudden change in attitude, at times they perceived benefits. Mario Tagliacozzo found that invoking his Jewishness could be useful. A few days after Rome's liberation, he tried to get some tobacco. At first the shopkeeper appeared reluctant, but "for once the word 'Jew' was magical and helped me solve the problem."[143]

Tagliacozzo's diary entry does not tell us why the shopkeeper changed his opinion upon learning of his customer's Jewishness, but it shows that being Jewish suddenly could be an asset rather than a liability. In Germany the population's newfound enthusiasm for anything Jewish resulted in an increase in clients for Jewish professionals. In a letter to relatives in the United States, Peter Reiche described how "everybody is now trying to get help through the Jews. *Vati* said that people come to him from miles around, even when they are not ill, just so they can say: 'But I have not been a Nazi, I even go to a Jewish doctor.'"[144] Similarly, Moskowitz reported that "a Jewish lawyer was swamped by his old clientele. A Jewish physician now enjoys a lucrative practice among his old neighbors."[145]

Reclaiming Belongings

The complex postwar relations between Jews and non-Jews also shaped conflicts over Jewish property after the war, though real or pretended sympathies to the Jewish plight seldom went far enough to ensure the return of stolen assets. Jews across Europe encountered hostility when trying to get their belongings back, and their attempts to retrieve or be compensated for what had been stolen often proved unsuccessful.[146] A number of Italian Jews recounted the cold reception they received upon returning to their house or apartment, realizing that their neighbor or porter, who had moved into their place, had not expected them to return.[147] In such situations, Jews often had to deal with antisemitic insults. Emma Tagliacozzo, for example, asked the Roman Jewish community for assistance with her ongoing battle to regain her assets. Without going into detail, Tagliacozzo remarked in a letter to the community that her adversary used "various insulting words for my membership in the so-called Jewish race."[148] The postwar housing shortage and desperate economic circumstances turned some of these conflicts into heated fights.[149]

In the immediate aftermath of the war, the Italian government passed a law that restored Jewish property rights. Yet the return of assets turned out to be a lengthy and difficult process.[150] The restitution laws were vague and ambiguous and could easily be interpreted in various ways. A report on Jewish assets from the Joint described the property law as "without teeth because no effort had been made nor machinery devised by the Italian government to carry the law into effect."[151] To the dismay of the victims, the same public agency that had previously managed the property confiscated

126 | *Home after Fascism*

by the Fascist regime—EGELI (Ente di Gestione e Liquidazione Immobiliare [Organization for the Management and Liquidation of Property])—oversaw restitution, and now demanded that Italian Jews reimbursed them for any administrative costs associated with the storage and return of their property.[152] Jews protested this practice. One of the Jewish victims asserted in his reply to EGELI that "we wish to point out that we did not name you our guardians."[153] Another explained that he refused to pay "the sum of L.18,650 for the administration of my home . . . during the Nazi-Fascist period . . . holding that the EGELI . . . functioned as a sort of concentration camp for our possessions."[154]

Italian Jews also faced difficulties regaining assets they had entrusted to a fake "Aryan" partner in order to get around the racial laws or assets they had sold under duress.[155] People who went to court to reclaim their property lost in most cases, and the majority decided against pursuing the matter in front of the law.[156] Some took the matter into their own hands and asked for their belongings directly from the new owners. Giancarlo Sacerdoti, then a young man, remembers going around with his mother, asking for the return of their possessions: "In this wandering from house to house I learned many things and among them that people pour hot tears over those who die, but woe betide those who open their eyes and ask for the restitution of their belongings."[157] Others were more successful. Rita Guetta Brüll had entrusted her possessions to Catholic friends and recalls how when she came back home, "the neighbors . . . brought our things to us few at a time. . . . We had left everything because we had left unexpectedly, in a matter of hours."[158]

Like Brüll, Emilia Piperno's family succeeded in regaining their home and their possessions, but only after a fierce fight with the woman who had settled in their house during their absence. Piperno recounts her mother gleefully watching while the occupants left:

> I think few people have gained the satisfaction to witness the complete annihilation of the enemy. This was given to my mother who personally went to assist "the Bonaglia" [the woman who had occupied their home]. Young, brilliant, and victorious, she sat down in a chair in her kitchen to see the Bonaglia knocked down, crying, and packing her things, making sure that she would not carry off any of ours too. At one point the Bonaglia took a metal box in which we stored coffee, a blue metal box with green mirrors that had always been in our kitchen and that we called the peacock box. My mother pointed at it and she left it. Later, when we lived again in our home, and she picked up the peacock box to make coffee, she felt sorry about it. She told me: "I was petty

with the Bonaglia, I could have left her this box; after all it has no value and no importance." My mother never threw the Peacock box away, in part because it was one of those things that gave you the idea of home, like a box of biscuits or one with buttons, and in part because looking at it, each time there was a warning, because she had not acted according to the teachings of the sacred texts, according to which a Jew has to remember what Amalek did, but should never rejoice in the humiliation of his enemy.[159]

In Piperno's story, the metal box embodies their home. It symbolizes its loss, the process of regaining it, the conflict with the non-Jewish occupant, the wish for vengeance, and regret.

Some German Jews likewise received their property back directly, without needing to involve authorities. Peter Reiche reported to relatives in the United States that some of his mother's clothes had been at the dressmaker's when she was deported and that all of them were still there when he and his parents went to ask for them. His former nanny had also kept some of their belongings. He wrote, "These people are terrifically good and have kept all the stuff that was given to them and are not trying to make out that it now belongs to them." But the Reiche family suspected one of their neighbors of having kept some of their things, which the neighbor claimed had gotten lost. As the woman had supported his parents while they were in Theresienstadt, they did not want to ask to search her apartment.[160]

Some Germans returned Jewish property without the owners even needing to ask. After Hans Frankenthal and his brother returned from Auschwitz to their home, numerous people came by to bring them clothes and food, and "Café König brought not only cakes, but also all those things that our parents had given them after the pogrom night for storage. My parents had not written anything down back then, but König had a list of all the furnishings and belongings—every piece of furniture, every spoon, every cup and each dish—and gave me and Ernst [his brother] the things. We were very thankful for their trustworthiness."[161]

Most Germans, however, rejected restitution and reacted aggressively when Jews tried to regain their assets.[162] Like in Italy, the destruction of much of the prewar housing stock made it particularly difficult to repossess apartments and houses. Walter Spier, a survivor of Auschwitz, recounted that their home was occupied when he and his brother returned but that they managed to kick the inhabitants out and move back in.[163] Many others struggled to get their own "Aryanized" homes back.[164] The western Allies promulgated restitution laws a few years after the end of the war, though the

128 | *Home after Fascism*

legislation seems to have impeded rather than facilitated the restitution demands of returning Jews. Before 1947 individual demands were frequently handled relatively quickly and without much bureaucratic hassle. However, after the issuing of the military law concerning restitution in the US zone, and in particular after the foundation of the Federal Republic in 1949, returning Jews faced lengthy court procedures. Like Jews in Italy, German Jews struggled, in particular, with regaining property that they had been forced to sell under the Nazi regime.[165]

In the Soviet occupied zone, a number of mostly Jewish Communists aimed to ensure the restitution of Jewish property. However, while the SED leadership initially agreed with the proposal for a restitution bill, the final version of a decree regarding pension and welfare rights of those persecuted under Nazism provided additional pensions and support payments but no restitution. The political leadership claimed that returning property would only serve the restoration of capitalism. While stolen assets in general were returned to the Jewish communities, individuals in most cases could not reclaim their property.[166] For many surviving Jews, whether in East or West Germany or in Italy, the inability to reclaim their stolen possessions, as well as the destruction and occupation of their houses and apartments, made returning *home* difficult, if not impossible.

Hopes and Disappointments

The inability to reclaim their belongings and move back into their homes constituted one of the major disappointments for Italian Jews. Their main wish had appeared simple: they hoped for "life to return to normalcy," to how things had been before the racial laws.[167] Persistent antisemitism and the struggle to regain assets made this more difficult. They pointed to their rights as Italian citizens and voiced their anger in response to the unjust treatment they received in the aftermath of the war. Their hopes and efforts to bring perpetrators to justice likewise brought few results. A Milanese Jew voiced his anger about the leniency toward "our worst persecutors with broad amnesties, defense committees, and repelled purges" in a letter to the community.[168] Italian defascistization came to an abrupt halt with the amnesty of 1946. Justice Minister Palmiro Togliatti, head of the Italian Communist Party whose wife, Rita Montagnana, was Jewish, issued the amnesty decree on June 22, 1946, probably in the hopes of making the Communist Party more appealing to the middle class. The amnesty applied to all political crimes, with the exclusion of those that were unusually cruel. While the special courts had prepared over twenty thousand trials and given severe sentences for the crime of collaboration, most of the sentences were later appealed and revoked.[169] Within six years of the end of the war, no Italian citizen remained in prison for having contributed to the persecution of Jews.[170] By and large, the judiciary, the prefects, and the police remained untouched by defascistization.[171]

Most Fascist intellectuals who had signed the *Manifesto della razza*, the theoretical basis for the subsequent racial persecution, likewise escaped prosecution.[172] Nicola Pende, an endocrinologist and cosigner of the manifesto, was among those who benefitted from the lax prosecution. In May 1946 the Roman court of appeals acquitted Pende, on the grounds that he had no responsibility in the proclamation of the racial laws following the manifesto.[173] The Milanese Jewish paper protested against Pende's acquittal, arguing that his participation in the racist campaign had contributed to the murder of millions. In a letter to the journal *Israel*, Pende defended himself, stating that he "never signed the infamous racial manifesto in 1938, and never joined or contributed to the Fascist antisemitic campaign."[174] Carlo Alberto Viterbo replied that it was "incontrovertible and demonstrated that Pende with his dark science put himself in the service of racism and the regime that imposed it." In line with the Italian Jewish discourse at the time, Viterbo framed his protest in the context of a betrayed Italian nation and not as part of the particular experience of Italian Jews, arguing that "Italy suffered much, and still suffers, because too many people, for too long, have closed their eyes, their heart, and their brain and bent their backs."[175] The protest against Pende went beyond the publication of critical articles. When Pende returned to the university in December 1948, several Jewish students attended his first lecture with the aim of disturbing it. Giorgio Sabbadini, a young medical student, remembered, "Democrats, communists, and Jews: all present."[176] But they were not the only ones who came. The noise of whistles was "the signal, for them, for the fascists. They began punching us." With the help of a friend, Sabbadini made it out, though barely.[177]

Like Pende's acquittal, racial theorist Giulio Cogni's successful evasion of punishment frustrated Italian Jews. Giulio Cogni, whose 1936 book *Il Razzismo* had been an influential text, returned to his hometown of Siena in the spring of 1946.[178] His reappearance troubled the Jewish community. In a letter to his uncle, Raffaele Cantoni, Luigi Sadun wrote in May 1946 that Cogni's return "reminded us of all his past activities and how they may

130 | *Home after Fascism*

have contributed to the tragedy that has destroyed us."[179] Two members of the community denounced Cogni, who then wrote an apologetic letter to Cantoni.[180] Cogni was exculpated because, as he himself explained, "the accusations did not include any crime, and so the matter was moot."[181] The Jews in Siena concluded that the only remaining hope was in divine justice, as humans were often "in a hurry, as in this case, to acquit."[182] While they argued that Cogni's role in spreading racism contributed to their persecution, the postwar judiciary system did not see this as a punishable crime. Neither did his racist past diminish his reputation or postwar career. The Turinese publishing house Einaudi hired Cogni as a consultant and translator in 1949.[183] Like Cogni, Pende remained successful. Both fashioned themselves as devout Catholics, and the public quickly forgot their contributions to Fascist racism.[184] Lino Businco, another "racist scientist," even received the Commenda al merito della Repubblica in 1963.[185]

Several Italian Jews, prominently among them Massimo Adolfo Vitale, voiced outrage over the state's lenient treatment of perpetrators.[186] Bruno Fiorentini, who had joined the resistance during the war, expressed outrage over the "scandalous verdict" in the trial against collaborators involved in the arrest and subsequent deportation of his sister and her family. The court had acquitted all of the accused on the grounds that they had merely obeyed orders. In an article published in January 1947, Fiorentini protested the verdict, arguing that the orders as well as the entire RSI were unlawful. He opined that at least these men should be fired from their posts. "WE DO NOT WANT THEM," he exclaimed. With "we," he did not refer to the Italian Jews whom the collaborators had harmed but rather "we citizens, who pay for this service." He added, "We partisans also do not want them because tolerating them would insult our thousands of dead dear ones and ourselves."[187] When he voiced his frustrations, Fiorentini did not see himself as part of a wronged minority but rather as representing Italians' opinions, placing himself firmly within the Italian nation.

Italian Jews largely remained invested in the postwar state, though at times it fell short of their idealized version. The status of religion within society proved another point of friction. Italian Jews hoped that the state would return to its pre-Fascist laicism. During the Union of Italian Jewish Communities' first congress after the end of the war, the leadership voiced the expectation that the postwar state would embrace religious equality.[188] However, when the Constituent Assembly's draft for a constitution for the new republic became public, their hopes dwindled. After the draft had been publicized, individual Italian Jews expressed fears and disappointment with the constitution and its lack of religious equality.[189]

The Union of Italian Jewish Communities, while supporting the political activism of individual members, generally tried to refrain from actively engaging in Italian political life, but it took a stand in the discussion over the status of religion and the confirmation of the Lateran Pacts in the constitution. The UCII, represented by Raffaele Cantoni, sent a memorandum to the deputies in the Constituent Assembly in March 1947, asking for revisions. It rejected two main aspects: First, the UCII stated that the constitution violated the equality of religions. Following the principles of the concordat between the church and the state from 1929 (the so-called Lateran Treaties), Catholicism remained the state religion, and the constitution merely tolerated other religious sects. The memorandum emphasized that equality of all citizens constituted "the essential point of the constitution of a democratic state" and demanded "absolute equality of worship and complete equality of the citizens." Jews feared the impact that the preference for Catholicism would have on the education of children, stating that in the past, "children of non-Catholics have found themselves at school in conditions of inequality, inferiority, and uneasiness."[190] Second, the memorandum took issue with the constitution's assertion of the indissolubility of matrimony. The Jewish leaders objected because Catholic ecclesiastical principles would be applied to Jewish marriages even though Jewish religious law allowed divorce.[191] Cantoni joined forces with other leaders of religious minorities in Italy and sent a letter directly to Enrico de Nicola, the provisional head of state, a few weeks later, reiterating the points made in the memorandum to the Constituent Assembly. The letter also pointed, if rather carefully, to the past in order to substantiate their case, arguing that considering the status of religious minorities carefully was crucial, "especially after the recent persecutions suffered by some of these minorities."[192] In their memorandum to the Constituent Assembly, the representatives of the UCII likewise backed their demands by noting the crimes of the Fascist regime: "Recent painful experiences prove that Italian legal provisions can approve of the monstrosities and excesses that put us Jews, Italian citizens, into the condition of 'outlaws.'" The text also stressed the importance of a return to the country's tradition. The Constituent Assembly had the responsibility, the UCII argued, "to outline in a constitution the fundamental rules of civil life that are worthy of Italy, her traditions and the new era which she is about to inaugurate for herself and mankind."[193] The language

132 | *Home after Fascism*

with which the Jewish leadership criticized the draft stressed the narrative of a true Italy, temporarily overshadowed by Fascism but to which Italian Jews now expected to return.

Beyond appealing to the Constituent Assembly directly, the UCII also recruited the help of international Jewish organizations such as the World Jewish Congress and the Joint.[194] In a letter to the WJC from March 1947, the UCII explained its situation and asked the former "to take appropriate action immediately in order that, especially in the non-Jewish press, the problem is discussed, pointing out the injustice of the proposed discrimination in the treatment of religious beliefs of the Italians. We hope that your action will make the Italian legislators realize that in 1947 world public opinion disapproves a preferential treatment of one faith in comparison with others."[195] In his reply, Meir Grossman, director of the Department of Overseas Relations of the WJC, asserted that "your stand on the question of religious equality in Italy has been widely publicized in the general American and Jewish press and has been given sympathetic consideration."[196] At the same time, the UCII seemed to fear the potential impact of overly aggressive public involvement of foreign Jews in the affair. In an internal letter dated June 19, 1947, a representative from the AJC explained that they "were informed that the Italian Jewish community would disapprove of any overt action by non-Italian Jewish communities with respect to the proposed Italian Constitution. The reasoning was that the Italian people, while perhaps freer from antisemitism than any other nation in Europe, would resent the involvement of foreigners in Italian domestic affairs."[197] The letter reveals the often-contradictory depiction of the status of Jews within Italy: an emphasis on the supposed absence of antisemitism paired with a fear that a strong reaction against overt discrimination could lead to hostility toward Jews. While intervening with state authorities on the matter of the constitution, the UCII voiced their complaint carefully, and while insisting on religious equality, they at the same time pointed to the gratitude of Italian Jews toward the Catholic Church. The Constituent Assembly enacted the Constitution on December 22, 1947, and in spite of the UCII's appeal, the Lateran Treaties were confirmed and Catholicism remained a privileged religion in the postwar Italian state. The indissolubility of marriage, however, failed by a few votes and was omitted from the constitution.[198]

While Italian Jews framed their postwar expectations within a discourse around a return to the true Italy, most German Jews, both in the East and the West, wanted radical change. Some saw it as their duty to herald that transformation.[199] "We the survivors," remembered actress Steffie Spira, who returned to Berlin, "would build a new world, without war, filled with the ideas of communism."[200] The dream of a better country built on Socialist ideals attracted not just members of the Communist Party. Others shared the antifascist sentiments propagated by East German postwar leaders, and some felt convinced that, unlike West Germany, "antifascists were in charge" in the Soviet occupied zone.[201] Hans Mayer, who did not join the Communist Party but felt close to Communism, remembered that "we allowed ourselves to hope a lot, back then, when the war had ended and everything seemed possible."[202] Also in West Germany, some hoped for a new beginning. Dietrich Goldschmidt, who had been interned in a forced labor camp as what the Nazis termed Mischling 1. Grades, remembered his thoughts after liberation: "A new beginning was before us, for us, for all our loved ones, for the country, things could only get better, and we wanted to play our role in this." However, Goldschmidt, writing about his postwar hopes decades later, foreshadows their imminent disappointments: "but we had no idea, back then, how difficult, not to say, how long and in many respects completely unsatisfactory the reconstruction of the German statehood, which we hoped would be a new start, would be."[203]

The dancer Valeska Gert voiced her disappointment about the difficulties returning emigrants faced in postwar Germany in a piece titled "The Remigrant." In other cabaret numbers she criticizes political opportunism and people's unwillingness to face the past. Gert was not able to revive the success she had enjoyed in the 1920s and in 1956 she left Berlin for the small town of Kampen on the island of Sylt.[204] The 1949 film Der Ruf (The last illusion) provides a fictional account of the frequent disappointment returnees faced. In the film, Fritz Kortner, an Austrian Jewish actor who had lived in Berlin before the rise of the Nazis, plays a German Jewish professor who returns from the United States to his former university but soon faces antisemitism among colleagues and students. The fight against the persistent prejudice and ideological delusions wears him down, and he dies at the end of the film. Kortner himself returned from exile, and the film is based on the actor's experience.[205] In his memoir, Kortner wrote of his disappointment with Germans' unwillingness to show empathy to the victims of Nazi persecution.[206]

Jews in West Germany who had hoped for a radical break with the Nazi past voiced increasing disappointment. Articles published in Der Weg echo these sentiments, adopting an increasingly pessimistic and angry tone.

134 | *Home after Fascism*

Instead of apologies, regret, and help with rebuilding their lives, returning Jews faced denial of guilt, unwillingness to acknowledge their difficulties, and latent antisemitism.[207] The United States' Office of Military Government noted a growing sense of disappointment and frustration, especially among younger German Jews.[208] At a press conference in the fall of 1948, Kurt Epstein, president of the regional association of Jewish communities in Hesse, maintained that "the desacralization of cemeteries and defamations were evidence of the lack of good will." Another participant, Rabbi Wilhelm Weinberg, the first post-Holocaust chief rabbi of Hesse and Frankfurt, added that "the real reasons for the bitterness and disappointment of the Jews in Germany have to be sought in the years after 1945."[209] A few years later, Rabbi Weinberg left, as he explained in his final sermon, "in bitterness."[210] In an article published in the *Jüdisches Gemeindeblatt für die britische Zone* in April 1947, on the occasion of the first postwar election, the journalist Karl Marx described this sense of disappointment, which led him to consider leaving Germany.[211] He criticized the political players' lack of engagement with the question of German guilt and the absence of objections to antisemitic insults and incidences, such as the desacralization of cemeteries.[212]

Jews in West Germany frequently criticized the failed denazification and prosecution of perpetrators. With the impending Cold War, Communism replaced Nazism as the main threat in the eyes of the Western Allies. Allied pressure for denazification decreased and allowed for a rapid rehabilitation of former party members.[213] Hans Frankenthal, who served as a witness in a denazification lawsuit, complained that denazification showed few results, as former Nazis were either acquitted or released after a few weeks. "They just ignored us and our history," Frankenthal wrote, "and it got worse with the beginning of the Cold War. Denazification was a farce."[214] Joseph Wulf, a German-born Polish Jew and Auschwitz survivor who moved to Berlin in the early 1950s, published several works on Nazi Germany and Nazi perpetrators, hoping to push the country toward a reckoning with its crimes. Deeply disappointed with the postwar country and traumatized by his experiences in the camp, he took his own life in 1974.[215]

In 1949 West Germans elected Konrad Adenauer, a chancellor who supported amnesty as a method of integrating party members into society. With the subsequent passage of generous amnesty laws, former Nazis returned to their old positions within a few years.[216] The population had insisted on wiping slates clean since the end of the war, and the newly elected government legitimized such thinking. It gradually delegitimized the prosecution of Nazi criminals, with the result that few perpetrators faced trial after the FRG's foundation.[217] By 1950 most of the Nazi judges had regained their positions. As author Hermann Kesten laconically commented, "the judge under Hitler is the judge under Adenauer."[218]

Living in Soviet-occupied Germany, Victor Klemperer likewise frequently criticized denazification's shortcomings.[219] But the hopes he and others had set in the Communists seemed to hold up, at least to some extent.[220] For the first year of occupation, the Soviet authorities followed a stringent denazification policy, instituting thorough changes in social and economic structures. The much-smaller Soviet occupied zone scrutinized almost twice as many people in the course of its denazification process as the three other zones. Comparing the numbers of sentences in East and West Germany, Mary Fulbrook concludes that East Germany pronounced almost double the number of sentences as the West, for a much smaller population.[221]

While numerous former members of the Nazi Party similarly continued their professional careers in East Germany, changes in elites and leadership were more radical than in the West. Former members of the resistance and emigrants, among them several of Jewish origin, played a larger role in the GDR. Indeed, the initial success of many Communists of Jewish origin who were part of the Soviet occupied zone's cultural and political elite further strengthened their belief in the possibility of creating a home in the emerging Socialist state.[222] The writer Anna Seghers commented in a letter that in spite of her mistrust of the German population, she could sense that "a new world was built."[223] Communist and antifascist Jews believed that as politicians, writers, and artists, they would be able to contribute to making a new society.[224]

Yet they soon suffered setbacks. After an initial phase in which the Soviet occupied zone seemed to promise a reckoning with the past and an openness to discussing German crimes, the situation deteriorated. In the spring of 1946, the Soviets adopted a new policy of differentiating between "nominal Nazis" and "active Nazis," and by March 1948, all "nominal" Nazis had been reprieved and a large number of NSDAP members had been integrated into the new society. Denazification officially ended in 1948.[225] Around the same time, the Soviet Union, which had initially supported the foundation of a Jewish state in Palestine, shifted course and rejected and vilified Zionism. Israeli flags were no longer publicly displayed at official

136 | *Home after Fascism*

commemoration events.[226] Initiatives for restitution failed, and party members who had supported the foundation of Israel or restitution efforts found themselves accused of disloyalty.[227] Antisemitic hostility spread over the Eastern Bloc, culminating in an anti-Jewish witch hunt in the early 1950s.[228]

Following the show trial against Rudolf Slansky and other high-ranking Czech Communists of Jewish origin in 1952, the SED leadership initiated a thorough purge. People of Jewish origin were accused of connections with the "Zionist movement," the American secret service, or the "Trotzkiite-Jewish movement."[229] Paul Merker, a leading member of the Communist party who had advocated for the restitution of Jewish property but was not Jewish, became the prime victim of the purge.[230] In December 1952, Merker was arrested as a spy and charged with acting as an agent for American imperialism and Zionism. The court sentenced him to eight years in prison. Soon after Merker's arrest, the Central Party Control Commission detained Julius Meyer, president of the Association of Jewish Communities in the GDR. SED agents searched Jewish community offices, and the party accused several of its Jewish members of being Zionists.[231] After his release, Meyer warned others, and within a week, Meyer, Leo Zuckermann, and most of the heads of the Jewish communities fled. In total, more than four hundred Jews left the GDR in January 1953.[232]

On January 4, 1953, the *Neues Deutschland*, the GDR's official newspaper, published an article titled "Lehren aus dem Prozeß gegen das Verschwörerzentrum Slansky" (Lessons from the trial against the Slansky conspiracy). The article reported the revelation of "Zionists as agents of American imperialism."[233] Using antisemitic stereotypes such as the "capitalist Jew," the article rejected claims for restitution and validated the anti-Jewish feelings and envy of Jewish victims that prevailed among the party elites as well as in the population.[234] One month later, the VVN, which had provided assistance to Jewish survivors, spoken out against antisemitism, and contributed to the commemoration of the Holocaust, was dissolved. In an investigation two years earlier, the party leadership had concluded that some of the VVN's members should be considered enemies of the party—about one-third to one-half of the VVN's members were Jewish. The VVN was replaced with the Committee of Antifascist Resistance Fighters (Komitee der Antifaschistischen Widerstandskämpfer).[235]

Even while spreading hostility against Jews, the political leadership denied antisemitism. The article in *Neues Deutschland* emphasized the supposed lack of antisemitism among the population: "The speculation of American imperialism aims to make use of the fact that especially the working people in the people's democracies, who are brought up in a spirit of friendship among peoples and proletarian internationalism, do not tolerate antisemitism and feel solidarity with the Jews, who had been so severely persecuted by fascism."[236] Heinz Brandt, born to a Jewish family in Posen in 1909 and a Communist Party member since 1931, remembered an SED functionary explaining to him in the days following the Slansky affair: "As a result of the teachings of the Slansky trial we had to examine functionaries who returned from the West emigration especially. Is it not a fact— and this has absolutely nothing to do with racist antisemitism—that Jews stemmed mostly from lower middle classes [kleinbürgerlichen Schichten], have no social connection with the working class, and have relatives and friends everywhere in the West?"[237] While denying antisemitism, this SED functionary relied on antisemitic stereotypes of Jews as disloyal cosmopolitans and embodiments of bourgeois culture to justify the disproportional attack on Communists of Jewish origin. Stereotypes of Jews as foreign and conspiratorial and as imperialists and capitalists were widespread in the SED, making Jews a likely target when fears about the regime's stability soared.[238] With their antisemitic campaign, the SED leadership reacted to developments in the Soviet Union and at the same time aimed to stabilize the regime and consolidate its power. Attitudes and motivations among the political leadership, however, differed considerably, which led to an incoherent message.[239]

The strict denial of antisemitism, contradictory actions, and muddled language conflating Jewishness and Zionism made it difficult for Jews in the GDR to decipher the situation. The party's anti-Jewish propaganda and an increase in antisemitic insults gave them cause to worry. At the same time, however, East German courts, in accordance with the GDR's constitution, gave prison sentences for spreading antisemitic propaganda in January 1953.[240] Jews in East Germany responded differently to the purges. In a reply to his friend and colleague Lion Feuchtwanger, who wrote with concern, Arnold Zweig depicted the accusations of antisemitism primarily as Western propaganda and stressed that "there can be no racial hatred in a place where the fight between the classes . . . has been resolved."[241] He admitted, however, that his wife, Bea, and his son read the situation differently. Similarly to Zweig, Victor Klemperer reassured a friend, "You must know that we cannot possibly have antisemitism—our theory . . . our liberation by the Russians . . . this is against Zionism in league with the US, with capitalism."

Klemperer welcomed the party's anti-Zionism, as it was in line with his own reservations.[242] Others believed the accusations against Paul Merker and primarily thought (or at least depicted) this phase as a purge of traitors or *Westemigranten*, referring to people who had fled, for instance, to the United States, England, or Mexico in the Nazi period, apparently unaware or unwilling to discuss the antisemitic undertones.[243] In her memoir Lotte Winter briefly mentions the flight of her friend Leo Zuckermann. She sets his sudden disappearance within the context of party purges but does not refer to Zuckermann's Jewishness or the party's antisemitism, which she discussed in other parts of her memoir.[244]

While some denied that antisemitism played a role in the purges, others highlighted that the purges created feelings of fear and mistrust toward party and state and linked the experience with the most recent past.[245] The writer Alfred Kantorowicz noted in his diary in response to the Slansky affair, "This—this is monstrous. This is Streicher's language, Himmler's attitude, the atmosphere of the Gestapo interrogations . . . the 'morality' of the murderers of Dachau and Buchenwald, of those who gassed people in Auschwitz and Maidanek."[246] The renewed experience of being excluded, othered, discriminated against, wrongly accused of disloyalty, and persecuted came as a shock for some of the party's Jewish members.[247] They feared the loss of their positions, arrest, and worse. Exclusion from the party led to social isolation as people tended to fear that contact with traitors could endanger them.[248] For Charlotte Holzer, a member of a Jewish resistance group who had been interrogated and tortured by the Gestapo, party examination brought back traumatic memories. The SED investigators accused her and her husband of having been Gestapo agents and suspected the latter of working for the American secret service. During her interrogation in April 1952, Holzer both incriminated others and expressed her absolute loyalty to the Communist Party, declaring that she had recognized that it "was her duty to tell the party everything."[249]

Stalin's death in March 1953 marked the endpoint of the persecution. By then, the Jewish communities had shrunk significantly and had lost most of their leading personnel. Most Jewish members of the SED had opted out of the Jewish communities.[250] But the GDR staged no show trials.[251] The specific German situation prevented the GDR's antisemitic campaign from becoming as virulent as in the Soviet Union or Czechoslovakia.

In 1953 Alfred Kantorowicz did not yet give up on the Communist state, though he struggled at various points. Already by 1949 he had been forced to end his journal, titled *Ost und West*, which, as the title suggests, had aimed to form a bridge between intellectuals of both camps.[252] After the journal's closure, Kantorowicz assumed a position as professor of literature at the Berlin Humboldt University, which he held until he fled the GDR in 1957. In an article published in the West German newspaper *Die Zeit* after his flight, he described the "painful process of my progressive disillusionment."[253] His hopes for Socialist Germany were shattered, yet West Germany with its restorative tendencies appalled him.[254] Others shared these feelings of loss and disappointment. Leo Löwenkopf, head of the Dresden community, wrote to friends who remained in the GDR about his flight in 1953, "I was always a decent person and have worked hard on building our home. But we could no longer endure the defamation and so we made the decision to give up our home and leave. Apparently, what we have suffered during the Nazi era was not enough! Now we are faced with the question of where to? And with what?"[255] After living in Düsseldorf for several years, Löwenkopf moved to Zurich in 1957. Others also left Germany a second time after fleeing to the West; Leo Zuckermann immigrated once again to Mexico. After West Berlin refused to acknowledge Julius Meyer as a political refugee, he immigrated to Brazil.[256] For these disillusioned Communist Jews, the West German state—anticommunist and reactionary, with former NSDAP members still holding high positions—could not provide a home.

While Klemperer ultimately defended the SED leadership against the accusations of antisemitism, his diary entries reveal mixed feelings. In January 1953, contemplating the problems of the state and the mistakes of its leadership, he concluded that it was not better in the West and that at least "we [East Germans] have great aims, they have mean ones."[257] Others likewise found comfort in the thought that while life might be difficult in the GDR, things were worse in West Germany.[258] They remained invested in the project of building a better state, and not all considered the project failed. Looking back, Lotte Winter declared that she had "through persistent fighting against the reactionary heritage, professionally, politically and personally conquered for [herself] a new home."[259]

Conclusion

Winter's expression "conquered . . . a new home" reveals the extent to which her own effort played a role in her regaining a sense of home. She did not simply return home. She created a home. Other returning Jews, in Italy as well as in both Germanies, likewise tried to actively reclaim or remake their homes. They focused on getting rid of perpetrators, reeducating the population, and regaining their belongings. Jews in Italy and both Germanies reacted to persistent antisemitism, reported incidents, wrote articles condemning prejudice, and appealed to local authorities. They reminded others that antisemitism was no longer a publicly acceptable attitude. Such an active approach, and in particular an involvement in politics, could strengthen a sense of belonging to the emerging postwar states. However, it also frequently resulted in disappointment.

Jews in all three postwar states depicted such disappointments, though German Jews more frequently voiced their disillusionment. German and Italian Jews had held radically different expectations. While most Italian Jews looked forward to resuming their lives, Jews in both Germanies hoped for change. Italian Jews felt disappointed when the return to their idealized past did not occur as seamlessly as they had hoped but by and large believed that a return to normalcy remained possible. Jews in West Germany felt dissatisfied with the failed denazification, lack of remorse, and latent antisemitism, and a number left the country in the late 1940s and early 1950s. Numerous Jews in East Germany fled the state in which they had set high hopes after the anti-Jewish purges in 1952. They had seen radical change, but for many the new regime fell short of their ideal version of an antifascist, better Germany. Still, others remained attached to their home country despite these disappointments. Feelings of attachment and belonging, hope and disappointment, were neither simple nor fixed.

4

BELONGING

FEELINGS OF BELONGING WERE VERY MUCH IN FLUX in the aftermath of the war. The Nazis and Fascists had not merely stolen Jews' property and attacked their lives; they had also shaken their self-understanding.[1] Shortly after the war, the Italian novelist Alberto Moravia, whose father was Jewish, described how the Fascist racial laws had robbed him of his right to self-definition: "Finally, excluded but always suspect, I was prohibited from signing my own name in newspapers. I then took the transparent pseudonym of Pseudo. All of this by way of saying that in those years, for reasons wholly connected with Fascism, day by day my identity became more uncertain, more problematic, more ephemeral."[2] For Jews in Germany and Italy, the racial laws, as Moravia suggests, constituted an attack on their self-understanding.

For some being categorized as Jewish came as a surprise. They had not identified as Jewish; some had considered themselves atheists, while others had converted to Christianity. But even those who understood themselves as Jewish mostly thought of themselves as *Italians* or *Germans* of the Jewish faith. The Fascist and Nazi states' efforts to categorize people had forced some to consider their Jewish origin for the first time. Reflecting on her Jewishness, Lotte Winter concluded, "My personal relationship with Judaism was forced upon me by Hitler and the Nuremberg laws."[3] Like Winter, other Jews who survived, both in Germany and Italy, felt that the racial laws had forced them to redefine their relationships with their Jewish origins.[4] The Italian writer Natalia Ginzburg, born to a Catholic mother and a Jewish father in 1916, stated in an interview, "My Jewish identity became extremely important to me from the moment the Jews began to be persecuted. At that point I became aware of myself as a Jew. . . . While I did not have any sort of formal Jewish upbringing, I nevertheless felt my Jewishness very acutely

142 | *Home after Fascism*

during the war years (my first husband, Leone Ginzburg, was a Jew) and after the war, when it became known what had been done to the Jews in the camps by the Nazis. Suddenly my Jewishness became very important to me."[5] For many Jews, in Italy and Germany as elsewhere in Europe, persecution led to a strengthening of their self-understanding as Jewish. In some cases a sense of Jewishness supplanted the lost sense of national belonging. Indeed, existing literature suggests that after the Holocaust, "the Jewish identification with the various host nations, and with Europe as a whole, had faded."[6] While this holds true for many but not all German Jews, it does not accurately represent Italian Jews' postwar self-representation. The racial legislations had defined Jews as no longer German or Italian, and many in both countries depicted a sense of loss, betrayal and outrage when they recounted how the state with which they had identified suddenly marked them as outcasts.[7] However, after the war, they evaluated the moment of exclusion differently. While German Jews mostly preferred to distance themselves from a national community that had excluded them, Italian Jews aimed to reintegrate.

Categories such as "Jewish," "Italian," or "German" lack clear definitions and are constantly evolving. This chapter explores how Italian and German Jews defined these categories and focuses on their introspective reassessments of their place within their home. Examining Jews' ideas of what being German or Italian meant to them highlights the fractured and fluid nature of national belonging.[8] Fascists and Nazis had claimed the right to define the nation and had excluded those deemed unfit. In Fascism's aftermath the three former Fascist states reinvented themselves in distinct ways, and those who had been ostracized reacted to, and aimed to influence, this process. They reclaimed, repossessed, reshaped, or purposefully inhabited the margins of the nation. They found individual answers of how to formulate their belonging to the imagined national collective—some reinventing its past, others idealizing its future, and still others formulating a selective belonging to those aspects of the nation they considered least tainted. Rather than focusing on the public discourse of nationalism, the aim here is to examine these personal and individual identifications with the nation that, while influenced by broader discourses, developed in distinct ways.[9]

Like Germanness and Italianness, Jewishness lacks a clear definition. Relying on competing understandings of Jewishness, Italian and German Jews debated what being Jewish meant. The racist systems of categorization remained in people's heads and continued to influence their experiences in the postwar period. At the same time, Jewish institutions insisted on reclaiming the right to define Jewishness and the right to draw boundaries to decide who could and who could not belong to the Jewish collective. Indeed, the process of redefining and remaking this group highlights its fluid, rather than fixed and homogenous, character.[10] Zionist activists hoped to create a cohesive group and to convince others that their internal differences did not matter, but not all German and Italian Jews agreed with this view, and not all accepted institutional definitions of Jewishness. Zionism, the newly founded Israel, and the Shoah all played a crucial role in expressions of Jewish self-identification in the postwar period, though individual Jews evaluated their importance differently.

The immense rupture caused by exclusion, ostracism, and persecution reinforced the fluid nature of self-understanding. "I needed to find myself again," explained Mariella Milano, an Italian Jew, after the war.[11] Surviving Jews like Mariella searched for and renegotiated their place of belonging within and without these different collectives. The war, moreover, had created new categories—such as victim, survivor, and resistance fighter—that influenced Jews' self-understanding. In Germany, definitions of national belonging increasingly differed between East and West. For many Jews in the East, a sense of national belonging became intertwined with a self-understanding as antifascist. Self-definitions as a fighter against Fascism and as a resister also played crucial roles in postwar Italy.

Foremost Italian

On the surface, Fascist exclusion had hardly affected Italian Jews' self-depiction. Most Italian Jews continued to describe themselves as Italians of the Jewish faith. Italian Jewish leadership, keen to move reintegration forward, publicly emphasized Italian Jews' self-perception as Italians. The head of the Roman community, for instance, explained in a letter in June 1944 that he wished to "declare in the most formal and clearest manner, that Roman Jews, as believers, are faithful to the belief of their fathers; as citizens they feel, like the others, profoundly and exclusively Italian."[12] Others likewise emphasized the prominence of Italy within their self-understanding; Amelia Pincherle Rosselli, a Venetian writer and the mother of antifascist resisters Carlo and Nello Rosselli, explained, "[we are] Jews, but first and foremost Italians," and the writer Primo Levi described himself as "80% Italian and 20% Jewish."[13]

144 | *Home after Fascism*

Most Italian Jews had kept their citizenship throughout the war, which helped them maintain their self-understanding as Italian. Fascist Italy did not revoke Jews' citizenship in 1938. The racial legislation had declared them outsiders, yet legally they remained Italians. Only Jewish immigrants who had gained their citizenship after 1918 lost it with the racial laws.[14] In November 1943 the Fascist Republican Party's Manifesto di Verona declared Jews enemy aliens. However, the RSI authorities did not codify the proposal into law. Historian Michele Sarfatti speculates that they either considered it superfluous or did not actually want Italian Jews to be considered foreigners out of concern that the Germans might use this as a pretext to claim Jewish assets.[15]

After the war, some Jews who had acquired foreign citizenship as emigrants and wished to return and resume their Italian citizenship faced bureaucratic difficulties.[16] Others, like Bruno Di Cori, found the process to be relatively easy. He remembered that the authorities explained that after two uninterrupted years of living in Italy, he would automatically regain his citizenship.[17] Enzo (Heinz) Arian, who had been born in Germany but immigrated to Italy in 1933, struggled for decades to obtain Italian citizenship. He first tried to do so, unsuccessfully, in 1937, before he and his wife, Giorgina Levi, left Italy. After their return he renewed his application every year starting in 1946. As he had no interest in regaining his German citizenship, he remained stateless until 1962, when, three years before his death, he was finally granted Italian citizenship.[18] While the Germany he left when he was in his early twenties could no longer be a home for which he felt affection, he felt deeply attached to Italy. Even though the racial laws had forced them into exile, their persecution under Fascism had not significantly affected the couple's identification with Italy.[19]

Others pointed to their exclusion from the Italian nation in 1938 as a turning point in their relation to their home country. One Italian Jew wrote soon after the war that the racial campaign had not only "constricted their professional and economic activities, their civil and domestic life, their very individual liberty, . . . and finally the lives of entire families with arrests, deportations and massacres, but also and *above all their sense of being Italian.*"[20] Eugenia Servi, a young Tuscan Jew, explained, "In 1938, I was marginalized, today it is me who feels different."[21] Some felt they no longer belonged. Franco Schönheit, who had been arrested by Italian police and deported to Auschwitz, explained, "I no longer identify myself with the country."[22]

Born in 1868, Emma de Rossi Castelli was seventy years old when the racial laws were issued, and the persecution hit her hard. She had considered herself a fervent patriot and felt particularly connected to her hometown of Livorno. In her diary she described her conflicting feelings toward her home country. In June 1945 she wrote, "With the racial laws I felt excluded from my homeland, I said that I no longer felt Italian. But you cannot so easily betray the attachment to the land where you were born, and now I suffer to see Italy so dilapidated, ruined, with its half-destroyed cities."[23] She continued to love her home, despite her disappointment. In the end she found it difficult to see herself as anything other than Italian. By and large, Italian Jews looked back at the time of exclusion with pain, but it ultimately did not negate their wish to self-identify as Italian.

Italian Jews remained attached to the food, the language, and the culture and often felt deeply connected to a specific region or town. Fulvia di Segni Jesi highlighted her love for Trieste and the local dialect throughout her memoirs.[24] In his *Periodic Table*, Primo Levi wrote about his relation to Piedmont: "It was in Piedmont, in Turin, that we had, in effect, our roots, not massive, but deep, wide ranging and fantastically intertwined."[25] Roman Jews in particular emphasized their identification with the city and with the neighborhood where many of them still lived: the "ghetto." The mostly lower-class inhabitants of the ghetto, who were also united by distinct rituals and a common dialect, the Giudaico-Romanesco, primarily considered themselves to be Romans and in some ways different from Jews in other parts of the country.[26]

While Italian Jews largely remained deeply connected to their hometowns and home country, some expressed feeling more distant from the state and its institutions after the war. The racial legislation had barred Jews from employment with the state, and after the war Italian Jews appeared more reluctant to seek public employment or a career in the military, while the number of Jews employed within commerce grew.[27] Italian Jews' loyalty to the royal house also had received a severe blow, even if some, particular elderly, Italian Jews remained attached to the House of Savoy.[28] In an editorial for *Israel*, published in May 1946, Carlo Alberto Viterbo conveyed the disappointment of Italian Jews with "Vittorio Emanuele III who, without resistance and against the sentiment of the Italian people, signed the so-called racial laws, depriving citizens who had faithfully served their country in peace and war of any security and abandoning them to the Nazi-fascists' thirst for blood and robbery." Viterbo indicated that consequently,

146 | *Home after Fascism*

the majority of Jews would vote for the republic in the upcoming referendum because "Italy, dear to our heart, needs a radical renewal."[29] Thus, in his article, Viterbi distanced himself from the monarchy while emphasizing his belief in Italy and the Italian people, who, in his view, had opposed the racial laws, in contrast to the king and the Fascist regime.

Italian Jews considered themselves as belonging to what they referred to as the true Italy, which was as much a nostalgic idealization of the past as a vision for the future determined by their current needs.[30] Giacomo Viterbo described this true Italy in an article from May 1945:

> Italy has returned to being Italy. For many, many years, but especially in recent times, it seemed to have lost its ancient soul. . . . Especially us, Jews born and raised in Italy, we, Jews who remained in hiding in the . . . Italian Social Republic, could have believed that by now Italy meant no more than Fosse Ardeatine, S. Vittore, Fossoli, Bolzano, that the Italian nation could no longer be properly represented if not by Pavolini, Saletta, Colombo, Mussolini. But none of us Jews . . . have ever believed such a thing. Everyone knew that the *true Italy* was represented by other places, by other ideas, by other people. We . . . recognized this Italy during the days of the resistance, in the faces of the *volontari della libertà* [freedom volunteers] and in the proclamations of the CLN [Comitato di Liberazione Nazionale, the National Liberation Committee].[31]

In Viterbo's article the antifascist forces represent the true Italy, its present as well as a resurrection of its past, of the country's "ancient soul." Only with the antifascist resistance and the end of the war did Italy return to its essential self; the time in between is rendered unrepresentative, or, in the words of philosopher Benedetto Croce, a "parenthesis."[32] While Viterbo lists sites of Jewish suffering, he strongly rejects the notion that Italian Jews considered these as representative of their home country—"none of us . . . have ever believed such a thing." Italian Jews' imagination of Italy was built on an evocation of a return to the country's tradition (which remained vague in most depictions), a rejection or denial of its Fascist past, and an affirmation of antifascism.[33]

After the war Italian elites promoted the narrative of national unity in antifascist resistance as the basis for the nation's self-image. Such myths played a crucial role in unifying nations in Europe after the war.[34] For Italian Jews the myth of antifascist resistance rendered their past meaningful and affirmed their belonging within the national collective. They frequently structured their own self-understanding around this antifascist image of the new republic and consequently preferred a self-depiction as resisters rather than as victims. In his *Eight Jews*, Giacomo Debenedetti asks for

Jewish victims to be remembered as having played their part in the fight for liberation: "If there is a right that Jews claim, it is only this: that those of their dead who had died of violence and hunger . . . should be ranked with all other dead—all the other victims of this war. They too were soldiers, alongside every other soldier . . . *Soldier Coen, Soldier Levi, Soldier Abramovic, Soldier Chaim Blumenthal, age five, fell at Leopoli amid his family with his hands tied behind his back, while still defending and bearing witness to the cause of liberty.*"[35] For Italian Jews, who had been violently excluded from the national community under Fascism, the antifascist narrative and their role within it lent weight to their efforts to reconstruct themselves as Italian. If the antifascist fight represented the true Italy, Jewish inclusion in it made it possible for them to return to the national community; as merely victims of Fascist persecution, they would have remained outside.

Italian Jews tended to emphasize that they had been part of the resistance movement as Italians and not as Jews.[36] Italian Jewish postwar discourse framed Jewish participation in the resistance as foremost a sign of their dedication to their home country, less frequently mentioned political aspirations, and rarely perceived it as Jewish resistance. The Fascists had arrested Vittorio Foa as a political opponent in 1935. After his release in 1943, he joined the resistance movement. He explained, "There were many Jews in the Resistance with me, but I always felt their commitment was not so much an expression of their Jewishness as a sign of their integration."[37] The *Bollettino della comunità israelitica di Milano* (Bulletin of the Jewish Community of Milan) published a series in the immediate aftermath of the war honoring Jewish partisans. Under the headline "Our Heroes," it dedicated a weekly article to an Italian Jewish resistance fighter who had lost his life in the resistance. Often merely the remark that the young man was buried in the Jewish cemetery pointed to the deceased's Jewishness.[38] Most articles underlined the men's Italianness. One of the articles in the *Bollettino*, dedicated to Walter Rossi, described the young man with the following words: "He did not know about weapons, knew no hatred, but only pity, pity for the battered and betrayed Italy, beaten, mocked, and tortured he was able to endure and to be silent about his parents' hiding place, the name of his companions and their places of refuge. He died as a hero, the name of his mother and of Italy on his lips."[39] While the text relates that he and his family were persecuted, nowhere does it state the background for this persecution or the reason his parents had to go into hiding. At the same time, the text strongly underlines Rossi's (assumed) patriotism.[40] By contrast, the

148 | *Home after Fascism*

more private commemoration of his family emphasized Rossi's Jewishness. They created a postcard with a Star of David in his honor.[41]

No Longer German?

In contrast to Italian Jews, most German Jews lost their citizenship between 1933 and 1945. Some were deprived of their citizenship under the Law on the Revocation of Naturalizations and the Deprivation of German Citizenship of July 14, 1933. But the largest number lost theirs with the Eleventh Decree to the Law on the Citizenship of the Reich in November 1941, which stated that Jews who took up residence in a foreign country lost their citizenship as soon as they crossed the border. Deportation to the East counted as a change of residence, making both Jewish refugees and deportees stateless.[42] In a world that functioned in national categories, they were officially marked as belonging nowhere.[43] Freia Eisner, the adopted daughter of Kurt Eisner, remembered "crying bitterly" when she was officially informed that she was no longer German. She described it as if "a part of me died."[44]

In the fall of 1945, soon after the establishment of the Allied Control Council, German citizenship could be restored to Jews at their request.[45] However, renaturalization proved a complicated and contested subject.[46] Resistance to automatic restoration came not from German authorities but rather from the Jewish communities. Jewish organizations opposed the automatic return of citizenship since they rejected the reconstruction of Jewish life in Germany. The World Jewish Congress stressed that "persons who do not wish to become German nationals again *may* remain stateless."[47] Some Jews of German origin preferred remaining stateless, even if they lived in their former home country.[48] In his 1947 article in *Commentary*, Moses Moskowitz explained that "with the abolition of Nazi discriminatory legislation, they [German Jews] regained their former rights of German citizenship; but that is no particular privilege today, and its liabilities are great."[49] An automatic return to German citizenship would have also caused problems for returnees who still had property in their countries of exile since German assets were frequently confiscated.[50]

In the Soviet zone, the different regions had already issued decrees regarding renaturalization in 1946, and returnees were soon able to regain their citizenship without facing many problems. The US zones passed legislation in the spring of 1948. In the French and British zones, which lacked an official legislation, many returnees regained citizenship in an informal way until the *Grundgesetz* (Basic Law) came into effect in the newly founded Federal Republic of Germany, FRG in May 1949. According to clause 116, paragraph 2 of the Basic Law: "Former German citizens whose nationality has been withdrawn on political, racial, or religious grounds between January 30, 1933, and May 8, 1945, and their descendants, shall be naturalized upon application. They shall be deemed never denaturalized, as long as they have established residence in Germany after May 8, 1945 and have not expressed a contrary intention."[51] The clause differentiated between persons who lived in Germany and those who remained in their countries of exile. Whereas the former regained their citizenship automatically, the latter had to apply to the German authorities to again become German citizens.

In some cases, Jewish remigrants who had acquired a different citizenship during their time in exile chose to keep their non-German passports. Theodor Adorno retained his American citizenship even though it forced him, due to American immigration laws, to return to the United States for ten months in 1952, when he would have preferred to stay in Frankfurt.[52] Käte Hamburger, a literary scholar who had fled to Sweden in 1934, kept her Swedish citizenship after she returned to Germany in 1956.[53] The writer Wolfgang Hildesheimer returned to Germany to work at the Nuremberg trials as a Palestinian citizen. In the spring of 1948, he began to worry about becoming stateless or needing to return to what was now Israel.[54] His fears became reality, and in April 1948 he wrote to his sister, "What at the moment shakes me the most is that I apparently will become stateless by May 15. I hope that my new position in the British zone will allow me to be naturalized later on [as British]."[55] Hildesheimer's letters make it clear that he had no intentions of officially becoming German again, but his hopes for British citizenship did not materialize. In the early 1950s, he began the process of regaining his German citizenship.[56] Others, such as Wolfgang Fischer, who returned from Shanghai in 1947, looked forward to getting back their "German citizenship with all its rights and duties."[57]

The hesitation among many German Jews to regain German citizenship was linked to their reluctance to identify as German.[58] Many preferred to create distance between themselves and the country in which they again lived. Jurek Becker remembered that his father taught him to live "like a spectator" and to "let them feel that you do not belong to them, they will anyhow never forget it."[59] The journalist Karl Marx, who published the *Jüdisches Gemeindeblatt für die Nord-Rheinprovinz und Westfalen* and after 1948 the *Allgemeine Wochenzeitung für Juden in Deutschland*, likewise underlined the spectator role of Jews in Germany. In an article from 1947, he argued that "our newspaper is a Jewish paper. It is a paper that does not have to concern itself with German party politics."[60] Tellingly, the postwar Jewish organization, founded in the summer of 1950, named itself Zentralrat der Juden in Deutschland (Central Council of Jews in Germany): a radical shift from pre-Nazi predecessors, such as Central-Verein deutscher Staatsbürger jüdischen Glaubens (Association of German Citizens of the Jewish Faith) or Verband der deutschen Juden (Association of German Jews). Some still spoke of themselves as German Jews, but self-description as "Germans of the Jewish faith" had become rare.

In the spring of 1946, *Der Weg* published an article entitled "Jews in Germany or German Jews." Its author argued that German Jews had the right to self-identify as Germans. The author reminded his coreligionists that they had once proudly called themselves "German citizens of the Jewish faith" and fought for "the social, governmental, economic, and cultural emancipation of Jews in Germany, because we were Germans and knew how to combine this fact with our Jewish faith." The article took on a defensive tone, insisting that "we are not worse Jews, just because we believe we are good and true Germans."[61] Preempting criticism, the author defended his views before an audience that he knew would in many cases see Jewish and German identifications as incompatible. His choice of words—that they "believed [themselves] to be," rather than *were* "good and true Germans"—points to his own uncertainties. As late as 1968, Siegmund Weltlinger, whose experiences in hiding had made him perhaps more optimistic about Jewish life in Germany, admitted that most would not understand when he declared that he "never regretted being a German Jew." Weltlinger told his audience that "two things make him especially thankful to his creator. . . . First, that I was born a Jew. . . . And second that I was born as a German and was allowed to grow up in German culture."[62]

While few Jews shared Weltlinger's enthusiasm, others likewise remained attached to German culture. Feelings of national belonging are more complex than an abstract sense of attachment to the nation. While most Jews in Germany rejected patriotic statements, they remained connected to aspects of Germanness, to what I call niches of belonging. They felt connected to their mother tongue—to familiar expressions, songs, and jokes—and remained intimately familiar with the country's culture.[63] Above all, language played a crucial role in their sense of self and belonging; language, as Eva Hoffman writes, "constitute[s] us."[64] Literary scholar Käte

Hamburger, who returned from Sweden, explained in an interview: "I did not give up German even after I had emigrated. . . . After all I am identical with this language. I believe the mother tongue is what ultimately decides whether one feels that one belongs to a nation."[65]

In a speech in Paris in 1949, Alexander Abusch reminded his audience that his mother tongue was not primarily Hitler's language: "Allow me to speak to you in my mother tongue, even though your memories of Hitler are still a near, and for my people [*mein Volk*] shameful past. It is the language of that great humanist poet whose 200th birthday we will celebrate this year far beyond our borders: the language of Goethe."[66] By talking about *his people*, Abusch clearly stressed his belonging to Germany, which he tried to refashion as the land of "poets and thinkers." After the Nazis had appropriated German culture, such efforts to reclaim language and literature were common among German Jews. Jewish publications from the immediate postwar period were filled with articles that sought to free the German "greats," such as Goethe and Nietzsche, from suspicions of antisemitism. In an article published in the journal *Zwischen den Zeiten* in October 1947, August Kruhm writes, "Goethe's relationship to the Jews, in the last decade, tendentiously distorted and deliberately falsified by Nazi literature, is reexamined [here] with the surprising result that Goethe's tolerant attitude knew no religious and racial prejudices. Indeed, his personal intercourse with Jews was extensive."[67] Thus, Kruhm as well as other German Jews reclaimed the author who meant so much to them from the Nazis.[68] Other articles focused on Jewish contributions to German culture, pointing to their rootedness in Germany. The *Jüdisches Gemeindeblatt für die britische Zone*, one of the earliest Jewish postwar publications, contained a series titled *Juedischer Anteil an der Deutschen Kultur* (Jewish contributions to German culture). The German people must "remember what Jews have done for the international reputation of German culture," writes Siegbert Kahn in his *Antisemitismus und Rassenhetze*, providing a long list of German Jewish scientists, artists, and authors.[69]

Numerous Jews, among them Anna Seghers, Arnold Zweig, Victor Klemperer, Jürgen Kuczynski, Alexander Abusch, and Klaus Gysi, became active in the Cultural League for the Democratic Renewal of Germany (Kulturbund zur demokratischen Erneuerung Deutschlands), which, founded in the Soviet occupation zone in June 1945, promoted classical German literature as well as the works of emigrated German authors. German Jews in both the East and West, such as Hermann Kesten, Hans Wolffheim, and Alfred Kantorowicz, tried to make the literature of exiled authors known to German audiences.[70] Valeska Gert published her memoirs with the hope that she could reclaim her place within the history of German dance and theatre. She complained about the widespread ignorance about her contribution to modern dance and demanded a "spiritual restitution."[71] These artists aimed to bring the "other," exiled Germany back home and ensure its imprint on postwar cultural developments. However, their efforts had limited success.[72]

With their emphasis on culture and language, these German Jews hung onto a nonterritorial idea of Germanness.[73] But such niches of belonging were not limited to language and culture but also had a spatial dimension. Some expressed their love for a particular part of Germany. Grete Weil wrote in 1946 that Bavaria was still the place "to which she belonged in the deepest way."[74] Weil distinguished between the "rubble of the cities" and "the countryside," remaining attached to the latter.[75] She perceived nature as untouched and uncorrupted by Nazism.[76] Fritz Bauer wrote of his "Swabian homesickness." After his return, he went to eat Spaetzle (a Swabian specialty) and Sauerkraut: "I missed them for 12 years!"[77] Ursula Bernhardt maintained that while she no longer felt German, she continued to see herself as a "Berlinerin,"[78] and in a letter to his friend Johannes Becher, the composer Hanns Eisler emphasized that "even the destroyed Berlin, remains for me Berlin."[79] Many shared this loyalty to a specific region or city, in particular Berlin, while asserting that they no longer had a strong connection to the country as a whole.[80] Language, culture, food, and landscapes remained sources of comfort in spite of their general sense of distance.

Germans of Jewish origin who did not identify strongly as Jewish and had distanced themselves from the Jewish community were more likely to self-identify as German. This holds especially true for Socialists and Communists from Jewish families, who tended to be more positive about a future in Germany and whose political community provided them with a network. Kurt Goldstein remembered that after his liberation from Auschwitz, a French comrade asked him why he wanted to return to Germany, suggesting he should instead join him in France. But Goldstein countered that "I am a German, that is my language, that is my culture. I began my life in the German workers movement." He added that French Fascists had tortured him and handed him over to the Nazis, while German Communists had helped him survive.[81] The dream of a better future allowed people like Goldstein to envision a place where they would belong; their vision of Germany was, above all, the Socialist, antifascist Germany. While belonging to the Communist collective would have potentially allowed for a sense of belonging to an international community of antifascists, many German Jewish Communists, like Goldstein, felt strongly tied to the German Communist movement and to the wish of building the first "socialist state on *German* soil."[82]

In particular in the aftermath of the 1952 purges, German Communists of Jewish origin who did not flee the GDR emphasized their closeness to party, state, and their German homeland to prevent accusations of disloyalty and "cosmopolitanism."[83] However, such loyalty to state and party was not merely political posturing. Many were deeply invested in the party and the state and perceived them as important protectors against a renewed rise of Fascism and antisemitism. Such feelings become apparent in reactions to the uprising of June 1953. Many Jews in the GDR felt uneasy when confronted with the masses who demonstrated on June 17, even if some felt sympathetic toward the people's demands.[84] Seeing excited Germans demonstrating and voicing nationalist as well as antisemitic sentiments triggered memories of the Nazi period, and some welcomed the suppression of the uprising.[85] Hans Mayer wrote that after June 17, he felt relief for having overcome this threat.[86]

Imagined Communities

Fear and suspicion of other Germans was widespread among German Jews in the East and West. While they could feel a sense of belonging to some aspects of Germany, most struggled with feeling connected to the Germans. "Finally, it is imagined as a community, because, regardless of the actual inequality and exploitation that may prevail in each, the nation is always conceived as a deep, horizontal comradeship," writes Benedict Anderson in his seminal work on nationalism.[87] For most German Jews, antisemitic violence had destroyed any belief in such comradeship with other members of this imagined, national community. They could no longer feel connected to an abstract mass of people when they knew the majority were implicated in the persecution and murder of their friends and family. As with other aspects of national belonging, German Jews tended to feel part of selected groups, rather than connected to Germans more broadly.

Hans Frankenthal explained that it was very "difficult for us [him and his brother] to even speak with people, unless we were one hundred percent sure that they had been on our side."[88] Others shared the feeling that

154 | *Home after Fascism*

they could only trust those whom they knew to have been opposed to the regime. Anna Seghers's letters from the first years after her return reveal both her strong wish to build a new society in Germany and the immense difficulty of living among Germans. In the spring of 1947, she wrote:

> I started looking for a fixed point in all the confusion. . . . You know how to behave when you meet a Nazi. But what when you meet a democrat who has taken a democratic stance on some question for an hour, and when you go home with him, he suddenly rambles about *Lebensraum*, of *verjudete Gesinnung*, of *vernegerte* Frenchmen? And if you confront him, he apologizes that he has been fed these expressions for so long that he cannot get rid of them so quickly. I began looking for people who hadn't even let themselves be fed; who refused this food from the start. I came across friends I had known many years ago.[89]

Like most other Communist Jews, Seghers associated with people who shared her political convictions. The party offered the comfort of being among the like-minded. After years of isolation, they needed a collective with whom they could share their resentments and qualms regarding other Germans.[90] While a sense of belonging to the German people proved difficult, they felt strongly connected to the Communist community.[91] Recha Rothschild, for example, described her comrades as her "family of choice," and Lea Grundig declared the party her "true home."[92]

Some Jews in West Germany who engaged in politics also felt connected to people who shared their political outlook while remaining distant from other Germans.[93] In a letter to a friend written shortly before his return from Sweden, Fritz Bauer admitted that he "shuddered" when thinking about personal interactions. But Bauer felt close to fellow Social Democratic remigrants.[94] German Jews in both East and West Germany also continued to feel connected to non-Jewish friends whom they knew to have behaved decently during the war.[95] Journalist Ernest Landau, a camp survivor, depicted these often tentative connections in an essay published in 1951: "Frequently he [the German Jew] finds old friends or at least people he knows and who know him, people to whom a relationship of trust either exists or can at least be initiated without major difficulties because of cultural and social connections."[96] There were too few Jews in Germany to allow living entirely secluded. Those who wanted to avoid encounters with non-Jews at any cost left the country. Those who remained tended to, as Landau suggests, rebuild friendships with those they had known before the war or with people whose record of the past they trusted. When Wolfgang

Hildesheimer first returned in 1946, he struggled to build relationships with the non-Jews around him. In July 1947 he wrote to his parents, who had remained in Palestine, "I have an irresistible antipathy against the Germans. . . . Still, I'm friends with some very cultured Germans and am in contact by correspondence with several others. In personal relationships you overcome the animosity after all."[97]

Still, while they inevitably came in close contact with the population, most German Jews did not feel part of an imagined community of Germans. Rather, they emphasized feeling distant, indifferent, or estranged from the non-Jewish majority.[98] Alfred Meyer, who had left Germany in 1939 and returned as an Allied soldier, felt "torn between hate towards all Germans, pity for some of them, and indifference. The last attitude will probably win."[99] Marga Spiegel, who survived the war hidden with her husband and young daughter, described her lack of any emotions. In her memoir, written fifteen years after the end of the war, she explained that they had "no strength to be happy, no strength to hate, or revenge ourselves. This wasn't only the case for us. Everywhere where a Jewish person re-emerged, it was the same: They were too numbed, too weak, to feel real joy about the regained freedom. We did not even have strength for feelings of hatred and vengeance."[100] Spiegel ascribed her lack of hatred to fatigue after the years of suffering, but there also seemed to have been a general unwillingness to emotionally engage the non-Jewish population, even in a negative way.

Like Spiegel, most surviving Jews in Germany denied feeling any hatred toward non-Jews.[101] In a short essay written in 1946, Kurt Hirschfeld picked up on the surprising absence of hatred among German Jews, writing that "our hatred *should* be deadly." Asking what became of their hatred, he explained that it "weakened to dislike and suspicion."[102] Others pointed out that "hatred was alien to Judaism."[103] They discussed hatred when describing the Nazis' attitudes or when they wrote about the latent antisemitism of the postwar years.[104] Antisemites hated; they did not. With their rejection of hatred as an emotional response, they distanced themselves from the perpetrators. This emphasis on a lack of emotion was consistent with the dominant emotional regime of the postwar period, which, as historian Frank Biess explains, "was one of restraint and anti-intensity." He perceives the general call for emotional restraint as a result of "the real and perceived emotional excesses of the wartime period."[105] After the war, memories of Nazi hatred, passion, and more generally an excess of feelings led to a turn away from radical emotions as the norm. For German Jews, distancing

156 | *Home after Fascism*

themselves from Nazism and emphasizing their own emotional disengagement with Germans proved important.

Such an emotionally distant relationship to the non-Jewish German population became the emotional norm at least on the discursive level. Jewish community leaders encouraged distance from Germans, in particular those who had been members of the NSDAP. In May 1947 the head of the Dortmund community, Siegfried Heimberg, wrote to a member, Rosi Nathan, inquiring about a rumor he had heard about her having a relationship with a denazified police officer. He made it clear that the community disapproved by stating, "After the cruelties of the past years, our members do not get involved with former activists." If she indeed was seeing the officer, they would "be forced to draw the consequences."[106] Heimberg did not specify what the consequences would be, but probably he meant exclusion from the community and therefore from any help they provided to their members. Nathan decisively rebuffed the accusations and asked Heimberg to "name the person who dragged my and my children's honor through the dirt."[107] The exchange reveals the extent to which the Jewish postwar discourse condemned any personal relationship with former NSDAP members. As Jews could not always be sure whether the Germans they encountered had been party members, such a taboo contributed to the need to be careful with social interactions.

People who were of Jewish descent but not members of the Jewish community tended to be less invested in keeping distance. Elisabeth T., a young woman whose mother was Jewish, mixed mainly with non-Jews in the aftermath of the war. In her memoir she described her shock upon realizing that the young man with whom she had become close had been a member of the Waffen-SS. But after considering an end to the friendship, she explained his past away:

> The young man had been indoctrinated since his youth, at school, in youth organizations like *Jungvolk* and *Hitlerjugend* with the slogans and ideologies of the Third Reich, he knew nothing else. So, it was almost unavoidable that he had joined the supposed elite group in his youthful enthusiasm. Moreover, I was sure that he had done nothing bad. He had a gentle mind and was a good-natured and helpful person—sometimes too helpful, as I realized later. Moreover, the Waffen-SS was a fighting unit and was not connected with the beasts of the general SS of the KZs (concentration camps).[108]

Either unaware or purposely ignorant of the crimes committed by the Waffen-SS, she became engaged to the young man in 1946, and they married soon after. Her relatively protected experience as the daughter of a non-Jewish father certainly shaped how she evaluated her future husband's past. Elisabeth lived quite removed from Jewish life and the Jewish community. Had she been a member of the Jewish community, her marriage to a former SS officer would have been met with disapproval. There may well have been differences between the more condemning outlook of the Jewish leadership and journalists and a more forgiving sentiment in parts of the Jewish population—that is, a distance between an emotional regime that promoted distance and the social reality of people who often felt close to neighbors and friends. While a marriage to a former member of the SS just a few years after the Holocaust remains well outside the norm, intermarriage remained common, and the numbers of intermarriages continued to rise. The small number of Jews in Germany (throughout the first postwar decades, the number of registered community members remained below thirty thousand) made intermarriage practically unavoidable.[109]

In Italy intermarriage rates likewise increased.[110] Yet some preferred a Jewish partner. Giancarlo Spizzichino, a Roman Jew, explained, for instance, that while "his best friend . . . was a Catholic," he wanted to marry a Jew: "Looking for a girl to marry, I have always had the wish to have a Jewish family, because of what I had suffered; if I did not, this would have been Nazism's victory. I wanted it for my father, who died in a concentration camp."[111] His wish, however, did not stem from mistrust toward the non-Jewish population but rather from wanting to keep Jewishness alive within his family.

Like many German Jews, Italian Jews wished to regain a sense of belonging, but in contrast to the former, they by and large did not feel the need to carve out a specific group of the population among whom they felt comfortable. They simply wished to be part of the imagined national community again. After liberation, Margherita Morpurgo, who unlike her sister Alma had not emigrated but survived in hiding, described regaining her sense of belonging: "Finally we have achieved what we always wanted, not being divided by others, being able to participate in the life of those around us, sharing their anxieties, their fears, and their hopes."[112]

Italian Jews tended to describe the revival of friendships after the war years as uncomplicated. In their depiction of postwar life, they seamlessly picked up relationships where exile and war had interrupted them. They wrote about renewing old friendships and working closely with non-Jewish colleagues.[113] Even if reintegration, in particular in the workplace, often

158 | *Home after Fascism*

proved difficult and sometimes painful, with former employers and colleagues showing little interest in making amends, the public discourse at the time remained largely positive.[114] In contrast to the German Jewish leadership and press, Italian Jewish community leaders as well as newspapers promoted a positive emotional attitude and stressed the importance of reintegration and working closely together in the reconstruction of the country.[115] For instance, Raffaele Cantoni, president of the Union of Italian Jewish Communities, declared in an essay that "the Italian people who have heroically resisted the poison of racial hatred deserve to be treated with great respect."[116]

The myth of the good Italian set the tone for Italian Jews' relationship with the majority population, and a strong attachment to the imagined community remained the emotional norm in the aftermath of the war. Still, some Italian Jews, in particular younger ones, described feeling estranged from the people around them.[117] Eugenia Servi, then in her early twenties, felt distant from the people in her small Tuscan village—a feeling that over the first postwar years became stronger: "Over time, rather than adapt, there was a growing sense of estrangement from the rest of the villagers."[118]

Jewishness

Estrangement from fellow Italians and Germans caused surviving Jews to feel more closely connected to an imagined national or international Jewish community. In particular for German Jews who had no political affiliation and could no longer see themselves as German, Jewishness became essential to their self-understanding. One survivor of Auschwitz exclaimed in a letter to his parents written in the immediate aftermath of the war, "We are not Germans. We are Jews."[119] Indeed, many German Jews embraced their Jewishness more strongly after the war.[120] When the rabbi of the Frankfurt community left for Detroit in 1946, the community leader thanked him for rekindling "the Jewish spirit and Jewish piety" among those who "unfortunately had been estranged."[121]

The experience of persecution under the Fascist regime and the Holocaust also affected Italian Jews' relationships with their Jewishness. Before the war most had regarded Judaism as a mainly private affair, but the experience of being persecuted caused many to feel more strongly connected to a Jewish collective.[122] In the late 1940s and early 1950s, Jewish culture in Italy flourished—the number of Jewish publications, newspapers, and books rose, and Italian Jews spent considerable money and effort to rebuild synagogues and invested in Jewish education.[123] A memorandum from American Jewish Committee representative Z. Shuster described an increase of "Jewish consciousness." He further remarked that Italian Jews showed "greater attachment to Jewish tradition, learning, and education."[124] In a letter written in May 1944, Lelio Vittorio Valobra likewise expressed the change that had occurred among Italian Jews and emphasized his belief in a Jewish collective: "The Jews have a common fate. We cannot remove ourselves from this, not even with a separate nationality, or attitude. It is a mistake made by Italian Jews who lived in a country that never knew antisemitism. Too long we believed that we have a separate fate, and perhaps because of this we never entirely understood the suffering of our brothers and did not try enough to alleviate it."[125] This idea that their previous distance from Judaism had been a mistake comes up frequently in the postwar writings of Italian Jews. Rome's chief rabbi, David Prato, called on his community to reaffirm their Judaism and to avoid the "fatal mistake of the past that led to the loss of your conscience, reducing your Judaism to a fading idea."[126] Some even perceived the Holocaust as a consequence of Jews' "assimilation," as a kind of divine punishment.[127] Others asserted that the persecution had uncovered the limits of integration.[128]

The end of the war allowed those who had hidden their Jewishness to openly reclaim it. Mario Tagliacozzo remembered the liberating feeling of becoming himself again after years in hiding: "One made one's identity public again by saying or hearing one's own last name. . . . In front of the Palazzo dell'Esposizione I heard myself called by my last name after so many months. It was the first time and it moved me. . . . I went to the food agency to collect my ration card: what a joy to be able to say my own name with an open face and to be able to call out without fear: 'I'm a Jew!'"[129]

Others who had done their best to hide their Jewishness in order to survive suddenly faced the challenge of proving that they were Jewish. Hertha Pineas and her husband, Hermann Pineas, a neurologist, had lived in Berlin until going underground with false documents to avoid persecution. They settled in Memmingen, Allgäu, where Hermann assumed the name Hans Günther and worked as a salesman at a tool and machine factory. In 1957 Hertha wrote a short report in which she described the difficulties they faced after their liberation when trying to reclaim their original names and prove their Jewish identity, in part to secure housing: "After liberation in 1945 we assumed our real names again, but the American military

160 | *Home after Fascism*

government was of the view that we should now again be regarded as German and had no claims as Jews, and no right to housing assistance. Only after fighting for half a year we were allocated an apartment. Then, the city of Memmingen testified in August 1945 to us that we would have a special status as Jews."[130] Numerous memoirs of German Jews who survived in hiding recount their first encounter with Allied soldiers and the need to prove their Jewishness. They all follow, more or less, the same story line: Russian or American soldiers find them in their hiding place, assume they are Germans, and tell them that no Jews had survived. Upon their insistence, the soldiers then ask them to prove their Jewishness, which they usually do by reciting the Sh'ma Yisrael (Hear, [O] Israel), the central prayer of the Jewish liturgy, though sometimes they mention a different prayer or use a Yiddish word. One of the soldiers then reveals his own Jewishness, which is followed by embracing and celebrating.[131] The trope of this encounter points to the wish of surviving German Jews to establish their belonging to a larger Jewish world. Klaus Gysi's story of his first encounter with Russians soldiers after he had survived in hiding resembles the stories so many other Jewish survivors told, with one crucial difference. He proved his innocence of Nazi crimes not by reciting a prayer but by showing the soldiers a book by Marx, thus highlighting his self-identification as a Communist.[132] These different ways of recounting the first encounter in which those persecuted could reveal their true selves reveal how such narratives are constructed to affirm belonging to different groups.

After the war Jewish communities in Germany as well as in Italy received requests for readmission from persons who had left the community as well as from others who had never been members but now wanted to join. Over two thousand people applied to become members of the Berlin Jewish community alone.[133] Neither the Italian nor the German community leaders perceived these applications in an entirely positive light. In an exchange with Gustavo Castelbolognesi, chief rabbi of Milano, Lelio Vittorio Valobra emphasized that "as much as I disapproved of those who left their ancestors' faith in difficult times, I can have no sympathy for those who, in the hope of material benefits, now knock on our door."[134] Emilio Canarutto expressed his rejection more sharply: "You will do well to keep your distance from the converts who in my opinion smell like cadavers. There can be no antidote that will bring them back to life, and even less that will return to them the honorary title 'Jew.' They could commit treason again."[135] Italian and German community leaders suspected that people joined merely in order to benefit from the support the communities and the Joint provided to members.[136] The head of the community in Erfurt turned to Rabbi Neuhaus in Frankfurt, asking for advice on how they should deal with the many applicants, stating that he assumed most of them were "opportunists."[137] In his reply Rabbi Neuhaus confirmed that they were facing the same issue in Frankfurt and explained that they did not accept anyone who had left the community before 1933 and refused the applicant if given the impression that they were "opportunists who want to join for some canned milk or half a pound of butter." He suggested that each individual case needed to be scrutinized.[138]

The requests for admittance forced Jewish leaderships to formulate criteria about whom to admit—and thus to define Jewishness. Both the Italian and German Jewish communities wanted to emphasize a sharp turn from the racial definitions of Nazism and Fascism and so defined Jewishness as a religious category. In February 1946 the Jewish community in Berlin sent a letter to the city magistrate in order to emphasize that "the term 'Jew' is again to be understood exclusively in the religious sense."[139] However, while both the Italian and German leaderships defined religion as the criterion of admittance, the communities in Italy seemed more willing to accept new members, likely because they received fewer applicants. While the German communities were flooded with readmission requests, Italian communities received a comparatively small number. Conversion rates decreased after the war, but most of the four thousand or so Jews who had converted to Catholicism under Fascism did not wish to rejoin Judaism.[140] Both Italian and German Jewish communities aided their members after the war, and economically Italy fared no better than Germany. Consequently, if requests for readmission depended only on a wish for material aid, Italians of Jewish origin should not have been less keen to join the Jewish community. One can speculate that they had less need to become part of the Jewish collective because they still felt comfortable with identifying as Italians. In contrast to many German Jews, they were not in search of a place of belonging.

Giuseppe Nathan, extraordinary commissioner of the Union of Italian Jewish Communities since November 1944, provided some general guidelines about the readmission process. Generally speaking, Italian communities were willing to readmit children, those who had left involuntarily, and those who "sincerely regret their mistake and give unequivocal proof of repentance and determination to return to the Jewish *faith*."[141] Rabbis should only allow the return to Judaism if they could personally assure

162 | Home after Fascism

themselves of the seriousness of the request. In practice, the communities seemed to readmit people without giving them too many difficulties, though in some cases they requested a ritual bath for the newcomer or returnee.[142] The German communities were more selective in their admittance. Rabbi Nathan Peter Levinson, who served as a rabbi in Berlin between 1950 and 1953, estimated that only about 5 percent of applicants were allowed to join the Berlin community.[143] The communities tended to readmit people who had withdrawn after 1933 but were more reluctant to let in those who had left earlier or those who had never registered as Jewish. In May 1948 the Frankfurt community, for instance, explained to an applicant, "We regret that we have to reject your request for admission, as we can only accept religiously Jewish persons [*Religionsjuden*]. . . . For us Jewish descent on the father's side plays no role."[144]

As in this case, communities turned away people who were of partial Jewish origin, as well as those who had not registered with a Jewish community prior to 1933. German Jews needed to refute Nazism's racial definition of Jewishness, but the shift in the official definition of the category caused problems. In a memo from December 1946, Joint representative Philip Skorneck highlighted this issue: "Practically everyone in Berlin wants to be a Jew today in order to participate in the relief distributions which the JDC makes through the *Gemeinde* [community]. Because of Hitler's Nazi ideology which defined Jewishness as a race, there are thousands of people in Berlin today who call themselves Jewish Catholics and Jewish Protestants because although they are adherents of a Christian religion they are descendants of Jews. They have thus adopted the Nazi idea of racism."[145] Having been persecuted as Jews, people of Jewish origin who had left the community or had never been community members hoped to receive aid from international Jewish organizations such as the Joint via the local Jewish community. But while they saw their persecution as Jews as proof of their Jewishness, the community did not, as this would have meant following Nazi racial criteria. Rejecting them, however, often meant refusing aid to those who had suffered alongside Jews who were defined as such by their religion. Some who were refused admittance reacted with anger and bitterness, feeling that they were treated unfairly.[146] After receiving a rejection, one German Jew underlined that he had been "considered a not-privileged full-Jew" under the Nazis and that he had been forced to join the Reich's Association of Jews in Germany and pay membership fees. But the community leadership did not change their view, replying that the community was not the "legal heir of the Reich's Association of Jews in Germany, which was founded by the infamous Gestapo."[147]

However, the communities did not decide alone who would be able to receive support; the Joint, as the biggest supplier of assistance to German Jews, had an important say in the matter. Indeed, at times the communities pointed to the American donors when justifying their strict policies regarding who should be counted as Jewish and thus receive support.[148] At the same time, the Joint referred to *Gemeinde* policies in its replies to letters from concerned donors who asked why the non-Jewish partners of their relatives did not receive any support. In June 1947 Mrs. Ernst Jonas requested information regarding the Joint's policy toward wives in a "mixed marriage" who had supported their husbands. "For instance—," Jonas wrote, "I have a letter from a relative (who I have long known) surviving at 70—who complains bitterly to me—that his ARYAN wife who faithfully and devotedly fed and cherished and saved him—cannot now receive LIKE treatment from him, for when he goes to receive food, he is permitted a portion for himself ALONE."[149] In reply, the Joint representative explained that they decided to let the communities choose to whom they gave aid. In another reply to a similar inquiry, a Joint official underlined that German Jews had a different understanding of what it meant to be a *Gemeinde* member than American Jews and declared that the Joint needed to respect the local habits. The letter continued, "Now, one of the most sensitive things in dealing with the Jewish people who have survived the holocaust in Germany is the way in which the people who never renounced their Judaism or never married out of the faith or separated themselves from the official Jewish community feel about the others."[150] The Joint worker explained that these Jews did not wish the others to join the community, as they felt they had suffered less. It appears that the Joint restricted its support to community members, and community leadership limited membership to religiously Jewish persons. When pressed, each institution made the other responsible for the exclusion of numerous racially persecuted persons or non-Jewish spouses.

In 1946, the foundation of the aid office for racially persecuted Christians (Hilfsstelle für rassisch verfolgte Christen) ameliorated the situation, but it still limited support to those associated with a religion, as one frustrated "half-Jew" pointed out. In a letter addressed to the Jewish community in Frankfurt as well as to the Hilfsstelle, Gerhard Bender raised the question of who would take care of him, as he "would need to see myself as

164 | *Home after Fascism*

a 'racially persecuted heathen.'" In his letter Bender described his suffering under the Nazis that ended with his internment in a concentration camp. He also aired his grievances over the Jewish community's behavior toward people like him. "At the Jewish community," Bender wrote, "I am looked at with a more or less dismissive eye and I am treated accordingly. I often then have the same feeling as with the Nazis, who labelled me a 'half-Jew.'"[151] For Bender, the community's policy meant that he was still categorized as a "half-Jew" and consequently as not entirely belonging.

In Hamburg, those who were persecuted as Jews but were not religiously Jewish founded the Emergency Society for People Affected by the Nuremberg Racial Laws (Notgemeinschaft der durch die Nürnberger Gesetze Betroffenen), which supported "Jews who had to wear the star, Jews in privileged mixed marriages, Aryans in mixed marriages and first-degree *Mischlinge*."[152] Similar organizations were soon founded in other German cities, and in 1952 they united as the Central Association of those not of Jewish Faith Affected by the Nuremberg Laws (Zentralverband der durch die Nürnberger Gesetze Betroffenen nichtjüdischen Glaubens).[153] But while such organizations helped people like Bender who did not self-identify as Jewish but expected support because the Nazis had persecuted them, it made little difference for those who wished to join a Jewish community not merely for the aid they would receive but because their experience of persecution as Jews had caused them to see themselves as belonging to a Jewish collective. Some Germans of Jewish origin, as well as some married to Jews, insisted that they wished to join not to receive material support but rather because they wanted to belong.[154] Having been ostracized by the majority "Aryan" community, their connection with Judaism, however marginal, offered a way to become part of a community.

Given the small number of children in the community, it appears surprising that communities frequently refused children of "mixed marriages." Inge Lewin was born in 1933 to a non-Jewish mother; her Jewish father was murdered in a concentration camp when she was only four years old. She tried to join the local Jewish community in January 1946, but her request was rejected. A penciled message on her application form reads: "Inge Lewin came to the classes after I asked her to do so. She knows no Hebrew and has no clue about Judaism. Who should educate the child in the Jewish religion? In her own words she had never seen a synagogue."[155] It seems that her lack of knowledge of Judaism, rather than the fact that by Jewish law Inge would not be considered Jewish, motivated the rejection.

The hesitation of Jewish communities in Germany to admit children who had not grown up in Jewish homes stood in contrast to the situation in France, where Jewish communities battled over the custody of Jewish children who had been educated in the Christian faith, aiming to keep them as Jews.[156] In Inge's case, her mother, who had filled out the form, did not show the sensitivities the Jewish communities may have expected. Under religion she wrote, "Jewish, in consequence of the Nazi persecution, since 1939 pro forma Roman Catholic."[157] Apparently the mother had baptized her daughter in the hope of protecting her from anti-Jewish persecution. More striking, however, is her statement that Inge was "Jewish as consequence of the Nazi persecution." The idea that the Nazis had made her daughter Jewish stood at odds with the aim of the communities to disconnect Jewishness from Nazi racism. Widespread pessimism about a future for Jews in Germany also explains their reluctance to admit the young girl. The question of who should educate the child in Judaism points to such insecurities. With almost no religious teachers left, the task of educating children who did not live in Jewish homes may have seemed daunting.

After 1945 German Jewish communities lacked religious leadership.[158] In East Germany the situation was especially desperate. Beyond Berlin, most communities could only hold synagogue services on the high holidays, as they lacked both rabbis and the required ten men to form a minyan. Martin Riesenburger, who led the first services in Berlin after the war, became chief rabbi of East Germany in 1961. He had studied at the Hochschule für die Wissenschaft des Judentums, but some doubted whether he had ever been ordained as a rabbi.[159] The situation in West Germany was somewhat better, although the demand for rabbis also exceeded supply. In May 1947, Max Meyer, head of the Frankfurt congregation, emphasized their need for a rabbi and their difficulties in finding someone who "more or less could fulfil the requirements we used to ask for previously."[160] Meyer made it clear that they would be willing to lower their standards while still hoping to find someone able to connect with German Jewish tradition, meaning that they would prefer a liberal rabbi. Rabbi Leopold Neuhaus had returned to Frankfurt from Theresienstadt, but he left in 1946 for Detroit, leaving the community without religious leadership. Most rabbis who survived the war in exile could not imagine returning. Many had found new positions in their adopted countries, and they often shared the international Jewish community's condemnation of Germany. Only four rabbis returned permanently, but a few more resettled in Germany for limited periods. In the

166 | *Home after Fascism*

immediate aftermath of the war, Jews in Germany could also rely on Allied military rabbis, as well as rabbis sent from Jewish organizations, but the deficit remained a concern.[161]

Italian Jews also struggled with a lack of religious leaders in the postwar years; the Nazis had murdered nine of Italy's twenty-one chief rabbis.[162] Small communities, in particular, were unable to find rabbis.[163] In February 1945 the UCII reopened the Rabbinical College to train desperately needed religious leaders.[164] The conversion of Israel Zolli, chief rabbi of Rome, exacerbated the crisis in religious leadership.[165] The Allies had reinstated Zolli as the chief rabbi after liberation, but most Italian Jews had lost faith in him.[166] Zolli had managed to hide during the war, leaving Roman Jews feeling abandoned, and after Rome's liberation, Zolli and the Roman community were in constant conflict.[167] Zolli and his wife were baptized in Santa Maria degli Angeli on February 13, 1945. His decision to convert seemed to have stemmed largely from his wish for revenge against the Jewish community, whom he believed had treated him poorly and unjustly after liberation.[168] Italian Jews reacted with shock and indignation to the news of the rabbi's conversion. Some became hostile, and Zolli received threatening phone calls.[169] An article published in *Israel* on February 15, 1945, condemned the rabbi's decision to convert and emphasized that his actions had angered the community.[170] David Pranzieri, the assistant rabbi of the Roman community, was elderly, frail, and deaf. In response to the desperate need for a new leader, David Prato, who had served as chief rabbi of Rome in the 1930s, returned to Italy.[171]

Perhaps it was partially due to the limited religious leadership and teaching, but neither in Italy nor in Germany did the increased importance of Jewishness lead to a drastic shift in attitudes toward religion. The Italian Jewish communities remained Orthodox after the war, although members were lenient in their religious practice. They celebrated life cycle events, attended synagogues on holidays, and were invested in rebuilding synagogues.[172] But they mostly took religious observance lightly, to the dismay of the Roman rabbi, David Prato, who criticized the lack of religious education and knowledge among the members of his community.[173]

In parts of Germany, in particular in the South, religious services changed because the mainly eastern European Jews who formed a majority in a number of the communities there preferred an Orthodox service. Before the war, liberal synagogues with German-language sermons and organ music had prevailed, but Orthodox ritual dominated postwar religious life.[174] The Orthodox service felt foreign to many German Jews who had grown up in liberal communities and caused some to live their Jewishness in the private realm.[175] Käte Hamburger, for instance, had been educated in liberal Judaism, but the Stuttgart community she joined after the war was Orthodox. She decided to be a member but did not attend synagogue services.[176]

Whereas the communities defined Jewishness as belonging to a religious community, individual Jews found myriad different ways to feel Jewish. Most Jews in Germany and Italy (as elsewhere) considered their Jewishness as more than a religion. While the Holocaust played an important role, the majority also went beyond the minimal understanding of Jewishness as the shared fate of a persecuted minority. Reasserting their self-understanding as Jewish, they emphasized different aspects, such as habits, sensibilities, and mentality; their belonging to a Jewish nation; or the importance of a shared history and culture.[177] *Der Weg* published old Jewish stories and folktales, emphasizing that these were "characteristically Jewish" and highlighting "Jewish humor."[178] The magazine *Frau in der Gemeinschaft* (Woman in the community) published a series of traditional Jewish recipes, suggesting that the "appetite for the special Jewish dishes that grandmother could make like no other is more relevant than ever in many families."[179] Italian Jews likewise expressed interest in Jewish cooking.[180]

Sometimes people's sense of being Jewish was diffuse. After years of persecution, individuals contemplated in what ways they considered themselves Jewish. In a long letter to the Jewish community, Franz Hesdörffer, a Frankfurt Jew who had survived in a "mixed marriage," pondered whether to rejoin the community he had left in the late 1930s, when he had hoped to improve the situation of his wife and children under the Nazis. Hesdörffer explained that as far as was traceable, all his ancestors had been "purely Jewish," a statement reminiscent of the Nazis' obsession with a "pure" ancestry. He also referred to the "racial togetherness" of German Jews. Hesdörffer explained that he was not religious and would feel out of place in Palestine, but on the other hand, he considered that his experiences as a "helper at the evacuation transports" and in Dachau and Theresienstadt had made him understand the "great value of religious belief for many who otherwise surely would have collapsed."[181] In the end, after corresponding further with the head of the Frankfurt community, he decided to join. For Hesdörffer Jewishness was not defined by religion but rather by shared ancestry and a shared fate.

168 | *Home after Fascism*

Like Hesdörffer, Emil Carlebach, who after his survival of Buchenwald returned to his hometown of Frankfurt, contemplated whether to join the local Jewish congregation, but he ultimately decided against it, explaining that as an atheist, he did not wish to join a group that defined itself as a religious community. At the same time, however, he did not wish to obfuscate his Jewish origin:

> Although I feel far more like a German than a Jew, I've never tried to keep my origin a secret . . . and I will not do so in the future. In the long difficult years in the camp, I believe I have shown that if necessary, I will defend with my life those threatened from fascism and antisemitism. So please do not take my rejection as "rejection," but only as an expression of ideological purity. Moreover, I stress again that I, as far as my influence allows it, will at any time be willing to defend the interests of our Jewish fellow humans [*Mitmenschen*] who have been so cruelly persecuted in the past.[182]

While friendly and respectful, Carlebach's letter shows the distance he felt from the Jewish community. In some ways similar to Hesdörffer, he understood his Jewishness as a question of origin. He also referred to his experience of persecution as an important part of his sense of belonging, or rather sense of responsibility, to the Jewish collective. Indeed, for many German as well as Italian Jews, the sense of a shared fate under Fascism and Nazism played a crucial role in their self-understanding as Jews. The writer Natalia Ginzburg held onto her sense of Jewishness in spite of her conversion to Catholicism in 1950. She defined Jewishness as a sense of solidarity with all victims of oppression.[183] A connection to Jewishness as part of a collective fight against racial oppression and Fascism, or out of solidarity with the victims of Nazi persecution, was particularly common among Communist and Socialist atheists who could not relate to Judaism as a religion.[184]

Helmut Eschwege grew up in a religious family but was also exposed to leftist ideas as a young boy, and he joined the Communist Party during his years of exile in Palestine. After his return to the Soviet occupied zone, he joined the local Jewish community even though he was not religious. In a party questionnaire, Eschwege stated his nationality as "Jewish," explaining that the experience of persecution made him regard himself as Jewish rather than German.[185] Eschwege's self-understanding as Jewish in national terms was an exception, although others shared his sense of loyalty to a Jewish collective. When Leo Zuckermann, a Jewish lawyer and member of the Communist Party and then the SED, had to justify his decision to join the Jewish community during party examinations in November 1950, he identified his solidarity with the victims as the main reason: "Of course I had not become religious or anything like this. However, the Nazi massacres of Jews, in addition to the other atrocities and the extermination of relatives had agitated me. . . . I took it at the time as an act of solidarity towards the Jewish population."[186] Journalist Hilde Eisler also joined the community after her return. She argued that being Jewish played no role in the GDR but that "there is solidarity and the feeling of belonging [among Jews], especially after the Holocaust."[187]

Other Communists with a Jewish background decided against joining the Jewish communities, such as Carlebach, who explained that as a member of the Communist Party, he struggled to reconcile membership in a religious community with his political outlook.[188] Two years after his return from England to East Germany in 1946, Siegbert Kahn published his *Antisemitismus und Rassenhetze* (antisemitism and racial hatred). In the book he laid out his position that Jews form "merely a religious community."[189] Kahn's definition matched the community's emphasis on religion as the criteria defining Jewishness, but it excluded Communist atheists like himself from the Jewish Community and depicted Communism and Jewishness as ultimately incompatible identificatory categories.

Yet Communists of Jewish origin related to their Jewishness in complex and sometimes contradictory ways. Recha Rothschild's memoir, for instance, reveals a self-understanding and self-fashioning as a German antifascist "who having long revoked religious rites, felt a member of the German people whose language she spoke and whose culture she had adopted."[190] At the same time, Rothschild writes with pride about her Jewish ancestors and her Jewish upbringing. In a semi-fictional biography, the photographer Abraham Pisarek is depicted as similarly holding onto elements of Jewishness while rejecting religion as well as Zionism after becoming a Marxist.[191] His work likewise bridges between different aspects of his self-understanding. With his photographs Pisarek chronicled the foundation of the antifascist state—his photos of the handshake of Otto Grotewohl and Wilhelm Pieck, symbolizing the merger of the SPD and KPD in 1946, are probably his most famous images. He also photographed Allied victory parades and German soldiers returning home. Yet many of his photographs depict Jewish life in postwar Germany. Pisarek took pictures of Jewish relief organizations providing food, the reopening of prayer rooms, children playing in displaced person camps, Jewish exiles returning from Shanghai, and the inauguration of early Holocaust monuments. His photographs

170 | Home after Fascism

from 1945 to 1950 create an image of the postwar years in which Jews and the rebuilding of Jewish life form a central part, in which the building of an antifascist state and a Jewish past and present coexist, and in which the Star of David stands next to antifascist symbols.

Initially, such a multifaceted self-understanding combining Jewishness and Communism seemed possible in the emerging East German state. Yet the SED leadership began to stress the mutual exclusiveness of Jewish and Communist self-understandings as the atmosphere shifted at the end of the 1940s. Kurt Goldstein remembers that Jewish Communists who returned from emigration joined Jewish communities only for a short time, since in the 1950s, the SED decided "that with an atheist world view and a political commitment to the party one could not belong to a religious community."[192] Communist Jews' relationships to their Jewish origin became a matter of interest of the Central Party Control Commission (Zentrale Parteikontrollkommission), established in 1948, which investigated, interrogated, and purged party members.[193] As in the examination of Leo Zuckermann and in the interrogation of Alexander Abusch, relation with one's Jewish origin became a central issue. Abusch, who lost all of his positions in July 1950, insisted that he had not displayed interest in Jewish questions since his eighteenth birthday. In his letter to the examining authorities, he chose an apologetic tone and stressed that he had freed himself from the "influence of Judaism" as a young man.[194] Most Communists of Jewish origin, especially if they wanted to climb the party ladder, tended to obfuscate any connection with Jewishness after 1952 and constructed life stories that emphasized distance from their Jewish background.[195] Others, like Zuckermann, left the GDR. Abraham Pisarek moved to West Berlin and turned almost exclusively to theater photography.

For those who did not want to make a political career, it was easier to combine a Communist worldview with membership in the Jewish community. While Abusch and others publicly distanced themselves from their Jewish origins, the Dutch Communist Yiddish-singing Auschwitz survivor Lin Jaldati combined antifascism and Jewishness on the stage, with not merely the approval but also the support of the East German state.[196] Similarly, other Communist Jews insisted on publicly identifying as Jewish *and* Communist and remained members of the Jewish community, despite party pressure.[197] Helmut Eschwege quarreled with both the community and the party about defining his Jewishness. The community had initially rejected his application since he did not understand Jewishness in religious terms, though they eventually admitted him, and the party, scrutinizing his questionnaire, disapproved of his self-definition as Jewish in national terms. After pressure, Eschwege renounced this self-definition, but a few weeks later, he sent a letter of complaint to the Committee for the Examination of Party Members insisting on his right to be a Jewish Communist.[198]

In West Germany and Italy, Communists and Socialists frequently combined their political outlook with a self-identification as Jewish.[199] In her Bolivian exile, Giorgina Levi immersed herself in Communist literature. She became a member of the Partito Comunista Italiano (PCI) when she returned to Italy in 1946.[200] While Levi stated that she never had "a religious belief" but rather a "profound political belief," she remained an active member of the Turin Jewish community and founded the periodical *Ha Kellilah*, which covered Jewish culture, Israel, and political life.[201] Levi saw no difficulty in combining Communism with a strong sense of Jewishness, and she did not see any difficulties in being an Italian patriot and a Jew. She described her aunt Rita Montagnana a member of the Italian Communist Party since its foundation and the wife of PCI leader Palmiro Togliatti, as similarly holding onto her Jewishness: "Despite her long exile . . . Rita . . . had never forgotten her Turin dialect and her Jewish identity. Sometimes she was pleased to remember Hebrew words, she was troubled at the sight of the miserable conditions of the Jews of Riga in 1921; it was she who Hebraicized her first granddaughter's name Enrichetta to Rivkà (Rebecca)."[202] Natalia Ginzburg linked Jewishness to the need to support all who were marginalized and oppressed and considered the Communist party as the best expression for this self-understanding as a Jew. Similarly, the journalist Sergio Camillo Segre explained that his Jewishness and his experience of persecution motivated his becoming a Communist.[203] For these Jewish Communists, Communism and Jewishness remained intertwined, rather than contradictory aspects of their self-perception.

Zionism

Few Italian or German Jews became more religious after the war, yet they found other ways to express Jewishness. Above all, advocating Zionism took on an important role.[204] Most Jews in Italy and Germany fervently supported the creation of a Jewish homeland in Palestine, considering it both a necessity for the many refugees as well as a precaution for the future. For some, even if they continued to live in Europe, the Holocaust had

172 | *Home after Fascism*

challenged the perception of Europe as a successful locus of Jewish existence. "The events proved Zionism and its followers right," wrote Georg Glücksstern in *Der Weg* in March 1946. Enthusiastic advocates of the Zionist project among the DPs, Jewish soldiers, and representatives of aid organizations likewise contributed to this strengthening of Zionism after the war.

Jewish Brigade soldiers who were stationed in Northern Italy at the end of the war and arrived in Germany by the summer of 1945 spread the Zionist message among the DPs and the local Jewish populations. They provided Zionist educational activities and aided in people's often-illegal immigration to Palestine.[205] In total about nine thousand Jewish soldiers arrived in Italy between 1943 and 1945.[206] Young Jewish Italians felt intrigued by the sight of Jewish soldiers and listened eagerly to their message of the "promised land."[207] More strongly than the older generation, they felt a need to redefine themselves after the war, and the project of building a Jewish state offered a path to self-transformation.[208] The soldiers paid particular attention to young people and helped establish schools, youth centers, scout troops, and *hachsharoth* (agricultural training camps), with the aim to plant the Zionist message and convince young people to emigrate to Palestine.[209] Eugenia Servi remembered that leaving for Palestine became an important topic of debate among her friends in the aftermath of the war. Feeling lost and estranged, she herself considered emigrating: "Perhaps that was the task that awaited me, to collaborate in the reconstruction of the State of Israel. In Palestine I would certainly find my natural environment, my identity, a purpose for living."[210] But none of her family members shared her feelings; they perceived Israel as an unrealistic utopian adventure, and her parents told her not to leave. Other young Jews likewise faced their parents' disapproval when considering immigration to Palestine.

Leone Diena, who saw himself as representative of the attitudes of young, middle-class Italian Jews, embraced Zionism after the war. Diena, a Socialist who had joined the resistance, emphasized his distance from Jewish religion as well as his general disdain of nationalism but argued in an article from June 1946 that he supported Zionism because of the need to provide for Jewish refugees and also because, as a minority, Jews were not able to live freely in the diaspora.[211] Yet Diena, as well as many others, while supportive of the idea, did not immigrate to Palestine. The Jewish Brigade soldiers were disappointed that while they seemed to influence young Italians, few actually left Italy.[212]

By contrast, Dan Vittorio Segre had already immigrated to Palestine before the war. He returned to Italy as a member of the Jewish Brigade and there reunited with his father, who had opposed Zionism. In Segre's depiction their meeting reflects the generational conflict and cements the success of Zionism over diaspora nationalism, though his father may have depicted it differently:

> We had both emerged unscathed from the same conflict, in which he had lost his country, Italy, and I had found a new one, Israel. I had returned home a victor in a foreign uniform; he, having survived six years of civilian ignominy and two hiding in the mountains, had witnessed the defeat of his country. Humiliated by the King he had personally served, persecuted by the Fascist regime to whose creation he had contributed, he had no other reason for pride if not in my participation in the Zionist cause which he had tenaciously opposed as an Italian nationalist.[213]

In the 1920s and 1930s, opposition to or at least distance from Zionism had been common in Italian Jewish communities since both the Fascist press as well as government representatives accused Zionists of disloyalty.[214] After the war, as in Segre's depiction here, many former supporters of Fascism and virulent anti-Zionists reconsidered their position. The leadership of the Italian Jewish community underwent significant changes, as those who had supported Fascism became untenable as leaders after the war. Dante Almansi, for instance, president of the Union of Italian Jewish Communities from 1939 to 1945, was forced out because of his Fascist past.

Yet while Fascism was discredited beyond doubt, not all immediately embraced Zionism; the fights of the 1930s over the direction of the communities lingered for a little while. On June 10, 1944, a few days after Rome's liberation, a group named Jewish Italian Action (Azione ebraica italiana) distributed a flyer that emphasized that "the fatherland of the Italians of Jewish religion—IS ITALY—those who do not feel this absolute imperative cannot be considered Italians; they will only be able to live in Italy as members of another nationality"[215] The flyer reveals that some Italian Jews continued to see Zionism as incompatible with Italian nationalism and illustrates the deep-seated fears that its promotion would prove dangerous to successful reintegration, leading to a surge in antisemitism. Others shared such sentiments. In an angry letter to the Roman Jewish community, one of its members, Sergio Bondi, complained about a meeting of young Jews in front of the synagogue in Via Balbo that aimed, according to him, to "bring the greatest possible mass of young people into contact with Zionism."

174 | *Home after Fascism*

Bondi took offense to several speeches given at the occasion that expressed views such as "our homeland is Palestine." He questioned whether the young people had any authorization to carry on their meeting in the space that belonged to the community and voiced his fear that they might harm Italian Jews' public image:

> I want to point out that at a time when the free Italian press reopens its arms to all Italian Jews . . . creating and flaunting a Jewish hyper-nationalism seems to me at least inappropriate. If Jews feel themselves as such not only from a religious perspective, but also from a national viewpoint, they may hold their meetings in a non-official way, and not affect, at such a delicate moment, the position of all those who feel themselves Italians of the Jewish religion, who intend to give to their homeland Italy without hesitation their modest social and, if possible, also military contribution.[216]

Some among the leadership also initially felt hesitant about an overt embrace of Zionism. Giuseppe Nathan, extraordinary commissioner of the Union of Italian Jewish Communities, warned in a meeting of community representatives in July 1945 that the Union of Italian Jewish Communities should not officially embrace Zionism but rather needed to obtain a clearly Italian national character since they depended on the Italian government.[217] In contrast, Raffaele Cantoni constructed a self-understanding that both perceived Zionism as an essential aspect of Jewishness and stressed its compatibility with belonging to Italy: "There is no need to pose the question of Zionism or not Zionism because it goes without saying that a community leader must feel the Zionist problem as a Jew must feel it, even if he is Italian and meets all his duties as an Italian citizen."[218] The election of David Prato as chief rabbi of the Roman Jewish community in April 1945 strengthened the Zionist position. In an open letter to Italian Jews, Prato fiercely promoted the idea of Italian Jews' return to Palestine—if not physically, at least spiritually.[219] Prato published his call to Zionism in the weekly newspaper *Israel*, a traditional organ of Italian Zionism that resumed publication in 1944. Editor Carlo Alberto Viterbo provided Jewish leaders such as Prato and Cantoni with a platform to advocate for Zionism and call Italian Jews to support the community in Palestine/Israel.[220] Soon anti-Zionist notions became irrelevant among the postwar leadership.[221]

Italian Jews reacted enthusiastically to the news of the UN's adoption of a resolution recommending the implementation of a partition plan of Mandatory Palestine on November 29, 1947. The journal *Israel* dedicated a jubilant special edition to the news, and in December 1947, Jews in Rome organized a rally and celebrated by passing under the Arch of Titus. Legend had banned Jews from walking under the arch, which had been erected in 81 CE to celebrate the sacking of Jerusalem and the destruction of the temple. The Jewish march underneath the arch symbolized the return of the Jewish people to their homeland.[222] When the state of Israel was officially founded in May 1948, the celebrations continued. Fabrizio Roccas, a Roman Jew, remembered, "When the state of Israel was proclaimed, there was a strong emotion [among Jews]; it was an event that has changed the lives of all Jews: this event has lifted the uncertainty that surrounded us for centuries."[223]

While they greeted the foundation of the state in Israel with euphoria, few Italian Jews wished to emigrate. In their eyes Israel remained a faraway country with an unbearable climate.[224] Moreover, the difficult economic situation in Israel, in contrast to Italy's recovering economy, made emigration unappealing.[225] Historian Bernard Wasserstein assumes that between 1948 and 1951, 1,305 Italians moved to Israel, and Sergio Della Pergola estimates the number of emigrants between 1944 and 1951 to be 2,084.[226] Overall, the initial enthusiasm over Zionism spurred by the presence of the Jewish Brigade and the foundation of the state appeared to wane in the early 1950s. Community leaders complained about the indifference of their constituents toward Zionism.[227] A Joint official described the gap between the leading figures of Italian Jewry and most Italian Jews, who ultimately remained fairly unimpressed by Zionism, suggesting that "a course should be steered midway between the enthusiastic Zionism of its leadership and the extreme lethargy of the bulk of the community."[228]

Italian philologist Cesare Segre, born in 1928, recalled how the Jewish Brigade soldiers had inspired him as a young man. But looking back at his life, he emphasized how short lived his attachment to Zionism, and more broadly to Jewishness, had been:

> There was, for a short time, a completely different life, which certainly constituted a self-contained stratum. It was the recovery of Judaism, which was intense for all those who had survived the Shoah. . . . I thought . . . that only there [in Israel] I would have been able to raise a family, something which seemed madness in the Europe of the concentration camps. . . . If I didn't allow myself to be seduced it's because, despite everything, the ties with Europe and Italy are, for me, unquestionable; I know by now, from experience, that any country can take away your nationality even if you live there, like my family, for centuries and centuries, but I want to stay here as long as humanly possible.[229]

176 | *Home after Fascism*

Segre's choice of words—he did not allow himself to be "seduced"—points to his later conviction that Zionism and a move to Israel would have been foolish. For a while Segre participated in activities the Jewish communities organized for young people, but he, "soon [I] said goodbye to the Jewish circles. Now I only have very sporadic contacts."[230]

Like Segre, other Italian Jews also positioned their Italianness above a self-identification as Zionists. They saw themselves primarily as Italians, as "citizens like all the others,"[231] and had little intention of leaving Italy for the "Jewish homeland." Roberto Milano explained his and his wife's attitudes: "We never had this feeling of Zionism, and still are of the view that in reality the Jews, after so many generations in the country in which they live, have more of an Italian culture, a Latin culture, than a Jewish culture."[232] Milano's statement highlights the emotional nature of belonging—he *felt* Italian, more than Jewish or Zionist. While many Italian Jews supported Zionism financially and the Italian Zionist Federation grew significantly in the postwar period, Italian Jews by and large perceived this as a means to help Jews in other countries.[233] Zionism also played a role as a secular expression of Jewishness, but it did not supplant their sense of *national* belonging to Italy.

Patriotism ran deep among Italian Jews. Even fierce Zionists believed in the importance of rebuilding Jewish life in Italy. The Zionist journal *Israel*, for instance, published numerous articles dedicated to the reconstruction and rebuilding of Jewish life in Italy. Support for Zionism did not go as far as to ask Italian Jews to leave their home country and start new lives in Palestine/Israel, and Italian Zionists often remained deeply invested in developments in Italy. Rabbi David Prato returned when the community was in need, even though he would have preferred to remain in Palestine. Another Zionist, Hebrew scholar Augusto Segre, son of a rabbi from Casale Monferrato, eventually immigrated to Israel in the late 1970s. In his memoirs he explained his decision to remain in Italy in the immediate aftermath of the war: "The small Italian Jewish world, which was torn to pieces by the war, awaited the active commitment of every survivor. Maybe I was fooling myself once again; but I felt the duty of forgoing my many dreams of Erez Israel—at least temporarily. . . . Proceeding in this way, I felt above all, was fulfilling a moral obligation toward so many friends with whom I had shared risks and dangers and who had died in the Nazi camps or fallen fighting for freedom during the Resistance."[234] His sense of owing his loyalties to the Italian Jewish community, intertwined with a strong belief in the resistance, made him push his Zionism temporarily aside.

In some ways Jews in West Germany resembled Italian Jews in their attitudes to Zionism. They supported the foundation of a Jewish state enthusiastically, but relatively few chose to emigrate. However, the distinct position of the German community in the Jewish world after the war, as well as German Jews' fraught relationship with their German homeland, made for a different discourse. Anti-Zionist voices played no role in German Jewish postwar discussions; most had distanced themselves too much from Germany to see a potential accusation of disloyalty as a concern. Yet German Jews struggled with being accepted as Zionists within the broader international community. The widespread disapproval of the existence of Jews in Germany often led to hostile reactions to German Jews' Zionist efforts, particularly after the foundation of Israel in 1948. The World Zionist Organization refused to admit the German Zionist Organization among its members, and the Jewish National Fund (Keren Kayemet LeYisrael) initially rejected donations from Germany.[235] The pressures to leave what many thought of as the country of murderers intensified after 1948. The Jewish Agency published a manifesto addressing Jews in Germany, stating their concerns and concluding with a plea for them to leave the country.[236] Articles in German Jewish papers evoked the end of the diaspora and hopes for the day "of the final return of the entire Jewish people to their own country Israel."[237] But most Jews who had resettled in Germany did not leave for Israel.[238]

While Italian Jews aimed to show that their support of Zionism did not minimize their patriotism for Italy, Jews in West Germany needed to prove that their living in Germany did not diminish their Zionism and thus their belonging to a transnational Jewish collective. The latter tried to assert their belonging to a group that largely rejected their life choices, resulting in feelings of guilt and intense efforts to prove themselves. Public discourse within the press, as well as speeches, articles, and letters of Jewish representatives, highlighted German Jews' emotional attachment and absolute loyalty toward Israel. After 1948 German Jews in the West contributed considerable effort and time to raise funds for the newly founded state.[239] Being supportive of Israel became a crucial part of their self-understanding. Some spoke of one day moving there or hoped their children would emigrate, while others perceived Israel as their emotional or true home.[240]

At the onset of the Arab-Israeli War of 1948, Julius Dreifuss, head of the Düsseldorf community, called on members to support the Jews fighting in Palestine: "As far as we have young people they too must be mobilized

178 | *Home after Fascism*

to *fight for our country*. We others have to join the line of defense and show that we are willing to sacrifice everything that helps us realize our most desired goal. . . . Remember the 6 million dead we would not have lost if we had had a Jewish state."[241] People's willingness to die for their country shows the depth of emotional attachments to the national community; what Anderson terms " a deep, horizontal comradeship."[242] As discussed, few German Jews felt such fraternity to other Germans, but the discourse of community leaders such as Dreifuss constructed, in theory at least, a deep comradeship with Israeli Jews.

Yet when it came to concrete life choices, individual Jews judged the matter differently. Wolfgang Hildesheimer, who as a Jewish Palestinian citizen probably felt considerable pressure to leave Germany and return to Palestine, defended his choice to stay in a letter to his parents: "I certainly think it's great that the youth in Palestine would rather die than give up the idea of their country, but I also do not know if that's right; I don't want to have a country, and I am not in favor of dying. I am in favor of life and as long as I live, I won't give up my hope for a better humanity. . . . I think it is perfectly right that the Jews want to and must have a state for themselves. But I would not like to work for it."[243] Hildesheimer, while supportive of the Zionist project, emphasized his universal, humanist outlook. Individual Jews had a more complex relationships with Zionism than the expressions of absolute loyalty that dominated the public discourse within West German Jewish communities.

In East Germany there was no similar public embrace of Zionism. Many Jews with close ties to Communism had a more critical stance toward the newly founded state, and political realities in the GDR soon made it difficult to openly embrace a pro-Israeli attitude. Initially, however, there had been little reason to assume that Jewish enthusiasm for the Zionist project would be a problem in the Soviet occupied zone. In the immediate aftermath of the war, the Soviet Union still supported the foundation of a Jewish state in Palestine, and in 1948 the Jewish communities in the SBZ celebrated its foundation.[244] Yet soon after its foundation, the GDR, following the Soviet Union, adopted a hostile stance toward Israel. While the flag of the newly found state flew visibly in official memorial events in the late 1940s, it was no longer displayed outside the Jewish community after 1950.[245] During the 1952 purges, Zionism became one of the main charges.[246]

Jewish communities in the GDR avoided public statements about Israel, and on a practical level, the hostility toward Israel caused difficulties for

GDR citizens who wished to visit their relatives.[247] Individual Jews voiced ambivalent attitudes. Victor Klemperer had been opposed to Zionism before the rise of Nazism and remained so after 1945.[248] After 1948 he became exceedingly critical of the newly founded state. He compared Israel's attitude toward the Arab population with Nazism, and while he concluded that there "are graduations of Dantean hells and Auschwitz was the ultimate of such depths of hell," he maintained, without going into detail, that the Jews had gotten rather close and that "especially as Jews they should not."[249] Klemperer argued that their experiences should have made Jews more aware of and more sympathetic toward the suffering of others.[250] Helmut Eschwege shared the critique of Israeli politics but he also protested against the GDR's often antisemitic attacks on the Israeli state.[251] While in exile in Palestine the writer Arnold Zweig had become increasingly disillusioned with the Zionist idea. Still, he did not wish to entirely discredit Zionism, and he argued that there was an "idealistic element" within the movement "that is still pulsating and throbbing among the Israeli people today."[252]

Conclusion

In contrast to other prominent Jews in the GDR, Zweig continued to affirm his Jewish background, which he did not perceive as counteracting but rather as mutually constitutive with his Socialism and antifascism.[253] Other Jews in Germany found it more difficult to combine different categories of identification. In the GDR contradictions in the state's policy toward its Jewish minority complicated Jews' relationship with both their Jewish origins as well as with their self-understanding as Communists. In West Germany some felt it was no longer possible to be both Jewish and German. The widespread condemnation of Jewish life in Germany within the international Jewish community exacerbated such feelings, and some defended their self-understanding as German facing a critical public. West German Jews felt pressure to show their attachment to Zionism, even if they had no wish to emigrate, while in East Germany, some kept their admiration for the Jewish state quiet.

Some Jews in Germany felt they did not belong anywhere. Victor Klemperer entitled his diary of the years 1945–1959 "Between the chairs" (*Zwischen den Stühlen*), emphasizing the sense of not fitting in.[254] Using similar words, the writer Karl Jakob Hirsch, who used the pseudonym Joe Gassner, described himself in a letter to a friend in 1948 as a "sick, helpless

180 | *Home after Fascism*

old man, sitting between all chairs, named J.G. Unpopular with both Jews and Christians."[255] After his return from the United States in the immediate aftermath of the war, Hirsch had hoped to resume his career as a writer, but he had little success and grew increasingly disappointed and frustrated.[256] Neither self-identified strongly as Jewish, and the memories of Nazi persecution troubled their relationships with other Germans. These examples illustrate how some Jewish returnees continued to feel displaced after the end of the war. Even though no longer persecuted, they still inhabited what Edward Said has termed "the perilous territory of not-belonging."[257] Alienation, in these cases, became an ongoing condition; an otherness that could be negotiated but not resolved.

Jews in Italy generally found it easier to combine different aspects of their self-understanding. Their identities as Italian and Jewish remained intertwined, rather than contrasting, aspects of their self-understanding. They remained Italian patriots in spite of Fascist persecution, were Zionists without ever wanting to move to Palestine/Israel, and attended Orthodox synagogue services while never considering eating kosher. Persecution made them more aware of their difference, and some felt greater solidarity with Jews in Italy and abroad, but in most cases, the Holocaust did not break their self-understanding as Italians who were also Jewish. Fractures in Italian Jews' sense of belonging to the nation caused by their persecution under Fascism are visible only with scrutiny, in the fear of once again being accused of disloyalty and in a greater distance to the state and its institutions.

CONCLUSION

The Old House and Its Shadows

HANS JACOBUS GREW UP IN BERLIN. LOOKING BACK at his childhood, he remembers his grandparents' house, the meals his grandmother prepared, and the hot chocolate they used to drink. But he also depicts how he had to move school, how his grandfather lost his business, and how they became poorer and increasingly frightened. In 1938, then fifteen-year-old Hans left Berlin with a Kindertransport. His mother, grandfather, and aunt did not survive.[1] In 1947, Hans Jacobus returned to his hometown. He remembered asking himself "if and how we could live and help here—after all that had happened."[2] Jacobus stayed in Berlin, made a career as a journalist, joined the SED, and saw the wall fall in 1989. He found a way "to live and help," but he did not forget. His grandparents' house still stood when he returned in 1947, but he no longer had any pictures of them. In 2002 the then seventy-nine-year-old Jacobus went to the archives to find out more about his family's fate. He learned that his mother had been denounced when riding the streetcar, covering the yellow star on her coat. She was punished with deportation to the Lodz ghetto and was sent there together with her sister and father. Jacobus's how could we live here? dominated much of German Jewish discourse in the immediate aftermath of the war. Jews looking in from the outside could not fathom the decisions of those who chose to remain in or return to Germany. Many who returned had doubts. Still, they lived in Germany and increasingly asserted their right to feel at home there.

In 1996 Israeli president Ezer Weizmann asked German Jewish students during a visit how Jews could still live in Germany after the Holocaust. The students protested his question and the underlying assumptions: the notion that Jews should not and could not live in the "country of perpetrators" had lost much of its validity.[3] What had once seemed unthinkable had become acceptable, and German Jews responded more confidently to those questioning their belonging.[4] German Jews' relationship to their home country changed after living in Germany for decades and witnessing the process of democratization.[5] In particular the so-called second generation of younger

182 | *Home after Fascism*

Jews promoted different views when it came to questions such as intermarriage or loyalty to Israel, and living in Germany assumed a more positive meaning for them.

While Jews continued to live in Germany, the dream of the Socialist state that Communists of Jewish origin hoped to build in the eastern part of the country ended abruptly in 1989.[6] For most of them, the fall of the wall came as a disappointment.[7] Asked about the collapse of the state in which she had invested so much, Hilde Eisler replied, "Of course I am sad it has come to this. We had believed in the idea of building a democratic, better, actually more just, humanistic Germany. That was the reason the people returned. That was the great hope of the people who came from the KZs, who were persecuted as antifascists. Naturally, it's a great defeat, a defeat we have suffered. We have to live with that."[8] East German Jews like Eisler now felt forced to become part of a country that they perceived critically. While Eisler had previously understood herself as a "GDR Jew," she still identified as Jewish, but not as German, after 1989.[9]

The year 1989 brought significant change for the wider German Jewish community, in both East and West Germany. After the opening of Soviet borders, a large number of Russian Jews moved to Germany. This immigration of Jews from the Soviet Union brought challenges as well as opportunities. Communities struggled with the integration of the newcomers; at the same time, the influx reinvigorated Jewish life in Germany. Mainly due to this immigration wave, Germany's Jewish community now numbers over one hundred thousand members.[10] Other Jews, among them an increasing number of young Israelis—estimates range from three thousand to twenty thousand, including some who reclaimed the citizenship their grandparents had lost—live in Germany outside the official Jewish community.[11] Whereas the Jewish population in most European countries decreased in the last five decades, the German Jewish population has grown significantly.[12] In 2003 the head of the Munich Jewish community, Charlotte Knobloch, declared on the occasion of setting the cornerstone for the new Jewish community center, "Today I feel I came home—and can finally unpack my bags."[13]

In the same year, the construction of the Memorial to the Murdered Jews of Europe began in Berlin. The monument was inaugurated in May 2005. Public memory of the Holocaust had changed significantly since the end of the war.[14] The Eichmann trial in 1961 and the subsequent Auschwitz trial triggered debates around German guilt, and media events such as the 1978 soap opera *Holocaust: The Story of Family Weiss* led to a greater awareness of the murder of the European Jews. Yet the fierce discussions during the *Historikerstreit* ("historians' dispute") in the late 1980s and around the Wehrmacht exhibition in the mid-1990s proved the persistent reluctance within the population to confront German guilt. The Holocaust has assumed a central role in Germany's national narrative, and Germans publicly commemorate the victims. Still, a reckoning with guilt and implication remains rare, and in the past decade, voices that claim a surfeit of memory and push for moving away from commemorating the Holocaust have become louder.[15] The electoral success of the Alternative für Deutschland in 2017—the first Far Right party to enter the German parliament since 1945—troubled German Jews.[16] Following an attack on a synagogue in Halle in October 2019, historian Michael Brenner published an article in the *Sueddeutsche Zeitung* suggesting it may be time to consider packing the proverbial suitcases.[17] While the rise of a populist Right and an increase in antisemitic attacks are not merely German problems, the country's past heightens the sense of threat.

In contrast to Germany Italy saw a decrease of the numbers of members in its Jewish communities over the postwar years despite the arrival of a few thousand Libyan and Persian Jews in the late 1960s. The community today counts about twenty-seven thousand members.[18] Despite the membership numbers slightly decreasing, Italian Jewish leaders believe in the strength of their community. They see a rise in cultural activities, which builds on the long history of Jews in Italy, and they emphasize the amicable relationship Italian Jews have with their non-Jewish neighbors.[19] Indeed a recent study that combined polling data and policy information to assess life quality for Jews in various European countries has placed Italy first on its list.[20]

Economic reasons, rather than fear of antisemitism, drive young Italian Jews' to consider emigration as high unemployment rates cause them to seek opportunities elsewhere.[21] Yet while most do not consider antisemitism a reason to leave the country, Italian Jews have been troubled by a rise of hostilities.[22] Studies by the Institute for Jewish Policy Research and the Milan-based Centro di Documentazione Ebraica Contemporanea (Center of Contemporary Jewish Documentation) suggest that contemporary antisemitism cuts across the political spectrum and relies on new as well as old stereotypes.[23]

Catholic antisemitism remains present, even though relations with the Catholic Church have improved over the course of the twentieth century. In

1965, the Second Vatican Council issued a declaration on the relation of the church with non-Christian religions (*Nostrae Aetate*), which changed the Roman Catholic Church's traditional teachings about Judaism and marked the church's partial effort to disavow antisemitism. Antisemitism has also taken on new forms. Since 1967 the Israeli-Palestinian conflict has fueled antisemitic sentiments in Italy and elsewhere in Europe. In Rome, a terrorist attack during the 1982 Lebanon War on the city's synagogue killed two-year-old Stefano Taché and injured several others. The attack triggered a press campaign that pushed Italian Jews to sever their connection to Israel and brought back accusations of disloyalty. Individual Italian Jews held different positions regarding Israel's war in Lebanon, but, independent of their view, they were frequently blamed for Israeli politics.[24]

As in Germany, the end of the Cold War reshaped the Italian political landscape. With the crisis of the political system between 1992 and 1994, following a corruption scandal known as *Tangentopoli*, the country's main political parties either lost their influence or disappeared entirely. The election of Silvio Berlusconi as prime minister in 1994 brought new impetus to revisionist perspectives of the Fascist past.[25] While the resistance lost its importance, the Holocaust gained a more central role in Italy's cultural memory.[26]

The status of the Holocaust within Italian memory had already begun to shift in response to events such as the Eichmann trial and the screening of the TV series *Holocaust*. These, as well as a number of Italian films and books, contributed to the growth of public awareness of the Shoah, though they did not lead to a reconsideration of Italy's role in the persecution.[27] Indeed, the 1986 documentary by Nicola Caracciolo, *Il coraggio e la pietà: Gli ebrei e l'Italia durante la guerra 1940–1945* (The Courage and the Pity: The Jews and Italy during the War of 1940–1945)—in contrast to its French counterpart, *Le chagrin et la pitié* (The Sorrow and the Pity)—affirmed postwar myths of Italians' benevolent and courageous conduct.[28] A critical reassessment of Italian Fascism eventually came from historians. Starting in 1988 with the fiftieth anniversary of the racial legislation, a younger generation of Italian historians began to challenge prevailing misconceptions about the legislation as well as the army's conduct in the colonies and occupied territories during the Second World War.[29]

In 2000 Italy introduced a national Holocaust memorial day, the so-called *Giorno della memoria* (day of memory), set on January 27, the liberation of Auschwitz.[30] The law instituting the memorial day both openly acknowledges "the Italian persecution of Jewish citizens" and highlights the role of Italian rescuers, naming the people who "opposed the extermination project and, risking their own lives, saved others, and protected the persecuted," among those who should be remembered.[31] The 2000s saw an acceleration in public commemoration of the Holocaust, marked not only by the increase of public events and media attention but also with plans for three Jewish Museums. In the early 2000s Rome's City Council approved plans for the construction of a national Museum of the Shoah. However, political controversy and other difficulties delayed the completion of the project.[32] In the meantime the *Museo Nazionale dell'Ebraismo Italiano e della Shoah* (National Museum of Italian Judaism and the Shoah) opened its doors in Ferrara in 2017.[33] Milan inaugurated its Shoah Memorial four years earlier, in 2013. The *Memoriale della Shoah* is located at the underground platform within the city's Central Station from where the Jewish deportees were loaded onto trains.

One of them was Liliana Segre, who was deported to Auschwitz when she was just thirteen years old. In 2018 President Sergio Mattarella named Segre Senator for Life, and it was in this role that Segre chaired the opening session of the Italian Senate of the parliament on October 13, 2022, after Italians had elected the most right-wing government since World War Two the previous month. In her speech Segre, deeply aware of the symbolic value of her role in this historic moment, recalled the 1938 racial laws, spoke of Giacomo Matteotti, the Socialist who was killed by the Fascists in 1924, and emphasized the importance of the *Festa della Liberazione* (Liberation Day), which commemorates the victory of the Italian resistance.[34] Segre thus set her speech within an antifascist framework.

A few weeks later, Giorgia Meloni, the newly elected far-right Prime Minister whose party, Brothers of Italy, has neo-fascist roots, likewise recalled the racial laws—depicting them as "the worst moment in Italian history."[35] Thus, Meloni joins the effort of other Italian right-wing leaders to distance themselves from antisemitism in order to legitimize the far-right.[36] Unlike Segre, Meloni did not refer to the resistance against Fascism in her speech, rather highlighting the threat of "totalitarianism" and the political violence of the 1970s.[37] Meloni thus set the racial laws within a broader frame of political violence committed from both sides of the political spectrum, erasing the historic specificity of Fascist violence.

Liliana Segre is part of a generation of Italian Jews whose perception of the past was impacted by an antifascist narrative that while never

186 | *Home after Fascism*

all-encompassing dominated public discourse in the aftermath of the war. Now, as Italy commemorates the centenary of the Fascist seizure of power, what has been termed the "anti-fascist paradigm" has lost much of its power.[38] The myth of the good Italian, the other pillar on which much of postwar Italian memory rested, appears more stable. Scholars of Italian Memory culture, such as Luisa Passerini and Filippo Focardi, have emphasized the strength and longevity of the myth though they also see some shifts in recent years.[39] Historians, but also contemporary Italian writers, address Fascist crimes, and both the Jewish and non-Jewish press have picked up such efforts to dismantle the myth of the good Italian. Still, both among Jews and non-Jews, in Italy and abroad, a belief that Italy was a safe haven for Jews, and that the Germans alone are to blame for the persecution remains common.[40]

The narrative of the good Italian crucially shaped the Italian postwar experience. Italians having "merely" been collaborators in the Holocaust made the construction of the myth possible. An understanding of the past that depicted the population as united in its resistance against the Nazi occupier, enabled Italian Jews in the immediate aftermath of the war to feel at home after violent exclusion. They framed their own experiences as part of a larger Italian story of war and suffering and the postwar years as a return to the true Italy. Many held onto a narrative that inserted their story within a narrative of resistance against Fascism, assuming the role of defenders of the nation rather than that of victims of its hostilities. For the majority of Italian Jews, their persistent attachment to their homeland pushed aside concerns about the past.

Silvia Lombroso, who survived in hiding in Italy while her children had escaped to the United States, wrote about the impossibility of disconnecting herself from her home: "The *patria*, even when you wrench yourself from her in order to survive, stays with you, strong, subtle, beyond suspicion; because your country is a nostalgia which assails you when you least expect it . . . your country is you, and your youth, it is the woman you have loved, and the old house and its shadows . . . the sweet rhythm of everyday life, it is the voice of things."[41] In the end, her love for and nostalgic memories of her home outweighed the memories of persecution.

Survival of the *home of memory* depended on the construction of postwar narratives; nostalgic feelings toward home could be retained within the vague and malleable conceptions of the true Italy or the other Germany, which promised that Fascism and Nazism could not alter or touch their essence. Because of Germany's overwhelming responsibility for the genocide and the country's inability or unwillingness to confront its past in the aftermath of the war, holding onto this notion of the other Germany proved difficult. The writer Hermann Kesten, who at the end of his life considered himself a lifelong emigrant, looked back to his postwar hopes: "We had not been emigrants.... We all had hoped to return to a better Germany, but for many it had, after all, been difficult to discover this better Germany."[42] Kesten, though he frequently visited the country, never returned. While most Italian Jews claimed the survival of their home of memory within the true Italy, German Jews by and large considered the home they remembered as destroyed or tainted beyond recognition.

By narrating and partially silencing the past, surviving Jews shaped their postwar relationship to their home countries. Italian Jews' efforts to fit their memories within a narrative of Italian resistance and depict a shared, national history of Italian suffering placed them squarely within the national community. By comparison, for most Jews in Germany the recent past created an unbridgeable rift with their home. Some Communists of Jewish origin who returned to the eastern part of the country constructed a shared past of antifascist resistance that de-emphasized the particularity of their own fate as persecuted Jews. In all three postwar states Jews thus positioned themselves vis-à-vis and aimed to shape larger, national narratives. Narratives spun above as well as below the national level likewise affected how individual Jews could tell their story.[43] Italian community leaders and cultural elites promoted the brava gente myth, while the German Jewish press and leadership criticized and pushed back against Germans' claims of innocence. While international Jewish organization supported the narrative of the good Italian, German Jews faced widespread disapproval of their choice to live in the country of murderers. German Jews who wanted to return home after the war were told that their home was destroyed or that it had never existed.

Two decades after liberation, the German-born scholar Gershom Scholem commented in an article on Jewish German relations that German Jews' sense of home had been a delusion:

> The fact that he [the German Jew] was not really at home, however much and emphatically he might proclaim himself to be—the "homelessness" which today is sometimes accounted to his glory, in that it is taken as an image of the *condition humaine* —constituted, at a time when alienation was still a term of abuse, a powerful accusation. And it is in keeping with so distorted a state of

188 | *Home after Fascism*

> affairs that the great majority of Jews, and especially those who had the highest degree of awareness, concurred in this judgment of their situation; this is why, in the very teeth of the skepticism, which was a part of their German environment, they aspired to or claimed a deep attachment to all things German, and a sense of being at home.... By and large, then, the love affair of the Jews and the Germans remained one-sided and unreciprocated; at best it awakened something like compassion.[44]

Scholem, a Zionist who had immigrated to Palestine in 1923, looked at the question of belonging from a particular viewpoint.[45] Most Jews who returned to Germany after 1945 did not see their past attachment to Germany as a delusion. While many could no longer love their home country, they did not discount the love they had felt in the past. Rather, they described Germany before the Nazis as idyllic and emphasized their strong attachment and the lack of hostilities between Jews and non-Jews before the rise of Nazism.[46] Rabbi Max Eschelbacher, who had immigrated to England but frequently visited Germany after the war, pointed out that "we really had once a home here, later it became the cruelest disappointment of our lives."[47] Most believed that their home had been destroyed, not that it had never existed. But this idealized home of memories was no longer attainable as a physical space.

Memories of Germany's crimes made it difficult for German Jews to feel or express attachment, and the widespread disapproval of Jewish life in Germany further exacerbated feelings of distance.[48] Among German Jews, love for their homeland remained outside their emotional community's "norms of emotional expression and value."[49] Still, there remained myriad ways in which they felt German. A sense of Germanness was not limited to patriotic expressions of an unqualified love for the fatherland. German Jews continued to feel attached to landscapes, language, and culture. Such niches of belonging allowed them to express their attachment to these specific remnants of home and create some continuity between their past and their present.

Belonging to a place and a larger community provides comfort and security; it also affects our sense of self. Our language and culture play a role in making us who we are. The attachment to home runs deep, and its loss is traumatic. While physical return after displacement was possible for German and Italian Jews, the re-creation of a sense of home proved, in many cases—mainly for German Jews but also for some Italian Jews—complicated and sometimes impossible. The effort Italian Jews put into declaring Fascism an exception in Italian history, freeing fellow Italians from blame, and playing down Italian collaboration, as well as German Jews' wish to rebuild, make a new home, resurrect some remnants of their previous lives, reclaim German culture from the Nazis, and find a space of belonging, need to be understood in this context. After all, as Jean Améry observed, "it is not good to have no home."[50]

NOTES

Introduction

1. See Geve, *Es gibt hier keine Kinder*; also ibid, *The Boy Who Drew Auschwitz*.
2. Thomas Geve, email to the author, May 10, 2019.
3. The Israeli writer Aharon Appelfeld raises this question in his *To the Edge of Sorrow*. At the end of the novel a survivor asks a partisan, Felix, where they should go now. "Home, he answers right away. 'Which home?' asks the survivor. 'There's only one home we grew up in and loved, and we're returning to it.' The survivor is astonished by Felix's answer. A smile, thin and unintended, spreads across his face." Thus, the novel ends and the reader never learns where exactly this home is and whether the Jewish survivors can return to it. See Appelfeld, *To the Edge of Sorrow*, 291.
4. Winterfeldt, *Deutschland*, 417. Unless otherwise noted, translations all are mine.
5. Bauer, "Una Vita Segnata," 19; see also conversation with Goti Bauer at "Goti Bauer," Fondazione Memoriale della Shoah di Milano, http://www.memorialeshoah.it/goti-bauer /?lang=en. Accessed December 28, 2022.
6. On German Jews' reactions to the rise of Nazism, see Miron, "Emancipation and Assimilation."
7. Kaplan, *Between Dignity and Despair*, 4.
8. Wildt, *Volksgemeinschaft als Selbstermächtigung*, 68; Miron, "The Home Experience," 183.
9. Kaplan, *Between Dignity and Despair*, 5, also 150.
10. Famous Jewish supporters of the PNF were Guido Jung, from 1932 to 1935 minister of finance; Aldo Finzi, member of the Grand Council of Fascism; and Margherita Grassini Sarfatti, Benito Mussolini's biographer as well as one of his mistresses. Both Jung and Sarfatti converted to Catholicism.
11. Sarfatti, "Autochthoner Antisemitismus," 236–237; Pavan, "An Unexpected Betrayal?," 137.
12. Historians have concluded that the anthropologist Guido Landra drafted the manifesto, which was then edited by Mussolini and other leading Fascists. On the origins of the manifesto, see Gilette, "The Origins of the 'Manifesto of Racial Scientists.'"
13. On racial theories in Italy, see Gilette, *Racial Theories in Fascist Italy*.
14. There is significant literature on the reasons behind the issuing of the racial laws. See for instance, Gentile, *The Sacralization of Politics in Fascist Italy*; Sarfatti, *The Jews in Mussolini's Italy*; Adler, "Jew as Bourgeois"; Sòrgoni, "Defending the Race"; Gilette, "The Origins of the 'Manifesto of Racial Scientists.'"
15. Pavan, *Tra Indifferenza e Oblio*, 174.
16. Visani, "The Jewish Enemy," 175.
17. Fascist Jews in particular felt humiliated and betrayed. See Pavan, "An Unexpected Betrayal?," 128; see also the letters in Maryks and Venturi, *"Pouring Jewish Water into Fascist Wine."*
18. Sarfatti, *The Jews in Mussolini's Italy*, 145.
19. Klein, *Italy's Jews from Emancipation to Fascism*, 95, 96.

191

192 | *Notes to pages 5–9*

20. Sarfatti, *The Jews in Mussolini's Italy*, 158.

21. See, for instance, oral history interview with Ida Rudley, RG-50.462.0097, United States Holocaust Memorial Museum Archive (hereafter USHMM); oral history interview with Evelyn Arzt Bergl, RG-50.030.0498, USHMM.

22. Osti Guerazzi, "Die ideologischen Ursprünge," 448.

23. Manifesto of Verona as in Schnapp, Sears, and Stampino, *A Primer of Italian Fascism*, 199.

24. Klinkhammer, "Polizeiliche Kooperation," 477.

25. Wildvang, "The Enemy Next Door"; Osti Guerrazzi, "Kain in Rom."

26. Regarding Italian Jews' survival, see Picciotto, *Salvarsi.*

27. Bertilotti, "Italian Jews and the Memory of Rescue," 127. Sarfatti and Schwarz estimate that about 8,000 Jews were killed, and Della Pergola lists the number as 7,500. See Sarfatti, *The Jews in Mussolini's Italy*; G. Schwarz, *Ritrovare se stessi*; Della Pergola and Staetsky, *From Old and New Directions.* Picciotto states that "7,186 are known to have been . . . killed on Italian soil or deported to Nazi camps" see Picciotto, "Italian Jews Who Survived the Shoah."

28. Grossmann and Lewinsky, "Erster Teil: 1945–1949, Zwischenstation," 123.

29. Grossmann, *Jews, Germans, and Allies*, 260. Frictions between eastern European and German Jews, however, played out mainly in the organization of communal life, in elections of community leadership, and in organizing services and religious life. In their memoirs, letters, and diaries, German Jews seldom mention the presence of the DP population, and in particular, those German Jew who did not join any Jewish community seemed to have barely noticed their presence.

30. Regarding Switzerland see: Broggini, *Frontier of Hope*, 361–374; Reuben Resnik to Comunità Israelitica, Milan and Turin, June 28, 1945, AR 45/54 # 629, American Jewish Joint Distribution Committee (hereafter JDC Archives), New York. About 12 percent of those who had emigrated to Palestine returned after the war, and only 1,041 Italian Jews left for Palestine/Israel between 1945 and 1955; 161 of them later returned. See Marzano, *Una terra per rinascere*, 361–371.

31. The estimates of how many DPs lived temporarily in Italy differ slightly. See Chiara Renzo, "Our Hopes Are Not Lost Yet," ;Kokkonen, "Jewish Displaced Persons"; Kohanski, "Italy," 387–90; Goldbloom, "Italy," 298; Tablet, "Italy," 349.

32. Schwarz, *Ritrovare se stessi*, 5.

33. Sinn, "Returning to Stay?," 395.

34. Buchanan, "'Good Morning, Pupil!'"

35. Schwarz, *Ritrovare se stessi*, 6.

36. Italian Communities Bureau Quarterly Report, January–March 1948, AR 45/54 # 626, JDC Archives, New York. See also Report on the Activity of the Italian Communities 1947, AR 45/54 # 627, JDC Archives, New York.

37. The literature on Jews in postwar Germany has grown significantly in the past decades; in particular, there are numerous works in German. See, for instance, Brenner, *Nach dem Holocaust*; Brenner et al., *Geschichte der Juden in Deutschland*; Mertens, *Davidstern unter Hammer und Zirkel*; Grossmann, *Jews, Germans, and Allies*; Geller, *Jews in Post-Holocaust Germany*; Zieher, *Im Schatten von Antisemitismus*; Sinn, *Jüdische Politik und Presse*; Burgauer, *Zwischen Erinnerung und Verdrängung*; Schönborn, *Zwischen Erinnerung und Neubeginn*; Kauders, *Unmögliche Heimat*; Geller and Meng, ed., *Rebuilding Jewish Life in Germany.* The history of DPs who temporarily resided in Germany after the war has received significant at-

tention. See, for instance, Konigseder and Wetzel, *Waiting for Hope*; Lavsky, *New Beginnings*. There is much less literature on Jews in postwar Italy; the most comprehensive study is Guri Schwarz's *Ritrovare se stessi*, translated into English as *After Mussolini*. Work that privileges the private and personal over the public remains scarce; see G. Schwarz et al., "Premessa." Regarding Italian Jews' struggle to retrieve their property, see D'Amico, *Quando l'eccezione diventa norma*; Pavan, *Persecution, Indifference, and Amnesia*. For the German case: Hockerts, Moisel, and Winstel, *Grenzen der Wiedergutmachung*; Goschler, *Schuld und Schulden*.

38. Fried, "Grieving for a Lost Home"; Marcus, *House as a Mirror of Self*; Joisten, "Heimat und Heimatlosigkeit"; Fenster, *The Global City*; Wise, "Home: Territory and Identity"; Wood and Beck, *Home Rules*; Applegate, *A Nation of Provincials*.

39. Regarding the importance of space as an analytical category in Jewish history, see Gromova, Heinert, and Vogt, *Jewish and Non-Jewish Spaces*; Lässig and Rürup, *Space and Spatiality*.

40. Hoffman, "The New Nomads," 50.

41. Améry, "How Much Home Does a Person Need?," 43.

42. Améry, "How Much Home Does a Person Need?," 47.

43. See, for instance, Plamper, *The History of Emotions*; Reddy, *The Navigation of Feeling*; Rosenwein, *Generations of Feeling*; Matt and Stearns, *Doing Emotions History*; Frevert, *Emotions in History*.

44. Regarding the importance of integrating emotions into historical research more broadly, beyond the subfield of history of emotions, see J. Lang, "New Histories of Emotion."

45. Regarding the phrase "emotional communities," see Rosenwein, *Emotional Communities*, 2.

46. Recent scholarship on other European countries as well as on the United States has shown that Jews found myriad ways to convey their experiences during the Second World War. See Poznanski, "French Apprehensions"; Doron, *Jewish Youth*; Jockusch, *Collect and Record!*; Grossmann, *Jews, Germans, and Allies*; H. Diner, *We Remember with Reverence and Love*; Azouvi, *Le mythe du grand silence*; Fritz, Kovács, and Rásky, *Before the Holocaust Had Its Name*.

47. "Ein Andenken an meine Lagerzeit vom 27.06.1943 bis 11.04.45 in Auschwitz O/S Gross / Breslau und Buchenwald / Weimar gezeichnet vom 26. Mai 45–5. Juni 45 in Buchenwald," *Es war einmal*, Vicissitudini dei singoli, 1.2.N.140, Archivio Centro di Documentazione Ebraica Contemporanea (hereafter ACDEC). Later published as Geve, *Es gibt hier keine Kinder*.

48. For a discussion of the emphasis on public and political representation on the past in memory studies, see Fulbrook, "History-Writing and Collective Memory"; Confino, *Germany as a Culture of Remembrance*.

49. On dominant postwar memory narratives in Italy and Germany, see, for example, Del Boca, *Italiani, Brava Gente?*; Bidussa, *Il mito del bravo italiano*; Herf, *Divided Memory*; Jarausch and Geyer, *Shattered Past*.

50. See, for instance, Cohen, "Personal Nationalism," 804.

51. Fulbrook writes, "In the course of the Nazi persecution, distinctive 'communities of experiences' were formed." Fulbrook, *Reckonings*, 8. Rather than seeing these communities as formed according to particular experiences, I highlight the active role Jewish survivors played in shaping communities after the war.

52. Forti, *Il Caso Pardo Roques*, 243.

194 | *Notes to pages 13–19*

53. G. Schwarz, *After Mussolini*; Klein, *Italy's Jews from Emancipation to Fascism*.

54. See Focardi, *La guerra della memoria*; Dunnage, "Making Better Italians"; Pezzino, "The Italian Resistance"; Fogu, "Italiani Brava Gente."

55. Applegate, *A Nation of Provincials*, 19.

56. For an emphasis on contested memories, see for instance Frei, *Adenauer's Germany*; Olick, "What Does It Mean to Normalize the Past?" Foot, *Italy's Divided Memory*.

57. Berger and Niven, *Writing the History of Memory*, 11.

58. Geller, Meng, *Rebuilding Jewish Life in Germany*, 248.

59. The literature on Jews in postwar Europe has grown significantly in recent decades. For accounts on Jews returning to Belgium, France, Hungary, the Netherlands, Poland, Romania, Slovakia, and the Soviet Union, see Bankier, *The Jews Are Coming Back*. For Poland and Slovakia, see Cichopek-Gajraj, *Beyond Violence*; on Czechoslovakia, see, for example, Láníček, "What Did It Mean to Be Loyal?"; on Jews in central Europe, see also Čapková and Rechter, "Germans or Jews?" For France, see, for example, Hand and Katz, *Post-Holocaust France and the Jews*; on Austria, see Anthony, *The Compromise of Return*.

60. Despite the differences between Fascism and Nazism, and despite the difficulties to clearly define Fascism, Nazi Germany and Fascist Italy are widely considered the most prominent Fascist regimes and are frequently used as the prime case studies in literature on Fascism. See Passmore, "A and not A: What Is fascism?"; Paxton, *The Anatomy of Fascism*; Payne, *A History of Fascism*; Griffin, *The Nature of Fascism*.

61. Two recent edited volumes offer comparative and transnational perspectives; see Bohus et al., *Our Courage*; Fischer, Riemer, and Schüler-Springorum, *Juden und Nichtjuden nach der Shoah*. Maude Mandel has compared the postgenocide experiences of Jews and Armenians in France in Mandel, *In the Aftermath of Genocide*. Rebecca Clifford has compared Holocaust Memory in France and Italy in Clifford, *Commemorating the Holocaust*. In a recent volume on *Rebuilding Jewish Life in Germany*, the editors Jay Howard Geller and Michael Meng call for examining postwar Jewish life from a comparative or transnational angle to "reconstruct more deftly the richness and plurality of Jewish experiences in Germany and Europe." See Geller, Meng, *Rebuilding Jewish Life in Germany*, 248.

62. See Goeschel, "A Parallel History?"

63. De Felice, Ledeen, and Petersen, *Renzo De Felice*, 57, 69, 75, 77, 89, 91.

64. Bessel, "Introduction: Italy, Germany and Fascism."

65. Lyttleton, "The 'Crisis of Bourgeois Society,'" 13.

66. See Sullam, *The Italian Executioners*; Reichardt, "Faschistische"; Del Boca, *I gas di Mussolini*; Mattioli, *Experimentierfeld der Gewalt*; Santarelli, "Muted Violence"; F. Levi, *L'ebreo in oggetto*; Maiocchi, *Scienza italiana e razzismo fascista*; Wildvang, "The Enemy Next Door"; Schneider, *Mussolini in Afrika*; Zimmerman, *Jews in Italy*; Sarfatti, *The Jews in Mussolini's Italy*; Collotti, *Razza e fascismo*; Finzi, *L'università italiana*; Fabre, *L'elenco*; Israel and Nastasi, *Scienza e razza nell'Italia fascista*.

67. See Steege, "Holding on in Berlin."

68. For comparative and transnational studies. see Jockusch, *Collect and Record!*; Mandel, *In the Aftermath of Genocide*; Zahra, *The Lost Children*; Biess, *Homecomings*; Meng, *Shattered Spaces*.

69. On the importance of memoirs and diaries as sources, see Miron, "The Home Experience," 181; Kaplan, "Revealing and Concealing"; Fulbrook, *Reckonings*, 327.

70. Schwarz, *Ritrovare se stessi*, 44; Zieher, *Im Schatten von Antisemitismus*, 123–125.

1. Returning Home?

1. See Heinz (Enzo) Arian to Giorgina Levi, October 9, 1944, in Enzo Arian, Giorgina Levi, *Una coppia di ebrei e il nazifascismo* (1934–1962), Epistolario, E/92, Archivio Diaristico Nazionale di Pieve Santo Stefano (Arezzo) (hereafter ADN); Giorgina Levi to Francesco Lemmi, December 25, 1940, and August 11, 1941, Lemmi Francesco and Giorgina Levi, *Caro Professore, eccomi di nuovo viva* (1940–1948), Epistolario, E/And, ADN. Regarding the couple's story, see also Passerini, *Women and Men in Love*, 279–321.

2. Giorgina Levi to Francesco Lemmi, December 25, 1940, Lemmi Francesco and Giorgina Levi, *Caro Professore, eccomi di nuovo viva* (1940–1948), Epistolario, E/And, ADN.

3. Kantorowicz, *Deutsches Tagebuch*, 102; Kantorowicz to Heinrich Mann, August 1946, Nachlass Alfred Kantorowicz, F 230/1, Institut für Zeitgeschichte (hereafter IFZ).

4. Kantorowicz, *Deutsches Tagebuch*, 63. See also letter from Lion Feuchtwanger to Alfred Kantorowicz, March 5, 1946, Nachlass Alfred Kantorowicz, F 230/1, IFZ.

5. Alfred Kantorowicz to Heinrich Mann, August 1946, Nachlass Alfred Kantorowicz, F 230/1, IFZ.

6. See, for example, Rolf Hertz, *Macht und Ohnmacht*, ME 387, 10, Leo Baeck Institute, Center for Jewish History, New York (hereafter LBI); Jürgens, *"Wir waren ja eigentlich Deutsche,"* 48.

7. Viktor Karfunkel to Vorstand der jüdischen Gemeinde in Frankfurt, January 14, 1948, Frankfurt – B.1/13, Serie A 728, Blatt 30, Zentralarchiv zur Erforschung der Geschichte der Juden in Deutschland, Heidelberg (hereafter ZA).

8. Webster, "Jüdische Rückkehrer in der BRD," 50.

9. Winterfeldt, *Deutschland*; also Walter Spier and his brother, see Junge, "'Go Back to Your Hometown,'" 24.

10. Grundig, *Gesichte und Geschichte*, 324–327.

11. Holzer, *Lebenserinnerungen von 1909–1951*, vol. 1.

12. On those who did not go back, see Grossmann, "German Jews as Provincial Cosmopolitans," 161.

13. For example, Irene Runge's parents; compare Runge, *Dreiundsechzig*; see also Kantorowicz, *Deutsches Tagebuch*, 96–98; Borneman and Peck, *Sojourners*, 81–101. See also Schrecker, *Many Are the Crimes*, 124–128.

14. Rapoport, *Meine ersten drei Leben*, 211–212, 270–280.

15. See Schrecker, *Many Are the Crimes*, 124–128.

16. Interview with Hilde Eisler in Borneman and Peck, *Sojourners*, 93.

17. Brunhilde Eisler to Gerhart Eisler, March 4, 1947, NY 4117/125, Bundesarchiv, Berlin (hereafter BArch).

18. Brunhilde Eisler, June 13, 1949, NY 4117/125, BArch.

19. Brunhilde Eisler, June 15, 1949, NY 4117/125, BArch.

20. Zweig, *Werk und Leben*, 394.

21. See also Gordon, "Against Vox Populi."

22. Gordon, "Widersprüchliche Zugehörigkeiten," 192–193.

23. Jürgens, "Wir waren ja eigentlich Deutsche," 95, 170, 220, 221; Bernhardt and Lange, *Der Riss durch mein Leben*, 269; Proskauer, Berghahn, and Wickert, *Erna Proskauer*; Schmuckler, *Gast im eigenen Land*, 117.

196 | Notes to pages 24–28

24. See Kaplan, *Between Dignity and Despair*, 64, 65; Einhorn, "Nation und Identität," 107, 108; Tyrolf, "'You Can't Go Home Again,'" 118.

25. Thomas Kornbichler, "Camilla und Steffie Spira, Schauspiel West – Schauspiel Ost, Zwei Leben in Deutschland" (unpublished manuscript, no date), 186, Steffie Spira Archiv, Stiftung Archiv der Akademie der Künste, Berlin (hereafter AAK).

26. Kornbichler, "Camilla und Steffie Spira," 186.

27. H.H. "'Berlin ist noch immer wunderbar' Steffi und Camilla Spira sind heimgekehrt" in *Nacht-Express: Die illustrierte Abendzeitung* [1948], Spira 33, Steffie Spira Archiv, AAK.

28. Spira, *Trab der Schaukelpferde*, 228.

29. Giordano, "Ich bin geblieben—warum?," 120.

30. Giordano, "Ich bin geblieben—warum?," 123, 125.

31. For examples see Martin Hollender, "Was wäre die Arbeiterbewegung ohne ihn? Ein inspirierter Außenseiter: Dem Historiker Helmut Hirsch zum hundertsten Geburtstag," *Frankfurter Allgemeine Zeitung*, August 31, 2007; see also Tauchert, *Jüdische Identitäten*, 33, 34; Krauss, "Jewish Remigration," 107; Lehmann, "Rückkehr nach Deutschland?," 43.

32. Heinz Galinski in conversation with Michael Brenner. See Brenner, *Nach dem Holocaust*, 148.

33. Leo Loewenstein to communities in Germany, November 13, 1945, Mainz – B.1/18, 61, Allgemeine Korrespondenz, ZA.

34. For examples see Wilhelm Meier, "Auswanderer–Rückwanderer," *Der Weg*, February 7, 1947; Benz, "'Für den Vater war es sehr schwer,'" 330. See also Sinn, "Aber ich blieb trotzdem hier," 86, 87.

35. Deutschkron, *Mein Leben nach dem Überleben*, 21–22, 92–97.

36. Quoted in Wojak, *Fritz Bauer*, 232. Written in 1962, this statement hints at Bauer's disappointment about the country's development in the decades following his return.

37. Krauss, "Jewish Remigration," 107.

38. See Dreifuss, *Ensemblespiel des Lebens*.

39. Alfred Dreifuss, *Über die jüdische Emigration in Schanghai*.

40. For examples see Rothschild, *Memoirs*, 173; Wroblewsky, *Zwischen Thora und Trabant*, 27; Kantorowicz, *Exil in Frankreich*, 9; see also Krauss, *Heimkehr in ein Fremdes Land*, 13.

41. See also Nolan, "Antifascism under Fascism," 50.

42. Interview with Ruth Benario in Borneman and Peck, *Sojourners*, 37–60; Rothschild, *Memoirs*, 173; interview with Sophie Marum in Wroblewsky, *Zwischen Thora und Trabant*, 27.

43. See Schloer, *Jüdisches Leben in Berlin 1933–1941*, introduction.

44. Rothschild, *Memoirs*, 171. See similar also Walter Sack, "Berliner Portraets, 'Bist Du nicht der Oskar?': Juedischer Arbeiterjunge, antifaschistischer Kämpfer, Emigrant, Handwerker, Bürgermeister," in *Berliner Zeitung*, December 17/18, 1988.

45. Brandt, *Ein Traum der nicht entführbar ist*, 169.

46. Stern, "The Return to the Disowned Home," 60, 61; Lagrou, "Return to a Vanished World," 17.

47. Fragebogen 38, Mannheim – B.1/36, ZA.

48. Wolfgang Fischer, "Heimkehr aus Heimweh," *Nacht-Express*, March 6, 1948.

49. Long and Oxfeld, *Coming Home?*, 5.

50. Améry, "How Much Home Does a Person Need?," 51.

51. See, for example, Meier, "Auswanderer–Rückwanderer"; Fritz Corsing, "Das Tor in die Welt," *Der Weg*, March 8, 1946.

52. Winterfeldt, *Deutschland*, 426.

53. Meier, "Auswanderer–Rückwanderer."

54. Grete Weil to Walter Jokisch, August 5, 1946, GW B 96, Literaturarchiv Monacensia, Munich (hereafter Monacensia).

55. Grete Weil to Walter Jokisch, July 6, 1946, GW B 96, Monacensia.

56. Regarding the role of emotions in decision-making processes, see Frevert, "Was haben Gefühle in der Geschichte zu suchen?"; Lerner et al., "Emotion and Decision Making."

57. Passerini, *Women and Men in Love*, 279.

58. Di Cori, *Memorie di un italiano in Medio Oriente*, 36.

59. Di Segni Jesi, *La lunga strada azzurra*, 141.

60. Ottolenghi, *Ricordi e impressioni di un'internata*, 148.

61. Smolensky and Jarach, *Tante voci, una storia*, 334; Steindler, *Viandante del XX secolo*, 111–113.

62. Zevi, "La mia autobiografia politica," 83–89.

63. Account of Arrigo Levi in Smolensky and Jarach, *Tante voci, una storia*, 374.

64. Interview with Piero Terracina, Roma, June 3, 2004, as in Strani, "Gli ebrei romani," 163.

65. Broggini, *Frontier of Hope*, 361. See also Longhi, *Exil und Identität*, 432–462.

66. Fondo Valobra, 1/140.3.1, ACDEC.

67. Andrea Bises in Smolensky and Jarach, *Tante voci, una storia*, 348.

68. Beer, *Va' Fuori d'Italia*, II.

69. Quoted in Barozzi, "L' uscita degli ebrei di Roma dalla clandestinità," 41.

70. The Italian Jewish press, however, considered it difficult or impossible for German and eastern European Jews to return and emphasized the need to help them settle in Israel. An article published in August 1945, for instance, maintains that "there is no way to return to Germany, Poland, Romania." See "Un popolo torna alla sua casa," *Bollettino della Comunità Israelitica di Milano*, August 31, 1945.

71. See, for example, British Broadcasting Corporation, *Ecco Radio Londra*; Virgina Lee Warren, "Jews' Future Seen Better in Europe," *New York Times*, June 18, 1945; Milton Bracker, "Italians Apologetic," *New York Times*, August 26, 1945; Delbert Clark, "Fascist Rescues of Jews Revealed," *New York Times*, May 22, 1946.

72. Bertilotti, "Italian Jews and the Memory of Rescue," 132.

73. Letter from Reuben B. Resnik, AJDC, Rome to American Jewish Joint Distribution Committee, New York and Paris, November 8, 1945, AR 45/54 # 629, JDC Archives, New York. Similar also the Joint report from May 19, 1946, AR 45/54 # 629, JDC Archives, New York.

74. "I patrioti italiani e gli ebrei," Bollettino d'informazione, published by the Italian Representative Committee of the World Jewish Congress, Nr. 6., June 1945, ACDEC. See also Memorandum by David Bernstein, March 22, 1947, American Jewish Committee, Record Group 347.7.1, YIVO Institute for Jewish Research, Center for Jewish History (hereafter YIVO Archives), New York; *American Jewish Year Book*, vol. 46 (September 18, 1944, to September 7, 1945), 230–236.

75. Papers from the World Jewish Congress Second Plenary Assembly, 1948, World Jewish Congress, January 1, 1948, Berman Archive, https://www.bjpa.org/search-results/publication /22287; also quoted in Brenner, *Nach dem Holocaust*, 66.

76. Harry Greenstein, *Heidelberg Conference: The Future of the Jews in Germany 1949*, MS 168, LBI.

198 | Notes to pages 32–36

77. Greenstein, *Heidelberg Conference*.

78. D. Diner, "Im Zeichen des Banns," 23.

79. Rede Leo Baeck, October 14, 1948, Frankfurt – B.1/13, Serie A 722, Blatt 39, ZA.

80. Sitzungsprotokoll der Interessenvertretung der jüdischen Gemeinden, June 8, 1947, RG 14.053 M, USHMM.

81. "Die problematische Stellung der Juden in Deutschland," *Der Weg*, March 1, 1946.

82. Letter of a German Jewish returnee to the German Jewish representative committee affiliated with the World Jewish Congress, September 18, 1946, C3/349, Central Zionist Archives (hereafter CZA).

83. See Chernow, *Die Warburgs*, 707; L. Winter, *Unsere Vergangenheit*, 244; Kantorowicz, *Deutsches Tagebuch*, 63; Bernhardt and Lange, *Der Riss durch mein Leben*, 284; Letters from Wolfgang Hildesheimer to his parents, Wolfgang Hildesheimer Archiv, 456, AAK; Hannah Arendt to Gertrud Jaspers, May 30, 1946, in Arendt and Jaspers, *Hannah Arendt, Karl Jaspers Briefwechsel*, 77.

84. Deutschkron, *Mein Leben nach dem Überleben*, 91.

85. Alfred Döblin to Hermann Kesten, Baden-Baden, December 3, 1948, in Kesten, *Deutsche Literatur im Exil*, 286.

86. Frankenthal, *Verweigerte Rückkehr*, 13.

87. Kauders, *Unmögliche Heimat*, 14.

88. Grete Weil to Walter Jokisch, February 24, 1946, GW B 96, Monacensia. Weil kept this feeling for decades. In an interview conducted in the late 1980s, she contended, "Und ich habe immer das Gefühl, sie [andere Juden] mißbilligen, daß ich in Deutschland lebe." Interview in Koelbl, *Jüdische Portraits*, 256.

89. Wolfgang Hildesheimer to his parents, December 7, 1947, Wolfgang Hildesheimer Archiv, 663, AAK.

90. For a discussion on the antiemigration sentiment in pre-state Israel more broadly, see Yehudai, "Displaced in the National Home."

91. Proskauer, Berghahn, and Wickert, *Erna Proskauer*, 99.

92. Grundig, *Gesichte und Geschichte*, 321.

93. Mendel, "The Policy for the Past in West Germany and Israel," 132.

94. Regarding the phrase "emotional regime," see Reddy, *The Navigation of Feeling*, 129.

95. "Juden in Deutschland oder Deutsche Juden," *Der Weg*, April 5, 1946.

96. Ganther, *Die Juden in Deutschland*, 1.

97. However, her memoir, written in the 1960s, foreshadows Gert's later disappointment when she writes, "Surely Berlin must be as lively as after the First World War." Gert, *Ich bin eine Hexe*, 180, 210, 219.

98. Ottolenghi and De Rossi Castelli, *Nei tempi oscuri*, 205.

99. Klemperer, *Ich will Zeugnis ablegen*, 770.

100. Klemperer, *So sitze ich denn zwischen allen Stühlen*, 7.

101. Account of Josef Warscher in Brenner, *Nach dem Holocaust*, 112.

102. August Adelsberger, Rechenschaftsbericht, Frankfurt – B.1/13, Serie A 114, Blatt 27, ZA; Max Jacobson depicts his waiting for transport and the lengthy journey home from Theresienstadt. See Jacobson, *Mein Leben und Erinnerungen*, 46–47.

103. See Guida, *La strada di casa*.

104. P. Levi, *La tregua*.

105. Testimonianza di Piero Terracina, "Io, deportato ad Auschwitz," Triangolo Viola, last updated July 11, 2002, http://www.triangoloviola.it/terracina.html.

Notes to pages 37–41 | 199

106. Letter in full quoted in Guida, *La strada di casa*, 168.

107. Guida, *La strada di casa*, 168–169.

108. See Carpi, Segre, and Toaff, *Scritti in memoria di Nathan Cassuto*.

109. Letter from Anna Di Gioacchino Cassuto, Viareggio, August 12, 1945, quoted in Guarnieri, *Intellettuali in fuga dall'Italia fascista*.

110. The USHMM designates the location as "Czechoslovakia?" but the ACDEC description states that the picture was taken at the Neustadt camp. The three women are named as Anna Di Gioacchino Cassuto, Amalia Navarro, and Emma Zarfatti but elsewhere Enrica Zarfati. See http://digital-library.cdec.it/cdec-web/storico/detail/IT-CDEC-ST0005-000210/cassuto-anna.html and http://digital-library.cdec.it/cdec-web/fotografico/detail/IT-CDEC-FT0001-0000018410/wiener-neustadt-campo-concentramento-anna-gioacchino-cassuto-amalia-navarro-ed-enrica-zarfatti.html.

111. Barthes, "The Rhetoric of the Image," 159,

112. Winterfeldt, *Deutschland*, 402–440.

113. For example, Karl Marx, see Sinn, *Jüdische Politik*, 74 and Lea Grundig, *Gesichte und Geschichte*, 320; also Valeska Gert, see Gert, *Ich bin eine Hexe*, 189, 228; see also Foitzik, "Politische Probleme der Remigration," 104; Krauss, "Westliche Besatzungszonen," 1163, 1164.

114. Victor, *Kehre wieder über die Berge*, 392.

115. See Victor, *Kehre wieder über die Berge*, 393–394 and 457.

116. See Einhorn, "Gender, Nation, Landscape," 711.

117. Rothschild, *Memoirs*, 175–176.

118. Alexander Abusch, SgY 30/1084/1, BArch.

119. Dreifuss, *Über die jüdische Emigration in Schanghai*, 31. HICEM was formed with the merger of three resettlement organizations: HIAS, an American organization ; the Paris-based Jewish Colonisation Association; and Emigdirect, based in Berlin. Regarding the difficulties of German Jews in Shanghai who wanted to return, see also "Ein Brief aus Schanghai," *Der Weg*, November 29, 1946.

120. L. Winter, *Unsere Vergangenheit*, 260, 275.

121. See, for example, the account of Holzer, *Lebenserinnerungen*, 244.

122. For Italy, see, for example, the letters in the following folders: Privati 1944–1947, Busta 02B, Fascicolo O2B-15, O2B-15e, and O2B-16, all Archivio Unione delle Comunità Ebraiche Italiane (hereafter AUCEI); see also Corrispondenza Comitato ricerche deportati, Busta 42, Fondo Comunità Israelitica di Roma, 1944–1948, Fascicolo 2, 5B1-1 (5), Archivio Storico della Comunità Ebraica di Roma (hereafter ASCER). For Germany, see Verband der Jüdischen Gemeinden in der DDR, 1945–1991, 5B1-1 (6), Historische Archiv der Stiftung Neue Synagoge Berlin–Centrum Judaicum (hereafter CJA); Frankfurt – B.1/13, Serie A 588, ZA.

123. Moritz Eisenstaedt to head of Jewish community Frankfurt/Main, April 25, 1949, Frankfurt – B.1/13, Serie A 727, 53, ZA.

124. Quoted as in Wojak, *Fritz Bauer*, 220.

125. "Bericht der Abteilung Emigration. Anlage zum VSJF Tätigkeitsbericht November 1, 1944 to May 31, 1945," 1.1.2.1. VE 3–6, 3748, Verband Schweizerischer Jüdischer Fürsorgen/Flüchtlingshilfen Archiv, Archiv für Zeitgeschichte, Zürich.

126. Ottolenghi, *Ricordi e impressioni di un'internata*, 148.

127. Ottolenghi, *Ricordi e impressioni di un'internata*, 149.

128. Kantorowicz, *Deutsches Tagebuch*, 101.

129. F. Levi, *I giorni dell'erba amara*, 238. See similarly also G. Morpurgo, *Diario di un rifugiato in svizzera*, and Donati, *Diario d'Esilio*.

200 | *Notes to pages 41–46*

130. Levi Coen, *Ebrei nell'occhio del ciclone*. Guido Levi likewise depicted the patriotic feelings of the returning refugees: "When we entered Italy, we were all singing, someone exited the train after it had stopped to kiss the Italian ground." Guido Levi, Fondo Broggini. Bell4-128u, Archivio di Stato del Canton Ticino, Bellinzona.

131. Regarding the traumatic experience of the border crossing, see Kaplan, *Hitler's Jewish Refugees*, 37–39.

132. See Davidson and Bondi, "Spatialising Affect; Affecting Space," 7–10.

133. Sahl, *Memoiren eines Moralisten*, 217.

134. Marcuse to Harold von Hofe and Townsend, June 17, 1949, in Marcuse, *Briefe*, 64. Marcuse described the same moment differently in his memoir: "When we reached the German border, I felt overwhelmed." Marcuse, *Mein zwanzigstes Jahrhundert*, 361.

135. Peter Gay depicts his "emotional numbness" during his first return visit to Berlin, the city in which he had grown up. See P. Gay, *My German Question*, 8.

136. Marcuse to Harold von Hofe and Townsend, June 22, 1949, in Marcuse, *Briefe*, 363. Another German Jew described feeling similarly overwhelmed upon her arrival: "The first time? Horrible! I was standing at the train station in Kassel, looked down Bahnhof Street. (Pause) It was - one cannot - one was foreign. Foreign and afraid." See Kliner-Fruck, *Es ging ja ums Überleben*, 202.

137. Victor, *Kehre wieder über die Berge*, 393, 394.

138. Di Camerino, *R, come Roberta*, 65–66. Alba Soliani Rabello similarly related how on the day of her return from Switzerland, her son was leaning out of the train's window when it arrived at the station. A soldier on guard duty asked him if he was from Italy. When the boy replied yes, the soldier hugged him, "his eyes bright with tears." Soliani Rabello, *Diario*, 44.

139. Paepcke, *Ich wurde vergessen*, 121.

140. Noack-Mosse, *Theresienstaedter Tagebuch*, 139.

141. See, for instance, Max Jacobson, who writes about a number of people who welcomed and helped him upon his return from Theresienstadt and also depicts an amicable relationship with his employer, who rehired him. See Jacobson, *Mein Leben und Erinnerungen*, 47–49.

142. Letter from Rabbi Dr. Neuhaus to Dr. Haeger, Frankfurt – B.1/13, Serie A 154, Blatt 8, 9, ZA; Siegmund Weltlinger described his first meeting with "old Christian friends" in his hometown of Kassel as joyful. Siegmund Weltlinger to Max Elb, October 29, 1954, Siegmund Weltlinger, E Rep. 200–22, Landesarchiv Berlin (hereafter LAB).

143. Alexander Abusch, *Erinnerungen an die ersten Jahre der Kulturrevolution 1946–1950*, 43, no date, SgY 30/1084/1, BArch.

144. Quoted in Guida, *La strada di casa*, 178.

145. For examples see Guida, *La strada di casa*, 192–193.

146. Di Camerino, *R, come Roberta*, 62.

147. Di Cori, *Memorie di un italiano in Medio Oriente*; Di Segni Jesi, *La lunga strada azzurra*; Anonymous, "Un' italiana reduce da Auschwitz racconta," Vicissitudine dei singoli, Saralvo Corrado, Busta 2, Fascicolo 663, ACDEC.

148. Di Segni Jesi, *La lunga strada azzurra*, 149.

149. A. Morpurgo, *Queste mie figlie*, 72.

150. Di Cori, *Memorie di un italiano in Medio Oriente*, 112.

151. Hoffman, "The New Nomads," 49, 50.

152. Regarding the links between habits, home, and identity, see Wise, "Home: Territory and Identity," 303.

153. Di Cori, *Memorie di un italiano in Medio Oriente*, 113.

154. L. Levi, *Se va via il re*, 21–23.

155. See Nicolaysen, *Siegfried Landshut*, 344; Kesten, "Die vergebliche Heimkehr," 17.

156. Quoted in Brenner, *Nach dem Holocaust*, 112.

157. Letter Dr. Neuhaus to Dr. Hirsch, November 4, 1945, Frankfurt – B.1/13, Serie A 153, Blatt 116–118, ZA.

158. Interview with Hans Mayer in Koelbl, *Jüdische Porträts*, 183. Similar also Karl Jakob Hirsch: "The former Germany no longer exists." KJH to Dr. Boesch, February 21, 1950, Nachlass Karl Jakob Hirsch, Universitätsbibliothek der LMU München.

159. See, for instance, the interview with Ernest and Renata Lenart in Jürgens, *Wir waren ja eigentlich Deutsche*, 93.

160. Seghers, "Der Besuch," 1956, quoted in Seghers, *Hier im Volk der kalten Herzen*. In her "The Outing of the Dead Schoolgirls" (Ausflug der toten Mädchen), written in Mexico in 1944, Seghers depicted this longing for the landscapes of her youth. In the autobiographical story, Seghers dreams about an outing with her school friends. She finds herself back in Mainz and describes her feelings: "As I continued to look around me I found I could breathe more freely and my heart filled with a wave of happiness. The heavy burden of depression that had weighed on every breath I drew had vanished without my noticing it. As a seed draws life from the earth in which it is planted, so too the gentle curves of this countryside filled my very being with joy and gladness." Seghers, "The Outing of the Dead Schoolgirls," 619–620.

161. Kantorowicz, *Deutsches Tagebuch*, 117.

162. Knowles, Cole, and Giordano, *Geographies of the Holocaust*, 4.

163. Mayer, *Ein Deutscher auf Widerruf*, 316.

164. Lothar Orbach, "Neues Leben Aus Totem Stein," *Der Weg*, March 22, 1946.

165. Luzzati, *La mia vita*, 59.

166. Donati, *Diario d'Esilio*, 321. Similar also Di Camerino, *R, come Roberta*, 65; Tagliacozzo, *Metà della vita*, 317.

167. Di Segni Jesi, *La lunga strada azzurra*, 149.

168. Steindler, *Viandante del XX secolo*, 123.

169. Marcuse to von Hofe and Townsend, July 17, 1949, in Marcuse, *Briefe*, 80. See also interview with Ms. C. in Kliner-Fruck, *Es ging ja ums Überleben*, 297; Kantorowicz, *Deutsches Tagebuch*, 121. I came across only one Italian Jew who described the weather negatively. Edda Ulmann, who had immigrated with her parents to São Paulo, did not want to return. She explained, "The following day, we arrived in Genoa, . . . it was cold! Or was it just my impression?" Edda Ulmann, "L'angelo e la bimba ebrea," MP/Adn2, ADN.

170. Behar, *Diary 1943–1947*; Ottolenghi, *Ricordi e impressioni di un'internata*, 153.

171. Di Segni Jesi, *La lunga strada azzurra*, 140.

172. Kantorowicz, *Deutsches Tagebuch*, 144. Similar also Marcuse, *Mein zwanzigstes Jahrhundert*, 361, 363. In 1939, as part of the plan to redesign Berlin into the imperial capital of the world, the Nazis relocated the *Siegessäule* (victory column) from Königsplatz to the new Grosser Stern.

173. For another example, see Döblin, *Destiny's Journey*, 299–304.

174. The Kindertransport (Children's Transport) was the informal name of a British scheme that brought Jewish children from Nazi Germany, Austria, and Czechoslovakia to Great Britain between 1938 and 1940.

175. Letter from Peter Reiche to relatives, January 1, 1946, Sammlung Peter H Reiche, 2005/51/01-14, Archiv Juedisches Museum Berlin (hereafter AJM).

176. Orbach and Orbach-Smith, *Soaring Underground*, 316.

202 | Notes to pages 49–52

177. L. Winter, *Unsere Vergangenheit*, 275.

178. Kesten, "Die vergebliche Heimkehr," 24.

179. Anna Seghers to unknown, no date [Frühjahr 1947], in Seghers and Berger, *Hier im Volk der kalten Herzen*, 39.

180. Vansant, *Reclaiming Heimat*, 101.

181. Hans-Erich Fabian, "Liquidationsgemeinden?," *Der Weg*, May 2, 1947.

182. On Marx see Sinn, *Jüdische Politik*.

183. Quoted in Blaschke, Fings, and Lissner, *Unter Vorbehalt*, 155. The writer Stefan Heym, who returned from the United States to East Germany in 1953, similarly explained that he had mixed feelings when he went back to his hometown of Chemnitz, "but not this sense of home, which is so frequently discussed. This was, after all, also the place in which I had been treated especially poorly." Interview with Stefan Heym in Koelbl, *Jüdische Porträts*, 116. Similar also Hermann Kesten to Joseph Wittlin, February 5, 1950, HKB 2510, Monacensia.

184. Anna Seghers to Lenelore Wolf, Berlin, November 1, 1947, in Seghers and Berger, *Hier im Volk der kalten Herzen*, 162. Rabbi Nathan Peter Levinson described the connection between sad memories and his former home similarly to those mentioned here. See Levinson, *Ein Ort ist, mit wem du bist*, 106.

185. Letter to the Jewish community Frankfurt, August 22, 1948, Frankfurt – B.1/13, Serie A 585, Blatt 22, ZA. See, for instance, also the letter from Heinrich Alexander to the Hamburg Jewish community, August 27, 1948, edited in: "Key Documents of German-Jewish History," Institute for the History of German Jews, November 16, 2022, https://jewish-history-online .net/source/jgo:source-177.

186. L. Winter, *Unsere Vergangenheit*, 228.

187. Letter from Doctor Hirsch to Julius Meyer, May 3, 1949, Verband der Jüdischen Gemeinden in der DDR, 1945–1991, 5B1-1 (4), Blatt 285, 286, CJA.

188. Regarding the interconnection between health and place, see Williams, *Therapeutic Landscapes*.

189. Eugenia Servi, *Ed ora, 50 anni dopo . . .* , ADN, 44, 49.

190. Servi, *Ed ora, 50 anni dopo . . .* , 44; also Luzzati, *La mia vita*.

191. Bauer, "Una Vita Segnata," 19.

192. On the displacement of Italians from the border zone between Italy and Yugoslavia, and the memories and narratives created around these events, see Ballinger, *History in Exile*.

193. Frankenthal, *Verweigerte Rückkehr*, 96.

194. Gert, *Ich bin eine Hexe*, 7; see also Hylenski, "Ich will leben, auch wenn Ich tot bin," 46.

195. Cited as in A. Villa, *Dai lager alla terra promessa*, 21.

196. See, for example, Emilio Levi, Vicissitudini dei singoli, Busta 14, Fascicolo 410, ACDEC; Junge, "'Go Back to Your Hometown'"; Dello Strologo, "Pensa che bambina fortunata," 34; Steindler, *Viandante del XX secolo*, 118–119; Di Cori, *Memorie di un italiano in Medio Oriente*, 119; also, Valeska Gert's return to her home in Kampen. See Gert, *Ich bin eine Hexe*, 240.

197. Fried, "Grieving for a Lost Home," 365.

198. Marcus, *House as a Mirror of Self*, 241.

199. Marcus, *House as Mirror of Self*; also Auslander, "Coming Home?"; Csikszentmihalyi and Rochberg-Halton, *The Meaning of Things*.

200. Levi Coen, *Ebrei nell'occhio del ciclone*; Di Camerino, *R, come Roberta*, 66.

201. Albert Meyer to Rudolf Meyer, May 13, 1945, Nachlass Albert G. Meyer, R-2003/197 /01-17, AJM.

202. Varsano, "Personal Memories," July 2, 1954, in "Examples of Material Losses Suffered by the Jews in the Period 1938–1945: Testimony, Reports, Documents," in Commissione per la ricostruzione delle vicende che hanno caratterizzato in Italia le attività di acquisizione dei beni dei cittadini ebrei da parte di organismi pubblici e privati (Commission aiming to study the acquisition of goods of Jewish citizens by private and public bodies in Italy), General Report (April 2001). http://presidenza.governo.it/DICA/beni_ebraici/index.html. Accessed 03.01.2015. On Samule Varsano, see also Saban, "Da Salonicco a Napoli."

203. Bassani, *L'anzulon*, 47, 48.

204. Regarding the meanings of objects in a home, see Adler and Hamilton, *Homes and Homecomings*, 460; Marcus, *House as Mirror of Self*.

205. Vitale, *Una bambina ebrea*, 15.

206. See Hirsch and Spitzer, "Testimonial Objects."

207. See also Auslander, "Coming Home?," 239.

208. Miranda Avigdor to her cousin, October 31, 1945, Vicissitudine dei singoli, Busta 1, Fascicolo 37, ACDEC; for more examples, see Ottolenghi and De Rossi Castelli, *Nei tempi oscuri*, 196; Leone Leoni to Reuben Resnik, July 6, 1945, AR 45/54 # 629, JDC Archives, New York.

209. Massimo della Pergola, letter to the mayor of Gorizia, January 27, 1992, in "Examples of Material Losses Suffered by the Jews in the Period 1938–1945: Testimony, Reports, Documents," in Commissione per la ricostruzione delle vicende che hanno Caratterizzato in Italia Le Attività Di Acquisizione Dei Beni Dei Cittadini Ebrei Da Parte Di Organismi Pubblici E Private, Rapporto Generale (April 2001).

210. Oberdorfer, *A Marco*, 29.

211. See, in particular, Hirsch, *The Generation of Postmemory*.

212. Sara Corcos, Statement, May 13, 1945, in "Examples of Material Losses Suffered by the Jews in the Period 1938–1945: Testimony, Reports, Documents," in Commissione per la ricostruzione delle vicende che hanno Caratterizzato in Italia Le Attività Di Acquisizione Dei Beni Dei Cittadini Ebrei Da Parte Di Organismi Pubblici E Private, Rapporto Generale (April 2001).

213. Regarding the social aspect of emotions, see Frevert, "Was haben Gefühle in der Geschichte zu suchen?," 197; Rosenwein, *Emotional Communities*, 2.

214. Rosenwein, *Emotional Communities*, 2.

2. Entangled Memories

1. Vittorio Fano, November 27, 1945, Busta 442, Biblioteca Archivio Renato Maestro Venice (hereafter BARM).

2. Scholars and writers began using the term *Holocaust* widely in the 1960s, and it took the 1978 TV series *Holocaust* to push it into widespread use. See Petrie, "The Secular Word 'Holocaust'"; "In contemporary Italy, *Shoah* is more commonly used than *Olocausto*. See R. Gordon, "From Olocausto to Shoah."

3. See, for example, Young, *The Texture of Memory*; Friedländer, *Memory, History, and the Extermination of the Jews of Europe*; Hartman, *Holocaust Remembrance*; Goldberg and Hazan, *Marking Evil*; Schlemmer and Steinweis, *Holocaust and Memory in Europe*.

4. Niven, "On the Use of 'Collective Memory,'" 427.

5. On scholars' neglect of individual memory in favor of collective memories, see Fulbrook, "History-Writing and Collective Memory," 68.

204 | Notes to pages 57–60

6. Fulbrook, "History-Writing and Collective Memory," 73.

7. Assmann, "Transformations between History and Memory."

8. Halbwachs, *On Collective Memory*, 23.

9. Halbwachs, *On Collective Memory*, 33.

10. Fulbrook, *Reckonings*, 8.

11. Quoted as in Picciotto, "L'attività del Comitato ricerche deportati ebrei," 77.

12. Picciotto, "La ricerca del Centro di documentazione ebraica," 76–77.

13. L. Levi, *Se vai via il re*, 6. See also Di Cori, *Memorie di un italiano*; Servi, *Ed ora, 50 anni dopo . . .* ; interview with Giulia Cohen in Strani, "Gli ebrei romani e la ricostruzione," 203.

14. Kosmala, "Zwischen Ahnen und Wissen," 140.

15. Testimonies in Tagliacozzo and Di Castro, *Gli ebrei romani raccontano la "propria" Shoah*, 272, 275; John Richter to Fritz Selbiger, November 14, 1945, Nachlass Fritz Selbiger, 6.2, Nr. 25, CJA.

16. Letter from Maria Simonetta, Corrispondenza Comitato ricerche deportati, Busta 42, Fondo Comunità Israelitica di Roma, ASCER; Kurt Grote to Jewish community, June 5, 1947, Frankfurt – B.1/13, Serie A 1185–1204, Blatt 14, ZA.

17. See among numerous examples: letters in Busta 442, BARM; letters in Frankfurt – B.1/13, Serie A 1185–1204, ZA; also ads in *Der Weg*, March 22, 1946.

18. Letter from B.K. to anonymous, March 22, 1946, Bestand 5A 1: Jüdische Gemeinde zu Berlin, 1945–1990, 0257–0279, CJA.

19. For instance, Jewish community to Norbert Gans, December 2, 1947, Frankfurt – B.1/13, Serie A 1185–1204, ZA.

20. August Adelsberger, "Rechenschaftsbericht ueber seine Zeit als Betreuer der Juden und Mischlinge in Frankfurt, zwischen April 1945 und Juli 1945," Frankfurt – B.1/13, Serie A 114, Blatt 27, ZA.

21. Testimony of Giorgio Bemporad, Archivio Storico Pratiche Requisizioni Ebraici, Fascicolo 25, Busta 142, D 14.1, Archivio Storico della Comunità Ebraica di Firenze, Florence (hereafter ASCEF); Marisa Bemporad, *Dall'ostilità all'ospitalità*, MP/T2, ADN, 6. See also interview with Giulia Cohen in Strani, "Gli ebrei romani e la ricostruzione," 203; testimony of Aldo Tedeschi, Fascicolo 12, Busta 142, D 14.1, ASCEF.

22. Simonov, "Atroci Realtà: Il più grande mattatoio umano dell'Europa," December 7, 1944, *Israel*.

23. Sharples, *Postwar Germany and the Holocaust*, 11–14; Fantini, *Notizie dalla Shoah*, 332; R. Gordon, *The Holocaust in Italian Culture*, 45.

24. E. Morpurgo, *Diario dell'esilio*, 147.

25. See, for example, Editta Levi, *Una vita, la famiglia, il lavoro, e poi . . .* , MP/00, ADN, 15; interview with Giancarlo Spizzichino in Archivio Storico della Comunità Ebraica di Roma, *La Comunita Ebraica*, 119.

26. See, for instance, letter of Sally Aumann to the Jüdische Beratungsstelle, Frankfurt/Main, October 31, 1945, Frankfurt – B.1/13, Serie A 147, Blatt 3.2, ZA; the papers of Giulio Finzi, 1.2.N.251, ACDEC; interview with Hans Radziewski, in Heenen-Wolff, *Im Haus des Henkers*, 69; Nachlass Dr. Erich Cohn, 6.6, Nr. 120, CJA.

27. Winterfeldt, *Deutschland: Ein Zeitbild*, 443.

28. Interview with Heinz Galinski in Koelbl, *Jüdische Portraits*, 74.

29. The community archives in both Italy and Germany contain numerous search requests from community members; see Frankfurt – B.1/13, Serie A 115, Frankfurt – B.1/13, Serie A 1185–1204 ZA; Busta 165, ACF/Corrips./Varie anno 1944, Fascicolo 7; ACF/Corrips./

Varie anno 1945, Fascicolo 8, ASCER. For newspapers see *Der Weg*; "Le Notizie dei deportati" in *Israel*; *Bollettino della Comunità Israelitica di Milano*. Regarding survivors as source for information, see letter from Corrado Saralvo to Dott.ssa Bianca Morpurgo, April 5, [1945]; Letter from Donato Ottolenghi to Corrado Saralvo, October 3, 1946; Dario Mini to Corrado Saralvo, March 15, 1946, all in Fondo Corrado Saralvo, 1.2.N.700, ACDEC; for another example, see Walter Cohen to Dr. Lewin, April 4, 1946, Düsseldorf Allgemeine Korrespondenz, Düsseldorf – B.1/5, 76, ZA.

30. See, for instance, the exchange between Ebe Castelfranchi Finzi and Raffaele Cantoni in July and August 1948, Busta 44A, Comitato ricerche deportati ebrei, Fascicolo 44A-2, AUCEI, and also Soppelsa, *Diciamo pane al pane*, 245–246.

31. Alfredo Sarano, Segretario Comunità Israelitica di Milan to Anna Cassuto, May 10, 1947, Cassuto Nathan, 1.2.N.119, ACDEC; Verband Schweizerischer Juedischer Fluechtling-shilfen to Anna Cassuto, October 12, 1945, 2.N.119, ACDEC.

32. Nathan Cassuto was sent on a death march to Gross Rosen, where he was murdered by the Nazis in February 1945.

33. Correspondence between Raffaele Cantoni and Anna Cassuto, 1.2.N.119, ACDEC; see also letter from Sara Corcos Di Gioacchino to Ottolengho, Presidente del Comitato per la celebrazione della Resistenza, Communita Israelitica Milano, November 4, 1955. 1.2.N.119, ACDEC. The two sisters reunited in Palestine; Sara had survived the war in Morocco. Sara and her husband returned to Italy in 1948 after Anna had been killed during an attack on the Hadassah Hospital in Jerusalem, where she worked as a lab technician during the 1948 war.

34. Kugelmass and Boyarin, *From a Ruined Garden*, 34.

35. Ellen Rathé, Entschaedigung, Nachlass Ellen Rathé, 6.23, Nr. 4, CJA; Dr. Neuhaus to Dr. Hirsch, Frankfurt – B.1/13, Serie A 153, Blatt 116–118, ZA; Testimony of Aldo Tedeschi, Archivio Storico Pratiche Requisizioni Ebraici, Busta 142, D 14.1/2, Fascicolo 12, ASCEF; Editta Levi, *Una vita, la famiglia*, 15; Jacobson, *Mein Leben und Erinnerungen*.

36. Ottolenghi Minerbi, *Colpa*, 8; quoted also in von Treskow, *Judenverfolgung in Italien*, 76.

37. In Chile relatives of the desaparecidos faced similar uncertainties. A research team is working on identifying the victims, and relatives can visit the bones of their loved ones, which helps them in their mourning process. Tylim, "Skyscrapers and Bones," 467.

38. Tylim, "Skyscrapers and Bones," 468.

39. Regarding the role of the body in funerals, see Hoy, *Do Funerals Matter?*, 106.

40. Fritz Selbiger, Nachlass Fritz Selbiger, 6.2, Nr. 3, CJA; see similar also Riesenburger, *Das Licht verlöscht nicht*, 97–98.

41. Vera Bessone, "Auschwitz, 50 anni fa/Una storia. 'Li ci uccisero 19 familiari.' Due sorelle di Riccione," *Corriere di Rimini*. April 25, 1996; see also Zaban and Zaban, *Diario di due Sfollate*.

42. Lebenslauf Ellen Rathé, Aufzeichnungen nach Ilse Truninger Rathe, 6.23, Nr. 3, CJA.

43. Bassani, *The Garden of the Finzi-Continis*, 7 (my emphasis).

44. Clifford, "The Limits of National Memory," 129.

45. Tagliacozzo and Di Castro, *Gli ebrei romani raccontano la "propria" Shoah*, 283.

46. Testimony of Henry Bauer, 1996.A.0211, USHMM.

47. Walter Windspach to Vitale, June 3, 1948, Comitato ricerche deportati ebrei, Busta 44A, AUCEI.

48. Beginning in 1946, survivors' federations elsewhere in Europe organized such visits to concentration camps. See Dreyfus, "The Transfer of Ashes after the Holocaust," 21–35, 25. The Italian Jewish community also organized visits to the camps, starting a year after

206 | *Notes to pages 63–68*

Windspach's suggestion. In 1955 the journal *Israel* reported that such a trip organized by the Union of Italian Jewish Communities was canceled due to lack of interest, suggesting that, ultimately, few Italian Jews wanted to visit the camps. See Mazzini, "Memory of the Shoah," 214–215.

49. On the ritual significance of monuments, see Connerton, *How Societies Remember*, 42.

50. Similarly, Winter argued that First World War memorials "were built as places where people could mourn. . . . Their ritual significance has often been obscured by their political symbolism which, now that the moment of mourning has long passed, is all that we can see." J. Winter, *Sites of Memory*, 95.

51. Oberdorfer, *A Marco*, 29.

52. Puvogel, *Gedenkstätten für die Opfer des Nationalsozialismus*, 42.

53. See, for instance, the invitations to memorial services in Genoa and Milan, in Comitato ricerche deportati ebrei, Busta 44, AUCEI; and to a ceremony in Venice, in Corrispondenza—1946, Busta 442, BARM; see also Mainz – B.1/18, 60, ZA; see also Jüdische Gemeinde Schwerin, http://www.juden.de/gemeinden/juedische_gemeinde_schwerin.html. Accessed January 14, 2023; Jüdische Gemeinde Cottbus, http://www.juedische-gemeinde-cottbus.de/de/node/16. Accessed January 14, 2023.

54. C. Villa, ". . . e Mnemosine, confusa e smarrita," 187; R. Gordon, *The Holocaust in Italian Culture*, 117; G. Schwarz, *After Mussolini*, 55–57; Kister, *Olam She Kulo Tohar*.

55. "Il Monumento al sacrificio ebraico," *Bollettino della Comunità Israelitica di Milano*, August 1947.

56. Clifford, *Commemorating the Holocaust*, 97. About the victims see also L. Segre, *Le Fosse Ardeatine*.

57. Puvogel, *Gedenkstätten für die Opfer des Nationalsozialismus*, 109.

58. "Fürth gedenkt der Kedoschim!," *Nachrichten für die Jüdischen Bürger von Fürth*, December 1949.

59. "Fürth gedenkt der Kedoschim!"

60. Quoted in Schmid, *Antifaschismus und Judenverfolgung*, 27, 28.

61. There is a rich literature cataloging and analyzing these myriad memorials and monuments. The volume *Gedenkstätten für die Opfer des Nationalsozialismus* by Ulrike Puvogel lists more than three thousand monuments, memorials, and plaques erected after the war to commemorate the racially and politically persecuted in Germany. For further examples of early Italian Jewish monuments, see Mazzini, "Memory of the Shoah"; R. Gordon, *The Holocaust in Italian Culture*. For an analysis of monuments, see, among others, Milton and Nowinski, *In Fitting Memory*; Young, *The Texture of Memory*; Miller, *One, by One, by One*; Marcuse, Schimmelfennig, and Spielmann, *Steine des Anstosses*; Koshar, *From Monuments to Traces*.

62. See Zerubavel, *Recovered Roots*, 6–12.

63. Torriglia, *Broken Time, Fragmented Space*, x, xi; Goeschel, "A Parallel History?," 617–618. Palmiro Togliatti, leader of the Italian Communist Party, shared the view that the Italian people never embraced Fascism since it stood in contrast to their culture and traditions.

64. There is substantial literature on the myth of the good Italian. See, for instance, Focardi, *L'immagine del cattivo tedesco*; Ben-Ghiat, "A Lesser Evil?"; Del Boca, *Italiani, Brava Gente?*; Bidussa, *Il mito del bravo italiano*; Focardi and Klinkhammer, "The Question of Fascist Italy's War Crimes"; Fogu, "Italiani Brava Gente."

65. Italians suffered immensely under German occupation. The German occupying forces murdered over fifteen thousand Italian civilians in massacres and homicides. See Focardi, "Italy's Amnesia over War Guilt," 18.

66. There is vast literature on the narrative of an Italy unified in its resistance against the German occupier. See, for example, Dunnage, "Making Better Italians"; Pezzino, "The Italian Resistance"; Focardi, *La guerra della memoria*; Poggiolini, "Translating Memories of War."

67. Pezzino, "The Italian Resistance."

68. Foot, *Italy's Divided Memory*, 155–157.

69. Clifford, *Commemorating the Holocaust*, 81, 87–88.

70. R. Gordon, "Gray Zones," 116.

71. See G. Schwarz, "On Myth Making and Nation Building."

72. Declaration of the first Italian Zionist Congress in the liberated part of Italy, Rome, March 1945, Fondo Valobra, 7A/147-11, ACDEC. Also quoted in G. Schwarz, "On Myth Making and Nation Building," 8.

73. For another example that portrays the rescue efforts of the Catholic Church without questioning the role of the pope and the church more broadly, see Minerbi Ottolenghi, *Colpa*, as well as von Treskow's analysis of the work, in *Judenverfolgung in Italien*, 76. On the Catholic Church, see Zuccotti, *Under His Very Windows*; Phayer, *The Catholic Church and the Holocaust*.

74. Fulbrook, *Reckonings*, 174.

75. See, for instance, Di Camerino, *R, come Roberta*, 65; Ravenna, *Relazione*, Testimonianze sui campi di concentramento, Fascicolo 44A-3, AUCEI.

76. Oberdorfer, *A Marco*, 30.

77. "Liberazione," *Israel*, December 7, 1944. On Viterbo see Schächter, "Carlo Alberto Viterbo."

78. Debenedetti, *October 16, 1943: Eight Jews*, 84; similar also Lombroso, *Si può stampare pagine vissute*, 198; quoted in G. Schwarz, *After Mussolini*, 177, 118.

79. G. Schwarz, "On Myth Making and Nation Building," 112. Also see, for instance, "Commemorazione dell'Anniversario della Liberazione e dei Martiri Ebrei," *Bollettino della Comunità Israelitica di Milano*, May 1947.

80. Radio show from April 30, 1944. Printed in Cantoni, "Il saluto dell'unione delle comunità israelitiche italiane a Riccardo Bachi," 22; similarly also Raffaele Cantoni, "Non perdiamo altro tempo!," *Israel*, July 12, 1945.

81. See also Toscano, "The Abrogation of Racial Laws," 165. The Risorgimento (literal resurgence) was the cultural, social, and political movement for Italy's unification culminating in the establishment of Kingdom of Italy in 1861. The notion of the resistance as the Second Risorgimento was challenged by right-wing and neofascist forces that considered the resistance as "anti-national" and not compatible with the ideals of the Risorgimento. See Forlenza, "Sacrificial Memory and Political Legitimacy."

82. Letter Valobra to Saly Mayer, January 19, 1945, Joint/Saly Mayer Coll, Archiv für Zeitgeschichte, ETH Zurich.

83. Paepcke, *Ich wurde vergessen*, 122.

84. Jacobus, "Man wollte ein Zuhause," 88. See also the interview with Clara Berliner in Ostow, *Jews in Contemporary East Germany*, 83–90; L. Winter, *Unsere Vergangenheit*, 300.

85. See, for instance, Holzer, *Lebenserinnerungen*; interview with Richard Bodenheimer in Morris, *The Lives of Some Jewish Germans*, 190; Schmuckler, *Gast im eigenen Land*, 202;

208 | *Notes to pages 72–75*

Deutschkron, *Mein Leben*, 118, 127; interview with Ernest und Renata Lenart in Jürgens, *Wir waren ja eigentlich Deutsche*; Bernhardt and Lange, *Der Riss durch mein Leben*, 286; Hans Erich Fabian, "Purim das Los der Juden," *Der Weg*, March 15, 1946.

86. Albert Meyer to Rudolf Meyer, May 13, 1945, Nachlass Albert G. Meyer, R-2003/197/01-17, AJM.

87. Another German Jew, Kurt Hirschfeld, wrote, "We have seen party members—however very few—who risked their lives to help Jews, who only joined the party in order to do so. We know others who, without having been party members, were scoundrels, who denounced, enriching themselves at our plight. We have had black sheep among us who, in order to be released from deportation, sold their souls and their brothers." Kurt Hirschfeld, [1946], Nachlass Siegmund Weltlinger, E Rep. 200-22, Nr. 112, LAB.

88. There are some noteworthy exceptions, such as, for instance, philosopher Karl Jaspers, who delivered lectures to students in 1946 that were later on published under the title *The Question of German Guilt*. However, while he discusses German guilt, Jaspers does not write about the Jewish victims. In their correspondence, Hannah Arendt criticizes this omission. See Sznaider, *Gedächtnisraum Europa*, 71, 72.

89. Jarausch and Geyer, *Shattered Past*, 315–318. This narrative of German victimization emerged already in the immediate aftermath of the war. See D'Erizans, "Securing the Garden."

90. Moeller, *War Stories*, 20.

91. Posener, *In Deutschland*, 53.

92. Ernst Günter Fontheim, "Bemerkung zum Thema Entnazifizierung," *Der Weg*, July 12, 1946.

93. Klemperer, *So sitze ich denn zwischen allen Stühlen*, 9, 16, 17, 29, 41, 59, 60, 82.

94. Hannah Arendt, "The Aftermath of Nazi Rule—Report from Germany," *Commentary*, October 1950; see also Kesten to Anton Troll, N.Y., August 17, 1947, in Kesten, *Deutsche Literatur im Exil*, 255, 256.

95. "Authentischer Bericht über die Lage der Juden in Berlin," *Aufbau*, September 21, 1945.

96. Lewin, "Kurzes Gedaechtnis oder . . . ?," *Jüdisches Gemeindeblatt für die britische Zone*, December 10, 1946.

97. Richarz, "Biographie und Remigration," 342–343.

98. Moses Moskowitz, "The Germans and the Jews: Postwar Report," *Commentary*, January 7, 1946.

99. Nelly Cohn-Leschzer, "Verantwortung der Deutschen," *Der Weg*, July 7, 1950.

100. Richard May, "Falschmünzerei," *Der Weg*, November 29, 1946.

101. See also the chapter on "Kollektivschuld" in Geis, *Übrig sein*.

102. Giordano, *Die Zweite Schuld*.

103. Giordano, "Zwei Männer sehen die Deutschen," 13.

104. Wilhelm Meier, "Kollektivschuld," *Der Weg*, July 5, 1946 (my emphasis).

105. Fulbrook, *Reckonings*, 9; Rothberg, *The Implicated Subject*.

106. D'Erizans, "Securing the Garden," 186.

107. Klemperer, *So sitze ich denn zwischen allen Stühlen*, 29.

108. Deutschkron, *Mein Leben*, 218.

109. Moritz Goldschmidt to Oberstaatsanwalt Köln, April 13, 1948; Bestand 5B 1, Verband der Jüdischen Gemeinden in der DDR, 1945–1991, Nr. 2, CJA.

110. Assmann, "Transformations between History and Memory," 52.

111. Berg, "Hidden Memory and Unspoken History," 49.

Notes to pages 76–79 | 209

112. The phrase "the other Germany" conveyed the idea that the emigrants represented a true Germany and its cultural tradition and spoke on behalf of the silenced people. See Krauss, *Heimkehr*, 19; Lehmann, "Rückkehr nach Deutschland?," 43; Stephan, "Die intellektuelle, literarische und künstlerische Emigration," 30; also Fröschle, "Das andere Deutschland;" Nolan, "Antifascism under Fascism," 50; Shiloh-Dayan, "On the Point of Return," 43–44.

113. Kantorowicz to Heinrich Mann, July 28, 1941, Nachlass Alfred Kantorowicz, F 230/1, IFZ.

114. Kantorowicz to Heinrich Mann, March 24, 1945, Nachlass Alfred Kantorowicz, F 230/1, IFZ.

115. Siegmund Weltlinger, *Erlebnisbericht: "In Hitlers 'tausendjährigem Reich,'"* Nachlass Siegmund Weltlinger, E Rep. 200-22, LAB.

116. Rosenthal, *Zwei Leben in Deutschland*, 79. After the war Hans Rosenthal made a career as a radio and television quiz show host and as the president of the Tennis Borussia Berlin soccer club. He also became a member of the Central Council of Jews in Germany.

117. Kaplan, *Between Dignity and Despair*, 87.

118. Kurt Hirschfeld, Nachlass Siegmund Weltlinger, E Rep. 200-22, LAB.

119. See, for example, Siegmund Weltlinger, "Die Jüdische Gemeinde zu Berlin, ihre Lage und ihre Wünsche," March 20, 1946, Nachlass Siegmund Weltlinger, E Rep. 200-22, LAB; Ralph Giordano, "Gedanken nach einer Fahrt durch Deutschland,"; Giordano, "Zwei Männer sehen die Deutschen."

120. Meier, "Kollektivschuld."

121. Fabian, "Purim das Los der Juden."

122. Cornelissen, "Der 20. Juli 1944 in der deutschen Erinnerungskultur," 19.

123. Thiess, "Die innere Emigration," 24.

124. "Literarische Welt: Eine Irreführung," *Aufbau*, October 1945; see also Thomas Mann, "Warum ich nicht nach Deutschland zurückgehe: Antwort auf einen Brief Walter von Molos in der deutschen Presse," *Aufbau*, September 1945.

125. Klemperer, *So sitze ich denn zwischen allen Stühlen*, 129.

126. Stern, "The Return to the Disowned Home," 60, 61; Lagrou, "Return to a Vanished World," 17.

127. Reuter and Hansel, *Das kurze Leben der VVN*, 193.

128. Herf, *Divided Memory*, 106, 159, 160; Burgauer, *Zwischen Erinnerung und Verdrängung*, 201.

129. Niven, "Remembering Nazi Anti-Semitism in the GDR"; Gerlof, *Tonspuren*; Walther, "Keine Erinnerung, nirgends?"; Bohus, Hallama, and Stach, *Growing in the Shadow of Antifascism*. Regarding the historiography of Jews in the GDR, see Goschler, "Tur Tur's Lantern on a Tiny Island."

130. Niven, "Remembering Nazi Anti-Semitism in the GDR," 206.

131. Peitsch, "Antifaschistisches Verständnis der eigenen jüdischen Herkunft," 125–127.

132. Huppert, Zweig, and Loeper, *Engpass zur Freiheit*; Mika and Zweig, *Im Feuer vergangen*.

133. Heymann, *Marxismus und Rassenfrage*, 50.

134. W. E. B. Du Bois, "The Negro and the Warsaw Ghetto," *Jewish Life*, May 1952, https://perspectives.ushmm.org/item/w-e-b-du-bois-the-negro-and-the-warsaw-ghetto. Accessed January 14, 2023. Cited also in Rothberg, "W. E. B. Du Bois in Warsaw."

135. Michael Rothberg highlights the early conjunction of Holocaust memory and decolonization in a different context and suggests that the emergence of Holocaust memory was

210 | Notes to pages 80–85

inflected by histories and memories of slavery, colonialism, and decolonization. See Rothberg, *Multidirectional Memory*, 7.

136. Abusch, *Der Irrweg einer Nation*, 250–251.

137. Abusch, *Der Irrweg einer Nation*, 250; Kahn, *Antisemitismus und Rassenhetze*, 7.

138. Letter from Julius Meyer to a student, October 24, 1950, Bestand 5B 1, Verband der Jüdischen Gemeinden in der DDR, 1945–1991, Nr. 2, CJA.

139. See Shneer, "An Alternative World"; Graf, "Taking Up the Cause of the Jewish Collective."

140. Ulbricht, *Reden und Aufsätze*, 27, 28; cited also in Kessler, *Die SED and die Juden*, 34; quoted in Schmid, *Antifaschismus und Judenverfolgung*, 23.

141. Fulbrook, *Reckonings*, 224, 225; Niven, "Remembering Nazi Anti-Semitism in the GDR."

142. Hartewig, *Zurückgekehrt*, 300–312; Monteath, "A Day to Remember," 200. In France a similar hierarchy emerged. The amount of financial aid and pensions depended on the deportee's status as either resister or nonresister. The latter category included the majority of surviving Jewish deportees. See Clifford, *Commemorating the Holocaust*, 35.

143. See for instance Holzer, *Lebenserinnerungen*, 249, 250.

144. Fritz Selbiger, Memoiren, Familienchronik, Nachlass Fritz Selbiger, 6.2, Nr. 3, CJA.

145. Interview with Kurt Goldstein in Herzberg, *Überleben heisst erinnern*, 326; see also Walter Sack, "Berliner Portraets, 'Bist Du nicht der Oskar?': Juedischer Arbeiterjunge, antifaschistischer Kämpfer, Emigrant, Handwerker, Bürgermeister," *Berliner Zeitung*, December 17/18, 1988.

146. Rothschild, *Memoirs*; Alfred Dreifuss, "In eigener jüdischer Sache . . ." (manuscript, no date), Alfred Dreifuss Archiv, 976, AAK.

147. DY55/V278/3/176, BArch.

148. DY55/V278/3/176, BArch.

149. For an exploration of agency within discursive structures, see G. Spiegel, introduction to *Practicing History*, 1–32. Since the end of the war, historians' understanding of how to define resistance has evolved, and the current understanding more closely matches the ideas of these survivors who suggested a broader definition. See Rozett, "Jewish Resistance."

150. Erich Simon, DY55/V278/4/56, BArch.

151. Landesverband VVN Brandenburg, Arnold Munter, DY55/V278/4/56, BArch. Such a wish to claim status as a resister was widespread. For another example, see Gilman, *Jurek Becker*, 25, 26.

152. Danyel, "Die geteilte Vergangenheit."

153. Dirks, *Die Verbrechen der anderen*, 330; Naimark, *The Russians in Germany*, 66, 361, 456; Fulbrook, *Reckonings*, 224, 243.

154. Cited as in Marlies Menge, "Zwei aus einer Straße," *Die Zeit*, October 21, 1988.

155. Anna Seghers to anonymous, no date [Spring 1947], in Seghers, *Hier im Volk der kalten Herzen*, 41.

156. Anna Seghers to Sally David Cramer, Berlin, July 31, 1947, in Seghers, *Hier im Volk der kalten Herzen*, 100, 101.

157. L. Winter, *Unsere Vergangenheit*, 314–315.

158. Holzer, *Lebenserinnerungen*, 244.

159. Interview with Kurt Goldstein in Herzberg, *Überleben heisst Erinnern*, 244; interview with Ilse Stillmann in Herzberg, *Überleben heisst Erinnern*, 197.

160. Interview with Ruth Gützlaff in Herzberg, *Überleben heisst Erinnern*, 129.

161. See, for example, testimony of Ascarelli Silvana in Castelnuovo, 1.2.N.31, ACDEC; "I collaboratori delle deportazione: Un processo alla Corte d'Assise di Roma," *Israel*, March 1, 1945; "Onoranze alle vittime dell'eccidio nazista," *Israel*, March 8, 1945.

162. Quoted as in Tagliacozzo and Di Castro, *Gli ebrei romani raccontano la "propria" Shoah*, 166.

163. As in Tagliacozzo and Di Castro, *Gli ebrei romani raccontano la "propria" Shoah*, 155.

164. Luigi Carmi to Unione, Pisa, November 9, 1946, "Privati 1944–1945," AUCEI.

165. Schiffer, *Non c'è ritorno a casa*, 193. Schiffer published his memoirs decades after the war when talking about Italy's implication became more common.

166. See the testimonies in Tagliacozzo and Di Castro, *Gli ebrei romani raccontano la "propria" Shoah*.

167. Bertilotti, "Italian Jews and the Memory of Rescue," 134; see also E. Momigliano, *Storia tragica e grottesca del razzismo fascista*.

168. Bauer, "Una Vita Segnata"; for more examples see Osti Guerrazzi, "Kain in Rom."

169. Millu, *I ponti di Schwerin*, 15 (my emphasis).

170. Millu, *I ponti di Schwerin*, 16 (my emphasis); for another example see Marta Ottolenghi Minerbi's autobiographical novel, *La colpa di essere nati*, which promotes the narrative of the good Italian while mentioning Italian perpetrators at various points. See also von Treskow, *Judenverfolgung in Italien*, 72–73.

171. See, for example, Debenedetti, *October 16, 1943: Eight Jews*, 26; Lattes, *Memoir*, 14; letter from Edoardo Forti to Vittorio Fano, November 1, 1946, Busta 442, BARM; Giorgio Bemporad, Archivio Storico Pratiche Requisizioni Ebraici D 14.1/2, Fascicolo 25, Busta 142, ASCEF; Liliana Briefel, *My Story of Life in Italy during the Holocaust*, 2005.387, USHMM.

172. Lutz Klinkhammer, "Le strategie tedesche di occupazione e la popolazione civile," 110.

173. D. Segre, *Memoirs of a Fortunate Jew*, 75.

174. "Farinacci," *Israel*, December 28, 1944.

175. See Ben-Ghiat, "A Lesser Evil?," 140; G. Schwarz, *Ritrovare se stessi*, 115.

176. According to De Felice, 10,370 Jews, or about 20 percent of the Jewish population, had been members of the PNF before 1938. De Felice, *Storia degli ebrei italiani sotto il fascismo*, 75. Michele Sarfatti estimates that Italian Jews made up about 2 to 3 percent of the PNF membership even though they were only about 1 percent of the population. He assumes that "the explanation lies not in a propensity of Italian Jews towards that particular party, but rather in the peculiarly Jewish tendency to engage in political life that arose out of their history as a minority, their higher level of education, and their living predominantly in towns." Sarfatti, introduction to "Italy's Fascist Jews."

177. See "A proposito di un nostro resoconto," *Israel*, December 6, 1945; see also Badrnejad-Hahn, "Wiederaufbau oder Neubeginn?," 175. Giorgio Bassani mentions the membership of Jews in the PNF frequently in his work. See Bassani, *Five Stories of Ferrara*, *The Garden of the Finzi-Continis*, and *Le parole preparate*. On Bassani's depiction of Fascist Jews, see also Neppi, "Giorgio Bassani e Arrigo Levi," 135–154.

178. Letters in Busta 442, BARM. See also Renato Almansi's defense of his father, Dante Almansi, who had been a PNF member: Renato Almansi, "Mio padre," in *Rassegna Mensile di Israel*, vol. 42, n. 5–6, (May–June, 1976); see also Raspagliesi, "Fascist Jews between Politics and the Economy." See also the essay by Silvia Berti on Arnaldo Momigliano where she emphasizes that Momigliano joined the party for professional reasons. Momigliano joined the PNF in 1932; party membership was a condition for the position as chair of Greek history at

212 | Notes to pages 88–91

the University of Rome that he assumed in the same year. He lost this position as a consequence of the 1938 racial laws and left Italy for the UK in 1939. The literary critic Carlo Dionisotto, Momigliano's close friend, asserted that Momigliano became a member "reluctantly." It seems that Momigliano himself did not reflect on his PNF membership after the war. Berti, "Arnaldo Momigliano."

179. On these letters see Orvieto, "Letters to Mussolini."

180. Von Treskow, *Judenverfolgung in Italien*, 19, 20, and 61–65, 107.

181. Briefel, *My Story of Life in Italy during the Holocaust.*

182. See, for example, E. Momigliano, *Storia trágica e grottesca del razzismo fascista*; Emilio Levi, *Ricordo di Maria*, 3; Maestro, *Tempo di guerra / Tempo di pace*, 21–22; Luft, *La mia guerra da civile*, 2–4; see also von Treskow, *Judenverfolgung in Italien*, 68; "Mussolini," *Israel*, May 3, 1945.

183. Luzzati, *La mia vita*, 17–18.

184. Cantoni, "Il saluto dell'unione delle comunità israelitiche italiane," 22 (my emphasis).

185. Valobra to Giacomo Terracini, May 13, 1944, Fondo Valobra, 14/156-T, ACDEC; see also Vittorio Foa cited in Stille, *Benevolence and Betrayal*, 321.

186. L. Morpurgo, *Caccia all'uomo!*, 67.

187. "I patrioti italiani e gli ebrei," ACDEC.

188. Focardi, "La memoria del fascismo," 61–65; Focardi and Klinkhammer, "The Question of Fascist Italy's War Crimes," 339; Ben-Ghiat, "A Lesser Evil?," 140. Regarding ideas about Italians' national character in political and social discourse, see Patriarca, *Italian Vices.*

189. Focardi and Klinkhammer, "The Question of Fascist Italy's War Crimes," 335–337; also Focardi, "Italy's Amnesia over War Guilt," 9–11.

190. Carlo Calenda, "Appunto: Taluni aspetti internazionali della questione ebraica," 1–2, Archivio di Stato Ministero Afari Esteri, Gabinetto 1943–1948, pacco 107, cat. II 1944–1947, f. 84, "Comunità Israelitica Italiana." Quoted in Toscano, *La "porta di Sion,"* 17–21; also G. Schwarz, "On Myth Making and Nation Building," 9–10.

191. G. Schwarz, "On Myth Making and Nation Building," 10–13.

192. Even during the war, the BBC's Radio London portrayed the Italians as good people and Mussolini as a misguided puppet. See British Broadcasting Corporation, *Ecco Radio Londra*; Focardi, "Italy's Amnesia over War Guilt," 23.

193. See, for instance, Ottolenghi Minerbi, *Colpa*, 153, 157, see also von Treskow, *Judenverfolgung in Italien*, 127.

194. Leaflet "Agli Ebrei Italiani di Ginevra," no date [1945], signed by Renzo Ottolenghi and Vittorio Tedeschi, Fondo Valobra, 1/140, ACDEC; see similar also Adolfo Massimo Vitale, "Pellegrinaggio fra l'orrore," Busta 44A, Fascicolo 44A-4, AUCEI; DELASEM letter to Italian Jewish refugees, Fondo Valobra 1/140.3.1, ACDEC.

195. *American Jewish Year Book*, vol. 46 (September 18, 1944, to September 7, 1945), 233.

196. Maestro, *Tempo di guerra / Tempo di pace*, 21.

197. Blackshirts refers to the members of the armed squads of Italian Fascism who wore black shirts as part of their uniform.

198. The American Joint Distribution Committee to AJDC Lisbon (Copy to New York), May 19, 1946, AR 45/54, No. 629, JDC Archives, New York; see similar also "Riconoscenza degli ebrei verso l'Italia," *Bollettino della Comunità Israelitica di Milano*, February 24, 1946.

199. Memorandum by David Bernstein, March 22, 1947, American Jewish Committee, Box 82, Italy, Archives American Jewish Committee, Record Group 347.7.1, YIVO Archives, New York.

200. After the Second World War, numerous Jewish refugees sought to enter Palestine. Italy was their main transit country. The Union of Italian Jewish Communities assisted in the illegal immigration, and the Italian government likewise supported it as they hoped to undermine British control of the Mediterranean. Moreover, the Italian government did not want refugees to settle in Italy permanently. G. Schwarz, *After Mussolini*, 135; Porat, "One Side of a Jewish Triangle in Italy," 181–203.

201. G. Schwarz, *After Mussolini*, 136.

202. Processo Hoess a Varsavia, Busta 44 A, Fasc. 4, Fondo UCEI da 1934, "Pellegrinaggio fra l'orrore," AUCEI.

203. See Massimo Adolfo Vitale, "Les persécutions contre les juifs en Italie 1938–1945," http://digital-library.cdec.it/cdec-web/viewer/cdecxDamsHisto26/IT-CDEC-ST0026-000243#page/11/mode/1up. Accessed July 26, 2018; on the conference see Jockusch, *Collect and Record!*, 163.

204. Vitale, "Les persécutions contre les juifs"; see also Laura Brazzo, "L'ansia di sapere: Massimo Adolfo Vitale e il Comitato Ricerca Deportati Ebrei," http://digital-library.cdec.it/cdec-web/progetti/info/ansia-di-sapere.html. Accessed January 14, 2023.

205. Massimo Adolfo Vitale, Promemoria, November 1949, Fondo Massimo Adolfo Vitale, Busta 1, Fascicolo 3, Corrispondenza CRDE 1949, ACDEC.

206. Forti, *Il caso Pardo Roques*, 4.

207. Forti, *Il caso Pardo Roques*, 222–225.

208. Forti, *Il caso Pardo Roques*, 242.

209. Ernesto Canarutto to Signor Avv. Bruno Ascarelli, June 16, 1946, Fascicolo 65A8 "Privati 1944–1945," AUCEI. See also letter from G. B. to Vittorio Fano, December 6, 1945, Busta 442, BARM; letter from R. S. to Ministero l'Assistenza Postbellica, "Privati 1944–1945," 65A-8, AUCEI.

210. Letter from Aldo De Benedetti to the Jewish community of Rome, June 28, 1946, Busta 165, ACF/Corrips./Varie anno 1945, Fascicolo 9, ASCER; see also the letter from Raffaello Sacerdoti to Ministero l'Assistenza Postbellica, August 27, 1945, "Privati 1944–1945," Fascicolo 65A-8, AUCEI. See similar also Misul, *Fra gli artigli del mostro nazista*, 7.

211. Regarding the perception of the Holocaust in postwar Italy, see R. Gordon, *The Holocaust in Italian Culture*; Focardi, "La percezione della Shoah"; Clifford, *Commemorating the Holocaust*; Bravo, D'Amico, and Brunello Mantelli, *I campi di sterminio nazisti*; Bravo, "Social Perception of the Shoah in Italy."

212. Servi, *Ed ora, 50 anni dopo . . .*, 48.

213. Ravenna, *Relazione*.

214. Goti Bauer, Testimony, March 4, 1992, ACDEC.

215. R. Gordon, "Primo Levi," 49. Natalia Ginzburg, who at the time worked for Einaudi, rejected the book on the grounds that several other concentration camp memoirs had already been published. She later considered her rejection an error. See Castronuovo, *Natalia Ginzburg*, 117, 118. Her initial rejection may point to her lack of considering the particularity of the Jewish experience in the camps at the time.

216. Unlike in France, where the national narrative around the resistance included deported and murdered deportees, in Italy the public imagination focused on victorious resistance fighters and marginalized deportees. Clifford, *Commemorating the Holocaust*, 81.

217. Biess, "Feelings in the Aftermath," 35–36.

218. See Servi, *Ed ora, 50 anni dopo . . .*, 44; also Luzzati, *La mia vita*; "Viva," *Bollettino della Comunità Israelitica di Milano*, September 1945; Testimony of Shoshana Debenedetti, RG O.93, f. 42649, Yad VaShem Archives, Jerusalem (hereafter YVA).

214 | *Notes to pages 93–95*

219. Testimony of Luisa (Franchetti) Naor, RG O.3, f. 6755.371, YVA; Testimony of Laura Nahoum, RG O.93, f. 42763.103, YVA.

220. Zargani, *Per violino solo*, 55.

221. Paladini, "A colloquio con Primo Levi," 149.

222. Di Cori, *Memorie di un italiano in Medio Oriente*, 118.

223. See Foa, *Il cavallo e la torre*.

224. See Foa Yona, "Leaving Fascist Italy."

225. Lelia Foa to her daughter Anna Foa, May 21, 1946, quoted in Stille, *Benevolence and Betrayal*, 164. Ottolenghi Minerbi likewise emphasized forgiveness in her autobiographical novel; see von Treskow, *Judenverfolgung in Italien*, 72 and 151.

226. Tauchert, *Jüdische Identitäten in Deutschland*, 182.

227. Collotti, *Il fascismo e gli ebrei*, 162.

228. Regarding European Jews' efforts to witness and testify, see Feinstein, *Holocaust Survivors in Postwar Germany*; Jockusch, *Collect and Record!*; Cesarani and Sundquist, *After the Holocaust*; Poznanski, "French Apprehensions, Jewish Expectations"; H. Diner, *We Remember with Reverence and Love*; Doron, *Jewish Youth and Identity*.

229. See, for instance, Beth Cohen, "The Myth of Silence"; see also Mazzini, "Memory of the Shoah."

230. See, for example, the recollections by Lucie Adelsberger, "Psychologische Beobachtungen im Konzentrationslager Auschwitz" (1947), Lucie Adelsberger Collection 1947–1994, LBI; Jacobson, *Mein Leben und Erinnerungen*; Rothschild, *Memoirs*; Anonymous, "Lebensbericht: Nacht über Deutschland: Illegales Leben eines Mischehepaares in einer deutschen Kleinstadt 1941–1945" (1947), R-2005/7, AJM; see also the testimonies by Dott. Leonardo de Benedetti, dott. Primo Levi; Luciana Nissim, "Riccordi della casa dei morti"; Jenny Ravenna; Franca Lattes; Stella Valabrega; Avigdor Miranda, in "testimonianze sui campi di concentramento," Fascicolo 44A-3, AUCEI. For a listing of all early Italian Jewish memoirs, see Jäger, "Frühe Holocaustzeugnisse italienischer Jüdinnen," and Anna Baldini, "La memoria italiana della Shoah." Other survivors decided to recount their stories decades later. Numerous factors have encouraged Jews to write about their lives during the war in the last two decades. The memory culture in both Italy and Germany had changed, and interest in Holocaust testimonies had grown significantly. At the end of their lives, many memoirists felt this was their last chance to recount their stories and prevent them from being forgotten. Some were motivated by the questions of children and grandchildren or the wish to present their history to the following generations. Anita Lasker-Walfisch, for instance, explained in her preface, addressing her children directly, "We have never talked much about those dark days and how it came about that you do not have any grandparents. . . . I have recorded as much as I possibly could so that you should 'inherit,' as it were, and keep alive the memory of those terrible days." Anita Lasker-Walfisch, *Memoir*, ME 304, LBI. See similar also Vitale, *Una bambina ebrea*. Regarding the increase of interest in Holocaust testimonies in the 1970s and 1980s, see Wieviorka, *The Era of the Witness*.

231. Barozzi, "L'uscita degli ebrei di Roma dalla clandestinità," 44–45.

232. Frankenthal, *Verweigerte Rückkehr*, 113.

233. Frankenthal, *Verweigerte Rückkehr*, 115.

234. See Castronuovo, *Natalia Ginzburg*, 36.

235. Kaminer, "Spaetfolgen bei juedischen KZ Uerberlebenden," 22.

236. Jacobson, *Mein Leben und Erinnerungen*, 45.

237. Jonas Lesser to Nelly Cohn-Leschzer, May 22, 1946, Nachlass Dr. Erich Cohn, 6.6, CJA.

Notes to pages 96–102 | 215

238. Jonas Lesser to Nelly Cohn-Leschzer, June 1, 1946, Nachlass Dr. Erich Cohn, 6.6, CJA.

239. Victoria Schoenmaker to Fritz Selbiger, September 7, 1947, Nachlass Fritz Selbiger, 6.2, CJA.

240. Rosa Deutscher to H. Hartogson, December 11, 1947, Frankfurt – Frauenverein 1924, ZA.

241. Siegmund Weltlinger to Clothilde Daniel, September 14, 1950, E Rep. 200–22, LAB.

242. Primo Levi to Eugenio Ravenna, December 6, 1945, quoted in "Eugenio Ravenna (1920–1977)," Museo Ferrara, http://www.museoferrara.it/view/s/e929751d18df44baa721bb0 29foc2066. Accessed January 14, 2023.

243. See exchange between Enrico Rosenholz and Sofia Shafranov [Schafranov], Rosenholz, famiglia, 1.1.N.6, ACDEC; on Sofia Schafranov see also Cavaliere and Schafranov, *I campi della morte in Germania*. Alberto Cavaliere, Sofia Schafranov's brother-in-law, conducted this long interview, which was first published in 1945 and thus is one of the earliest testimonies published in postwar Italy.

244. Regarding the notion of emotional refuge, see Biess, "Feelings in the Aftermath," 35–36.

245. Alfredo Sarano, Segretario Comunità Israelitica di Milano, to Anna Cassuto, May 10, 1947, Fondo Cassuto Nathan, 1.2. N.119, ACDEC.

246. Letter from unknown to Erich Cohn, November 21, 1946, Nachlass Dr Erich Cohn, 6.6. Nr 35, CJA.

247. See Koch, "But There Is Always Hope in the Human Heart."

248. Quoted in Guida, *La strada di casa*, 196.

249. Noack-Mosse, *Theresienstaedter Tagebuch*, 1.

250. Eugenio Ravenna was Bassani's second cousin, and his return inspired the story. The plaque was erected in Via Mazzini in April 1949 and included the name of Ravenna's namesake: Eugenio Ravenna, son of Isacco Ravenna and Eloisa Polacco, who was born thirty years earlier. See Museo Ferrara, http://www.museoferrara.it/view/s/e929751d18df44baa721bb029foc2066 and ACDEC, http://digital-library.cdec.it/cdec-web/persone/detail/person-6410/ravenna -eugenio.html. Accessed January 14, 2023. On the Ravenna family, see Ravenna, *La famiglia Ravenna*. On Bassani's story see also D. Schwarz, "Why Giorgio Bassani Matters," 42.

251. Bassani, *Five Stories of Ferrara*, 78.

252. Bassani, *Five Stories of Ferrara*, 78, 81. Like Bassani, scholars have discussed the potential of monuments to serve forgetting rather than remembering the past; see Young, *The Texture of Memory*, 61.

253. Nelly Cohn-Leschzer, "Die Gezeichneten," *Der Weg*, August 11, 1950.

254. Quoted as in Stille, *Benevolence and Betrayal*, 346–347.

255. P. Levi, *Survival in Auschwitz*, 26 and 123.

256. See Friedländer, *Probing the Limits of Representation*.

257. On the difficulty of recounting traumatic experiences, see Culbertson, "Embodied Memory, Transcendence, and Telling," 170; Langer, *Holocaust Testimonies*; Laub, "An Event without a Witness," 75–92.

258. P. Levi, *The Drowned and the Saved*, 83–84.

259. Confino and Fritzsche, "Introduction: Noises of the Past," 5.

3. Reclaiming Home

1. L. Winter, *Unsere Vergangenheit*, 275.

2. E. Morpurgo, *Diario dell'esilio in Svizzera*, 46.

216 | Notes to pages 102–107

3. Venezia, "Perché è successo?," 139.

4. For a reassessment of Jewish agency in the prosecution of Nazi war criminals, see Bloxham, *Genocide on Trial* and "Jewish Witnesses in War Crimes Trials of the Postwar Era"; Douglas, *The Memory of Judgement*; Cohen, "Dr. Jacob Robinson"; Jockusch, "Justice at Nuremberg?"

5. Stern, *Im Anfang war Auschwitz*; Bergmann and Erb, *Antisemitismus in der Bundesrepublik Deutschland*; Rossi-Doria, "'Antisemitismo democratico'"; Goldstaub, "Appunti per uno studio sui pregiudizi antiebraici"; Toscano, *Ebraismo e Antisemitismo in Italia*.

6. There is vast literature on the topic of restitution. Regarding Italian Jews' struggle to retrieve their property, see D'Amico, *Quando l'eccezione diventa norma*; Pavan, *Persecution, Indifference, and Amnesia*. For the German case, see Winstel, *Verhandelte Gerechtigkeit*; Goschler, *Schuld und Schulden*; Hockerts, Moisel, and Winstel, *Grenzen der Wiedergutmachung*.

7. Frankenthal, *Verweigerte Rückkehr*, 109.

8. Orbach and Orbach-Smith, *Soaring Underground*, 330–334. Walter Spier and his brother also beat up a Nazi after the war. See Junge, "'Go Back to Your Hometown,'" 27.

9. This absence of a discourse or acts of revenge was not particular to German Jewish survivors but was common for Holocaust survivors more generally. See Roseman, "'No, Herr Führer!'"

10. Moses Moskowitz, "The Germans and the Jews: Postwar Report," *Commentary*, January, 1946.

11. Richard May, "Falschmünzerei," *Der Weg*, November, 29, 1946.

12. See Giordano, *Die zweite Schuld*, 294.

13. Roseman, "'No, Herr Führer!'" 73, 74.

14. Hannah Arendt, "The Aftermath of Nazi Rule—Report from Germany," *Commentary*, October 1950, 343.

15. Landau, "Wir Juden und unsere Umwelt," 148–149.

16. Wilhelm Meier, "Nürnberger Reflexionen," *Der Weg*, July 16, 1946.

17. Roseman, "'No, Herr Führer!'" 85.

18. See, for instance, Klemperer, *So sitze ich denn zwischen allen Stühlen*, 109; Paepcke, *Ich wurde vergessen*, 126; Nelly Cohn-Leschzer, "Antagonismen," *Der Weg*, October 20, 1950.

19. Moskowitz, "The Germans and the Jews."

20. Julius Meyer, "Das Nürnberger Urteil und wir," *Der Weg*, October 10, 1946.

21. Richard May, "Falschmünzerei," *Der Weg*, November, 29, 1946.

22. Meier, "Nürnberger Reflexionen."

23. Kessler, "Verdrängung der Geschichte," 35; Monteath, "Narratives of Fascism," 100.

24. Eschwege, *Fremd unter meinesgleichen*, 50.

25. Kurt Grobe to Adelsberger, May 20, 1945, Frankfurt – B.1/13, Serie A 115, Blatt 23, ZA.

26. Klemperer, *So sitze ich denn zwischen allen Stühlen*, 94. Klemperer joined in December 1945.

27. Raim, "Der Wiederaufbau der Justiz in Westdeutschland," 53–54.

28. Friedlander, "The Deportation of the German Jews," 202–203.

29. Fulbrook, *Reckonings*, 233; Rückerl, *NS-Verbrechen vor Gericht*, 110.

30. Jockusch, "Das Urteil der Zeugen," 653; see also Marrus, *The Holocaust at Nuremberg*, 6, 7.

31. Wolfgang Hildesheimer to his parents, February 5, 1947, Wolfgang Hildesheimer Archiv, 456, AAK. The Doctors' Trial (officially *United States of America v. Karl Brandt, et al.*)

considered the fate of twenty-three German physicians for their willing participation in war crimes and crimes against humanity. Sixteen of the defendants were found guilty, seven of whom were executed.

32. Zevi and Zevi, *Ti racconto la mia storia*, 54, 55.

33. Jockusch, "Das Urteil der Zeugen," 653; see also Marrus, *The Holocaust at Nuremberg*, 6, 7.

34. Jockusch, "Justice at Nuremberg?," 127.

35. Hans-Erich Fabian, "Vor dem Nürnberger Urteil," *Der Weg*, September 13, 1946.

36. See, for instance, Frankfurt – B.1/13, Serie A 618, Blatt 14, ZA; letter from A.M., April 29, 1947, in Jüdische Gemeinde Mainz – B.1/18, Blatt 61, ZA; Bestand 5B1 1, Verband der Jüdischen Gemeinden in der DDR, 1945–1991, Nr. 6, CJA; Singewald in Herzberg, *Überleben heisst Erinnern*, 65; see also Willingham, *Jews in Leipzig*, 144; Raim, "Der Wiederaufbau der Justiz in Westdeutschland," 53, 54; Friedlander, "The Deportation of the German Jews," 203; Wojak, *Fritz Bauer*, 191; Fulbrook, *Reckonings*, 237.

37. Geis, *Übrig sein*, 245–248.

38. Geis, *Übrig sein*, 248–249.

39. "Angstpsychose," *Der Weg*, April 10, 1947.

40. Raim, "Der Wiederaufbau der Justiz in Westdeutschland," 53, 54; Friedlander, "The Deportation of the German Jews," 203; See, for instance, Frankfurt – B.1/13, Serie A 618, Blatt 14, ZA; Willingham, *Jews in Leipzig*, 144; Letter from A.M., April 29, 1947, Jüdische Gemeinde Mainz – B.1/18, Blatt 61, ZA; Bestand 5B1 1, Verband der Jüdischen Gemeinden in der DDR, 1945–1991, Nr. 6, CJA.

41. "Auschwitzer SS-Aufseherin unschädlich gemacht," *Der Weg*, May 31, 1946.

42. Wojak, *Fritz Bauer*, 191.

43. Wojak, *Fritz Bauer*, 247.

44. Fulbrook, *Reckonings*, 254.

45. Singewald in Herzberg, *Überleben heisst Erinnern*, 65.

46. Letter from Erster Öffentlicher Kläger bei der Spruch- und Berufungskammer für den Bezirk Frankfurt A.M., December 22, 1948, Frankfurt – B.1/13, Serie A 618, Blatt 13, ZA.

47. "Entnazifizierung," *Der Weg*, May 31, 1946.

48. To Öffentlicher Kläger bei der Zentralberufungskammer Hesse, October 24, 1951, Frankfurt – B.1/13 Serie A 618, Blatt 33, ZA.

49. See, for instance, correspondence between Hans Fuchs and Leo Kohorn, February 1948, Frankfurt – B.1/13, Serie A 588, ZA.

50. Literally "Persil ticket"—Persil refers to a laundry detergent. This contemporary term for denazification certificates suggested the whitewashing of the past.

51. Klemperer, *So sitze ich denn zwischen allen Stühlen*, 94.

52. Klemperer, *So sitze ich denn zwischen allen Stühlen*, 15, 94.

53. For other examples see Lebenslauf Ellen Rathé, Nachlass Ellen Rathé, 6.23, Nr. 3, CJA; A.S. certificate for K., September 16, 1946, RG 14052 M Reel 11, USHMM; Scheer, *Im Schatten der Sterne*, 389.

54. Geis, *Übrig sein*, 259.

55. "Unsere Pgs," *Der Weg*, March 15, 1946.

56. Geis, *Übrig sein*, 258–259.

57. Margarete Landé to the Frankfurt Jewish community, April 10, 1946, Frankfurt – B.1/13, Serie A 595, Blatt 64–66, ZA.

218 | *Notes to pages 110–114*

58. On Clauss see Weingart, *Doppel-Leben*.

59. See the letters in Bestand 5B1, Verband der Jüdischen Gemeinden in der DDR, 1945–1991, CJA; Jüdische Gemeinde Mainz – B.1/18, 61, ZA; Frankfurt – B.1/13, Serie A 588, ZA; Frankfurt – B.1/13, Serie A 1191, ZA; Frankfurt – B.1/13, Serie A 1193, ZA.

60. Head of the Düsseldorf Jewish community to Adolf Caspari, January 21, 1948, Düsseldorf – B.1/5, 76, ZA.

61. Peter Hartmann to Waldmann, December 9, 1946, Jüdische Gemeinde Mainz – B.1/18, 61, Allgemeine Korrespondenz, ZA.

62. Domenico, *Italian Fascists on Trial*, 19–21.

63. Woller, "Die Anfänge der politischen Säuberung in Italien," 142–147.

64. Emilia Canarutto to Rita Calimani, April 26, 1945, Fondo Canarutto, 125, Privati diversi, ACDEC.

65. E. Morpurgo, *Diario dell'esilio in Svizzera*, 148.

66. For the fascinating history of Mussolini's corpse, see S. Luzzatto, *The Body of Il Duce*.

67. M. Pacifici, *Diario*, 5; see also E. Piperno, *Trattoria dei cacciatori*, 46.

68. Domenico, *Italian Fascists on Trial*, 174–175.

69. See, for instance, letter from Giacomo Sarfatti, Angelo Romanelli, et al. to Comando della Polizia Alleata, March 22, 1946, Fondo Famiglie Sarfatti, Cesana, Polacco, Busta 1, Fascicolo 2, ACDEC; Vittorio Fano to the heads of the Milan and Trieste community and the president of the Unione, February 24, 1947, Busta 44 A, 449, Comitato ricerche deportati ebrei, AUCEI.

70. Testimony of Vittorio Cremisini, July 6, 1946, Italy 116, Box 247, YIVO Archives.

71. Lea Pincherle, "Pro memoria (per il dopo guerra)," November 17, 1944, Fondo Valobra 5/144-8, ACDEC. I do not know whether she succeeded in ensuring that he would face trial.

72. Jockusch, "In Search of Retribution"; Person, "Building a Community of Survivors."

73. Emilio Canarutto to Bruno Küsnacht, February 15, 1945, Fondo Canarutto 125, Privati diversi, ACDEC.

74. Emilio Canarutto to Bruno Küsnacht, February 26, 1945, Fondo Canarutto 125, Privati diversi, ACDEC.

75. Sullam, *The Italian Executioners*, 86.

76. Vittorio Fano to the heads of the Milan and Trieste community. Venice, February 24, 1947. Busta 44A, Fascicolo 44-A-22, AUCEI.

77. Di Vita, "Gli Ebrei di Milano sotto l'occupazione nazista," 20; also Sullam, *The Italian Executioners*, 123.

78. See United Nations War Crimes Commission, *Law Reports of Trials of War Criminals*.

79. See Comunicato, March 14, 1947, Processo Hoess a Varsavia, Busta 44A, Fascicolo 44A-4, AUCEI.

80. Letter from Massimo Adolfo Vitale, February 28, 1947, Processo Hoess a Varsavia, Busta 44A, Fascicolo 44A-4, AUCEI.

81. Eugenio Ravenna to CRDE, March 5, 1947, Processo Hoess a Varsavia, Busta 44A, Fascicolo 44A-4, AUCEI.

82. See Fulbrook, *Reckonings*, 294, 300, 362. In a letter to Cologne's state attorney, a German camp survivor put his difficulties into words: "They demand of us that, if we claim to have been there, we must have seen and heard it all. But we were almost paralyzed with fear and terror, and our senses barely worked. They require us to name the hour, the day, but we had neither clock, nor calendar in the camp, we did not even know if it was Sunday or a holiday. We are supposed to describe the appearance of our executioners. But in their uniforms,

Notes to pages 114–118 | 219

they all looked the same to us." Quote in the original German in Rückerl, *NS-Verbrechen vor Gericht*, 253.

83. See, for instance, the letter from lawyer Pia Levi Ravenna to the Jewish community of Milan with information about the trial against collaborators Santa Maria Riva and Monticelli, January 27, 1949, Fondo Massimo Adolfo Vitale, Busta 5, Fascicolo 187, ACDEC; correspondence between Pia Levi Ravenna and the Jewish community of Milan on the trial against John Cornaggia, May–June 1949, Fondo Massimo Adolfo Vitale, Busta 5, Fascicolo 188, ACDEC.

84. "Un'altra triste pagina chiusa: Guide e confinari condannati per tradimento e vessazione agli ebrei," *La Prealpina*, February 20, 1947.

85. Altmann to Presidente Delle Comunità Israelitiche Italiane, Milano, August 27, 1948, Attività del Comitato ricerche deportati ebrei, Fascicolo 44A-2 449, AUCEI.

86. La Corte Straordinaria di Assise di Alessandria, Province of Alessandria, Italy 116, Box 247, YIVO Archives. The defendants received a sentence of five years and a fine of five thousand lira.

87. "Un'altra triste pagina chiusa"; the court sentenced the guides to prison terms of three to twenty years.

88. Renzo Levi to capo della pubblica sicurezza, October 23, 1946, Privati 1946–1948, Busta 02B, AUCEI.

89. G. Schwarz, *Ritrovare se stessi*, 10.

90. Goldstaub, "Appunti per uno studio sui pregiudizi antiebraici," 141. See also the report on the attack of the Jewish Quarter in Rome, February 1948, AR 45/54 # 626, Joint Archives, New York.

91. Interview with Liliana Spizzichino in *La Comunita Ebraica di Roma*, 118.

92. L. Levi, *Se vai via il re*, 11–15; Guido Hassan likewise recounted facing antisemitism when returning to school; see Broggini, *Frontier of Hope*, 385.

93. A. Villa, *Dai lager alla terra promessa*, 263–264.

94. Letter from Massimo Vitale to Massimo Mercurio, Direttore del giornale "Il Mattino d'Italia," October 3, 1947, Busta 44A, Fascicolo 44A-2, AUCEI.

95. Geom Giacomo Camerini to Raffaele Cantoni, June 9, 1948, Busta 85G, AUCEI.

96. Goldstaub, "Appunti per uno studio sui pregiudizi antiebraici," 174; for one example see letter from Zachariah Schuster to Foreign Affairs Department, June 16, 1950, American Jewish Committee, Record Group 347.7.1, YIVO Archives.

97. Mazzini, "Aspetti dell'antisemitismo cattolico dopo l'Olocausto," 325.

98. Elena Foa to Direzione dell' E.I.A.R, March 11, 1947, "Ricorso presentato dall'Unione ai deputati dell'Assemblea Costituente," Fascicolo 65B-10 654, AUCEI.

99. Vitale Milano to direzione degli ospedali riunti di Roma, July 8, 1945, Busta 72, Fascicolo 5, AUCEI. The archive contains no reply from the hospital, so its reaction, or lack thereof, remains unknown.

100. Memorandum on Italy from Z. Shuster, June 25, 1947, American Jewish Committee, Record Group 347.7.1, YIVO Archives.

101. Letter from Zachariah Schuster to Foreign Affairs Department, June 16, 1950, American Jewish Committee, Record Group 347.7.1, YIVO Archives.

102. In 1965 the Second Vatican Ecumenical Council, *Nostra Aetate*, finally rejected the church's traditional anti-Jewish attitude. The Declaration on the Relationship of the Church to Non-Christian Religions repudiated antisemitism and the charge that Jews were

220 | *Notes to pages 118–121*

collectively guilty for the crucifixion of Jesus Christ. See Phayer, *The Catholic Church and the Holocaust*, 208–215.

103. Zuccotti, *Under His Very Windows*, 139.

104. Goldstaub, "Appunti per uno studio sui pregiudizi antiebraici," 145.

105. Croce, Prefazione to *I pavidi*, xiii, xiv. See also G. Schwarz, *Ritrovare se stessi*, 11.

106. Rossi-Doria, "'Antisemitismo democratico,'" 258–261.

107. Dante Lattes, "Benedetto Croce e l'inutile martirio d'Israele," *Israel*, January 30, 1947.

108. A. Momigliano, *Essays on Ancient and Modern Judaism*, 139; see also G. Schwarz, *After Mussolini*, 8–9. After the war Momigliano did not return even though Benedetto Croce offered him a position in his institute in Naples; possibly Croce's remarks played a role here. Grafton, "Arnaldo Momigliano," ix–xvi.

109. Hillel [pseud.], "Antisemitismo Spicciolo," *Israel*, January 18, 1945.

110. "Liberazione," *Israel*, December 7, 1944.

111. "Ziel der Zeitschrift," *Der Weg*, March 1, 1946.

112. Wilhelm Meier, "Auswanderer—Rückwanderer," *Der Weg*, February 7, 1947; see also Ernst Landau, "Wir Juden und die Umwelt: Ein Beitrag zum Problem der Kollektivschuld," *Jüdische Rundschau* 6, July 1946, 23–25.

113. Albrecht, "Jeanette Wolff, Jakob Altmaier und Peter Blachstein," 238.

114. L. Winter, *Unsere Vergangenheit*, 278, 285, 300, 314; Grundig, *Gesichte und Geschichte*, 318.

115. Rothschild, *Memoirs*, 173.

116. See, for instance, Deutschkron, *Mein Leben nach dem Überleben*, 113, 116, 117; Morris, "Interview with Bodenheimer," 194; Schmuckler, *Gast im eigenen Land*, 155; Tapetenfabrik Strauven to Abraham Fischmann, September 25, 1948, Allgemeine Korrespondenz Düsseldorf – B. 1/5, 77, ZA; Carl Frowein, "Beschwerde über das Verhalten der für den Neusser Viehmarkt zuständigen Beamten," November 30, 1946, Allgemeine Korrespondenz Düsseldorf – B.1/5, 77, ZA.

117. Stern, *The Whitewashing of the Yellow Badge*, 210. In 1938 Nazi authorities had decreed that by January 1, 1939, Jewish men and women bearing first names of "non-Jewish" origin had to add the names "Israel" and "Sara" respectively, to their given names.

118. Hockenos, *A Church Divided*, 151; Stern, *The Whitewashing of the Yellow Badge*, 75, 157.

119. Kurt Schatter to Hauptausschuß OdF, Bad Liebenstein, 06/28/1947, Bestand 5B1, Verband der Jüdischen Gemeinden in der DDR, 1945–1991, CJA. Numerous OdFs were founded in German towns and cities in the immediate aftermath of the war to provide material assistance to the victims of Nazi persecution.

120. Günter Nobel to Meyer, May 24, 1949, Bestand 5B1 1, Verband der Jüdischen Gemeinden in der DDR, 1945–1991, Nr. 5, CJA.

121. R. Gay, *Safe among the Germans*, 102; Granata, "'Das hat in der DDR keine Rolle gespielt, was man war,'" 89, 90.

122. Quoted in Goldenbogen, "Leon Löwenkopf," 95.

123. On DPs' demonstrations see Grossmann, *Jews, Germans, and Allies*, 258–259.

124. Head of the Jewish community Düsseldorf to "Nordstern" All Versicherungs-Aktiengesellschaft, November 3, 1947, Allgemeine Korrespondenz Düsseldorf – B. 1/5, 77, ZA. The insurance company had written to the Jewish community as they did not have an address for Kurt Frank (emphasis in original).

125. Nordstern to Jewish Community Düsseldorf, November 5, 1947, Allgemeine Korrespondenz Düsseldorf – B.1/5, 77, ZA (emphasis in original).

Notes to pages 122–126 | 221

126. See Stern, *The Whitewashing of the Yellow Badge*, 90.

127. Stern, *The Whitewashing of the Yellow Badge*, 201–207.

128. Klemperer, *So sitze ich denn zwischen allen Stühlen*, 572.

129. See Jünger, "Farewell to the German-Jewish Past," 73.

130. Klemperer, *So sitze ich denn zwischen allen Stühlen*, 383.

131. Einhorn, *Nation und Identität*, 101–119; Winterfeldt, *Deutschland*, 428; Giordano, "Ich bin geblieben—warum?," 125; Grete Weil to Walter Jokisch, December 28, 1946, GW B 96, Monacensia; Paepcke, *Ich wurde vergessen*, 121; Klemperer, *So sitze ich denn zwischen allen Stühlen*, 148.

132. Klemperer, *So sitze ich denn zwischen allen Stühlen*, 55. Across western Europe, Jewish returnees experienced overstated support for their cause. On postwar philosemitism in western Europe, see Daniel Cohen, "Towards a History of 'Philosemitic' Europe since 1945," EuropeNow, November 2, 2017, http://europenowjournal.org/2017/11/01/towards-a-history-of -philosemitic-europe-since-1945/.

133. Debenedetti, *October 16, 1943; Eight Jews*, 66.

134. Harry Greenstein, *Heidelberg Conference: The Future of the Jews in Germany 1949*, LBI.

135. Moskowitz, "The Germans and the Jews," 10.

136. Stern, *The Whitewashing of the Yellow Badge*, xxi.

137. Altfelix, "The 'Post-Holocaust Jew'"; Stern, *The Whitewashing of the Yellow Badge*, 397–399.

138. Stern, *The Whitewashing of the Yellow Badge*, 397–399.

139. Cohen, "Towards a History of 'Philosemitic' Europe."

140. Dr. Neuhaus to Rechtsabteilung der Aktienbaugesellschaft, August 15, 1945, Frankfurt –B.1/13, Serie A 147, Blatt 27, ZA.

141. Vorstand der jüdischen Gemeinde Mainz to Marg. Lied, December 25, 1947, Jüdische Gemeinde Mainz – B.1/18, 60, ZA.

142. Becker, *Mein Vater, die Deutschen und ich*, 251.

143. Tagliacozzo, *Metà della vita*, 332.

144. Letter from Peter Reiche to relatives, January 1, 1946, Sammlung Peter H. Reiche, 2005/51/01-14, JMA.

145. Moskowitz, "The Germans and the Jews."

146. For a European perspective, see Dean, Goschler, and Ther, *Robbery and Restitution*; Diner, and Wunberg, *Restitution and Memory*; Pavan, "Neither Citizens nor Jews." For Viennese Jews see Anthony, "Return of Jewish Concentration Camp Survivors," 288; for Parisian Jews see Auslander, "Coming Home?," 244–245.

147. A. Villa, *Dai Lager alla terra promessa*, 19.

148. Letter from Emma Tagliacozzo to Ottolenghi, no date, Busta 165, ASCER.

149. See, for examples Report on Jewish Assets, Rome, February 18, Italy Summary of Reports (1945–1967), AR 45/54 # 629, JDC Archives; A. Villa, *Dai Lager alla terra promessa*; Testimonies of Bemporad Giorgio and Adolfo Orvieto, Fascicolo 25 and 23, Busta 142, ACEF.

150. D'Amico, *Quando l'eccezione diventa norma*; Fubini, "Die Rechtsstellung der jüdischen Gemeinde Italiens," 76.

151. Report on Jewish Assets, Rome, February 18, Italy Summary of Reports (1945–1967), AR 45/54 # 629, JDC Archives, New York.

152. The Fascist government had set up the EGELI, operating under the Ministry of Finance, in 1939. After the war the organization showed no remorse or sensitivity in its handling of the restitution. Indeed, its approach to the return process enraged the victims. For

222 | *Notes to pages 126–130*

instance, the EGELI demanded that Italian Jews reimburse them for all administrative costs associated with the storage and return of their property. Pavan, *Persecution, Indifference, and Amnesia*, 21.

153. Quoted in Pavan, *Persecution, Indifference, and Amnesia*, 22.

154. Letter from Arrigo Vita to the UCII, 1948, Vicissitudini dei singoli, Arrigo Vita, Serie I, b. 29, Fascicolo 782.

155. D'Amico, *Quando l'eccezione diventa norma*, 366; See also Pavan, *Persecution, Indifference, and Amnesia*, 18–19.

156. Pavan, *Persecution, Indifference, and Amnesia*, 18–19.

157. A. Villa, *Dai Lager alla terra promessa*, 18.

158. Cited as in Broggini, *Frontier of Hope*, 372.

159. E. Piperno, *Trattoria dei cacciatori*, 50.

160. Letter from Peter Reiche to relatives, January 1, 1946, Sammlung Peter H Reiche, 2005/51/01-14, AJM.

161. Frankenthal, *Verweigerte Rückkehr*, 97; see similar also letter from Clara Fischer to Jüdische Gemeinde Düsseldorf, June 28, 1947, Allgemeine Korrespondenz Düsseldorf – B.1/5, 77, ZA.

162. Stern, *Im Anfang war Auschwitz*, 337; Winstel, *Verhandelte Gerechtigkeit*, 389; Bergmann, *Geschichte des Antisemitismus*, 117–122. Junge "'Go Back to Your Hometown,'" 27.

163. Junge, "'Go Back to Your Hometown,'" 148.

164. Grossmann, *Jews, Germans, and Allies*, 95; Frankenthal, *Verweigerte Rückkehr*, 118.

165. Webster, "Jüdische Rückkehrer in der BRD nach 1945," 63–74.

166. Goschler, *Schuld und Schulden*, 361–364; Graf, "Twice Exiled," 8–20; Hartewig, *Zurückgekehrt*, 312–313.

167. Di Cori, *Memorie di un italiano in Medio Oriente*, 120; Balderi, *Tremarono i Lungarni*, 25; see also von Treskow, *Judenverfolgung in Italien*, 61.

168. Letter from Emilio Ernesto Canarutto to Signor Avv. Bruno Ascarelli c/o Unione, June 19, 1946, "Privati 1944-1945," Fascicolo 65A-8, AUCEI.

169. Woller, *Die Abrechnung mit dem Faschismus*, 405.

170. Pezzino and Schwarz, "From Kappler to Priebke," 310.

171. Ginsborg, *A History of Contemporary Italy*, 92.

172. The Manifesto of race was issued on July 14, 1938. It argued that Italy's population was of Aryan origin and that a distinct Italian race existed. Jews could not become members of this race. See Collotti, "Die Historiker und die Rassengesetze in Italien," 61.

173. Franzinelli, *L'amnistia Togliatti*, 208–210.

174. Pende, "Al Sig. Direttore di Israel" and "Processo a Pende," both in *Israel*, January 13, 1949.

175. Pende, "Processo a Pende."

176. Quoted in Tagliacozzo and Di Castro, *Gli ebrei romani raccontano la "propria" Shoah*, 282.

177. The *Giornale d'Italia* wrote that a small minority of students staged a protest against Pende but were opposed by the majority of the students. See A. Villa, *Dai Lager alla terra promessa*, 89.

178. Gilette, "The Origins of the 'Manifesto of Racial Scientists,'" 308, 313.

179. Luigi Sadun to Raffaele Cantoni, May 28, 1946, Busta 85G-12, AUCEI.

180. Letter from Mario Castelnuovo to Carlo Alberto Viterbo, May 18, 1946 and Luigi Sadun to Raffaele Cantoni, May 28, 1946, Busta 85G-12, AUCEI.

181. Letter from Giulo Cogni to presidente della comunità israelitica italiana per il tramite della comunità israelitica di Siena, May 18, 1946, Busta 85G-12, AUCEI.

182. Letter from Mario Castelnuovo to Carlo Alberto Viterbo, Siena, May 18, 1946; see also Luigi Sadun to Raffaele Cantoni, May 28, 1946, both Busta 85G-12, AUCEI.

183. Adler, "Jew as Bourgeois," 322–323.

184. Letter from Giulio Cogni to presidente della comunità israelitica italiana per il tramite della comunità israelitica di Siena, May 18, 1946, Busta 85G-12, AUCEI. See also A. Villa, *Dai Lager alla terra promessa*, 93.

185. A. Villa, *Dai Lager alla terra promessa*, 93.

186. Baiardi, "Sulle sofferenze," 303.

187. Bruno Fiorentini, "Sacandaloso verdetto del tribunale di Pistoia: Gli ordini di rastrellare gli ebrei sono da considerarsi legittimi," *Voce Partigiana, organo del comitato regionale dell'a.n.p.i*, January 21, 1947.

188. Badrnejad-Hahn, "Wiederaufbau oder Neubeginn?," 98; Toscano, "The Abrogation of Racial Laws," 157.

189. Giorgio Rossi to Unione, March 26, 1947, Fascicolo 65B-10 654 and Angelo Cavaglione to Unione, June 16, 1947, Privati 1944–1945, Fascicolo 65A-8, both AUCEI; also Carlo Alberto Viterbo, "Uguaglianza e rispetto," *Israel*, February 6, 1947.

190. Observations and suggestions submitted by the Union of Italian Jewish Communities to the Deputies of the Constituent Assembly, Files of the Commissions, Committees, and Departments of the Conference, Overseas Department / Department of Overseas Relations, Italy, C7/309, CZA.

191. "L'Unione delle comunità e il progetto di costituzione," *Israel*, March 13, 1947; Report of Administration Bureau, January 1 through March 31, 1947, AR 45/54 # 627, JDC Archives, New York.

192. "All'Onorevole Enrico de Nicola Capo provvisorio della Repubblica Italiana," Rome, March 22, 1947 and Ricorso presentato dall'Unione ai deputati dell'Assemblea Costituente, both Fascicolo 65B-10 654, AUCEI.

193. Observations and suggestions submitted by the Union of Italian Jewish Communities to the Deputies of the Constituent Assembly, Files of the Commissions, Committees, and Departments of the Conference, Overseas Department / Department of Overseas Relations, Italy, C7/309, CZA.

194. Joint Research Department Report No. 31, first quarter 1947, submitted by Jacob Trobe, AR 45/54 # 627, JDC Archives, New York.

195. Unione to WJC, March 1947, Files of the Commissions, Committees, and Departments of the Conference, Overseas Department / Department of Overseas Relations, C7/309, CZA.

196. Meir Grossman, Director Department of Oversees Relations to Unione delle Comunità Israelitiche Italiane, C7/309, CZA.

197. Letter from Simon Segal, Ass. Director, Foreign Affairs Department, June 19, 1947, American Jewish Committee, Record Group 347.7.1, YIVO Archives.

198. G. Schwarz, *After Mussolini*, 30, 31.

199. A. Winkler, *Hermann Kesten im Exil*, 36; Mertz, *Und das wurde nicht ihr Staat*, 24; Rothschild, *Memoirs*, 169–173; interview with Ruth Benario in John Borneman and Jeffrey M. Peck, *Sojourners*, 37–60; interview with Sophie Marum in Wroblewsky, *Zwischen Thora und Trabant*, 27.

200. Spira, *Trab der Schaukelpferde*, 228.

224 | Notes to pages 133–136

201. Becker, *Mein Vater, die Deutschen und ich*, 249; see similar also Helmut Eschwege, *Fremd unter meinesgleichen*, 50.

202. Mayer, *Ein Deutscher auf Widerruf*, 303.

203. Dietrich Goldschmidt, "8. Mai 1945, Erlebnisse, Taetigkeiten und Erfahrungen 1945–1949," ME1014, LBI.

204. The texts of the cabaret pieces "Der Remigrant," "Der Jubler," "Die Ratte," and "Ilse Koch" are included in Gert's memoir, *Ich bin eine Hexe*, 243, 248–250.

205. Josef von Báky, dir. *Der Ruf*. 1949. Bavaria Film Studios, Munich.

206. Brenner, "'We Are the Unhappy Few,'" 13.

207. E. G. Lowenthal, "Isolation und Unsicherheit," *Juedisches Gemeindeblatt*, October 15, 1948; Fritz Eschen, "Die überlebenden Juden," *Juedisches Gemeindeblatt*, November 27, 1946; Karl Jakob Hirsch to Hans [no surname], July 20, 1950, Nachlass Karl Jakob Hirsch, Universitätsbibliothek der LMU München; Hans-Erich Fabian, "Unheimliches Deutschland," *Der Weg*, January 31, 1947.

208. Stern, *The Whitewashing of the Yellow Badge*, 224.

209. Press conference with Rabbi Dr. Baeck, October 14, 1948, Frankfurt – B.1/13, Serie A 722, Blatt 38, ZA.

210. Rabbi Wilhelm Weinberg, "Abschiedspredigt," November 1951, RG 10.238, USHMM.

211. See "Ein Hotel im stillen Winkel? Nein: Im unterirdischen Bunker von Düsseldorf," *Zeitschrift Konstanze*, July 1948, quoted in Sinn, *Jüdische Politik*, 78. However, Marx decided to stay and eventually defended Jewish life in Germany. See Sinn, *Jüdische Politik*, 80, 81.

212. Karl Marx, "Nach den Wahlen," *Jüdisches Gemeindeblatt für die britische Zone*, April 30, 1947.

213. Frei, *Vergangenheitspolitik*, 303.

214. Frankenthal, *Verweigerte Rückkehr*, 103, 105. See also "Wir bemerken," *Der Weg*, July 12, 1946.

215. Brenner, "'We Are the Unhappy Few,'" 18.

216. H. Winkler, *Der lange Weg*, 167; Mitscherlich and Mitscherlich, *Die Unfähigkeit zu trauern*, 27, 36.

217. Frei, "Amnestiepolitik in den Bonner Anfangsjahren," 490.

218. Kesten, *Der Geist der Unruhe*, 239.

219. Klemperer, *So sitze ich denn zwischen allen Stühlen*, 71, 73, 80, 107, 118.

220. Klemperer, *So sitze ich denn zwischen allen Stühlen*, 94.

221. Fulbrook, *Reckonings*, 357.

222. See Goldenbogen, "Leon Löwenkopf," 98; Hartewig, *Zurückgekehrt*, 195.

223. Anna Seghers to Erika Friedländer, Paris, November 17, 1947, in Seghers and Berger, *Hier im Volk der kalten Herzen*, 162.

224. See also Peitsch, "Antifaschistisches Verständnis der eigenen jüdischen Herkunft," 125–127. On the GDR's self-understanding as antifascist, see Fulbrook and Port, *Becoming East German*; D. Diner, "On the Ideology of Antifascism"; Danyel, "DDR-Antifaschismus"; Grunenberg, *Antifaschismus—ein deutscher Mythos*.

225. Dirks, *Die Verbrechen der anderen*, 330; Naimark, *The Russians in Germany*, 66, 361, 456.

226. Graf, "Taking up the Cause of the Jewish Collective," 160.

227. Graf, "Twice Exiled," 19–20.

228. The schism with Tito's Yugoslavia in 1948 led to a hunt for alleged enemies within the Communist Parties and produced a series of show trials. Czechoslovak authorities investigated an alleged "Zionist" conspiracy, which culminated in a show trial against Rudolf Slansky

as well as several other leading Communists, the majority of whom were of Jewish origin. Soviet antisemitism culminated in the so-called Doctors' Plot of 1953. On January 13, 1953, the "Pravda" announced that a group of prominent Moscow doctors were under arrest and had confessed to murdering a high-ranking member of the politburo and planning the murder of several militaries. On April 3, after Stalin's death, the Pravda announced that the doctors were not guilty and had been freed. Kessler, *Die SED und die Juden*, 57–63; on Slansky see Gerber, *Ein Prozess in Prag*.

229. Kessler, *Die SED und die Juden*, 68; Herf, *Divided Memory*, 107.

230. Whether because of his interest in restitution or because the party accused him as a "Zionist agent," contemporaries thought of Merker as Jewish. See, for instance, Eschwege, *Fremd unter meinesgleichen*, 54; also in the secondary literature, see O'Doherty, "The GDR in the Context of Stalinist Show Trials," 308.

231. Timm, "The Burdened Relationship," 30; Offenberg, *Seid vorsichtig gegen die Machthaber*, 85.

232. Mertens, *Davidstern*, 56; Kessler, *Die SED und die Juden*, 100–102. The exact number of the remaining community members in the GDR is unclear. Compare Mertens, *Davidstern*, 59–73. In 1989 the five Jewish communities in the GDR had only about four hundred members. See http://www.zentralratdjuden.de/en/topic/134.html.

233. "Beschluss des SED-Zentralkomitees über die Lehren aus dem Prozess gegen das Verschwörerzentrum Slansky," *Neues Deutschland*, January 15, 1953.

234. Kessler, *Die SED und die Juden*, 105; Herbst, "Großmutter im Sterben," 27; Timm, "The Burdened Relationship," 32.

235. Reuter and Hansel, *Das kurze Leben der VVN von 1947 bis 1953*, 454.

236. "Beschluss des SED-Zentralkomitees über die Lehren aus dem Prozess gegen das Verschwörerzentrum Slansky," *Neues Deutschland*, January 15, 1953.

237. Brandt, *Ein Traum der nicht entführbar ist*, 192; on Brandt, next to his memoirs, see also Andresen, *Widerspruch als Lebensprinzip*.

238. Meng, *East Germany's Jewish Question*, 617–619.

239. For different interpretations of the motivations behind the SED's antisemitic campaign, see Kessler, *Die SED und die Juden*, 57–63; Haury, *Antisemitismus von links*, 391–398; Meng, *East Germany's Jewish Question*, 617–619; Monteath, "The German Democratic Republic and the Jews," 455.

240. Scheer, *Im Schatten der Sterne*, 424; O'Doherty, "The GDR in the Context of Stalinist Show Trials," 315. Article 6 of the GDR constitution states,

> All citizens have equal rights before the law. Incitement to boycott of democratic institutions or organizations, incitement to attempts on the life of democratic politicians, the manifestation of religious and racial hatred and of hatred against other peoples, militaristic propaganda and warmongering as well as any other discriminatory acts are felonious crimes within the meaning of the Penal Code. The exercise of democratic rights within the meaning of the Constitution is not an incitement to boycott. Whoever has been convicted of such a crime is disqualified from holding public office or a leading position in economic or cultural life. He also loses the right to vote and to stand for election.

See United States Department of State, *Documents on Germany 1944–1985*, Department of State Publication 9446 (Washington, DC: Department of State, n.d.), 278–306.

241. Arnold Zweig to Lion Feuchtwanger, January 24, 1953, in Feuchtwanger, Zweig, Hofe, *Briefwechsel*, 199.

226 | *Notes to pages 138–141*

242. Klemperer's attitude to the anti-Jewish campaign was also influenced by his strong dislike of Paul Merker, with whom he had had a harsh disagreement over the chapter about Zionism in his work on the language of the Third Reich. Klemperer gloated as he realized that with the new anti-Zionist stance of the regime, he would not need to omit this chapter after all. Klemperer, *So sitze ich denn zwischen allen Stühlen*, 353– 354.

243. See Klaus Gysi's memories depicted in Kaufman, *A Hole in the Heart of the World*, 121; Axen and Neubert, *Ich war ein Diener der Partei*, 116–120; interview with Sophie Marum in Wroblewsky, *Zwischen Thora und Trabant*, 28.

244. L. Winter, *Memoirs*, 303–304.

245. Mertens, *Davidstern*, 61; Kessler, *Die SED und die Juden*, 103; Schmid, *Antifaschismus und Judenverfolgung*, 38; Herbst, "Großmutter im Sterben," 27. Compare also Krause, *Zweimal verfolgt*, 122, 135, 147–163; Eschwege, *Fremd unter meinesgleichen*, 65–89; Brandt, *Ein Traum*, 179-199; Offenberg, *Seid vorsichtig gegen die Machthaber*, 91.

246. Kantorowicz, *Deutsches Tagebuch*, 353. Scholars have pointed to the possibility that Kantorowicz—who, after his flight, fashioned himself as a long-time opponent of repressive aspects of the regime—may have rewritten parts of his diary. See McLellan, "The Politics of Communist Biography"; Rohrwasser, *Stalinismus und die Renegaten*, 105–126.

247. Hartewig, *Zurückgekehrt*, 427; Eschwege, *Fremd unter meinesgleichen*, 73, 82.

248. Jürgen Kuczynski depicts the social isolation of Rudolf Herrnstadt, a journalist and politician of Jewish descent who was removed from his position in the SED's politbuuro in 1953. Kuczynski, *Ein linientreuer Dissident*, 47.

249. Scheer, *Im Schatten der Sterne*, 422–424.

250. Stern, "The Return to the Disowned Home," 65–66.

251. Kessler, *Die SED und die Juden*, 104.

252. Earlier that year, Kantorowicz, confronted with rumors that the party leadership doubted his integrity, had written to Wilhelm Pieck, the first president of the newly founded GDR. In this letter Kantorowicz asked for clarification on why the party leadership doubted his commitment and stressed his loyalty to the Socialist cause. Alfred Kantorowicz to Wilhelm Pieck, March 23, 1949, F 230/1, IFZ.

253. Alfred Kantorowicz, "Warum ich ging . . . ," *Die Zeit*, September 19, 1957.

254. Alfred Kantorowicz to Marta Feuchtwanger, December 24, 1958, Nachlass Alfred Kantorowicz, F 230/1, IFZ.

255. Quoted in the German original in Hartewig, *Zurückgekehrt*, 345.

256. Allen, *Befragung—Überprüfung—Kontrolle*, 79–86.

257. Klemperer, *So sitze ich denn zwischen allen Stühlen*, 349; see also 502, 589–90, 601, 637, 708.

258. Becker, *Mein Vater, die Deutschen und ich*.

259. L. Winter, *Unsere Vergangenheit*, 290.

4. Belonging

1. The concept of self-understanding refers to individuals' perspectives on what constitutes their self, based both on a person's identification with a larger group or community and on outside categorization since the way others see and categorize someone affects their self-understanding. The self is socially constructed. Regarding the various aspects of self-understanding and identification, often summarized under the vague term *identity*, see Brubaker and Cooper, "Beyond 'Identity,'" 29.

2. Preface by Alberto Moravia in Debenedetti, *October 16, 1943; Eight Jews*, 15.

3. L. Winter, *Unsere Vergangenheit*, 4.

4. Defez, *Memorie di un' ebreo napoletano*, 1–2; Emilio Levi, *Ricordo di Maria*, 4. Primo Levi stated in an interview that he became Jewish as a consequence of his persecution as a Jew. He points to both the racial legislation and his deportation to Auschwitz. His experiences in the camp also exposed him to eastern European Jewish culture and language, to which he felt connected, even though he did not speak Yiddish. Later on, Levi studied Yiddish and immersed himself in Jewish culture. See Castronuovo, *Natalia Ginzburg*, 115–119.

5. Boyers and Ginzburg, "An Interview with Natalia Ginzburg," 141.

6. Zwiep, "Goodbye to All That?" 229.

7. Regarding the crucial role national belonging plays in formulating people's self-understanding, see A. Cohen, "Personal Nationalism," 803. Of course, not all Europeans defined themselves in national terms as research on national indifference shows. However, most German and Italian Jews had strongly identified with their home country before Nazism and Fascism. On national indifference, see Zahra, "Imagined Noncommunities."

8. The notion that ethnic and national collectives are historically emergent and mutable rather than fixed is widely shared among scholars of nationalism. On the constructed nature of the nation, nationalism, and national belonging, see, among many others, Anderson, *Imagined Communities*; Hobsbawm and Ranger, *The Invention of Tradition*; Brubaker, "Ethnicity, Race, and Nationalism."

9. Regarding these different approaches, see Hearn, "National Identity."

10. Regarding the constructed and fluid character of groups, see Brubaker, "Ethnicity without Groups."

11. Interview with Mariella Milano in Strani, *Gli ebrei romani e la ricostruzione*. For an overview over the literature on Jewish identity, see E. Cohen, "Jewish Identity Research."

12. President of the Roman community to Comitato dell'Unione Proletaria, June 20, 1944, ACF/Corrips./Varie anno 1944, Fascicolo 7, ASCER.

13. Amelia Pincherle Rosselli, *Memoriale* (unpublished memoir), quoted in Pugliese, "Contesting Constraints"; Carpegna, "'Io non pensavo di scrivere' Intervista a Primo Levi," 356.

14. As a consequence, about 1,200 Italian Jews became stateless. For one example see Schiffer, *Non c'è ritorno a casa*, 37.

15. Sarfatti, "I caratteri principali della legislazione antiebraica in Italia," 209.

16. Contemporary Italian law did not allow dual citizenship. For examples see Pelini, "Appunti per una storia della reintegrazione," 118.

17. Di Cori, *Memorie di un italiano in Medio Oriente*, 131.

18. He probably was refused because of his membership in the Communist Party.

19. See Passerini, *Women and Men in Love*, 279–321.

20. Anonymous, "Epurazione," "Reintegrazioni patrimoniali e funzionari 1944–1945," Fascicolo 65A-5, AUCEI.

21. Servi, *Ed ora, 50 anni dopo . . .* , 43.

22. Quoted as in Stille, *Benevolence and Betrayal*, 349.

23. Ottolenghi and De Rossi Castelli, *Nei tempi oscuri*, 202.

24. Di Segni Jesi, *La lunga strada azzurra*.

25. Levi, *The Periodic Table*, 54. Fellow writer Giorgio Bassani was deeply connected to Ferrara, which plays a dominant role in his work.

26. Badrnejad-Hahn, "Wiederaufbau oder Neubeginn?," 100–103.

27. G. Schwarz, *After Mussolini*, 10.

228 | Notes to pages 145–148

28. G. Schwarz, *After Mussolini*, 98.

29. Carlo Alberto Viterbo, "Due giugno," *Israel*, May 23, 1946.

30. Regarding nostalgic visions for the future that are constructed according to needs in the present, see Boym, *The Future of Nostalgia*, xiv.

31. Giacomo Viterbo, "Messaggio dal Nord: Libertà e Pace," *Israel*, May 17, 1945 (my emphasis). The Fosse Ardeatine were the site of a mass killing on March 24, 1944; S. Vittore is a prison in Milan that held political prisoners as well as Jews before their deportation, the Fossoli camp was a concentration and transit camp for Italian Jews, and Bolzano was a transit camp. Pavolini, Saletta, and Colombo were prominent members of the Fascist Party.

32. Pombeni, "Il peso del passato," 390.

33. For other discussions of the true Italy, see "Liberazione," *Israel*, December 7, 1944; "Il Presidente dell'Unione, agli ebrei d'Italia," *Bollettino Della Comunità Israelitica Di Milano*, April 18, 1946; "I patrioti italiani e gli ebrei," *Bollettino d'Informazione: Pubblicato per cura del Comitato Rappresentativo Italiano del World Jewish Congress*, June 1945; Letter Cantoni to Cogni, June 18, 1946, Manifestazione delle stampa su ebrei e sull' Ebraismo 1945–1946, 85G-12, AUCEI.

34. Foot, *Italy's Divided Memory*, 17; Judt, "The Past Is Another Country"; Ben-Ghiat et al., "History as It Really Wasn't," 408.

35. Debenedetti, *October 16, 1943; Eight Jews*, 84–86 (italics in the original).

36. Longhi, *Die Juden und der Widerstand gegen den Faschismus in Italien*.

37. Quoted as in Stille, *Benevolence and Betrayal*, 321.

38. For instance, "Nostri Eroi: Sergio Piazza," *Bollettino*, September 25, 1945.

39. "Nostri Eroi: Walter Rossi," *Bollettino*, October 15, 1945 (reprinted from *Il Partigiano Alpino*, partisan periodical). Walter Rossi died in April 1944 at only nineteen years old. See Levi, Montagnana, and Luzzatto, *I Montagnana*, 129.

40. None of the articles in the series on "our heroes" in the *Bollettino* mentions female resistance fighters. Female partisans did not fit postwar Italy's understanding of gender roles. The resistance fighter was imagined as young, strong, and male. Consequently, women who had been in the resistance seldom recounted their experiences, and female resistance played no role in the antifascist discourse. See Jäger, "Frühe Holocaustzeugnisse italienischer Jüdinnen," 220; Bravo, "Armed and Unarmed." This holds true for the Jewish discourse around the resistance as well. Liana Millu and Luciana Nissim, two Jewish Auschwitz survivors, both wrote memoirs about their experiences as deportees in the immediate aftermath of the war. Both had been members of the resistance but did not mention this in their memoirs. This stands in contrast to the wish to emphasize a past in the resistance among male Italian Jews.

41. Klein, *Italy's Jews*, 201.

42. Majer, *"Non-Germans" under the Third Reich*, 120; Fraser and Caestecker, "Jews or Germans?," 394–395. During the war many refugees preferred statelessness over a status as a citizen of an enemy country.

43. Her own experiences as well as the larger refugee crisis shaped Hannah Arendt's political philosophy as she grappled with the enigma of statelessness and considered the vulnerable position of those who belonged nowhere. See, for instance, Arendt, *The Origins of Totalitarianism*, 177; Arendt, "We Refugees."

44. Nachlass Freia Eisner, 6.4, Nr. 9 Lebenslauf, CJA.

45. Boris Sapir, "Germany," *American Jewish Year Book*, 1947–1948.

46. Scholz, *Skandinavische Erfahrungen erwünscht?*, 83.

47. German Jewish representative committee affiliated with the World Jewish Congress, Dr. Gerhart Jacoby, Executive Secretary, May 20, 1946, C3/348-74, CZA (my emphasis).

48. See, for instance, Frankenthal, *Verweigerte Rückkehr*, 107.

49. Moskowitz, "The Germans and the Jews."

50. Scholz, *Skandinavische Erfahrungen erwünscht?*, 83.

51. Bundesministerium der Justiz, http://www.gesetze-im-internet.de/gg/BJNR000010949.html. Accessed January 17, 2023.

52. Rensmann, "Returning from Forced Exile"; similar also, Hans Rothfels retained his American passport until 1969 and repeatedly returned to his American refuge; see Bauer-kämpfer, "Americanisation as Globalisation."

53. Interview with Käthe Hamburger in Koelbl, *Jüdische Portraits*, 108.

54. Wolfgang Hildesheimer to Eva und Ernst Teltsch, March 10, 1948, Wolfgang Hildesheimer Archiv, 663, AAK.

55. Wolfgang Hildesheimer to Eva und Ernst Teltsch, April 7, 1948, Wolfgang Hildesheimer Archiv, 456, AAK.

56. Wolfgang Hildesheimer to Eva und Ernst Teltsch, no date [1952], Wolfgang Hildesheimer Archiv, AAK.

57. Wolfgang Fischer, "Heimkehr aus Heimweh," *Nacht-Express*, March 6, 1948. Leon Löwenkopf, who grew up in Dresden but was born in Poland, worked on gaining German citizenship immediately after his return to Dresden. Goldenbogen, "Leon Löwenkopf," 95.

58. See, for instance, the interview with Egon M. Kornblum in Jürgens, *Wir waren ja eigentlich Deutsche*, 169; interview with Hans Mayer in Koelbl, *Jüdische Portraits*, 183.

59. Becker, *Mein Vater, die Deutschen und ich*, 247–250. At the same time, Max, Jurek Becker's father, claimed after the war that he had been born in Fürth, turning himself from a Polish to a German Jew. See Gilman, *Jurek Becker*, 24.

60. Karl Marx, "Nach den Wahlen," *Jüdisches Gemeindeblatt für die britische Zone*, April 30, 1947. Though Marx changed this perspective; see Sinn, *Jüdische Politik*.

61. W.P.C., "Juden in Deutschland oder Deutsche Juden," *Der Weg*, April 5, 1946.

62. Siegmund Weltlinger, "Jugenderinnerungen und Alterserkenntnisse eines deutschen Juden," Vortrag gehalten am 10. Januar 1968 im Amerika Haus vor der Gesellschaft für christlich-jüdische Zusammenarbeit in Berlin. e.V, 12, E Rep. 200–22, LAB. Over the following decades, Jews became more comfortable with defining themselves as Germans. Ignatz Bubis, for instance, entitled his memoir, published in 1993, *Ich bin ein deutscher Staatsbürger jüdischen Glaubens* (I am a German citizen of the Jewish faith).

63. For an exploration of the concept of cultural intimacy, see Herzfeld, *Cultural Intimacy*.

64. Hoffmann, "The New Nomads," 47–48.

65. Interview in Koelbl, *Jüdische Portraits*, 110.

66. Abusch, "In Paris zur Welt gesprochen" (1949), in *Entscheidung unseres Jahrhunderts*.

67. August Kruhm, "Goethe und Felix Mendelsohn-Bartholdy," in *Zwischen den Zeiten*, October 1947.

68. Numerous articles in *Zwischen den Zeiten*, as well as Kantorowicz's *Ost und West*, are dedicated to Goethe.

69. Kahn, *Antisemitismus und Rassenhetze*, 91.

70. Hermann Kesten did not return to Germany but played an active role in German literary culture.

71. See Hylenski, "Ich will leben, auch wenn Ich tot bin," 51.

230 | Notes to pages 152–154

72. Regarding Kesten's effort and subsequent frustration, see Kesten, "'La doulce France,'" "Literatur im Exil," and "Die Gevierteilte Literatur"; also Kesten to Hans Sahl, December 25, 1959, HKB 2237, and Kesten to Fritz Landshoff, March 25, 1948, HKB 1949, both Monacensia.

73. Eigler, *Heimat Space, Narrative*, 2.

74. Weil to Jokisch, July 6, 1946, and November 28, 1946, GW B 96, Monacensia.

75. Weil to Jokisch, August 5, 1946, GW B 96, Monacensia.

76. Similarly, Walter Grünwald stated that he identified as a Swabian because all his ancestors had been Swabian farmers. Interview with Walter und Lotte Grünwald in Jürgens, *Wir waren ja eigentlich Deutsche*, 224.

77. Quoted as in Wojak, *Fritz Bauer*, 228.

78. Bernhardt and Lange, *Der Riss durch mein Leben*, 297.

79. Letter from Hanns Eisler to Johannes Becher, November 24, 1946, Nachlass Hanns Eisler, 5411, AAK.

80. Inge Deutschkron, Leon Spierer, Erich Cohn, and Helmut Stern expressed a strong connection with Berlin. Deutschkron, *Mein Leben nach dem Überleben*, 270, 271; interviews with Leon Spierer and Helmut Stern in Jürgens, *Wir waren ja eigentlich Deutsche*, 18, 27; interview with Erich Cohn in Grande and Literaturzentrum, *Sind allet Berlina*. In this regard see also Schloer, *Im Herzen immer ein Berliner*. Ralph Giordano described similar feelings for Hamburg; see Giordano, "Ich bin geblieben—warum?," 124; see also Fritz Bauer in Wojak, *Fritz Bauer*, 228; Hans Mayer in Koelbl, *Jüdische Portraits*, 183.

81. Goldstein in Herzberg, *Überleben heisst Erinnern*, 328.

82. Interview with Ruth Benario in Borneman and Peck, *Sojourner* (my emphasis); see also Rothschild, *Memoirs*, 173; interview with Sophie Marum in Wroblewsky, *Zwischen Thora und Traban*, 27; Völter, *Judentum und Kommunismus*, 254–255.

83. Hartewig, *Zurückgekehrt*, 429; Kessler, "Verdrängung der Geschichte," 45.

84. The uprising of 1953 started with the strike of East Berlin construction workers on June 16 and turned into a widespread uprising against the GDR government involving more than one million people.

85. Kessler, "Verdrängung der Geschichte," 46; Kühling, *Erinnerung an nationalsozialistische Verbrechen in Berlin*, 253–255.

86. Mayer, *Ein Deutscher auf Widerruf*, 53; similar Klemperer, *So sitze ich denn zwischen allen Stühlen*, 390.

87. Anderson, *Imagined Communities*, 6.

88. Frankenthal, *Verweigerte Rückkehr*, 98, 109.

89. Anna Seghers to anonymous, no date [Spring 1947], in Seghers and Berger, *Hier im Volk der kalten Herzen*, 42–43; see also Seghers to Magda Stern, June 12, 1947, and Seghers to Gisl and Egon Erwin Kisch, December 22, 1947, in Seghers and Berger, *Hier im Volk der kalten Herzen*, 65 and 189.

90. Hartewig, *Zurückgekehrt*, 108.

91. See, for instance, Jacobus, "Man wollte ein Zuhause," 88; Einhorn, "Nation und Identität," 101–119; interview with Clara Berliner in Ostow, *Jews in Contemporary East Germany*, 83–90; L. Winter, *Unsere Vergangenheit*, 300; Hermlin, *Gedichte*, 53; Mayer, *Ein Deutscher auf Widerruf*, 305.

92. Rothschild, *Memoirs*, 166; Grundig, *Gesichte und Geschichte*, 326.

93. See, for example, Albrecht, "Jeanette Wolff, Jakob Altmaier und Peter Blachstein," 236–254; Stefanie Zweig, "Bilder jüdischer Frauen: Jeanette Wolff," *Die Frau in der Gemeinschaft: Mitteilungsblatt des Jüdischen Frauenbundes in Deutschland*, June, July 1958.

Notes to pages 154–158 | 231

94. Wojak, *Fritz Bauer*, 185, 222.

95. For some examples see DY55/V278/4/56, BArch; Jacobson, *Mein Leben und Erinnerungen*; Lennert, "Zugehörigkeit, Selbstbewußtsein, Fremdheit," 394.

96. Landau, "Wir Juden und unsere Umwelt."

97. Wolfgang Hildesheimer to his parents, October 7, 1947, Wolfgang Hildesheimer Archiv, 662, AAK.

98. For some examples see Noack-Mosse, *Theresienstaedter Tagebuch*, 146; Proskauer, Berghahn, and Wickert, *Erna Proskauer*, 102; Landau, "Wir Juden und unsere Umwelt."

99. Albert Meyer to Rudolf Meyer, May 13, 1945, Nachlass Albert G. Meyer, R-2003/197/01-17, AJM.

100. Spiegel, *Bauern als Retter*, 139.

101. Interviews with Ruth K. and Theodor Goldmann in Morris, *The Lives of Some Jewish*, 78, 183; Bernhardt and Lange, *Der Riss durch mein Leben*, 285; "Hassen Wir?," *Der Weg*, April 19, 1946. For people who did not return to Germany, discussing hatred toward their former home country may have been more common. In his memoir, Peter Gay, who had no interest in returning to Germany and initially also rejected the idea of visiting the country, discusses his hatred of Germans. See P. Gay, *My German Question*, 6, 7.

102. Kurt Hirschfeld, Nachlass Siegmund Weltlinger, E Rep. 200–22, LAB (my emphasis). See also Andreas Brämer on Rabbi Schlomo Rülf, ". . . die Rückkehr eines Rabbiners nach Deutschland ist keine Selbstverständlichkeit," 177.

103. "Hassen Wir?"

104. For instance, Nelly Cohn-Leschzer, "Die Gezeichneten," *Der Weg*, August 11, 1950; Wilhelm Meier, "Nürnberger Reflexionen," *Der Weg*, July 16, 1946; Treves, "Mit tiefer Dankbarkeit blicke ich zurück"; Kantorowicz, *Deutsches Tagebuch*, 96.

105. Biess, "Feelings in the Aftermath," 34.

106. Siegfried Heimberg, Gemeinde Dortmund to Rosi Nathan, May 7, 1947, Dortmund-Bestand B.1/2, 11, ZA.

107. Rosi Nathan to Jüdische Kultusgemeinde, May 12, 1947, Dortmund-Bestand B.1/2, 11, ZA.

108. Elisabeth T., *Memoirs* (private archives).

109. Bodemann, "'How Can One Stand to Live There as a Jew . . .'"; Della Pergola, "Jewish Out-Marriage."

110. Della Pergola, *Jews in the European Community*, 25–82.

111. Interview with Giancarlo Spizzichino in Archivio Storico della Comunità Ebraica di Roma, *La Comunità Ebraica di Roma*, 118.

112. "Attraverso L'Italia in Fuga: Ricordi di Margherita Morpurgo," in Morpurgo and Morpurgo, *L'Esilio*.

113. Editta Levi, *Una Vita*; Di Camerino, *R, come Roberta*, 68; Smolensky and Jarach, *Tante voci*, 374; Tagliacozzo, *Metà della vita*, 317–319; Ottolenghi, *Ricordi e impressioni di un'internata*.

114. The psychologist Enzo Bonaventura, for instance, returned to Florence from Jerusalem in 1947 but found an environment unwilling to reintegrate him. He returned to Jerusalem where he was killed in 1948. Patrizia Guarnieri, who researched the story of Bonaventura's emigration and return, concludes that "what emerges here is that these self-defensive narratives began very early and not undeliberately within the academic community itself. . . . Close to the facts, the covering up of suffering and responsibility were activated intentionally with further responsibilities and, once again, without provoking any unanimous, effective protests capable of preventing it." See Guarnieri, *Italian Psychology and Jewish Emigration*, 153. See

232 | *Notes to pages 158–161*

also Lia Levi's depiction of her father's return to work, as he also struggled with an indifferent reception. L. Levi, *Se va via il re*, 26, 27.

115. See, for instance, "Liberazione," *Israel*, December 7, 1944.

116. Raffaele Cantoni, "Manifestazione delle stampa su ebrei e sull' Ebraismo 1947" (unpublished essay), no date, Fascicolo 85G-13, AUCEI.

117. See, for one example, L. Levi, *Se va via il re*, 26–27; see also R. Segre, *Venti mesi*, 51.

118. Servi, *Ed ora, 50 anni dopo . . .* , 45.

119. Anonymous diary, 6.14, Nr 2, CJA. For other examples see interview with Kurt Cohen in Jürgens, *Wir waren ja eigentlich Deutsche*, 51, 52; interview with Walter und Lotte Grünwald in Jürgens, *Wir waren ja eigentlich Deutsche*, 223.

120. See Brenner, "The Transformation of the German-Jewish Community," 51; also Tauchert, *Jüdische Identitäten in Deutschland*, 123.

121. "Zum Abschied von Herrn Rabbiner Dr. Leopold Neuhaus," Frankfurt – B.1/13, Serie A 597, Blatt 13, ZA.

122. G. Schwarz, *Ritrovare se stessi*, 180–181; Tagliacozzo and Di Castro, *Gli ebrei romani raccontano la "propria" Shoah*, 254.

123. Klein, *Italy's Jews*, 182.

124. Z. Shuster, "Memorandum on Italy, June 25, 1947," American Jewish Committee, Record Group 347.7.1, YIVO Archives.

125. Valobra to Giacomo Terracini, May 13, 1944, Fondo Valobra 14/156-T, ACDEC.

126. "Alla Torà e a Sion!," *Israel*, December 7, 1944.

127. For an example see Ottolenghi and De Rossi Castelli, *Nei tempi oscuri*, 11; on this issue see also Maifreda, "La riaggregazione," 623–624.

128. G. Schwarz, *Ritrovare se stessi*, 54–55.

129. Tagliacozzo, *Metà della vita*, 318. See also Maestro, *Tempo di guerra / Tempo di pace*, 25.

130. "Bericht von Frau Herta Pineas vom 17. Dezember 1957," Hermann Pineas Collection 1878–1975, # AR 94, LBI.

131. For instance, R. Gay, *Safe among the Germans*, 127; Degen, *Nicht alle waren Mörder*, 278–284; Spiegel, *Bauern als Retter*, 138; Michael Brenner, "'Die Bombardierung Dresdens 1945 rettete meiner Mutter das Leben' Historiker Michael Brenner schildert die Geschichte seiner Familie - und warnt vor dem wachsenden Antisemitismus 75 Jahre nach der Befreiung von Auschwitz," *Süddeutsche Zeitung*, January 23, 2020.

132. See Kaufman, *A Hole in the Heart of Darkness*, 38, 53.

133. Brenner, *Nach dem Holocaust*, 70.

134. Letter from Valobra to Rabbi Castelbolognesi, September 10, 1944, Fondo Valobra 3/142, ACDEC.

135. Canarutto to David Schaumann, December 5, 1944, Fondo Canarutto 4/103-S, ACDEC.

136. See, for instance, "Juedische Großmütter gefragt," *Der Weg*, March 22, 1946; see also "Jüdische Großmutter zu Schwarzmarktpreisen," *Jüdisches Gemeindeblatt für die Nord-Rheinprovinz und Westfalen*, Dezember 1946.

137. Head of the community in Erfurt to Rabbi Dr. Neuhaus, December 20, 1945, Frankfurt – B.1/13, Serie A 622, Blatt 4, ZA.

138. Rabbi Dr. Neuhaus to head of the community in Erfurt, January 28, 1946, B.1/13, Serie A 622, Blatt 3, ZA.

139. Letter of the Jüdische Gemeinde to the Magistrat der Stadt Berlin, February 11, 1946, Bestand 5A 1: Jüdische Gemeinde zu Berlin, 1945–1990, Nr. 73, CJA.

140. G. Schwarz, *Ritrovare se stessi*, 5.

141. Letter from Giuseppe Nathan to Giorgio Terni, May 19, 1945, "Abiure e conversioni 1944–1945–1946," Busta 72, Fascicolo 72-5, AUCEI (my emphasis).

142. "Abiure e conversioni 1947," Busta 72, Fascicolo 72-6, AUCEI.

143. Brenner, *Nach dem Holocaust*, 70.

144. M. Meyer to anonymous, May 28, 1948, Frankfurt – B.1/13, Serie A 604, Blatt 11, ZA.

145. Memorandum from Philip Skorneck to Ray Levy, November 12, 1946, 45/54 # 304 [45/64 # 378] Germany, Baptized Jews, 1946–1947, JDC Archives.

146. For instance letter to the Jewish community, January 8, 1945, Bestand 5A 1: Jüdische Gemeinde zu Berlin, 1945–1990, Nr. 0257, CJA; community to Enders, April 12, 1947, Jüdische Gemeinde Mainz – B.1/18, 61 Allgemeine Korrespondenz, ZA.

147. Albert Frank to Jewish community Düsseldorf, March 3, 1946. The Reich's Association of the Jews in Germany (Reichsvereinigung der Juden), a compulsory organization for all Jews in Nazi Germany, was established on July 4, 1939. The Gestapo functioned as controlling institution. See Meyer, "Handlungsspielräume regionaler jüdischer Repräsentanten," 65.

148. See, for instance, Jüdische Gemeinde Mainz – B.1/18, 61 Allgemeine Korrespondenz, ZA; also Grossmann, *Jews, Germans, and Allies*, 97.

149. Emphasis in original. Correspondence with Ms. Ernst Jonas, June 12, 1947, 45/54 # 304 [45/64 # 378] Germany, Baptized Jews, 1946–1947, JDC Archives, New York.

150. Letter to Amand Hecht, May 26, 1948, New York, 45/54 # 304 [45/64 # 378] Germany, Baptized Jews, 1946–1947, JDC Archives.

151. Gerhard Bender to Betreuungsstelle der Jüdische Gemeinde Frankfurt, June 18, 1946, Frankfurt – B.1/13, Serie A 148, Blatt 93, ZA.

152. Beate Meyer, "Notgemeinschaft der durch die Nürnberger Gesetze Betroffenen," in *Das jüdische Hamburg. Ein historisches Nachschlagewerk*, edited by the Institut für die Geschichte der deutschenJuden: https://www.dasjuedischehamburg.de/inhalt /notgemeinschaft-der-durch-die-nürnberger-gesetze-betroffenen. Accessed January 17, 2023.

153. Harald Schmid, "'Wiedergutmachung' und Erinnerung," 36–37.

154. For one example see Betty Scheuer to community, October 28, 1947, Frankfurt - B.1/13, Serie A 609, Blatt 57, ZA.

155. Antrag auf Aufnahme, Frankfurt – B 1/13, Serie A 596, Blatt 32, ZA.

156. Doron, *Jewish Youth and Identity in Postwar France*.

157. Antrag auf Aufnahme, Frankfurt – B 1/13, Serie A 596, Blatt 32, ZA.

158. See, for instance, Rede Leo Baeck, October 14, 1948, Frankfurt – B.1/13, Serie A 722, Blatt 39, ZA.

159. Riesenburger, *Das Licht verlöschte nicht*.

160. Gemeinde Frankfurt am Main to Hilfsverein für jüdische Auswanderung Zürich, May 23, 1947, Frankfurt – B.1/13, Serie A 585, Blatt 4, ZA.

161. Brämer, "'. . . die Rückkehr eines Rabbiners,'" 171–172.

162. Klein, *Italy's Jews*, 184.

163. Quarterly Report, January–March 1947, AR 45/54 # 627, JDC Archives.

164. Quarterly Report, January–March 1947, AR 45/54 # 627, JDC Archives; see also Weisbord and Sillanpoa, *The Chief Rabbi*, 134. Similar institutions reopened much later in Germany.

165. Israel Anton Zoller, born on September 27, 1881, in Galicia, was the chief rabbi of Rome from 1939 to 1945.

234 | *Notes to pages 166–168*

166. Tensions between Zolli and the members of the community existed from the onset, partially due to their different understandings of rituals and religious services. Zolli, who came from eastern Europe, had a different understanding of Judaism than the Roman Jews. Badrnejad-Hahn, "Wiederaufbau oder Neubeginn?," 61.

167. Weisbord and Sillanpoa, *The Chief Rabbi*, 130. About Zolli's conduct during the war, see also Badrnejad-Hahn, "Wiederaufbau oder Neubeginn?," 71. Apparently Zolli had tried to warn the community of the impeding danger but was considered alarmist.

168. There were several conflicts, among them a dispute about his pension, as he wished to go into early retirement. Weisbord and Sillanpoa, *The Chief Rabbi*, 151–152; Badrnejad-Hahn, "Wiederaufbau oder Neubeginn?," 71.

169. Weisbord and Sillanpoa, *The Chief Rabbi*, 137.

170. "Una clamorosa defezione," *Israel*, February 15, 1945.

171. Weisbord and Sillanpoa, *The Chief Rabbi*, 141; see also "Dr. David Prato Returns to Old Post as Chief Rabbi of Rome; Leaves Palestine," Jewish Telegraphic Agency, September 2, 1945, http://www.jta.org/1945/09/02/archive/dr-david-prato-returns-to-old-post-as-chief-rabbi-of-rome-leaves-palestine. To prove loyalty to the regime, the Fascists who dominated the Roman Jewish community leadership in the 1930s ousted Prato, whom the Fascist press had accused of antifascism. See Badrnejad-Hahn, "Wiederaufbau oder Neubeginn?," 7.

172. Klein, *Italy's Jews*, 196–198.

173. David Prato, "I problemi dell'istruzione," *La Voce*, March 17, 1949.

174. Brenner, *Nach dem Holocaust*, 70.

175. See Heinsohn, "'Aber es kommt auch darauf an, wie einen die Anderen sehen,'" 84; also Tauchert, *Jüdische Identitäten*, 265.

176. Interview with Käthe Hamburger in Koelbl, *Jüdische Portraits*, 108.

177. For various examples, see, for instance, "Eine alte Geschichte," *Der Weg*, March 22, 1946; Schmuckler, *Gast im eigenen Land*, 121; Brandt, *Ein Traum der nicht entführbar ist*, 71; Bruno Di Cori, *Memorie di un italiano in Medio Oriente*; letter by Giorgio Rossi, March 26, 1947, "Ricorso presentato dall'Unione ai deputati dell'Assemblea Costituente." Fascicolo 65B-10, AUCEI; Emilia Piperno, *Trattoria dei Cacciatori*, 17.

178. "Eine alte Geschichte."

179. Else Borchardt, "Fuer den juedischen Haushalt: Rezepte und Anregungen," *Frau in der Gemeinschaft*, Dezember 1956.

180. Klein, *Italy's Jews*, 194.

181. Franz Hesdörffer to Jewish community Frankfurt, December 26, 1945, Frankfurt – B.1/13, Serie A 593, Blatt 31, ZA.

182. Emil N. Carlebach to Jewish community Frankfurt, March 16, 1947, Frankfurt – B 1/13, Serie A 603, Blatt 76, ZA.

183. See Castronuovo, *Natalia Ginzburg*, 5, 74, 87.

184. See interviews with Ruth Benario and Hilde Eisler in Borneman and Peck, *Sojourners*, 37–60, 81–101; Eschwege, *Fremd unter Meinesgleichen*, 66. Interview with Florence Singwald in Herzberg, *Überleben heisst Erinnern*; Goldenbogen, "Leon Löwenkopf," 99–100; interview with Clara Berliner in Ostow, *Jews in Contemporary East Germany*, 85; see also Gilman about the motivation of Max Becker (who was not a Communist) to join the Berlin community after the war; Gilman, *Jurek Becker*, 25. The British historian Isaac Deutscher captures this sentiment when he describes his own relationship to Judaism: "Religion? I am an atheist. Jewish nationalism? I am an internationalist. In neither sense am I therefore a Jew. I am,

however, a Jew by force of my unconditional solidarity with the persecuted and exterminated." Deutscher, "Who Is a Jew?," 51.

185. Eschwege, *Fremd unter meinesgleichen*, 66.

186. Quoted as in Breitsprecher, "Die Bedeutung des Judentums und des Holocaust," 201.

187. Interview with Hilde Eisler in Borneman and Peck, *Sojourners*, 96.

188. See also Hartewig, *Zurückgekehrt*, 3.

189. Kahn, *Antisemitismus und Rassenhetze*, 91.

190. Rothschild, *Memoirs*, 31.

191. Unikower, *Suche nach dem gelobten Land*.

192. Kurt Goldstein in Herzberg, *Überleben heisst Erinnern*.

193. Kessler, *Die SED und die Juden*, 68. For another example see Eschwege, *Fremd unter meinesgleichen*, 66.

194. Kessler, *Die SED und die Juden*, 84.

195. See, for instance, Kaul, *Es Wird Zeit, Dass Du Nach Hause Kommst*; also Friedman, "The Cold War Politics of Exile"; Rothschild, *Memoirs*. On perceptions of Jewishness among Communists of Jewish origin, see also Hartewig, *Zurückgekehrt*, 512–515; Koch, "'After Auschwitz You Must Take Your Origin Seriously.'"

196. Shneer, "Eberhard Rebling, Lin Jaldati, and Yiddish Music."

197. For example, Helmut Eschwege, Günter Nobel, and Ruth Benario. See Eschwege, *Fremd unter Meinesgleichen*; Hartewig, *Zurückgekehrt*, 159; interview with Ruth Benario in Borneman and Peck, *Sojourners*, 37–60.

198. Eschwege, *Fremd unter meinesgleichen*, 66; Walther, "Helmut Eschwege and Jewish Life," 104.

199. For instance, Jeanette Wolff and Jakob Altmaier; see Albrecht, "Jeanette Wolff, Jakob Altmaier und Peter Blachstein." For Italy see Alberto Defez, *Memorie di un' ebreo napoletano*; Ajò, *Il bello ha odore*; Tagliacozzo and Di Castro, *Gli ebrei romani raccontano la "propria" Shoah*, 77–78; see also Castronuovo, *Natalia Ginzburg*.

200. Passerini, *Women and Men in Love*, 304.

201. Giorgina Levi to Francesco Lemmi, May 22, 1948, Lemmi and Levi, *Caro Professore*, ADN.

202. Levi, Montagnana, and Luzzatto, *I Montagnana*, 53.

203. See Castronuovo, *Natalia Ginzburg*, 100.

204. This was the case across western Europe; see Kristel, "Revolution and Reconstruction," 142; Zwiep, "Goodbye to All That?," 228.

205. A British military unit composed of Jews mainly from Palestine. On the Jewish Brigade in postwar Germany, see Patt, *Finding Home and Homeland*; Lavsky, *New Beginnings*; Mankowitz, *Life between Memory and Hope*.

206. Badrnejad-Hahn, "Wiederaufbau oder Neubeginn?," 158.

207. G. Schwarz, *After Mussolini*, 70; Klein, *Italy's Jews*, 208–209.

208. G. Schwarz, *After Mussolini*, 69.

209. Badrnejad-Hahn, "Wiederaufbau oder Neubeginn?," 157.

210. Servi, *Ed ora, 50 anni dopo . . .* , 46.

211. Leone Diena, "Perché sono diventato sionista," *Israel*, June 27, 1946.

212. Porat, *Israeli Society*, 199. For another example of a young Italian Jew who enthusiastically embraced Zionism but then opted to remain in Italy, see Ottolenghi, *Ricordi e impressioni*, 84.

236 | *Notes to pages 173–178*

213. D. Segre, *Memoirs of a Fortunate Jew*, 8. Also quoted in G. Schwarz, *After Mussolini*, 70.

214. Badrnejad-Hahn, "Wiederaufbau oder Neubeginn?," chap. 3.

215. Quoted in Badrnejad-Hahn, "Wiederaufbau oder Neubeginn?," 169.

216. Sergio Bondi to Roman community, June 18, 1944, ACF/Corrisp./Varie anno 1944, Fascicolo 7, ASCER.

217. Badrnejad-Hahn, "Wiederaufbau oder Neubeginn?," 176.

218. Quoted in Badrnejad-Hahn, "Wiederaufbau oder Neubeginn?," 176–177.

219. David Prato, "Alla Torà e a Sion!," *Israel*, February 1, 1945.

220. Raffale Cantoni, "Annata Storica," *Israel*, September 2, 1948; Prato, "Alla Torà e a Sion!"

221. G. Schwarz, *Ritrovare se stessi*, 33–35.

222. See Di Cori, *Memorie di un italiano in Medio Oriente*, 125; also the interview with Gino Fiorentino and Emma Alatri in Strani, "Gli ebrei romani e la ricostruzione," 249.

223. Interview with Fabrizio Roccas in Archivio Storico della Comunità Ebraica di Roma, *La Comunita Ebraica di Roma nel Secondo Dopoguerra*, 123.

224. G. Schwarz, *Ritrovare sa stessi*, 183; so also, for instance, Alma Morpurgo, see Hametz, "The Interstices of Life and Memory."

225. Klein, *Italy's Jews*, 211–212.

226. Wasserstein, *Vanishing Diaspora*, 92; Della Pergola and Tagliacozzo, *Gli Italiani in Israele*, 33.

227. Badrnejad-Hahn, "Wiederaufbau oder Neubeginn?," 222.

228. Report for October and November 1946, AR 45/54 # 628, JDC Archives, New York.

229. C. Segre, *Per curiosità*, 112–113; also in G. Schwarz, *After Mussolini*, 98–100.

230. C. Segre, *Per curiosità*, 112–113; G. Schwarz, *After Mussolini*, 98, 99.

231. Guido Lopez, Carte Personali e familiari, scheda no 49, ACDEC; similar also Tagliacozzo, *Metà della vita*, 316–317.

232. Interview with Roberto and Mariella Milano in Strani, "Gli ebrei romani e la ricostruzione," 187.

233. Klein, *Italy's Jews*, 213.

234. A. Segre, *Memories of Jewish Life*, 364.

235. Tauchert, *Jüdische Identitäten in Deutschland*, 145; Kauders, "West German Jewry."

236. Mendel, "The Policy for the Past in West Germany and Israel," 129.

237. E. Lindner, "Rückblick und Ausblick," *Jüdische Hefte: Ausgewählte Aufsätze*, October 1948.

238. Mendel, "The Policy for the Past in West Germany and Israel," 132.

239. Kauders, *Heimat ausgeschlossen*, 88–98.

240. See interviews with Boris Schachtel and Max Stein in Morris, *The Lives of Some Jewish Germans*, 81, 167; interview with Kurt Cohen in Jürgens, *Wir waren ja eigentlich Deutsche*, 52; see also Tauchert, *Jüdische Identitäten in Deutschland*, 127–129.

241. "Referat des Herrn Julius Dreifuss anlässlich des 15. April 1948," Vorsitzender der Synagogengemeinde Düsseldorf, Allgemeine Korrespondenz Düsseldorf – B.1/5, 77, ZA (my emphasis).

242. Anderson, *Imagined Communities*, 6.

243. Wolfgang Hildesheimer to his parents, January 15, 1948, Wolfgang Hildesheimer Archiv, 456, AAK.

244. Timm, "Ein ambivalentes Verhältnis," 24–26.

245. Graf, "Taking Up the Cause of the Jewish Collective," 160.

246. Timm, *Hammer, Zirkel, Davidstern*, 114; Italian Jewish members of the PCI also encountered hostility toward Israel and negotiated this difficult relationship. Umberto Terracini, a leading member of Italy's Communist Party and president of Italy's lower house of Parliament after the war, supported Israel throughout his life and criticized the PCI's position toward the Jewish state. Natalia Ginzburg, in contrast, criticized Israel and supported the Palestinian cause. On Terracini, Israel, and the PCI, see Di Figlia, *Israele e la sinistra*, 19–20, 56–60. On Ginzburg, see Castronuovo, *Natalia Ginzburg*, 7, 94.

247. Timm, "Ein ambivalentes Verhältnis," 24; Mertens, *Davidstern*, 332–336. Eschwege, *Fremd unter meinesgleichen*, 92, 114, 128; interview with Walter Besser in Herzberg, *Überleben heisst Erinnern*, 249.

248. Klemperer, *So sitze ich denn zwischen allen Stühlen*, 823; Aschheim, "'Genosse Klemperer,'" 202–204.

249. Klemperer, *So sitze ich denn zwischen allen Stühlen*, 661–662; for another comparison of Israel with Nazi Germany, see Hans Rodenberg to Martin Hellberg, January 18, 1972, NY 4204/54, BArch.

250. Natalia Ginzburg argues along similar lines; see Castronuovo, *Natalia Ginzburg*, 7.

251. Eschwege, *Fremd unter meinesgleichen*, 114, 128.

252. Arnold Zweig to Lion Feuchtwanger, January 24, 1953, in Feuchtwanger, Zweig, and von Hofe, *Briefwechsel*, 200.

253. A. Gordon, "Widersprüchliche Zugehörigkeiten," 172.

254. Klemperer, *So sitze ich denn zwischen allen Stühlen*, 637, also 131, 478, 504, 589, 670.

255. KJH to Hans [no last name], March 20, 1948, Universitätsbibliothek der LMU München / Nachlass Karl Jakob Hirsch.

256. KJH to Dr. Boesch, February 27, 1950, Universitätsbibliothek der LMU München / Nachlass Karl Jakob Hirsch.

257. Said, *Reflections on Exile*, 176.

Conclusion

1. Jacobus, "Man wollte ein Zuhause"; Hans Jacobus, "Kein Grab—nur die Felder von Chelmno: Erinnerung an meinen Grossvater: Eine Tasse Schokolade in der Tauentzienstraße," *Der Freitag*, November 15, 2002. https://www.freitag.de/autoren/der-freitag /kein-grab-nur-die-felder-von-chelmno.

2. Jacobus, "Man wollte ein Zuhause," 88.

3. Schönborn, *Im Wandel*.

4. Michael Brenner, "In the Shadow of the Holocaust: The Changing Image of German Jewry after 1945" (Ina Levine Annual Lecture, 2010), https://www.ushmm.org/m/pdfs/Publi cation_OP_2010-08.pdf.

5. Kauders, "The Emotional Geography of a Lost Space," 205–206. For others such a sense of home remained fractured. Härtling, "Die Macht der Verdränger," 178; Marcuse, "Lebe ich oder lebe ich nicht in der Bundesrepublik?" Regarding the history of the Jewish community from 1945 to today, see Brenner, *Geschichte der Juden in Deutschland von 1945 bis zur Gegenwart*. For a detailed study that shows how two leading figures, Karl Marx and Hendrik van Dam, contributed to building of the postwar Jewish community, see Sinn, *Jüdische Politik*.

238 | *Notes to pages 182–183*

6. A younger generation of East German Jews had, however, different feelings both toward their Jewishness and to the East German State. Disillusioned with both state and party, they rediscovered Judaism and tended to more strongly identify as Jewish. See Runge, *Dreiundsechzig*; Berger, *Mir langt's, ich gehe*, 197; Genin, *How the GDR*, 4. See also Stern, "The Return to the Disowned Home," 14; Granta, "The Cold War Politics of Cultural Minorities," 64.

7. Kaufman, *A Hole in the Heart of the World*; interview with Ruth Benario in Borneman and Peck, *Sojourner*, 37–60; "'Wir, so gut es gelang, haben das unsere getan,' Gespräch mit Steffie Spira," *Tribüne*, April 6, 1990; Runge, *Dreundsechzig*, 16; Lawrie, "'Es soll diese Spur doch bleiben . . .'"

8. Interview with Hilde Eisler in Borneman and Peck, *Sojourners*, 100.

9. Interview with Hilde Eisler in Borneman and Peck, *Sojourners*, 100.

10. Zentralrat der Juden in Deutschland, https://www.zentralratderjuden.de/service/faq/. Accessed January 18, 2023.

11. See von Mering, "Grenzgang als zögernde Wieder-Annäherung"; Anthony Faiola and Ruth Eglash, "Young Jews See Bright Future in Berlin but Past Weights Heavily in Israel," *Guardian*, November 10, 2014, http://www.theguardian.com/world/2014/nov/10/young-israelis -berlin-migration-antisemitism.

12. Sergio Della Pergola and Daniel Staetsky, "Jews in Europe at the Turn of the Millennium: Population Trends and Estimates," Institute for Jewish Policy Research, October 21, 2020, https://www.jpr.org.uk/reports/jews-europe-turn-millennium-population-trends-and -estimates?id=17623.

13. Quoted in the original German in Brenner, "Ein neues deutsches Judentum?," 421.

14. As I am completing this manuscript, a discussion on German memory politics that has been termed "catechism debate" or "Historikerstreit 2.0" has been playing out in German media as well as on social media and online blogs. The debate touches on several interrelated issues—the dominant role of the Holocaust in German memory politics, the relation of Holocaust memory to legacies of colonialism, German support for Israel, and the discussion of anti-Black racism and contemporary human rights struggles within German discourse. See "The Catechism Debate," The New Fascism Syllabus, August 20, 2021, http://newfascismsyl labus.com/category/opinions/the-catechism-debate/; Rothberg, "Lived multidirectionality."

15. On the avoidance of grappling with Germans' status as perpetrators, see Welzer, Moller, and Tschuggnall, *Opa war kein Nazi*; Nolan, "Air Wars, Memory Wars"; Fulbrook, *Reckonings*, 498. On the right-wing push against Holocaust memory, see "AfD-Mann Höcke löst mit Kritik an Holocaust-Gedenken Empörung aus," *Frankfurter Allgemeine Zeitung*, January 18, 2017; "Gauland: Hitler nur 'Vogelschiss' in deutscher Geschichte," *Süddeutsche Zeitung*, June 2, 2018.

16. The AFD also managed to attract some, if very few, Jews. In 2018 a few Jewish members of the AFD founded an organization called Jews in the AFD. The Central Council of Jews in Germany (Zentralrat der Juden in Deutschland) criticized the membership of Jews in the xenophobic and racist radical Right party. See "Jüdische AfD-Mitglieder gründen Vereinigung," *Zeit Online*, October 7, 2018, https://www.zeit.de/politik/deutschland/2018-10 /juden-afd-jafd-vera-kosova?utm_referrer=https%3A%2F%2Fde.wikipedia.org; "Zentralrat der Juden: Kein Verständnis für Engagement von Juden bei AfD," *Passauer Neue Presse*, September 27, 2018, https://www.pnp.de/nachrichten/politik/3085203_Zentralrat-der-Juden -Kein-Verstaendnis-fuer-Engagement-von-Juden-bei-AfD.html.

17. Michael Brenner, "Nach dem Anschlag von Halle: Packen wir die Koffer?," *Süddeutsche Zeitung*, October 12, 2019.

18. Della Pergola and Staetsky, "From Old and New Directions."

19. See, for instance Ben Sales, "Is There a Future for the Jews of Italy?" August 31, 2015, *Haaretz,* https://www.haaretz.com/jewish/despite-difficulty-italian-jews-upbeat-1.5393226.

20. See European Jewish Association, "Which European Countries Are Best for Jews?" · June 22, 2022, https://ejassociation.eu/eja/which-european-countries-are-best-for-jews-answers-may-surprise-you/.

21. "Italian Jewish Migration to Israel Booms," Agenzia Nazionale Stampa Associata, November 21, 2014, https://www.ansa.it/english/news/general_news/2014/11/21/italian-jewish-migration-to-israel-booms_48c946ce-bf4b-408e-89d3-9820e5204eaa.html; "Italian Emigration to Israel Expected to Double in 2014," *Haaretz,* November 23, 2014, https://www.haaretz.com/jewish/italian-aliyah-expected-to-double-1.5334079. While Jews in most European countries identified antisemitism and racism as the biggest problem in a recent survey, Italian Jews named unemployment and government corruption as the most pressing issues, see European Union Agency for Fundamental Rights, *Experiences and Perceptions of Antisemitism.* Still there is a slight increase of Italian Jews considering leaving the country because they feel unsafe. See Institute for Jewish Policy Research, "Young Jewish Europeans: Perceptions and Experiences of Antisemitism."

22. See for instance, Gadi Luzzatto Voghera, "Antisemitismo e derive da influencer," in Moked, July 2, 2021, https://moked.it/blog/2021/07/02/antisemitismo-e-derive-da-influencer/; see also CDEC, "L' Osservatorio antisemitismo," which is dedicated to recording antisemitic instances in Italy, https://www.osservatorioantisemitismo.it/episodi-di-antisemitismo-in-italia/. Accessed January 18, 2023.

23. Lichtner, "That Latent Sense of Otherness"; Betti Guetta e Stefano Gatti, "Alcune considerazione sull'antisemitismo 2007–2010," CDEC, "L' Osservatorio antisemitismo," December 9, 2010, https://www.osservatorioantisemitismo.it/approfondimenti/alcune-considerazioni-sullantisemitismo-2007-2010/; Della Pergola and Staetsky, "From Old and New Directions."

24. Della Pergola and Staetsky, "From Old and New Directions;" Lichtner, "That Latent Sense of Otherness," 466; Di Figlia, "Left-Wing Italian Jews," 85. On the attack and its ramifications for Italian society and the Jewish community, see Marzano and Schwarz, *Attentato alla sinagoga.* The event has left a mark on the Roman community; the city's Chief Rabbi Riccardo Di Segni referred to it as a "watershed" moment both for the city and the Jewish community at a commemorative ceremony in 2017. See Adam Smulevich, "35 anni dall'attentato terroristico palestinese contro il Tempio Maggiore di Roma," https://www.osservatorioantisemitismo.it/articoli/35-anni-dallattentato-terroristico-palestinese-contro-il-tempio-maggiore/.

25. Petersen, "Der Ort der Resistenza in Geschichte und Gegegnwart Italiens," 508; Mantelli, "Revisionismus durch 'Aussöhnung,'" 222; Mattioli, *"Viva Mussolini!"*; Focardi, "The Dispute over the Past."

26. Perra shows how the revisionist Right uses Holocaust memory in order to whitewash Fascism; see Perra, "Legitimizing Fascism."

27. On the reception of *Holocaust* in Italy, see Perra, "Narratives of Innocence and Victimhood"; on the Eichmann trial, see Galimi, "The Image of 'All Good Italians.'"

28. See Perra, "Legitimizing Fascism."

29. Bravo, "Social Perception of the Shoah in Italy," 391–392; Focardi, "The Dispute over the Past."

30. Regarding the discussion about the date, see Sarfatti, "Notes and Reflections on the Italian Law."

240 | *Notes to pages 185–186*

31. R. Gordon, "The Holocaust in Italian Collective Memory."

32. Initially the museum was to be built on the grounds of Villa Torlonia, formerly Mussolini's residence, then the Palazzo dell'Arte Moderna was suggested. See di Giulio, "Negotiations of Jewish Memory," 421. Di Giulio also suggests that the construction of the Holocaust monument in Berlin contributed to the perceived need to build a museum in Rome, highlighting the entanglement of commemorative cultures across national borders. He writes, "The German project rendered conspicuous the lack of a Holocaust museum in Italy, the first country to embrace Fascism and one of the first regimes to implement state-sponsored racist legislation in Europe." See di Giulio, "Negotiations of Jewish Memory," 419.

33. On the debate about the location of the Holocaust museum and the conflict between Rome and Ferrara see Di Giulio, "Negotiations of Jewish Memory," 420.

34. Corrado Augias, "Liliana Segre e la democrazia mite," *la Repubblica,* October 13, 2022, https://www.repubblica.it/commenti/2022/10/13/news/discorso_liliana_segre_senato_anti fascismo-369877273/; Concetto Vecchio, "Il discorso antifascista di Liliana Segre. Tanti applausi, ma su Matteotti, 25 aprile e Costituzione la destra è tiepida," *La Repubblica,* October 13, 2022, https://www.repubblica.it/politica/2022/10/13/news/discorso_liliana_segre_senato -369818390/; "Discorso di Liliana Segre al Senato della Repubblica, 13 ottobre 2022," Giustizia Insieme, October 13, 2022, https://www.giustiziainsieme.it/it/attualita-2/2490-discorso-di -liliana-segre-al-senato-della-repubblica-13-ottobre-2022.

35. Silvia Morosi, "Fascismo, leggi razziali, totalitarismi, violenza politica: così Meloni condanna gli errori del passato," *Corriere della Sera,* October 25, 2022, https://www.corriere .it/politica/22_ottobre_25/fascismo-leggi-razziali-totalitarismi-violenza-politica-storia -parole-meloni-camera-428c62d8-5453-11ed-a58a-ad027d5a5146.shtml. On Meloni's and the Brothers of Italy's Fascist roots see Ruth Ben-Ghiat, "The Return of Fascism in Italy," *The Atlantic,* September 23, 2022, https://www.theatlantic.com/international/archive/2022/09 /giorgia-meloni-italy-election-fascism-mussolini/671515/; Suzanne Cope, "Today's Far-Right Rise Echoes Mussolini's a Century Ago," *The Washington Post,* October 29, 2022, https://www .washingtonpost.com/made-by-history/2022/10/29/mussolini-fascism-italy-meloni/.

36. Meloni, like other far-right leaders such as Gianfranco Fini, aims to legitimize the far-right by distancing it from Mussolini's Fascist regime, and in particular from memories of the racial laws and the Holocaust. A condemnation of Fascist colonial violence plays no role in these attempts to mainstream the Right. While claiming to have moved beyond, or post Fascism and its ideology, these far-right leaders employ Fascist tropes and ideas. See also Perra, "Legitimizing Fascism;" George Newth, "Matteo Salvini, Giorgia Meloni, and 'Post-Fascism' as Political Logic," Political Studies Association, September 9, 2022, https:// www.psa.ac.uk/psa/news/matteo-salvini-giorgia-meloni-and-'post-fascism'-political-logic. On Meloni's effort to distance herself and her party from Italy's history of antisemitism, see also L'accensione con Giorgia Meloni: "Chanukkah, storia di un popolo che difende la sua identità," Moked, December 20, 2022. https://moked.it/blog/2022/12/20/laccensione-insieme -alla-premier-meloni-chanukkah-la-storia-di-un-popolo-che-combatte-per-lidentita/.

37. The one reference to antifascism in her speech aims to discredit it; she speaks about the political violence of "militant antifascism."

38. On the antifascist paradigm, see Consonni, *L'eclisse dell'antifascismo Resistenza.*

39. See the interviews with Luisa Passerini and Filippo Focardi in Bartolini, "Past, Present, and Future of the Italian Memory of Fascism," 306–307, 309.

40. Schwarz, *After Mussolini,* 186; Consonni, "The New Grammar of Otherness." Focardi, "Gedenktage und politische Öffentlichkeit in Italien," 219; Perra, "Between National and

Cosmopolitan Twenty-First-Century Holocaust Television." For recent examples that celebrate Italians' rescue of Jews, see the book by Elizabeth Bettina, *It happened in Italy* and in particular the video promoting the book, http://www.youtube.com/watch?v=uKNF9UyRSEc as well as the television series *Perlasca: un eroe italiano* (2002).

41. Lombroso, *Si può stampare*, 37; also quoted in G. Schwarz, *After Mussolini*, 98.

42. Hermann Kesten to Robert Neumann, November 16, 1962, HKB 2101, Monacensia; *Hermann Kesten-eine späte Annäherung*, Norbert Schmidt, (Medienwerkstatt Franken Film, Nürnberg, 1992).

43. Berger and Niven, *Writing the History of Memory*, 11.

44. Gershom Scholem, "Jews and Germans," *Commentary*, November 1966.

45. Much has been written on Scholem's refutation of the existence of a German Jewish dialogue before 1933, and his notion is frequently referenced and often qualified in the literature on German Jewish relations in the late nineteenth and early twentieth centuries; see Wiese, "Counter History"; L. Fischer, "Gershom Scholem and Postwar Germany Reconsidered."

46. For examples see Spiegel, *Bauern als Retter*; T. , *Memoirs*; interviews in Jürgens, *Wir waren ja eigentlich Deutsche*; interviews in Borneman and Peck, *Sojourners*.

47. Quoted in German in Geis, *Übrig sein*, 214.

48. Regarding the social aspect of emotions, see Frevert, "Was haben Gefühle in der Geschichte zu suchen?," 197; Rosenwein, *Emotional Communities*, 2.

49. Rosenwein, *Emotional Communities*, 2.

50. Améry, "How Much Home Does a Person Need?," 61.

BIBLIOGRAPHY

Archives

American Jewish Joint Distribution Committee, New York (JDC Archives, NY)
Archiv der Akademie der Künste, Berlin (AAK)
Archivio Centro di Documentazione Ebraica Contemporanea, Milan (ACDEC)
Archivio Diaristico Nazionale, Pieve Santo Stefano (ADN)
Archivio Storico della Comunità Ebraica di Firenze, Florence (ASCEF)
Archivio Storico Della Comunità Ebraica di Roma, Rome (ASCER)
Archivio Unione delle Comunità Ebraiche Italiane, Rome (AUCEI)
Archiv Jüdisches Museum, Berlin (AJM)
Biblioteca Archivio Renato Maestro, Venice (BARM)
Bundesarchiv, Berlin (BArch)
Central Zionist Archives, Jerusalem (CZA)
Historische Archiv der Stiftung Neue Synagoge Berlin – Centrum Judaicum (CJA)
Institut für Zeitgeschichte, Munich (IFZ)
Landesarchiv, Berlin (LAB)
Leo Baeck Institute, Center for Jewish History, New York (LBI)
Literaturarchiv Monacensia, Munich (Monacensia)
United States Holocaust Memorial Museum Archive, Washington, DC (USHMM)
Universitätsbibliothek der LMU München, Munich
Yad VaShem Archives, Jerusalem (YVA)
YIVO Institute for Jewish Research, Center for Jewish History, New York (YIVO)
Zentralarchiv zur Erforschung der Geschichte der Juden in Deutschland, Heidelberg (ZA)

Newspapers, Periodicals, and Magazines

American Jewish Yearbook
Aufbau
Berliner Zeitung
Bollettino della Comunità Israelitica di Milano
Commentary
Der Weg: Zeitschrift des Judentums
Die Zeit
Frankfurter Allgemeine Zeitung
Frau in der Gemeinschaft
Israel
Jüdische Hefte
Jüdische Rundschau

244 | *Bibliography*

Jüdisches Gemeindeblatt für die britische Zone
La Prealpina
La Rassegna Mensile di Israel
La Voce della Communità Israelitica di Roma
Mitteilungen der Gemeinschaft der durch die Nürnberger Gesetze Betroffenen–Niedersachsen
Nachrichten für die Jüdischen Bürger von Fürth
Nacht-Express
Neues Deutschland
Tribüne
Voce Partigiana
Zwischen den Zeiten

Unpublished Diaries and Memoirs

Ajò, Marta. *Il bello ha odore*. MP/96. Archivio Diaristico Nazionale.

Balderi, Gian Gaspare. Tremarono i Lungarni. MG/97. Archivio Diaristico Nazionale.

Bassani, Eugenia. L'anzulon, MG/95. Archivio Diaristico Nazionale.

Beer, Umberto. *Va' Fuori d'Italia*. Archivio Unione delle Comunità Ebraiche Italiane.

Behar, Becky. *Diary 1943–1947*. Vicissitudine dei singoli. Serie I, Busta 2. Archivio Centro di Documentazione Ebraica Contemporanea.

Bemporad, Marisa. *Dall'ostilità all'ospitalità*. MP/T2. Archivio Diaristico Nazionale.

Defez, Alberto. *Memorie di un' ebreo napoletano*. MG/99. Archivio Diaristico Nazionale.

Di Cori, Bruno. *Memorie di un italiano in Medio Oriente*. MP/94. Archivio Diaristico Nazionale.

Di Segni Jesi, Fulvia. *La lunga strada azzurra*. Archivio Unione delle Comunità Ebraiche Italiane.

Donati, Max. *Diario d'Esilio*. Vicissitudini dei singoli. Serie I, Busta 7. Archivio Centro di Documentazione Ebraica Contemporanea.

Dreifuss, Alfred. *Über die jüdische Emigration in Schanghai von 1939–1947*. SgY30 EA 1496. Bundesarchiv, Berlin.

Genin, Salomea. *How the GDR Turned a Jewish Self-hating Communist into a Jew : Or How I Returned to the Fold*. Leo Baeck Institute.

Holzer, Charlotte. *Lebenserinnerungen von 1909–1951*. EA 2014/1, SgY 30. Bundesarchiv, Berlin.

Jacobson, Max. *Mein Leben und Erinnerungen*. Leo Baeck Institute.

Lattes, Mario. *Memoir*. Vicissitudini dei singoli. Serie I, Busta 13. Archivio Centro di Documentazione Ebraica Contemporanea.

Levi, Editta. *Una vita, la famiglia, il lavoro, e poi . . .* MP/00. Archivio Diaristico Nazionale.

Levi, Emilio. *Ricordo di Maria*. MG/90. Archivio Diaristico Nazionale.

Levi Coen, Clara. *Ebrei nell'occhio del ciclone*. Vicissitudini dei singoli. Archivio Centro di Documentazione Ebraica Contemporanea.

Luft, Giuseppe. *La mia guerra da civile*. MG/91. Archivio Diaristico Nazionale.

Luzzati, Adriana. *La mia vita*. MP/02. Archivio Diaristico Nazionale.

Maestro, Leona. *Tempo di guerra / Tempo di pace*. DG/88. Archivio Diaristico Nazionale.

Morpurgo, Alma. *Queste mie figlie*. MP/86. Archivio Diaristico Nazionale.

Morpurgo, Gualtiero. *Diario di un rifugiato in svizzera 1943–1945*. DG/99. Archivio Diaristico Nazionale.

Noack-Mosse, Eva. *Theresienstaedter Tagebuch*. Leo Baeck Institute.

Bibliography | 245

Oberdorfer, Sonia. *A Marco.* MP/06. Archivio Diaristico Nazionale.
Ottolenghi, Lea. *Ricordi e impressioni di un'internata.* DG/92. Archivio Diaristico Nazionale.
Pacifici, Marcello. *Diario.* Vicissitudini dei singoli. Serie I, Busta 19. Archivio Centro di Documentazione Ebraica Contemporanea.
Piperno, Emilia. *Trattoria dei cacciatori.* MG/00. Archivio Diaristico Nazionale.
Rothschild, Recha. *Memoirs 1880–1947.* ME 243. Leo Baeck Institute.
Runge, Irene. *Dreiundsechzig.* ME 1514. Leo Baeck Institute.
Soliani, Alba Rabello. *Diario del periodo delle persecuzioni razziali 1943–45.* Vicissitudini dei singoli. Serie I, Busta 26. Archivio Centro di Documentazione Ebraica Contemporanea.
Soppelsa, Giorgio. *Diciamo pane al pane.* MG/07. Archivio Diaristico Nazionale.
Steindler, Livio. *Viandante del XX secolo.* MP/88. Archivio Diaristico Nazionale.
Ulmann, Edda. *L'angelo e la bimba ebrea.* MP/Adn2. Archivio Diaristico Nazionale.
Vitale, Enrica. *Una bambina ebrea.* MG/08. Archivio Diaristico Nazionale.
Winter, Lotte. *Unsere Vergangenheit, Unsere Zukunft 1933–1955.* ME 961. Leo Baeck Institute.
Winterfeldt, Hans. *Deutschland: Ein Zeitbild 1926–1945: Leidensweg eines deutschen Juden in den ersten 19 Jahren seines Lebens 1926–1969.* ME 690. Leo Baeck Institute.
Zaban, Luisa, and Silvia Zaban. *Diario di due Sfollate.* DG/And. Archivio Diaristico Nazionale.

Published Primary Sources

Abusch, Alexander. *Der Deckname: Memoiren.* Berlin: Dietz, 1981.
———. *Der Irrweg einer Nation: Ein Beitrag zum Verständnis deutscher Geschichte.* Berlin: Aufbau, 1946.
———. *Entscheidung unseres Jahrhunderts: Beiträge zur Zeitgeschichte 1921 bis 1976.* Berlin: Aufbau, 1977.
———. *Mit offenem Visier: Memoiren.* Berlin: Dietz, 1986.
Adorno, Theodor. "What Does Coming to Terms with the Past Mean?" In *Bitburg in Moral and Political Perspective*, edited by Geoffrey H. Hartman, 114–129. Bloomington: Indiana University Press, 1986.
Améry, Jean. "How Much Home Does a Person Need?" In *At the Mind's Limits: Contemplations by a Survivor on Auschwitz and Its Realities*, edited by Jean Améry, 41–61. Bloomington: Indiana University Press, 1980.
Arendt, Hannah. *Eichmann in Jerusalem: A Report on the Banality of Evil.* New York: Viking, 1963.
———. *The Origins of Totalitarianism.* New York: Harcourt, Brace & World, 1968.
———. "We Refugees." In *The Jewish Writings*, edited by Jerome Kohn and Ron H. Feldman, 264–275. New York: Schocken Books, 2007.
Arendt, Hannah, and Karl Jaspers. *Hannah Arendt, Karl Jaspers Briefwechsel, 1926–1969.* Edited by Lotte Köhler and Hans Saner. Munich: Piper, 2001.
Axen, Hermann, and Harald Neubert. *Ich war ein Diener der Partei: Autobiographische Gespräche mit Harald Neubert.* Berlin: Ost, 1996.
Bassani, Giorgio. *Five Stories of Ferrara.* Translated by William Weaver. New York: Harcourt Brace Jovanovich, 1971.
———. *The Garden of the Finzi-Continis.* Translated by William Weaver. New York: Harcourt, 1977.

246 | Bibliography

———. *Le parole preparate e altri scritti di letteratura*. Turin: Einaudi, 1966.

Bauer, Goti. "Una Vita Segnata." In *Voci dalla Shoah: Testimonianze per non dimenticare*, edited by Claudio Facchinelli and Liliana Segre, 11–20. Udine: Gaspari, 2020.

Becker, Jurek. *Mein Vater, die Deutschen und ich: Aufsätze, Vorträge, Interviews*. Frankfurt: Suhrkamp, 2007.

Berger, Gabriel. *Mir langt's, ich gehe. Der Lebensweg eines DDR-Atomphysikers von Anpassung zu Aufruhr*. Herder: Freiburg 1988.

Bernhardt, Ursula, and Peter Lange. *Der Riss durch mein Leben: Die Erinnerungen von Ursula Bernhardt*. Berlin: Tranvía, W. Frey, 2000.

Brandt, Heinz. *Ein Traum der nicht entführbar ist: Mein Weg zwischen Ost und West*. Berlin: Europäische Ideen, 1977.

British Broadcasting Corporation. *Ecco Radio Londra*. Wembley, UK: British Broadcasting Corporation, 1945.

Bubis, Ignatz, and Edith Kohn. *Ich bin ein deutscher Staatsbürger jüdischen Glaubens: Ein autobiographisches Gespräch mit Edith Kohn*. Cologne: Kiepenheuer & Witsch, 1993.

Cantoni, Raffaele. "Il saluto dell'unione delle comunità israelitiche italiane a Riccardo Bachi." In *Scritti in onore di Riccardo Bachi: La rassegna mensile di Israel, 5710–1950*. Città di Castello, Italy: Tipografia dell' "Unione Arti Grafiche," 1950, 20–22.

Cavaliere, Alberto, and Sofia Schafranov. *I campi della morte in Germania: Nel racconto di una sopravvissuta a Birkenau*. Milan: Paoline, 2010.

Croce, Benedetto. Prefazione to *I pavidi*, by Cesare Merzagora. Milan: Istituto editoriale Galileo, [1946].

Debenedetti, Giacomo. *October 16, 1943; Eight Jews*. Translated by Estelle Gilson. Notre Dame, IN: University of Notre Dame Press, 2001.

Degen, Michael. *Nicht alle waren Mörder: Eine Kindheit in Berlin*. Munich: Econ, 1999.

Dello Strologo, Pupa. "Pensa che bambina fortunata." In *Una gioventù offesa: Ebrei genovesi ricordano*, edited by Chiara Bricarelli, 25–35. Florence: Giuntina, 1995.

Deutscher, Isaac. "Who Is a Jew?" In *The Non-Jewish Jew and Other Essays*, edited by Tamara Deutscher, 25–41. London: Oxford University Press, 1968.

Deutschkron, Inge. *Mein Leben nach dem Überleben*. Munich: Deutscher Taschenbuch, 2001.

Di Camerino, Roberta. *R, come Roberta*. Milan: Mondadori, 1981.

Döblin, Alfred. *Destiny's Journey*. Plunkett Lake Press, 2019.

Dreifuss, Alfred. *Ensemblespiel des Lebens: Erinnerungen eines Theatermannes*. Buchverlag Der Morgen, 1985.

Eschwege, Helmut. *Fremd unter meinesgleichen: Erinnerungen eines Dresdner Juden*. Berlin: Ch. Links, 1991.

Feuchtwanger, Lion, Arnold Zweig, and Harold von Hofe. *Briefwechsel, 1933–1958*. Berlin: Aufbau, 1984.

Foa, Vittorio. *Il cavallo e la torre : Riflessioni su una vita*. Turin, Einaudi, 1991.

———. *Lettere della giovinezza: Dal carcere: 1935–1943*. Turin: Einaudi, 1998.

Foa Yona, Anna, "Leaving Fascist Italy." In *First Generation: In the Words of Twentieth-Century American Immigrants*, edited by June Namias, 109–16, Boston: Beacon, 1978.

Frankenthal, Hans. *Verweigerte Rückkehr*. Frankfurt: Fischer Taschenbuch: 1999.

Ganther, Heinz. *Die Juden in Deutschland: Ein Almanach*. Frankfurt: Neuzeit Verlag, 1953.

Gay, Peter. *My German Question: Growing Up in Nazi Berlin*. New Haven, CT: Yale University Press, 1998.

Bibliography | 247

Geve, Thomas. *The Boy Who Drew Auschwitz: A Powerful True Story of Hope and Survival.* Harpercollins, 2022.

——. *Es gibt hier keine Kinder.* Edited by Volkhart Knigge. Göttingen, Germany: Wallstein, 1997.

Giordano, Ralph. *Die zweite Schuld, oder von der Last Deutscher zu sein.* Hamburg: Rasch und Röhring, 1987.

——. "Gedanken nach einer Fahrt durch Deutschland," *Zwischen den Zeiten* 1 (1947): 17–23.

——. "Ich bin geblieben—warum?" In *Ich bin geblieben—warum?: Juden in Deutschland,* edited by Katja Behrens, 119–126. Gerlingen, Germany: Bleicher, 2002.

——. *Narben, Spuren, Zeugen: 15 Jahre Allgemeine Wochenzeitung der Juden in Deutschland.* Düsseldorf: Allgemeine Wochenzeitung der Juden in Deutschland, 1961.

——. "Zwei Männer sehen die Deutschen," *Zwischen den Zeiten* 6 (1948):3–13.

Glass, Martha, and Barbara Mueller-Wesemann. *"Jeder Tag in Theresin ist ein Geschenk": Die Theresienstädter Tagebücher einer Hamburger Jüdin 1943-1945.* Hamburg: Ergebnisse, 1996.

Grundig, Lea. *Gesichte und Geschichte.* Berlin: Dietz, 1984.

Härtling, Peter. "Die Macht der Verdränger." In *Literatur des Exils: Eine Dokumentation über die P.E.N.—Jahrestagung in Bremen vom 18. bis 20,* edited by Bernt Engelmann, 172–179. Munich: Goldman, 1981.

Hermlin, Stephan. *Gedichte und Nachdichtungen.* Berlin: Aufbau, 1990.

Heymann, Stefan. *Marxismus und Rassenfrage.* Berlin: Dietz, [1948].

Huppert, Hilde, Arnold Zweig, and Heidrun Loeper. *Engpass zur Freiheit: Aufzeichnungen der Frau Hilde Huppert über ihre Erlebnisse im Nazi-Todesland und ihre wundersame Errettung aus Bergen-Belsen.* Berlin: Kontext, 1990.

Jacobus, Hans. "Man wollte ein Zuhause." In *Skizzen der Gezeiten: Erlebte und Erträumtes,* 70–85. Berlin: Schkeuditz, 1998.

Jaspers, Karl. *The Question of German Guilt.* New York: Fordham University Press, 2000.

Kahn, Siegbert. *Antisemitismus und Rassenhetze.* Berlin: Dietz, 1948

Kantorowicz, Alfred. *Deutsches Tagebuch.* Munich: Kindler, 1964.

——. *Exil in Frankreich: Merkwürdigkeiten und Denkwürdigkeiten.* Bremen, Germany: Schünemann, 1971.

Kaul, Friedrich Karl. *Es wird Zeit dass du nach Hause kommst.* Berlin: Verl. Das Neue Berlin, 1961.

Kempner, Robert M. W., and Joerg Friedrich. *Anklaeger einer Epoche: Lebenserinnerungen.* Frankfurt: Ullstein, 1983.

Kesten, Hermann. "Denken deutsche Dichter?" In *Sind wir noch das Volk der Dichter und Denker? 14 Antworten,* edited by Gert Kalow. 79–87. Reinbek, Germany: Rowohlt, 1964.

——. *Der Geist der Unruhe. Literarische Streifzüge.* Kiepenheuer & Witsch, Köln, 1959.

——, ed. *Deutsche Literatur im Exil: Briefe europäischer Autoren 1933-1949.* Vienna: K. Desch, 1964.

——. "Die Gevierteilte Literatur." In *Der Geist der Unruhe. Literarische Streifzüge.* Cologne: Kiepenheuer & Witsch, 1959, 116–135.

——. "Die Nächstenliebe." In *Filialen des Parnass,* edited by Hermann Kesten, 117–127. Munich: Kindler, 1961.

248 | Bibliography

———. "Die vergebliche Heimkehr." In *"Ich hatte Glück mit den Menschen": Zum 100. Geburtstag des Dichters Hermann Kesten: Texte von ihm und über ihn*, edited by Wolfgang Buhl and Ulf von Dewitz, 15–24. Nuremberg: Stadtbibliothek, 2000.

———. "'La doulce France' oder Exil in Frankreich." In *Dichter—Literat—Emigrant: Über Hermann Kesten: Mit einer Kesten-Bibliographie*, edited by Walter Fähnders and Hendrik Weber, 227–236. Bielefeld, Germany: Aisthesis, 2005.

———. "Literatur im Exil." In *Der Geist der Unruhe: Literarische Streifzüge*. Cologne: Kiepenheuer & Witsch, 1959, 222–235.

———. "Zwanzig Jahre danach." In *Mit Menschen leben: Ein Nürnberger Lesebuch*, edited by Wolfgang Buhl, 134–156. Cadolzburg, Germany: Ars vivendi, 1999.

Klein, Dora. *Vivere e sopravivere Diario 1936–1945*. Milan: Mursia, 2001.

Klemperer, Victor. *Ich will Zeugnis ablegen bis zum letzten*. Berlin: Aufbau, 1995.

———. *So sitze ich denn zwischen allen Stühlen: Tagebücher*. Berlin: Aufbau, 1999.

Krause Johanna, Carolyn Gammon, *Zweimal Verfolgt: Eine Dresdner Jüdin erzählt*. Berlin: Metropolverlag, 2011.

Kuczynski, Jürgen. *Ein linientreuer Dissident: Memoiren 1945–1989*. Berlin: Aufbau, 1994.

Landau, Ernest. "Wir Juden und unsere Umwelt." In *Die Juden in Deutschland: Ein Almanach*, edited by Heinz Ganther. Frankfurt: Neuzeit, 1953.

Lennert, Rudolf. "Zugehörigkeit, Selbstbewußtsein, Fremdheit: Erinnerung an eine dunkle Zeit," *Neue Sammlung* 3/26 (1986): 381–395.

Levi, Franco. *I giorni dell'erba amara*. Genoa: Marietti, 1990.

Levi, Lia. *Se va via il re*. Rome: Edizioni e/o, 1996.

———. *Una bambina e basta*. Rome: Edizioni e/o, 1994.

Levi, Primo. *The Drowned and the Saved*. New York: Summit Books, 1988.

———. *La tregua*. [Turin]: Einaudi, 1963.

———. *The Periodic Table*. London: Penguin, 2012.

———. *Survival in Auschwitz*. New York: Touchstone, 1996.

Levi, Primo, Marco Belpoliti, and Robert Gordon. *The Voice of Memory: Interviews 1961–1987*. New York: New Press, 2001.

Levinson, Nathan. *Ein Ort ist, mit wem du bist: Lebensstationen eines Rabbiners*. Berlin: Hentrich, 1996.

Liepman, Heinz. *Ein deutscher Jude denkt ueber Deutschland nach*. Munich: Ner-Tamid, 1961.

Lombroso, Sylvia. *Si può stampare pagine vissute, 1938–1945*. Rome: Dalmatia, 1945.

Marcuse, Ludwig. *Briefe von und an Ludwig Marcuse*. Edited by Harold von Hofe. Zurich: Diogenes, 1975.

———. "Lebe ich oder lebe ich nicht in der Bundesrepublik?" In Hermann Kesten, *Ich Lebe Nicht in Der Bundesrepublik*, 107–113. Munich: List, 1964.

———. *Mein zwanzigstes Jahrhundert: Auf dem Weg zu einer Autobiographie*. Munich: List, 1960.

Mayer, Hans. *Ein Deutscher auf Widerruf*. Frankfurt: Suhrkamp, 1982.

Mika, Viktor, and Arnold Zweig. *Im Feuer vergangen: Tagebücher aus dem Ghetto*. Berlin: Rütten & Loening 1960.

Millu, Liana. *I ponti di Schwerin*. Genoa: Culturali Internazinali,1994.

Misul, Frida. *Fra gli artigli del mostro nazista: La più romanzesca delle realtà, il più realistico dei romanzi*. Livorno, Italy: Stabilimento Poligrafico Belforte, 1946.

Momigliano, Arnaldo. *Essays on Ancient and Modern Judaism*. Edited by Silvia Berti. Translated by Maura Masella-Gayley. Chicago: University of Chicago Press, 1994.

Momigliano, Eucardio. *Storia trágica e grottesca del razzismo fascista*. [Verona]: Mondadori, 1946.

Morpurgo, Alma, and Margherita Morpurgo. *L'esilio 1939–1955: Ricordi dal Cile*. Pasian di Prato, Italy: Campanotto, 1997.

Morpurgo, Elena. *Diario dell'esilio in Svizzera*. Pasian di Prato, Italy: Campanotto, 2005.

Morpurgo, Elena, Luisa Zaban, Silvia Zaban, and Paola Magnarelli. *Guerra, esilio, ebraicità: Diari di donne nelle due guerre mondiali*. Ancona, Italy: Lavoro, 1996.

Morpurgo, Luciano. *Caccia all'uomo!: Vita sofferenze e beffe: Pagine di diario 1938–1944*. Rome: Dalmatia, 1946.

Mortara, Giulio. *Lettere alla madre dall'esilio in Svizzera (1943–1945)*. Bellinzona, Switzerland: Salvioni, 2007.

Neumann, Robert. *Vielleicht das Heitere: Tagebuch aus einem andern Jahr*. [Munich]: K. Desch, 1968.

Nissim, Giorgio, and Liliana Picciotto Fargion. *Memorie di un ebreo toscano, 1938–1948*. Rome: Carocci, 2005.

Oppenheimer, Paul. *From Belsen to Buckingham Palace*. Newark, NJ: Beth Shalom, 1996.

Orbach, Larry, and Vivien Orbach-Smith. *Soaring Underground: Autobiographie eines jüdischen Jugendlichen im Berliner Untergrund 1938–1945*. Berlin: Kowalke, 1998.

Ottolenghi, Lea, and Emma De Rossi Castelli. *Nei tempi oscuri: Diari di Lea Ottolenghi e Emma de Rossi Castelli: Due donne ebree tra il 1943 e il 1945*. Livorno, Italy: Belforte, 2000.

Ottolenghi Minerbi, Marta. *La colpa di essere nati*. Milano: Gastaldi, 1954.

Pacifici, Emanuele. *Non ti voltare: Autobiografia di un ebreo*. Florence: Giuntina, 1993.

Paepcke, Lotte. *Ich wurde vergessen: Bericht einer Juedin, die das Dritte Reich ueberlebte*. Freiburg, Germany: Herder, 1979.

Paladini, Carlo. "A colloquio con Primo Levi." In *Lavoro, criminalità, e alienazione mentale: Richerche sulle Marche del primo Novecento*, edited by Paolo Sorcinelli, 147–159. Ancona, Italy: Lavoro, 1987.

Posener, Julius. *In Deutschland: 1945 bis 1946*. Berlin: Siedler, 2001.

Proskauer, Erna, Sabine Berghahn, and Christl Wickert. *Erna Proskauer: Wege und Umwege: Erinnerungen einer Rechtsanwaeltin*. Berlin: D. Nishen, 1989.

Rapoport, Ingeborg. *Meine ersten drei Leben: Erinnerungen*. Berlin: NORA, 2002.

Riesenburger, Martin. *Das Licht verlöschte nicht: Ein Zeugnis aus der Nacht des Faschismus*. Teetz, Germany: Hentrich & Hentrich, 2003.

Römer, Gernot. *Vier Schwestern: Die Lebenserinnerungen von Elisabeth, Lotte, Sophie und Gertrud Dann aus Augsburg*. Augsburg, Germany: Wissner, 1998.

Rosenthal, Hans. *Zwei Leben in Deutschland*. Bergisch Gladbach, Germany: Lübbe, 1980.

Sahl, Hans. *Memoiren eines Moralisten*. Frankfurt: Luchterhand, 1990.

Schiffer, Davide. *Non c'è ritorno a casa . . . memorie di vite stravolte dalle leggi razziali*. Milan: 5 Continents, 2003.

Schmuckler, Malka. *Gast im eigenen Land: Emigration und Rückkehr einer deutschen Jüdin*. Ratingen, Germany: Melina, 1997.

Seghers, Anna. "The Outing of the Dead Schoolgirls." *Kenyon Review* 31, no. 5 (1969): 613–642.

Seghers, Anna, and Christel Berger. *Hier im Volk der kalten Herzen: Briefwechsel 1947*. Berlin: Aufbau Taschenbuch, 2000.

Segre, Augusto. *Memories of Jewish Life : From Italy to Jerusalem 1918–1960*. Lincoln: University of Nebraska Press, 2008.

Segre, Cesare. *Per curiosità: Una specie di autobiografia*. Turin: Einaudi, 1999.

Segre, Dan Vittorio. *Memoirs of a Fortunate Jew: An Italian Story*. Bethesda, MD: Adler & Adler, 1987.

250 | *Bibliography*

Segre, Renzo. *Venti mesi*. Palermo: Sellerio 1995.

Spiegel, Marga. *Bauern als Retter: Wie eine jüdische Familie überlebte*. Berlin: Lit, 2009.

Spira, Steffie. *Trab der Schaukelpferde: Autobiographie*. Freiburg, Germany: Kore, 1991.

Tagliacozzo, Mario. *Metà della vita: Ricordi della campagna razziale 1938–1944*. Milan: Baldini & Castoldi, 1998.

Tedeschi, Giuilana. *There Is a Place on Earth*. New York: Random House, 1992.

Thiess, Frank. "Die innere Emigration." In *Die Grosse Kontroverse: Ein Briefwechsel um Deutschland*, edited by Johannes Franz Gottlieb Grosser, 24–26. Hamburg: Nagel, 1963.

Treves, Lotte. "Mit tiefer Dankbarkeit blicke ich zurück." In *Vier Schwestern: Die Lebenserinnerungen von Elisabeth, Lotte, Sophie und Gertrud Dann aus Augsburg*, edited by Gernot Römer, 135–228. Augsburg, Germany: Wissner, 1998.

Treves Alcalay, Liliana. *Con occhi di bambina: 1941–1945*. Florence: La Giuntina, 1994.

Ulbricht, Walter. *Reden und Aufsätze*. Hamburg: Blinkfüer, 1968.

Unikower, Inge. *Suche nach dem gelobten Land: Biographie*. Berlin: Verlag der Nation, 1978.

Venezia, Dora. "Perché è successo?" In *Una gioventù offesa: ebrei genovesi ricordano*, edited by Chiara Bricarelli, 121–136. Florence: Giuntina, 1995.

Victor, Walther. *Kehre wieder über die Berge*. Berlin: Aufbau, 1982.

Zargani, Aldo. *Per violino solo: la mia infanzia nell'Aldiqua, 1938–1945*. Bologna: Il Mulino, 2010.

Zevi, Tullia, and Nathania Zevi. *Ti racconto la mia storia: Dialogo tra nonna e nipote sull'ebraismo*. Milan: Rizzoli, 2007.

Zevi, Tullia Calabi. *La mia Autobiografia Politica*. Florence: Quaderni circolo Rosselli, Alinea.

Zweig, Arnold. *1887–1968: Werk und Leben in Dokumenten und Bildern*. Edited by Georg Wenzel. Berlin: Aufbau, 1978.

Books, Articles, Theses

Aberbach, David. *Surviving Trauma: Loss, Literature, and Psychoanalysis*. New Haven, CT: Yale University Press, 1989.

Adler, Franklin Hugh. "Jew as Bourgeois, Jew as Enemy, Jew as Victim of Fascism." *Modern Judaism* 28, no. 3 (2008): 306–326.

Adler, K. H., and Carrie Hamilton. *Homes and Homecomings: Gendered Histories of Domesticity and Return*. Oxford: Wiley-Blackwell, 2010.

Albrecht, Willy. "Jeanette Wolff, Jakob Altmaier und Peter Blachstein: Die drei jüdischen Abgeordneten des Bundestags bis zum Beginn der sechziger Jahre." In *Leben im Land der Täter: Juden im Nachkriegsdeutschland (1945–1952)*, edited by Julius H. Schoeps, 236–253. Berlin: Jüdische Verlagsanstalt, 2001.

Allen, Keith R. *Befragung Überprüfung Kontroll: Die Aufnahme von DDR-Flüchtlingen in West-Berlin bis 1961*. Berlin: Links, 2013.

Altfelix, Thomas. "The 'Post-Holocaust Jew' and the Instrumentalization of Philosemitism." *Patterns of Prejudice* 34 (2000): 41–56.

Anderson, Benedict. *Imagined Communities: Reflections on the Origin and Spread of Nationalism*. London: Verso, 2016.

Anderson, K., and S. Smith. "Editorial: Emotional Geographies." *Transactions of the Institute of British Geographers* 26, no. 1 (2001): 7–10.

Andresen, Knud. *Widerspruch als Lebensprinzip: Der undogmatische Sozialist Heinz Brandt (1909–1986)*. Bonn: Dietz, 2007.

Anthony, Elizabeth. *The Compromise of Return: Viennese Jews after the Holocaust*. Detroit: Wayne State University Press, 2021.

———. "Return of Jewish Concentration Camp Survivors to Vienna in the Immediate Post-war Period." *Jewish History Quarterly* 02 (2013): 286292.

Anthony, Tamara. *Ins Land der Väter oder der Täter?: Israel und die Juden in Deutschland nach der Schoah*. Berlin: Metropol, 2004.

Antonini, Sandro. *Delasem: Storia della piu grande organizzazione ebraica italiana di soccorso durante la seconda guerra mondiale*. Genoa: De Ferrari, 2000.

Applegate, Celia. *A Nation of Provincials: The German Idea of Heimat*. Berkeley: University of California Press, 1990.

Archivio Storico della Comunità Ebraica di Roma. *La comunita ebraica di Roma nel secondo dopoguerra: economia e societa (1945–1965)*. Rome: Camera di commercio, industria, artigianato e agricoltura di Roma, 2007.

Ascarelli, Roberta. *Oltre la persecuzione: Donne, ebraismo, memoria*. Rome: Carocci, 2004.

Aschheim, Steven. "'Genosse Klemperer' Kommunismus, Liberalismus und Jude sein in der DDR, 1945–1959." In *Zwischen Politik und Kultur: Juden in der DDR*, edited by Moshe Zuckermann, 184–209. Göttingen, Germany: Wallstein, 2002.

Assmann, Aleida. "Transformations between History and Memory." *Social Research* 75, no. 1 (2008): 49–72.

Assmann, Aleida, and Ute Frevert. *Geschichtsvergessenheit, Geschichtsversessenheit: Vom Umgang mit deutschen Vergangenheiten nach 1945*. Stuttgart: Deutsche. Verlag-Anstalt 1999.

Auslander, Leora. "The Boundaries of Jewishness, or When Is a Cultural Practice Jewish?" *Journal of Modern Jewish Studies* 8, no. 1 (2009): 47–64.

———. "Coming Home? Jews in Postwar Paris." *Journal of Contemporary History* 40, no. 2 (2005): 237–259.

Avagliano, Mario, and Marco Palmieri. *Gli ebrei sotto la persecuzione in Italia: Diari e lettere, 1938–1945*. Turin: Einaudi, 2011.

Azouvi, François. *Le mythe du grand silence: Auschwitz, les Français, la mémoire*. Paris: Fayard, 2012.

Badrnejad-Hahn, Hahle. "Wiederaufbau oder Neubeginn? Die Jüdische Gemeinde Rom von 1944/45–1960." PhD diss., Ludwig Maximilian University of Munich, 2013.

Baiardi, Marta. "Sulle sofferenze e sui danni subiti in questa guerra: Due memoriali dall'archivio storico della comunità ebraica di Firenze." *Annali di Storia di Firenze* 3 (2008): 1000–1034.

Bal, Mieke, Jonathan V. Crewe, and Leo Spitzer. *Acts of Memory: Cultural Recall in the Present*. Hanover, NH: University Press of New England, 1999.

Baldini, Anna. "La memoria italiana della Shoah (1944–2009)." In *Atlante della letteratura italiana*. Vol. 3, 758–763. Turin: Einaudi, 2012.

Ballinger, Pamela. *History in Exile: Memory and Identity at the Borders of the Balkans*. Princeton, NJ: Princeton University Press, 2018.

Bankier, David. *The Jews Are Coming Back: The Return of the Jews to Their Countries of Origin after WWII*. New York: Berghahn Books, 2005.

Bardgett, Suzanne. *Justice, Politics and Memory in Europe after the Second World War*. London: Vallentine Mitchell, 2011.

Barozzi, Frederica. "L'uscita degli ebrei di Roma dalla clandestinità." In *Il ritorno alla vita: Vicende e diritti degli ebrei in Italia dopo la seconda guerre mondiale*, edited by Michele Sarfatti, 31–46. Florence: Giuntina, 1998.

252 | Bibliography

Barthes, Roland. "The Rhetoric of the Image." In *Image, Music, Text,* translated by Stephen Heath, 152–163. New York: Hill and Wang, 1977.

Battini, M., and Stanislao G. Pugliese. *The Missing Italian Nuremberg: Cultural Amnesia and Postwar Politics.* New York: Palgrave Macmillan, 2007.

Bauerkämper, Arnd. "Americanisation as Globalisation: Remigrés to West Germany after 1945 and Conceptions of Democracy: The Cases of Hans Rothfels, Ernst Fraenkel and Hans Rosenberg." *Leo Baeck Institute Year Book* 49, no. 1 (January 2004): 153–170.

Belau, Linda, and Petar Ramadanovic. *Topologies of Trauma: Essays on the Limit of Knowledge and Memory.* New York: Other Press, 2002.

Ben-Ghiat, Ruth. "A Lesser Evil? Italian Fascism in/and the Totalitarian Equation." In *The Lesser Evil: Moral Approaches to Genocide Practices,* edited by Helmut Dubiel and Gabriel Motzkin, 137-153.New York: Routledge, 2004.

———. "The Secret Histories of Roberto Benigni's *Life is Beautiful.*" *The Yale Journal of Criticism* 14, no. 1 (2001): 253–266.

Ben-Ghiat, Ruth, Luciano Cafagna, Ernesto Galli della Loggia, Carl Ipsen, David Kertzer, and Mark Gilbert. "History as It Really Wasn't: The Myths of Italian Historiography." *Journal of Modern Italian Studies* 6, no. 3 (2001): 402–419.

Benz, Ute. "'Für den Vater war es sehr schwer.' Lucy Geigers Auswanderung und Rückkehr." In *Das Exil der kleinen Leute: Alltagserfahrung deutscher Juden in der Emigration,* edited by Wolfgang Benz, 326–331. Munich: Beck, 1991.

Benz, Wolfgang, and Werner T. Angress. *Zwischen Antisemitismus und Philosemitismus: Juden in der Bundesrepublik.* Berlin: Metropol, 1991.

Berg, Nicolas. "Hidden Memory and Unspoken History: Hans Rothfels and the Postwar Restoration of Contemporary German History?" *Leo Baeck Institute Yearbook* 49, no. 1 (January 2004): 195–220.

Berger, Stefan, and William John Niven. *Writing the History of Memory.* London: Bloomsbury Academic, 2014.

Bergmann, Werner. *Geschichte des Antisemitismus.* Munich: Beck, 2002.

Bergmann, Werner, and Rainer Erb. *Antisemitismus in der Bundesrepublik Deutschland: Ergebnisse der empirischen Forschung von 1946-1989.* Opladen, Germany: Leske and Budrich, 1991.

Berti, Silvia. "Arnaldo Momigliano (1908–1987): Judaism Past and Present." In *Makers of Jewish Modernity: Thinkers, Artists, Leaders, and the World They Made,* edited by Jacques Picard, Jacques Revel, Michael P Steinberg, Idith Zertal and Lydia Flem, 450–466. Princeton, NJ: Princeton University Press, 2016.

Bertilotti, Paola. "Italian Jews and the Memory of Rescue." In *Resisting Genocide: The Multiple Forms of Rescue,* edited by Jacques Sémelin, Claire Andrieu, and Sarah Gensburger, 127–144. New York: Columbia University Press, 2011.

———. "L'Unione delle comunita e la commemorazione della resistenza (1944-1948)." *La Rassegna Mensile di Israel* 24 (2008): 173–191.

Bertram, Juergen, and Helga Bertram. *Wer Baut, Der Bleibt: Neues Juedisches Leben Deutschland.* Frankfurt: Fischer Taschenbuch, 2008.

Bessel, Richard. "Introduction: Italy, Germany and Fascism." In *Fascist Italy and Nazi Germany: Comparisons and Contrasts,* edited by Richard Bessel, 1–12. Cambridge: Cambridge University Press.1996.

Bettina, Elizabeth. *It Happened in Italy: Untold Stories of How the People of Italy Defied the Horrors of the Holocaust*. Nashville: Thomas Nelson, 2009.

Bidussa, David. *Il mito del bravo italiano*. Milan: Il Saggiatore, 1994.

———. "Razzismo e antisemitismo in Italia: Fenomenologia e ontologia del bravo italiano." *La Rassegna Mensile di Israel* 59 (1992): 1–36.

Biess, Frank. "Feelings in the Aftermath: Toward a History of Postwar Emotions." In *Histories of the Aftermath: The Legacies of the Second World War in Europe*, edited by Frank Biess and Robert G. Moeller, 30–48. New York: Berghahn Books, 2010.

———. *Homecomings: Returning POWs and the Legacies of Defeat in Postwar Germany*. Princeton, NJ: Princeton University Press, 2009.

Bistarelli, Agostino. *La storia del ritorno: I reduci italiani del secondo dopoguerra*. Turin: Bollati Boringhieri, 2007.

Blaschke, Wolfgang, Karola Fings, and Cordula Lissner. *Unter Vorbehalt: Rückkehr aus der Emigration nach 1945*. Köln: Emons, 1997.

Bloxham, Donald. *Genocide on Trial: War Crime Trials and the Formation of Holocaust History and Memory*. Oxford: Oxford University Press, 2001.

———. "Jewish Witnesses in War Crimes Trials of the Postwar Era." In *Holocaust Historiography in Context: Emergences, Challenges, Polemics, and Achievements*, edited by David Bankier and Dan Michman, 539–553. New York: Berghahn Books, 2008.

Blunt, Alison, and Robyn M. Dowling. *Home*. London: Routledge, 2006.

Bodemann, Michal. "Die Endzeit der Märtyrer-Gründer: An einer Epochenwende jüdischer Existenz in Deutschland." *Babylon: Beiträge zur jüdischen Gegenwart* 8 (1990): 7–15.

———. "'How Can One Stand to Live There as a Jew . . .': Paradoxes of Jewish Existence in Germany." In *Jews, Germans, Memory: Reconstructions of Jewish Life in Germany*. 19–38. Ann Arbor: University of Michigan Press, 1996.

———. *In den Wogen der Erinnerung: Juedische Existenz in Deutschland*. Munich: Deutscher Taschenbuch, 2002.

Bohus, Kata, Atina Grossmann, Werner Hanak, and Mirjam Wenzel, ed. *Our Courage: Jews in Europe 1945–48*. Berlin: De Gruyter Oldenbourg, 2020.

Bohus, Kata, Peter Hallama, and Stephan Stach, ed. *Growing in the Shadow of Antifascism: Remembering the Holocaust in State-Socialist Eastern Europe*. Central European University Press, 2022.

Boll, Friedhelm. *Sprechen als Last und Befreiung: Holocaust, Ueberlebende und politisch Verfolgte zweier Diktaturen: Ein Beitrag zur deutsch-deutschen Erinnerungskultur*. Bonn: Dietz, 2001.

Borneman, John, and Jeffrey M. Peck. *Sojourners: The Return of German Jews and the Question of Identity*. Lincoln: University of Nebraska Press, 1995.

Bosworth, R.J.B. "Explaining 'Auschwitz' after the End of History: The Case of Italy." *History and Theory* 38, no. 1 (1999): 84–99.

Boyers, Peggy, and Natalia Ginzburg. "An Interview with Natalia Ginzburg," *Salmagundi* 96 (1992): 130–156.

Boym, Svetlana. *The Future of Nostalgia*. New York: Basic Books, 2016.

Brämer, Andreas. "'. . . die Rückkehr eines Rabbiners nach Deutschland ist keine Selbstverständlichkeit': Zur Remigration jüdischer Geistlicher nach Westdeutschland (1945–1965)." In *"Auch in Deutschland waren wir nicht Wirklich Zu Hause": Jüdische*

254 | Bibliography

Remigration Nach 1945, edited by Irmela von der Lühe, Axel Schildt, and Stefanie Schüler-Springorum, 169–190. Göttingen, Germany: Wallstein, 2008.

Brandt, Susanne, Christoph Cornelissen, Lutz Klinkhammer, and Wolfgang Schwentker. *Erinnerungskulturen: Deutschland, Italien und Japan seit 1945, Die Zeit des Nationalsozialismus*. Frankfurt: Fischer Taschenbuch, 2003.

Bravo, Anna. "Armed and Unarmed: Struggles without Weapons in Europe and in Italy." *Journal of Modern Italian Studies* 10, no. 4 (2005): 468–484.

———. "La memorialistica della deportazione dall'Italia (1945–1966)." In *I campi di sterminio nazisti: Storia, memoria, storiografia*, edited by Giovanna D'Amico, Brunello Mantelli, and Anna Bravo, 127–136. Milan: Angeli, 2003.

———. "Social Perception of the Shoah in Italy." In *The Jews of Italy: Memory and Identity*, edited by Bernard Dov Cooperman and Barbara Garvin. Bethesda: University Press of Maryland, 2008.

Bravo, Anna, Giovanna D'Amico, and Brunello Mantelli, eds. *I campi di sterminio nazisti: Storia, memoria, storiografia*. Milan: Angeli, 2003.

Bravo, Anna, Daniele Jalla, and Laura Maritano. *Una misura onesta: Gli scritti di memoria della deportazione dall'Italia, 1944–1993*. Milan: Angeli, 1994.

Breitsprecher, Ulrike. "Die Bedeutung des Judentums und des Holocaust in der Identitätskonstruktion dreier jüdischer Kommunisten in der frühen DDR—Alexander Abusch, Helmut Eschwege und Leo Zuckermann." *Jahrbuch für Historische Kommunismusforschung*, vol. 16, no. 23. (2010): 193–208.

Brenner, Michael. "Ein neues deutsches Judentum?" In *Geschichte der Juden in Deutschland von 1945 bis zur Gegenwart: Politik, Kultur und Gesellschaft*, edited by Michael Brenner, Dan Diner, Norbert Frei, Lena Gorelik, Constantin Goschler, Atina Grossman, Anthony Kauders, Tamar Lewinsky, and Yfaat Weiss, 419–434. Munich: Beck, 2012.

———. *Nach dem Holocaust: Juden in Deutschland 1945–1950*. Munich: Beck, 1995.

———. "The Transformation of the German-Jewish Community." In *Unlikely History: The Changing German-Jewish Symbiosis, 1945–2000*, edited by Leslie Morris and Jack Zipes, 49–61. New York: Palgrave, 2002.

———. "'We Are the Unhappy Few': Return and Disillusionment among German-Jewish Intellectuals," *Journal of Modern Jewish Studies* 13:1 (2014): 12–22.

Brenner, Michael, Dan Diner, Norbert Frei, Lena Gorelik, Constantin Goschler, Atina Grossman, Anthony Kauders, Tamar Lewinsky, and Yfaat Weiss. *Geschichte der Juden in Deutschland von 1945 bis zur Gegenwart: Politik, Kultur und Gesellschaft*. Munich: Beck, 2012.

Broder, Henryk M. *Der ewige Antisemit: Über Sinn und Funktion eines beständigen Gefühls*. Frankfurt: Fischer Taschenbuch, 1986.

Broggini, Renata. *Frontier of Hope: Jews from Italy Seek Refuge in Switzerland 1943–1945*. Milan: U. Hoepli, 2003.

Brown-Fleming, Suzanne. *The Holocaust and Catholic Conscience: Cardinal Aloisius Muench and the Guilt Question in Germany*. Notre Dame, IN: University of Notre Dame Press, 2006.

Brubaker, Rogers. "Ethnicity, Race, and Nationalism." *Annual Review of Sociology* 35 (2009): 21–42.

———. "Ethnicity without Groups." *European Journal of Sociology* 43, no. 2 (2002): 163–189.

Brubaker, Rogers, and Frederick Cooper. "Beyond 'Identity.'" *Theory and Society: Renewal and Critique in Social Theory* 29 (2000): 1–47.

Brumlik, Micha. *Jüdisches Leben in Deutschland Seit 1945*. Frankfurt: Juedischer Verlag bei Athenaeum, 1986.

Buchanan, Andrew. "'Good Morning, Pupil!' American Representations of Italianness and the Occupation of Italy, 1943–1945." *Journal of Contemporary History* 43, no. 2 (2008): 217–240.

Burgauer, Erica. *Zwischen Erinnerung und Verdrängung: Juden in Deutschland nach 1945*. Reinbek, Germany: Rowohlt, 1993.

Burleigh, Michael, and Wolfgang Wippermann. *The Racial State: Germany, 1933–1945*. Cambridge: Cambridge University Press, 1991.

Cannistraro, Philip V., and Brian R. Sullivan. *Il Duce's Other Woman*. New York: Morrow, 1992.

Čapková, Kateřina, and David Rechter. "Germans or Jews? German-Speaking Jews in Post-War Europe: An Introduction." *Leo Baeck Institute Year Book* 62 (2017): 69–74.

Caputo, Giuseppe. *Il pregiudizio antisemitico in Italia*. Rome: Newton Compton, 1984.

Carocci, Giampiero. *Storia degli ebrei in Italia: Dall'emancipazione a oggi*. Rome: Newton Compton, 2005.

Carpegna, Alessandra. "'Io non pensavo di scrivere' Intervista a Primo Levi." In *Mezzosecolo: Materiali di ricerca storica*, 355–358. Milan: Guanda, 1975.

Carpi, Daniel, Augusto Segre, and Renzo Toaff. *Scritti in memoria di Nathan Cassuto*. Jerusalem: Kedem, Yad Leyakkirenu, 1986.

Caruth, Cathy. *Trauma: Explorations in Memory*. Baltimore: Johns Hopkins University Press, 1995.

Castronuovo, Nadia. *Natalia Ginzburg: Jewishness as Moral Identity*. Leicester, UK: Troubador, 2010.

Cavaglion, Alberto. "Figure spettrali come i numeri negativi: Il ritorno dei deportati ebrei in alcune testimonianze (1945–1948)." In *Deportazione e internamento militare in Germania: la provincia di Modena*, edited by Giovanna Procacci and Lorenzo Bertucelli, 448–461. Milan: Unicopli, 2001.

———. "Sopra alcuni contestati giudizi intorno alla storia degli ebrei in Italia (1945–1949)." In *Il ritorno alla vita: vicende e diritti degli ebrei in Italia dopo la seconda guerra mondiale*, edited by Michele Sarfatti, 151–165. Florence: Giuntina, 1998.

Cesarani, David. *After Eichmann: Collective Memory and the Holocaust since 1961*. London: Routledge, 2005.

Cesarani, David, Tony Kushner, and Milton Shain. *Place and Displacement in Jewish History and Memory: Zakor V'makor*. London: Vallentine Mitchell, 2009.

Cesarani, David, and Eric J. Sundquist. *After the Holocaust: Challenging the Myth of Silence*. London: Routledge, 2012.

Chaumont, Jean-Michel. *Die Konkurrenz der Opfer: Genozid, Identitaet, Anerkennung*. Lüneburg, Germany: zu Klampen, 2001.

Chernow, Ron. *Die Warburgs: Odyssee einer Familie*. Berlin: Siedler, 1994.

Cichopek-Gajraj, Anna. *Beyond Violence: Jewish Survivors in Poland and Slovakia, 1944–48*. Cambridge: Cambridge University Press, 2014.

Clifford, Rebecca. *Commemorating the Holocaust: The Dilemmas of Remembrance in France and Italy*. Oxford: Oxford University Press, 2013.

———. "The Limits of National Memory: Anti-Fascism, the Holocaust and the Fosse Ardeatine Memorial in 1990s Italy." In *Forum for Modern Language Studies* 44, no. 2 (2008): 128–139.

256 | Bibliography

Cohen, Anthony P. "Personal Nationalism: A Scottish View of Some Rites, Rights, and Wrongs." *American Ethnologist* 23, no. 4 (1996): 802–815.

Cohen, Beth. "The Myth of Silence: Survivors Tell a Different Story." In *After the Holocaust: Challenging the Myth of Silence*, edited by David Cesarani and Eric J. Sundquist, 191–201. London: Routledge, 2012.

Cohen, Boaz. "Dr. Jacob Robinson, the Institute of Jewish Affairs and the Elusive Jewish Voice in Nuremberg." In *Holocaust and Justice: Representation and Historiography of the Holocaust in Post-War Trials,* edited by David Bankier and Dan Michman, 81–100. Yad Vashem Publications, 2010.

Cohen, Deborah, and Maura O'Connor. *Comparison and History: Europe in Cross-National Perspective.* New York: Routledge, 2004.

Cohen, Erik. "Jewish Identity Research: A State of the Art." *International Journal of Jewish Education Research* 1(1), (2010): 7–48.

Collotti, Enzo. "Die Historiker und die Rassengesetze in Italien." In *Faschismus und Faschismen in Vergleich: Wolfgang Schieder zum 60: Geburtstag,* edited by Christoph Dipper, 59–77. Vierow, Germany: SH-Verl, 1998.

———. *Il fascismo e gli ebrei: Le leggi razziali in Italia.* Rome: Laterza, 2003.

———, ed. *Razza e fascismo: La persecuzione contro gli ebrei in Toscana, 1938–1943.* Rome: Carocci, 1999.

Collotti, Enzo, and Patrizia Dogliani. *Arbeit macht Frei: Storia e memoria della deportazione: In occasione della mostra.* Carpi, Italy: Comune di Carpi, 1985.

Collotti, Enzo, and Lutz Klinkhammer. "Diskussionsforum zur Neubewertung des italienischen Faschismus, Enzo Collotti im Gespräch mit Luis Klinkhammer." *Geschichte und Gesellschaft* 26 (1997): 285–306.

Collotti, Enzo, Renato Sandri, and Frediano Sessi. *Dizionario della Resistenza: Storia e geografia della Liberazione.* Turin: Einaudi, 2000.

Colombo, Anna. *Gli ebrei hanno sei dita: Una vita lunga un secolo.* Milan: Feltrinelli, 2005.

Confino, Alon. *Germany as a Culture of Remembrance: Promises and Limits of Writing History.* Chapel Hill: University of North Carolina Press, 2006.

Confino, Alon, and Peter Fritzsche. "Introduction: Noises of the Past." In *The Work of Memory: New Directions in the Study of German Society and Culture,* edited by Alon Confino and Peter Fritzsche, 1–21. Urbana: University of Illinois Press, 2002.

Connerton, Paul. *How Societies Remember.* Cambridge: Cambridge University Press, 2012.

Consonni, Manuela M. "The Church and the Memory of the Shoah: The Catholic Press in Italy, 1945–1947." *Studies in Contemporary Jewry* 21 (2005): 21–34.

———. "The Impact of the 'Eichmann Event' in Italy, 1961." *Journal of Israeli History* 23 (2004): 90–99.

———. "The New Grammar of Otherness: Europe, the Shoah, and the Jews." *Jewish History* 24, no. 2 (2010): 105–126.

———. "The Santa Sede, the Shoah and Postwar Memory in Italy." In *Jews and Catholics in Dialogue and Confrontation: Religion and Politics since the Second World War,* edited by Eli Lederhendler, 132–153. Oxford: Oxford University Press for Institute of Contemporary Jewry, Hebrew University of Jerusalem, 2005.

———. "A War of Memories: De Felice and His Intervista sul Fascismo." *Journal of Modern Jewish Studies* 5, no. 1 (2006): 43–56.

———. "The Written Memoir: Italy 1945–1947." In *The Jews Are Coming Back: The Return of the Jews to Their Countries of Origin after WWII*, edited by David Bankier, 169–187. New York: Berghahn Books, 2005.

Cooperman, Bernard Dov, and Barbara Garvin. *The Jews of Italy: Memory and Identity.* Potomac: University Press of Maryland, 2000.

Cornelissen, Christoph. "Der 20. Juli 1944 in der deutschen Erinnerungskultur." In *Verräter? Vorbilder? Verbrecher?: Kontroverse Deutungen des 20: Juli 1944 seit 1945*, edited by Magnus Brechtken, Christoph Cornelissen, Christopher Dowe, Cornelia Hecht, Habbo Knoch, Bernhard Kroener, Alaric Searle, and Haus der Geschichte Baden-Württemberg, 15–42. Berlin: Frank et Timme, Verlag für wissenschaftliche Literatur, 2016.

Csikszentmihalyi, Mihaly, and Eugene Rochberg-Halton. *The Meaning of Things: Domestic Symbols and the Self.* Cambridge: Cambridge University Press, 1981.

Culbertson, Roberta. "Embodied Memory, Transcendence, and Telling: Recounting Trauma, Re-establishing the Self." *New Literary History* 26 (1995): 169–195.

D'Amico, Giovanna. *Quando l'eccezione diventa norma: La reintegrazione degli ebrei nell'Italia postfascista.* Turin: Bollati Boringhieri, 2006.

Danyel, Jürgen. "Die geteilte Vergangenheit. Gesellschaftliche Ausgangslagen und politische Dispositionen für den Umgang mit Nationalsozialismus und Widerstand in beiden deutschen Staaten nach 1949." In *Historische DDR-Forschung: Aufsätze und Studien*, edited by Jürgen Kocka, 11–14. Berlin: Akademie, 1993.

Davidson, Joyce, and Liz Bondi. "Spatialising Affect; Affecting Space: An Introduction." *Gender, Place & Culture: A Journal of Feminist Geography* 11, no. 3 (2004): 373–374.

Dean, Carolyn J. *Aversion and Erasure: The Fate of the Victim after the Holocaust.* Ithaca, NY: Cornell University Press, 2010.

Dean, Martin, Constantin Goschler, and Philipp Ther. *Robbery and Restitution: The Conflict over Jewish Property in Europe.* New York: Berghahn Books, 2007.

De Felice, Renzo. *Storia degli ebrei italiani sotto il fascismo.* Turin: Einaudi, 1972.

De Felice, Renzo, Michael A. Ledeen, and Jens Petersen. *Renzo De Felice: Der Faschismus: Ein Interview.* Stuttgart: Klett-Cotta, 1977.

Del Boca, Angelo. *I gas di Mussolini: Il fascismo e la guerra d'Etiopia.* Rome: Riuniti, 2007.

———. *Italiani, brava gente?: Un mito duro a morire.* Vicenza, Italy: N. Pozza, 2005.

Della Pergola, Sergio. "Jewish Out-Marriage: A Global Perspective." In *Jewish Intermarriage around the World*, edited by Shulamit Reinharz and Sergio Della Pergola. New Brunswick, NJ: Transaction, 2009.

———. *Jews in the European Community: Population Trends and Estimates.* Institute for Jewish Policy Research, European Jewish Demography Unit, 2020.

———. "A Note on Marriage Trends among Jews in Italy." *Jewish Journal of Sociology* 14 (1972): 197–205.

Della Pergola, Sergio, and L. D. Staetsky. *From Old and New Directions: Perceptions and Experiences of Antisemitism among Jews in Italy.* Institute for Jewish Policy Research, February 2015.

Della Pergola, Sergio, and Amedeo Tagliacozzo. *Gli Italiani in Israele.* Rome: Rassegna Mensile di Israel–Federazione Sionistica Italiana, 1978.

D'Erizans, Alex. "Securing the Garden and Longings for Heimat in Post-War Hanover, 1945–1948." *Historical Journal* 58, no. 1 (2015): 183–215.

258 | Bibliography

Di Figlia, Matteo. *Israele e la sinistra: Gli ebrei nel dibattito pubblico italiano dal 1945 a oggi.* Rome: Donzelli, 2012.

Dillmann, Hans Ulrich. *Jüdisches Leben nach 1945.* Hamburg: Europäische Verlagsanstalt, 2001.

Di Michele, Andrea. *Faschismen im Gedaechtnis = La memoria dei fascismi.* Innsbruck, Austria: Studien, 2005.

Diner, Dan. "Im Zeichen des Banns." In *Geschichte der Juden in Deutschland von 1945 bis zur Gegenwart: Politik, Kultur und Gesellschaft,* edited by Michael Brenner. Munich: Beck, 2012.

———. "On the Ideology of Antifascism." *New German Critique* 67 (1996): 123–132.

Diner, Dan, and Gotthart Wunberg. *Restitution and Memory: Material Restoration in Europe.* New York: Berghahn Books, 2007.

Diner, Hasia. *We Remember with Reverence and Love: American Jews and the Myth of Silence after the Holocaust, 1945–1962.* New York: New York University Press, 2009.

Dirks, Christian. *Die Verbrechen der anderen: Auschwitz und der Auschwitz-Prozess der DDR: Das Verfahren gegen den KZ-Arzt Dr. Horst Fischer.* Paderborn, Germany: Schöningh, 2006.

Di Sante, Costantino. *I campi di concentramento in Italia: Dall'internamento alla deportazione, 1940–1945.* Milan, 2001.

Di Vita, Dorina. "Gli Ebrei di Milano sotto l'occupazione nazista." *Quaderni del Centro studi sulla deportazione e l'internamento* 6 (1969–1971): 16–72.

Domenico, Roy Palmer. *Italian Fascists on Trial, 1943–1948.* Chapel Hill: University of North Carolina Press, 1991.

Doron, Daniella. *Jewish Youth and Identity in Postwar France: Rebuilding Family and Nation.* Bloomington: Indiana University Press, 2015.

Douglas, Lawrence. *The Memory of Judgement: Making Law and History in the Trials of the Holocaust.* New Haven, CT: Yale University Press, 2001.

Dreyfus, Jean-Marc. "The Transfer of Ashes after the Holocaust in Europe, 1945–60." *Human Remains and Violence* 1, no. 2 (2015): 21–35.

Dubiel, Helmut, and Gabriel Motzkin. *Lesser Evil: Moral Approaches to Genocide Practices.* Portland, OR: Frank Cass, 2004.

Dunnage, Jonathan. "Making Better Italians: Issues of National Identity in the Italian Social Republic and the Resistance." In *The Politics of Italian National Identity: A Multidisciplinary Perspective,* edited by G. Bedani and B. A. Haddock. Cardiff: University of Wales Press, 2000.

Easthope, Hazel. "Fixed Identities in a Mobile World? The Relationship between Mobility, Place, and Identity." *Identities* 16, no. 1 (2009): 61–82.

Eckhardt, Ulrich. *Jüdische Berliner: Leben nach der Schoa; 14 Gespräche.* Berlin: Jaron, 2003.

Eigler, Friederike Ursula. *Heimat Space Narrative : Toward a Transnational Approach to Flight and Expulsion.* Woodbridge: Camden House, 2014.

Einhorn, Barbara. "Gender, Nation, Landscape and Identity in Narratives of Exile and Return." *Women's Studies International Forum* 23, no. 6 (2000): 701–713.

———. "'Heimkehren' nach Ostdeutschland: Jüdische Rückkehrerinnen." In *Zur Geschichte des Frauenstudiums und Wissenschaftlerinnenkarrieren an deutschen Universität,* edited by Gabriele Jähnert. Berlin: Geschäftsstelle des ZiF, 2001.

———. "Nation und Identität: Erzählungen von Exil und Rückkehr." In *Zwischen Politik und Kultur: Juden in der DDR*, edited by Moshe Zuckermann. Göttingen, Germany: Wallstein, 2002.

Enardu, Maria Grazia. "L'aliyah bet nella politica estera italiana, 1945–1948." *Italia Judaica* 4 (1993): 514–532.

———. "L'immigrazione illegale ebraica verso la Palestina e la politica estera italiana, 1945–1948." *Storia delle Relazioni Internazionali* 2 (1986): 147–166.

Engel, David. "What Is the Holocaust?" In *A Companion to Europe, 1900–1945*, edited by Gordon Martel, 472–486. Malden, MA: 2006.

Epstein, Catherine. *The Last Revolutionaries: German Communists and Their Century*. Cambridge, MA: Harvard University Press, 2003.

European Union Agency for Fundamental Rights, *Experiences and Perceptions of Antisemitism: Second Survey on Discrimination and Hate Crime against Jews in the EU*, Luxembourg: Publications Office of the European Union, 2018.

Fabre, Giorgio. *L'elenco: Censura fascista, editoria e autori ebrei*. Turin: Zamorani, 1998.

———. "Mussolini and the Jews on the Eve of the March on Rome." In *Jews in Italy under Nazi and Fascist Rule, 1922–1945*, edited by J. D. Zimmerman. Cambridge: Cambridge University Press, 2005.

Fantini, Sara. *Notizie dalla Shoah: La stampa italiana nel 1945*. Bologna: Pendragon, 2005.

Fargion, Maria Luisa. *Beside Still Waters*. Ashfield, MA: Paideia, 1992.

Feinstein, Margarete Myers. *Holocaust Survivors in Postwar Germany, 1945–1957*. New York: Cambridge University Press, 2009.

Felman, Shoshana, and Dori Laub. *Testimony: Crises of Witnessing in Literature, Psychoanalysis, and History*. New York: Routledge, 1991.

Fenster, Tovi. *The Global City and the Holy City: Narratives on Knowledge, Planning and Diversity*. London: Routledge, 2004.

Ferrarotti, Franco. *La tentazione dell'oblio: Razzismo, antisemitismo e neonazismo*. Rome: Bari Laterza, 1993.

Filippa, Marcella. 1990. *Avrei capovolto le montagne: Giorgina Levi in Bolivia, 1939–1946*. Florence: Giunti.

Finzi, Roberto. *L'università italiana e le leggi antiebraiche*. Rome: Riuniti, 2003.

Fischer, Lars. "Gershom Scholem and Postwar Germany Reconsidered." In *Scholar and Kabbalist: The Life and Work of Gershom Scholem*, edited by Mirjam Zadoff and Noam Zadoff. Leiden, Netherlands: Brill, 2018.

Fischer, Stefanie. "Juden und Nichtjuden nach der Shoah: Begegnungen in Deutschland: Einleitung." In *Juden und Nichtjuden nach der Shoah: Begegnungen in Deutschland*, edited by Stefanie Fischer, Nathanael Riemer, and Stefanie Schüler-Springorum. Berlin: De Gruyter Oldenbourg, 2019.

Fischer, Stefanie, Nathanael Riemer, and Stefanie Schüler-Springorum, ed. *Juden und Nichtjuden nach der Shoah: Begegnungen in Deutschland*. Berlin: De Gruyter Oldenbourg, 2019.

Focardi, Filippo. "The Dispute over the Past: Political Transition and Memory Wars in Italy, from the Crisis of the First Republic until the Present Day." *Magazine of the European Observatory on Memories*, November 2020.

———. "Gedenktage und politische Öffentlichkeit in Italien: 1945–1995." In *Erinnerungskulturen: Deutschland, Italien und Japan seit 1945*, edited by Cristoph Cornelissen, Lutz Klinkhammer, and Wolfgang Schwentker. Frankfurt: 2003.

260 | *Bibliography*

———. "Italy's Amnesia over War Guilt: The 'Evil Germans' Alibi." *Mediterranean Quarterly* 25, no. 4 (2014): 5–26.

———. *La guerra della memoria: La Resistenza nel dibattito politico italiano dal 1945 a oggi.* Bari, Italy: Laterza, 2020.

———. "La memoria del fascismo e il 'demone dell'analogia.'" In *Faschismen im Gedächtnis*, edited by Andrea Di Michele and Gerald Steinacher. Innsbruck, Austria: Bozen, 2004.

———. "La percezione della Shoah in Italia nell'immediato dopoguerra: 1945–1947." In *Storia della Shoah in Italia: Vicende, memorie, rappresentazioni*, edited by Marcello Flores, Simon Levis Sullam, Marie-Anne Matard-Bonucci, and Enzo Traverso. Turin: UTET, 2010.

———. *L'immagine del cattivo tedesco e il mito del bravo italiano: La costruzione della memoria del fascismo e della seconda guerra mondiale in Italia.* Padua, Italy: Rinoceronte, 2005.

Focardi, Filippo, and Lutz Klinkhammer, "The Question of Fascist Italy's War Crimes: The Construction of a Self-Acquitting Myth (1943–1948)." *Journal of Modern Italian Studies* 9, no. 3 (2004): 330–348.

Fogu, Claudio. "Italiani Brava Gente: The Legacy of Fascist Historical Culture on Italian Politics of Memory." In *The Politics of Memory in Postwar Europe*, edited by Richard Ned Lebow, Wulf Kansteiner, and Claudio Fogu. Durham, NC: Duke University Press, 2006.

Foitzik, Jan. "Politische Probleme der Remigration." In *Exil und Remigration*, edited by Claus Dieter Krohn. Munich: Text + Kritik, 1991.

Foot, John. *Italy's Divided Memory.* New York: Palgrave Macmillan, 2009.

Forlenza, Rosario. "Sacrificial Memory and Political Legitimacy in Postwar Italy: Reliving and Remembering World War II." *History & Memory* 24, no. 2 (Fall/Winter 2012): 73–116.

Forti, Carla. *Il caso Pardo Roques: Un eccidio del 1944 tra memoria e oblio.* Turin: Einaudi, 1998.

Fox, Thomas C. "A 'Jewish Question' in GDR Literature?" *German Life and Letters* 44, no. 1 (1990): 58–70.

Frankel, Jonathan, and Dan Diner. *Dark Times, Dire Decisions: Jews and Communism.* Published for the Avraham Harman Institute of Contemporary Jewry by Oxford University Press, 2004.

Franzinelli, Mimmo. *L'amnistia Togliatti: 22 giugno 1946: Colpo di spugna sui crimini fascisti.* Milan: Mondadori, 2006.

Fraser, D., and Caestecker, F. "Jews or Germans? Nationality Legislation and the Restoration of Liberal Democracy in Western Europe after the Holocaust." *Law and History Review* 31, no. 2 (2013): 391–422.

Frei, Norbert. *Adenauer's Germany and the Nazi Past: The Politics of Amnesty and Integration.* Translated by Joel Golb. New York: Columbia University Press, 2010.

———. "Amnestiepolitik in den Bonner Anfangsjahren. Die Westdeutschen und die NS-Vergangenheit." *Kritische Justiz* 29.4 (1996): 484–494.

———. *Vergangenheitspolitik: Die Anfaenge der Bundesrepublik und die NS-Vergangenheit.* Munich: Beck, 1996.

Frei, Norbert, Christina Morina, Frank Maubach, and Maik Tändler. *Zur rechten Zeit: Wider die Rückkehr des Nationalismus.* Berlin: 2019.

Frevert, Ute. *Emotions in History: Lost and Found.* Budapest: Central European University Press, 2011.

———. "Was haben Gefühle in der Geschichte zu suchen?" *Geschichte und Gesellschaft* 35 (2009): 183–208.

Fried, Marc. "Grieving for a Lost Home: Psychological Costs of Relocation." In *Urban Renewal: The Record and the Controversy*, edited by James Wilson, 359–379. Cambridge, MA: MIT Press, 1966.

Friedlander, Henry. "The Deportation of the German Jews Post-War German Trials of Nazi Criminals." In *The End of the Holocaust*, 635–664. Berlin, New York: K. G. Saur, 1989.

Friedländer, Saul. *Memory, History, and the Extermination of the Jews of Europe.* Bloomington: Indiana University Press, 1993.

———. *Probing the Limits of Representation: Nazism and the "Final Solution."* Cambridge, MA: Harvard University Press, 1992.

———. *The Years of Extermination: Nazi Germany and the Jews, 1939–1945.* New York: Harper Collins, 2007.

———. *The Years of Persecution: Nazi Germany and the Jews, 1933–1939.* New York: Harper Perennial, 1998.

Friedman, Max Paul. "The Cold War Politics of Exile, Return, and the Search for a Usable Past in Friedrich Karl Kaul's Es Wird Zeit, Dass Du Nach Hause Kommst." *German Life and Letters* 58 (2005): 306–325.

Fritz, Regina Éva Kovács, and Béla Rásky, eds. *Before the Holocaust Had Its Name: Early Confrontations with the Nazi Mass Murder of the Jews.* Vienna: New Academic, 2016.

Fritzsche, Peter. "Fascism, Desire and Social Mechanics." In *"Faschismus" Kontrovers*, edited by Werner Loh, Wolfgang Wippermann, and Lothar Fritze, 76–81. Stuttgart: Lucius und Lucius, 2002.

Fröschle, Ulrich. "Das andere Deutschland: Zur Topik der Ermächtigung." In *Literarische und politische Deutschlandkonzepte 1938–1949*, edited by Gunther Nickel, 47–85. Göttingen, Germany: Wallstein, 2004.

Fubini, Guido. "Die Rechtsstellung der jüdischen Gemeinde Italiens: Rückblick auf ein halbes Jahrhundert (1945–1995)." In *Judentum und Moderne in Frankreich und Italien*, edited by Christoph Miething, 70–86. Tübingen, Germany: M. Niemeyer, 1998.

Fulbrook, Mary. "History-Writing and Collective Memory." In *Writing the History of Memory*, edited by Stefan Berger and William John Niven, 65–88. London: Bloomsbury Academic, 2014.

———. *Reckonings: Legacies of Nazi Persecution and the Quest for Justice.* Oxford: Oxford University Press, 2018.

Fulbrook, Mary, and Andrew I Port, ed. *Becoming East Germans: Socialist Structures and Sensibilities after Hitler.* New York: Berghahn Books, 2013.

Gagliani, Dianella, ed. *Donne, guerra, politica esperienze e memorie della Resistenza.* Bologna: CLUEB, 2000.

———. *Il difficile rientro: Il ritorno dei docenti ebrei nell'università del dopoguerra.* Bologna: CLUEB, 2004.

Galimi, Valeria. "I campi di concentramento in Toscana fra storia e memoria." In *I campi di concentramento in Italia*, edited by Costantino Di Sante, 207–227. Milan: Angeli, 2001.

———. "The Image of 'All Good Italians': The Eichmann Trial Seen from Italy." *Journal of Modern Italian Studies* 24, no. 1 (2019): 115–128.

Gay, Ruth. *Das Undenkbare tun: Juden in Deutschland nach 1945.* Munich: Beck, 2001.

262 | Bibliography

———. *Safe among the Germans: Liberated Jews after World War II*. New Haven, CT: Yale University Press, 2002.

Geis, Jael. *Übrig sein, Leben "danach": Juden deutscher Herkunft in der britischen und amerikanischen Zone Deutschlands 1945–1949*. Berlin: Philo, 1999.

Geller, Jay Howard. *Jews in Post-Holocaust Germany, 1945–1953*. Cambridge: Cambridge University Press, 2005.

Geller, Jay Howard, and Michael Meng. *Rebuilding Jewish Life in Germany*. Ithaca, NY: Rutgers University Press, 2020.

Gensch, Brigitte, and Sonja Grabowsky. *Der halbe Stern: Verfolgungsgeschichte und Identitätsproblematik von Personen und Familien teiljüdischer Herkunft*. Giessen, Germany: Haland & Wirth im Psychosozial, 2010.

Gentile, Emilio. *The Sacralization of Politics in Fascist Italy*. Cambridge, MA: Harvard University Press, 1996.

Gerber, Jan. *Ein Prozess in Prag: Das Volk gegen Rudolf Slánský und Genossen*. Göttingen, Germany: Vandenhoeck & Ruprecht, 2017.

Gerlof, Manuela. *Tonspuren: Erinnerungen an den Holocaust im Hörspiel der DDR (1945–1989)*. Berlin: De Gruyter, 2010.

Gilette, Aaron. "Guido Landra and the Office of Racial Studies in Fascist Italy." *Holocaust and Genocide Studies* 16 (2002): 357–375.

———. "The Origins of the 'Manifesto of Racial Scientists.'" *Journal of Modern Italian Studies* 6 (2001): 305–323.

———. *Racial Theories in Fascist Italy*. London: Routledge, 2002.

Gilman, Sander. *Jurek Becker: Die Biographie*. Munich: List, 2004.

Ginsborg, Paul. *A History of Contemporary Italy: Society and Politics, 1943–1988*. London: Penguin Books, 1990.

Goeschel, Christian. "A Parallel History? Rethinking the Relationship between Italy and Germany, ca. 1860–1945." *Journal of Modern History* 88 (2016): 610–632.

Goldberg, Amos, and Haim Hazan. *Marking Evil: Holocaust Memory in the Global Age*. New York: Berghahn Books, 2019.

Goldbloom, Maurice J. "Italy." *The American Jewish Year Book* 48 (1946): 298–99.

Goldenbogen, Nora. "Leon Löwenkopf, erster Vorsitzender der Jüdische Gemeinde zu Dresden nach der Shoah, Versuch einer Annäherung." In *Zwischen Erinnerung und Neubeginn: Zur deutsch-jüdischen Geschichte nach 1945*, edited by Susanne Schönborn. 91–102. Munich: Meidenbauer, 2006.

Goldstaub, Adriana. "Appunti per uno studio sui pregiudizi antiebraici nei primi anni del dopoguerra (1945-1955)." In *Il ritorno alla vita: Vicende e diritti degli ebrei in Italia dopo la seconda guerra mondiale*, edited by Michele Sarfatti, 139–149. Florence: Giuntina, 1998.

———. "L'antisemitismo in Italia." In *Storia dell'antisemitismo 1945–1993*, edited by Leon Poliakov, 425–471. Florence: La Nuova Italia, 1996.

Goodhart, Sandor. "The Witness of Trauma: A Review Essay." *Modern Judaism* 12, no. 2 (1992): 203–217.

Gordon, Adi. "Against Vox Populi—Arnold Zweig's Struggle with Political Passions." *Tel Aviver Jahrbuch für deutsche Geschichte* 38 (2010): 133–147.

———. "Widersprüchliche Zugehörigkeiten: Arnold Zweig in Ostdeutschland." In *"Ich staune, dass Sie in dieser Luft atmen können": Jüdische Intellektuelle in Deutschland nach 1945*, edited by Raphael Gross and Monika Boll, 171–294. Frankfurt: Fischer, 2003.

Gordon, Robert Samuel Clive. "From Olocausto to Shoah: Naming Genocide in 21st-Century Italy." *Modern Languages Open.* http://doi.org/10.3828/mlo.v0i0.75.

———. "Gray Zones: The Heterodox Left and the Holocaust in Postwar Italian Culture." *Jahrbuch des Simon-Dubnow-Instituts / Simon Dubnow Institute Yearbook*, 2015.

———. "The Holocaust in Italian Collective Memory: Il giorno della memoria, 27 January 2001." *Modern Italy* 11, no 2 (2006): 167–188.

———. *The Holocaust in Italian Culture, 1944–2010.* Stanford, CA: Stanford University Press, 2012.

———. "Holocaust Writing in Context: Italy 1945–47." In *The Holocaust and the Text, Speaking the Unspeakable*, edited by Andrew Leak and George Paizis, 32–50. New York: St. Martin's, 2000.

———. "Primo Levi: Primo Levi's 'If This Is a Man' and Responses to the Lager in Italy 1945–47." *Judaism* 48, no. 1 (1999): 49–83.

———. "Which Holocaust? Primo Levi and the Field of Holocaust Memory in Post-War Italy." *Italian Studies* 61, no. 1 (2006): 85–113.

Goschler, Constantin. *Schuld und Schulden: Die Politik der Wiedergutmachung für NS-Verfolgte seit 1945.* Göttingen, Germany: Wallstein, 2005.

———. "Tur Tur's Lantern on a Tiny Island: New Historiographical Perspectives on East German Jewish History." In *Rebuilding Jewish Life in Germany*, edited by Jay Howard Geller and Michael Meng, 181–190. Ithaca, NY: Rutgers University Press, 2020.

Goschler, Constantin, and Jürgen Lillteicher. *"Arisierung" und Restitution: Die Rückerstattung jüdischen Eigentums in Deutschland und Österreich nach 1945 und 1989.* Göttingen, Germany: Wallstein, 2002.

Gottfried Wagner, Abraham Peck. *Unsere Stunde Null: Deutsch und Juden nach 1945: Familiegschichte, Holocaust und Neubeginn.* Vienna: Böhlau, 2006.

Gotzmann, Andreas. "Historiography as Cultural Identity: Toward a Jewish History beyond National History." In *Modern Judaism and Historical Consciousness: Identities, Encounters, Perspectives*, edited by Andreas Gotzmann and Christian Wiese, 494–528. Leiden, Netherlands: Brill, 2007.

Graf, Philipp. "Taking Up the Cause of the Jewish Collective: Jewish Communists in Berlin's Soviet Sector during the 'Interregnum.'" In *Our Courage: Jews in Europe 1945–48*, edited by Kata Bohus, Atina Grossmann, Werner Hanak, and Mirjam Wenzel, 158–175. Berlin: De Gruyter Oldenbourg, 2020.

———. "Twice Exiled Leo Zuckermann (1908–85) and the Limits of the Communist Promise." *Journal of Contemporary History* 56, no. 3 (2021): 766–788.

Grafton, Anthony. "Arnaldo Momigliano: The Historian of History." In Arnaldo Momigliano, *Essays in Ancient and Modern Historiography*, ix–xvi. Chicago: University of Chicago Press, 2012.

Granata, Cora. "The Cold War Politics of Cultural Minorities: Jews and Sorbs in the German Democratic Republic, 1976–1989." *German History* 27 (2009): 60–83.

———. "'Das hat in der DDR keine Rolle gespielt, was man war': 'Ostalgie' und Erinnerungen an Antisemitismus in der DDR, 1949–1960." In *Zwischen Politik und Kultur: Juden in der DDR*, edited by Moshe Zuckermann, 82–100. Göttingen, Germany: Wallstein, 2002.

Grande, Petra, and Literaturzentrum. *Sind allet Berlina: Geschichten und Gedichte.* Berlin: Literaturzentrum, 1986.

264 | Bibliography

Greenspan, Henry. *On Listening to Holocaust Survivors: Recounting and Life History*. Westport, CT: Praeger, 1998.

Grenville, Anthony. *Jewish Refugees from Germany and Austria in Britain, 1933–1970: Their Image in AJR Information*. Edgware, UK: Vallentine Mitchell, 2010.

Griffin, Roger. *The Nature of Fascism*. London: Pinter, 1991.

Grinberg, León, and Rebeca Grinberg. *Psychoanalytic Perspectives on Migration and Exile*. New Haven, CT: Yale University Press, 1989.

Grobman, Alex, and L. Magnes Museum Judah. *Rekindling the Flame: American Jewish Chaplains and the Survivors of European Jewry, 1944–1948*. Detroit: Wayne State University Press, 1993.

Gromova, Alina, Felix Heinert, and Sebastian Voigt, eds. *Jewish and Non-Jewish Spaces in the Urban Context Berlin*. Berlin: Neofelis, 2015.

Grossmann, Atina. "German Jews as Provincial Cosmopolitans: Reflections from the Upper West Side." *Leo Baeck Institute Year Book* 53, no. 1 (2008): 157–168.

———. *Jews, Germans, and Allies: Close Encounters in Occupied Germany*. Princeton, NJ: Princeton University Press, 2007.

Grossmann, Atina, and Tamar Lewinsky. "Erster Teil: 1945–1949, Zwischenstation." In *Geschichte der Juden in Deutschland von 1945 bis zur Gegenwart: Politik Kultur und Gesellschaft*, edited by Michael Brenner et al. München: C.H. Beck, 2012.

Grunenberg, Antonia. *Antifaschismus Ein Deutscher Mythos*. Reinbek bei Hamburg: Rowohlt, 1993.

Guarnieri, Patrizia. *Intellettuali in fuga dall'Italia fascista: Migranti esuli e rifugiati per motivi politici e razziali*. Florence: Firenze University Press, 2019. English version 2020, *Intellectuals Displaced from Fascist Italy: Migrants, Exiles and Refugees Fleeing for Political and Racial Reasons*, https://intellettualinfuga.fupress.com/en/contenuti/238.

———. *Italian Psychology and Jewish Emigration under Fascism: From Florence to Jerusalem and New York*. New York: Palgrave Macmillan, 2016.

Guida, Elisa. *La strada di casa*. Rome: Viella, 2017.

Haan, Ido de. "Paths of Normalization after the Persecution of the Jews: The Netherlands, France and West Germany in the 1950s." In *Life after Death: Approaches to a Cultural and Social History of Europe during the 1940s and 1950s*, edited by D. S. Richard Bessel, 65–92. New York: Cambridge University Press, 2002.

Halbwachs, Maurice. *On Collective Memory*. Chicago: University of Chicago Press, 1992.

Hametz, Maura Elise. "The Ambivalence of Italian Antisemitism: Fascism, Nationalism, and Racism in Trieste." *Holocaust and Genocide Studies* 16, no. 3 (2002): 376–401.

———. "The Interstices of Life and Memory: Alma Morpurgo and the Central European Jewish Tradition." In *Jewish Intellectual Women in Europe, 1860–2000: Twelve Biographical Essays*, edited by Judith Szapor, Andrea Peto, Maura Hametz, and Maria Calloni, 349–375. Lewiston, NY: Edwin Mellen, 2012.

———. *Making Trieste Italian, 1918–1954*. Woodbridge, UK: Boydell, 2005.

Hand, Seán, and Steven T. Katz, eds. *Post-Holocaust France and the Jews, 1945–1955*. New York: New York University Press, 2016.

Hartewig, Karin. "A German Jewish Communist of the Second Generation: The Changing Personae of Klaus Gysi." In *Dark Times, Dire Decisions: Jews and Communism*, edited by Jonathan Frankel and Dan Diner, 255–275. New York: Oxford University Press, 2004.

———. *Zurückgekehrt: Die Geschichte der jüdischen Kommunisten in der DDR*. Cologne: Böhlau, 2000.

Hartman, Geoffrey, ed. *Holocaust Remembrance: The Shapes of Memory.* Oxford: Blackwell, 1994.

Hartman, Harriet, and Debra Kaufman. "Decentering the Study of Jewish Identity: Opening the Dialogue with Other Religious Groups." *Sociology of Religion* 67, no. 4 (2006): 365–385.

Haury Thomas. *Antisemitismus Von Links : Facetten der Judenfeindschaft.* Berlin: Aktion Courage e.V, 2019.

Hayse, Michael R. *Recasting West German Elites: Higher Civil Servants, Business Leaders, and Physicians in Hesse between Nazism and Democracy, 1945-1955.* New York: Berghahn Books, 2003.

Hearn, Jonathan. "National Identity: Banal, Personal and Embedded." *Nations and Nationalism: Journal of the Association for the Study of Ethnicity and Nationalism* 13, no. 4 (2007): 657–674.

Heenen-Wolff, Susann. *Im Land der Täter: Gespräche mit überlebenden Juden.* Frankfurt: Fischer Taschenbuch, 1994.

Heinsohn, Kirsten. "'Aber es kommt auch darauf an, wie einen die anderen sehen': Jüdische Identifikation und Remigration." In *Auch in Deutschland waren wir nicht wirklich zu Hause: jüdische Remigration nach 1945,* edited by Irmela von der Lühe, Axel Schildt, and Stefanie Schüler-Springorum,69–85. Göttingen, Germany: Wallstein, 2008.

Held, Steffen. *Jews in Leipzig, Germany under Nazism, Communism, and Democracy: Politics and Identity in the 20th Century.* Lewiston, NY: Edwin Mellen, 2011.

———. *Zwischen Tradition und Vermächtnis: Die Israelitische Religionsgemeinde zu Leipzig nach 1945.* Hamburg: Dilling und Galitz, 1995.

Herbst, Andreas. "Großmutter im Sterben: Die Flucht der Repräsentanten der Jüdischen Gemeinden 1953 aus der DDR." In *Helden, Täter und Verräter: Studien zum DDR-Antifaschismus,* edited by Annette Leo and Peter Reif-Spirek, 13–36. Berlin: Metropol, 1999.

Herf, Jeffrey. *Divided Memory: The Nazi Past in the Two Germanys.* Cambridge, MA: Harvard University Press, 1997.

———. "East German Communists and the Jewish Question: The Case of Paul Merker." Occasional Paper No. 11, Fourth Alois Mertes Memorial Lecture, German Historical Institute, Washington, DC, 1994.

Herman, Judith Lewis. *Trauma and Recovery.* [New York]: Basic Books, 1992.

Herzberg, Wolfgang. *Ueberleben heisst Erinnern: Lebensgeschichten deutscher Juden.* Berlin: Aufbau, 1990.

Herzfeld, Michael. *Cultural Intimacy: Social Poetics and the Real Life of States, Societies, and Institutions.* New York: Routledge, 2016.

Hirsch, Marianne. *The Generation of Postmemory: Writing and Visual Culture after the Holocaust.* New York: Columbia University Press, 2012.

Hirsch, Marianne, and Leo Spitzer. "Testimonial Objects: Memory, Gender, and Transmission." *Poetics Today* 27, no. 2 (2006): 353–383.

Hobsbawm, Eric, and Terence Ranger. *The Invention of Tradition.* Cambridge: Cambridge University Press, 2012.

Hockenos, Matthew D. *A Church Divided: German Protestants Confront the Nazi Past.* Bloomington: Indiana University Press, 2004.

Hockerts, Hans Günther, Claudia Moisel, and Tobias Winstel. *Grenzen der Wiedergutmachung: Die Entschädigung für NS-Verfolgte in West- und Osteuropa 1945-2000.* Göttingen, Germany: Wallstein, 2006.

266 | Bibliography

Hoffman, Eva. "The New Nomads." *Yale Review* 86, no. 4 (1998): 43–58.

Hoskins, Janet. *Biographical Objects: How Things Tell the Stories of People's Lives.* New York: Routledge, 1998.

Hoy, William G. *Do Funerals Matter? The Purpose and Practice of Death Rituals.* Hoboken, NJ: Taylor and Francis, 2013.

Hughes, Stuart. *Prisoners of Hope: The Silver Age of the Italian Jews, 1924–1974.* Cambridge, MA: Harvard University Press, 1983.

Illichmann, Jutta. *Die DDR und die Juden: Die deutschlandpolitische Instrumentalisierung von Juden und Judentum durch die Partei- und Staatsführung der SBZ/DDR von 1945 bis 1990.* Frankfurt: P. Lang, 1997.

Institute for Jewish Policy Research, "Young Jewish Europeans: Perceptions and Experiences of Antisemitism," London, Institute for Jewish Policy Research, 2019.

Israel, Giorgio. *Il fascismo e la razza: La scienza italiana e le politiche razziali del regime.* Bologna: Il Mulino, 2010.

Israel, Giorgio, and Pietro Nastasi. *Scienza e razza nell'Italia fascista.* Bologna: Il Mulino, 1998.

Jacobson, Kenneth. *Embattled Selves: An Investigation into the Nature of Identity through Oral Histories of Holocaust Survivors.* New York: Atlantic Monthly, 1994.

Jäger, Gudrun. "Frühe Holocaustzeugnisse italienischer Jüdinnen (1946–47)." In *Judentum und Antisemitismus im modernen Italien*, edited by Gudrun Jäger and Liana Novelli-Glaab, 219–237. Berlin: Trafo, 2007.

Jäger, Gudrun, and Liana Novelli-Glaab. *Judentum und Antisemitismus in modernen Italien.* Berlin: Trafo, 2007.

Jarausch, Konrad Hugo, and Michael Geyer. *Shattered Past: Reconstructing German Histories.* Princeton, NJ: Princeton University Press, 2003.

Jockusch, Laura. *Collect and Record!: Jewish Holocaust Documentation in Early Postwar Europe.* New York: Oxford University Press, 2012.

———. "Das Urteil der Zeugen: Die Nürnberger Prozesse aus der Sicht jüdischer Holocaustüberlebender im besetzten Deutschland." In *NMT: Die Nürnberger Militärtribunale Zwischen Geschichte, Gerechtigkeit und Rechtschöpfung*, edited by Kim Christian Priemel and Alexa Stiller, 653–684. Hamburg: Hamburger, 2013.

———. "In Search of Retribution: Nazi Collaborators Trials in Jewish Courts in Postwar Germany." In *Revenge, Retribution, Reconciliation: Justice and Emotions between Conflict and Mediation*, edited by Laura Jockusch, Andreas Kraft, and Kim Wünschmann, 127–145. Jerusalem: Hebrew University Magnes Press, 2017.

———. "Justice at Nuremberg? Jewish Responses to Nazi War-Crime Trials in Allied-Occupied Germany." *Jewish Social Studies* 19, no. 1 (Fall 2012): 107–147.

Joisten, Karen. "Heimat und Heimatlosigkeit: Philosophische Perspektiven." In *Religion und Migration heute: Perspektiven—Positionen—Projekte*, edited by Jürgen Manemann and Werner Schreer, 215–26. Regensburg, Germany: 2012.

Judt, Tony. "The Past Is Another Country: Myth and Memory in Postwar Europe." *Theoria: A Journal of Social and Political Theory* 87 (1996): 36–69.

———. *Postwar: A History of Europe since 1945.* New York: Penguin, 2005.

Jung, Thomas. "Nicht-Darstellung und Selbst-Darstellung: Der Umgang mit der 'Judenfrage' in der SBZ und der frühen DDR und dessen Niederschlag in Literatur und Film." *Monatshefte* 90, no. 1 (1998): 49–70.

Junge, Anna. "'Go Back to Your Hometown.': Jüdisch-nichtjüdische Konfrontationen im ländlichen Hessen 1945/1946." In *Juden und Nichtjuden nach der Shoah: Begegnungen in Deutschland*, edited by Stefanie Fischer, Nathanael Riemer, and Stefanie Schüler-Springorum, 13–29. Berlin: De Gruyter Oldenbourg, 2019.

Jünger, David. "Farewell to the German-Jewish Past: Travelogs of Jewish Intellectuals Visiting Post-War Germany, 1945–1950." In *Juden und Nichtjuden nach der Shoah: Begegnungen in Deutschland*, edited by Stefanie Fischer, Nathanael Riemer, and Stefanie Schüler-Springorum, 63–75. Berlin: De Gruyter Oldenbourg, 2019.

Jürgens, Franz J. *Wir waren ja eigentlich Deutsche: Juden berichten von Emigration und Rueckkehr*. Berlin: Aufbau Taschenbuch, 1997.

Kallis, Aristotle A. *Genocide and Fascism: The Eliminationist Drive in Fascist Europe*. New York: Routledge, 2009.

Kaminer, Isidor. "Spaetfolgen bei juedischen KZ Ueberlebenden." In *Geschichte als Trauma: Festschrift für Hans Keilson zu seinem 80: Geburtstag*, edited by Dierk Juelich and Hans Keilson, 19–33. Frankfurt: Nexus, 1991.

Kaplan, Marion. *Between Dignity and Despair: Jewish Life in Nazi Germany*. New York: Oxford University Press, 1998.

———. *Hitler's Jewish Refugees: Hope and Anxiety in Portugal*. New Haven, CT: Yale University Press, 2020.

———. "Revealing and Concealing: Using Memoirs to Write German-Jewish History." In *Text and Context: Essays in Modern Jewish History and Historiography in Honor of Ismar Schorsch*, edited by Ismar Schorsch, Eli Lederhendler, and Jack Wertheimer, 383–411. [New York]: Jewish Theological Seminary of America, 2005.

———. "What Is 'Religion' among Jews in Contemporary Germany?" In *Reemerging Jewish Culture in Germany: Life and Literature Since 1989*, edited by Sander L. Gilman and Karen Remmler. New York: 1994.

Kauders, Anthony. "The Emotional Geography of a Lost Space: Germany as an Object of Jewish Attachment after 1945." In *Heimat: At the Intersection of Memory and Space*, edited by Friederike Eigler and Jens Kugele. 193–207. Berlin: De Gruyter, 2012.

———. "Heimat ausgeschlossen: Von Schuldgefühlen im falschen Land." In *"Auch in Deutschland waren wir nicht wirklich zu Hause": Jüdische Remigration nach 1945*, edited by Irmela von der Lühe, Alex Schildt, and Stefanie Schüler-Springorum, 86–100. Göttingen, Germany: Wallstein, 2015.

———. *Unmögliche Heimat: Eine deutsch-jüdische Geschichte der Bundesrepublik*. Munich: Deutsche Verlags-Anstalt, 2007.

———. "West German Jewry: Guilt, Power and Pluralism." In "Jews in Europe after the Shoah: Studies and Research Perspectives," edited by Laura Brazzo and Guri Schwarz. Special issue, *Quest. Issues in Contemporary Jewish History: Journal of Fondazione CDEC* 1 (April 2010).

Kaufman, Jonathan. *A Hole in the Heart of the World: Being Jewish in Eastern Europe*. New York: Viking, 1997.

Kessler, Mario. *Die SED und die Juden: Zwischen Repression und Toleranz: Politische Entwicklung bis 1967*. Berlin: Akademie, 1995.

———. "Verdrängung der Geschichte: Antisemitismus in der SED 1952/53." In *Zwischen Politik und Kultur: Juden in der DDR*, edited by Moshe Zuckermann, 34–47. Göttingen, Germany: Wallstein, 2002.

268 | Bibliography

Kister, Yosef. *Olam She Kulo Tohar—Ledmuto Shel Israel Esptein (Gundar Aviel)* [A World That Is Entirely Pure—The Figure of Israel Epstein (Gundar Aviel)]. Jerusalem: Begin Heritage Center Press, 2013.

Klein, Shira. *Italy's Jews from Emancipation to Fascism*. Cambridge: Cambridge University Press, 2018.

Kliner-Fruck, Martina. *Es ging ja ums Überleben: Jüdische Frauen zwischen Nazi-Deutschland, Emigration nach Palästina und ihrer Rückkehr*. Frankfurt: Campus, 1995.

Klinkhammer, Lutz. "Der Resistenza-Mythos und Italiens faschistische Vergangenheit." In *Sieger und Besiegte: Materielle und ideelle Neuorientierungen nach 1945*, edited by Holger Afflerbach and Christoph Cornelissen, 119–139. Tübingen, Germany: Francke Verlag, 1997.

———. "Le strategie tedesche di occupazione e la popolazione civile." In *Guerra, guerra di liberazione, guerra civile*, edited by Massimo Legnani and Ferruccio Vendramini. Milan: Angeli, 1990.

———."Polizeiliche Kooperation unter deutscher Besatzung, Mechanismen der Repression in der Repubblica Sociale Italiana." In *Die "Achse" im Krieg: Politik, Ideologie und Kriegführung*, edited by Lutz Klinkhammer, Amedeo Osti Guerrazzi, and Thomas Schlemmer, 472–491. Paderborn, Germany: Schöningh, 2010.

Knowles, Anne Kelly, Tim Cole, and Alberto Giordano, eds. *Geographies of the Holocaust*. Bloomington: Indiana University Press, 2014.

Koch, Anna. "'After Auschwitz You Must Take Your Origin Seriously.' Perceptions of Jewishness among Communists of Jewish Origin in the Early German Democratic Republic." In *Jewish Lives Under Communism*, edited by Kateřina Čapková, Kamil Kijek, 111–130. New Brunswick, NJ: Rutgers University Press, 2022.

———. "'But There Is Always Hope in the Human Heart': Italian Jews' Search for the Deported in the Immediate Aftermath of the Holocaust." *Holocaust and Genocide Studies* 34, no. 2 (2020): 295–314.

Koelbl, Herlinde. *Jüdische Portraits: Photographien und Interviews*. Frankfurt: Fischer, 1989.

Kohanski, Alexander S. "Italy." *The American Jewish Year Book* 47 (1945): 387–90.

Kokkonen, Susanna. "Jewish Displaced Persons in Postwar Italy, 1945–1951." *Jewish Political Studies Review* 20 (2008): 91–106.

———.*The Jewish Refugees in Postwar Italy 1945–1951: The Way to Eretz Israel*. Saarbrücken: LAP Lambert Academic Publishing, 2011.

Kolinsky, Eva. *After the Holocaust: Jewish Survivors in Germany after 1945*. London: Pimlico, 2004.

Königseder, Angelika, and Juliane Wetzel. *Waiting for Hope: Jewish Displaced Persons in Post-World War II Germany*. Evanston, IL: Northwestern University Press, 2001.

Koonz, Claudia. *The Nazi Conscience*. Cambridge, MA: Belknap, 2003.

Koshar, Rudy. *From Monuments to Traces: Artifacts of German Memory, 1870–1990*. Berkeley: University of California Press, 2000.

Kosmala, Beate. "Zwischen Ahnen und Wissen: Flucht vor der Deportation (1941–1943)." In *Die Deportation der Juden aus Deutschland: Pläne–Praxis–Reaktionen 1938–1945*, edited by Birthe Kundrus and Beate Meyer, 135–159. Göttingen, Germany: Wallstein, 2004.

Krauss, Marita. *Heimkehr in ein Fremdes Land: Geschichte der Remigration nach 1945*. Munich: Beck, 2001.

———. "Jewish Remigration: An Overview of an Emerging Discipline." *Leo Baeck Institute Year Book* 49 (2004): 107–117.

Bibliography | 269

———. "Westliche Besatzungszonen und Bundesrepublik." In *Handbuch der deutschsprachigen Emigration 1933–1945*, edited by Claus-Dieter Krohn, Patrik von der Mühlen, Gerhard Paul, and Lutz Winckler, 1161–1171. Munich: K. G. Saur, 1999.

Kristel, Conny. "Revolution and Reconstruction: Dutch Jewry after the Holocaust." In *The Jews Are Coming Back: The Return of the Jews to Their Countries of Origin after WWII*, edited by David Bankier, 36–147. New York: Berghahn Books, 2005.

Krohn, Claus-Dieter, and Patrik von zur Muehlen. *Rueckkehr und Aufbau nach 1945: Deutsche Remigranten im oeffentlichen Leben Nachkriegsdeutschlands*. Marburg, Germany: Metropolis, 1997.

Kugelmass, Jack, and Jonathan Boyarin. *From a Ruined Garden: The Memorial Books of Polish Jewry*. New York: Schocken Books, 1983.

Kühling, Gerd. *Erinnerung an nationalsozialistische Verbrechen in Berlin: Verfolgte des Dritten Reiches und geschichtspolitisches Engagement im Kalten Krieg 1945–1979*. Berlin: Metropol, 2016.

Lagrou, Pieter. "Return to a Vanished World: European Societies and the Remnants of Their Jewish Communities." In *The Jews Are Coming Back: The Return of the Jews to Their Countries of Origin after WWII*, edited by David Bankier, 1–24. New York: Berghahn Books, 2005.

Lang, Berel. *Post-Holocaust Interpretation, Misinterpretation, and the Claims of History*. Bloomington: Indiana University Press, 2005.

Lang, Johannes. "New Histories of Emotion." *History and Theory* 57, no. 1 (2018): 104–120.

Láníček, Jan. "What Did It Mean to Be Loyal? Jewish Survivors in Post-War Czechoslovakia in a Comparative Perspective." *Australian Journal of Politics and History* 60, no. 3 (2014): 384–404.

Laqueur, Renata. *Schreiben im KZ: Tagebücher 1940–1945*. Hannover, Germany: Niedersächsische Landeszentrale für politische Bildung, 1991.

Lässig, Simone, and Miriam Rürup, eds. *Space and Spatiality in Modern German Jewish History*. New York: Berghahn Books, 2017.

Laub, Dori. "Bearing Witness, or the Vicissitudes of Listening." In *Testimony: Crises of Witnessing in Literature, Psychoanalysis, and History*, edited by Shoshana Felman and Dori Laub, 57–74. New York: Routledge, 1991.

———. "An Event without a Witness: Truth, Testimony and Survival." In *Testimony: Crises of Witnessing in Literature, Psychoanalysis, and History*, edited by Dori Laub and Shoshana Felman, 75–92. New York: Routledge, 1992.

———. *Knowing and Not Knowing the Holocaust*. Hillsdale, NJ: Analytic, 1985.

———. "Truth and Testimony: The Process and the Struggle." In *Trauma: Explorations in Memory*, edited by Cathy Caruth, 61–76. Baltimore: Johns Hopkins University Press, 1995.

Lavsky, Hagit. *New Beginnings: Holocaust Survivors in Bergen-Belsen and the British Zone in Germany, 1945–1950*. Detroit: Wayne State University Press, 2002.

Lawrie, S. W. "'Es soll diese Spur doch bleiben . . .': Hans Jacobus: Exile, National Socialism and the Holocaust." In *Refugees from the Third Reich in Britain*, edited by Anthony Grenville, 73–96. Leiden, Netherlands: Brill, 2002.

Lehmann, Hans Georg. "Rückkehr nach Deutschland? Motive, Hindernisse und Wege von Remigranten." In *Rückkehr und Aufbau nach 1945: Deutsche Remigranten im öffentli-*

chen Leben Nachkriegsdeutschlands, edited by Claus-Dieter Krohn and Patrik von der Mühlen, 39–70. Marburg, Germany: Metropolis, 1997.

Lerner, Jennifer S., Ye Li, Piercarlo Valdesolo, and Karim S. Kassam. "Emotion and Decision Making." *Annual Review of Psychology* 66, no. 1 (2015): 799–823.

Lerner, Paul. "Round Table Introduction: Jewish Studies Meets Cultural Studies." *Journal of Modern Jewish Studies* 8 (2009): 41–46.

Levi, Fabio. "Anti-Jewish Persecution and Italian Society." In *Jews in Italy under Fascist and Nazi Rule, 1922–1945*, edited by Joshua D. Zimmerman, 199–206. Cambridge: Cambridge University Press, 2005.

———, ed. *L'ebreo in oggetto: L'applicazione della normativa antiebraica a Torino, 1938–1943*. Turin: Zamorani, 1991.

———. *Le case e le cose: La persecuzione degli ebrei torinesi nelle carte dell'EGELI, 1938–1945*. Turin: Compagnia di San Paolo, 1998.

Levi, Giorgina, Manfredo Montagnana, and Amos Luzzatto. *I Montagnana: Una famiglia ebraica piemontese e il movimento operaio (1914–1948)*. Florence: Giuntina, 2000.

Lichtner, Giacomo. "That Latent Sense of Otherness: Old and New Anti-Semitisms in Postwar Italy." *Modern Italy* 23, no. 4 (2018): 461–472.

Lissner, Cordula. *Den Fluchtweg zurueckgehen: Remigration nach Nordrhein und Westfalen 1945–1955*. Essen: Klartext, 2006.

Long, Lynellyn, and Ellen Oxfeld. *Coming Home?: Refugees, Migrants, and Those Who Stayed Behind*. Philadelphia: University of Pennsylvania Press, 2004.

Longhi, Silvano. *Die Juden und der Widerstand gegen den Faschismus in Italien (1943–1945)*. Berlin: Lit, 2010.

———. *Exil und Identität: Die italienischen Juden in der Schweiz (1943–1945)*. Berlin: De Gruyter, 2017.

Lühe, Irmela von der, Axel Schildt, and Stefanie Schüler-Springorum, eds. *Auch in Deutschland waren wir nicht wirklich zu Hause: Jüdische Remigration nach 1945*. Göttingen, Germany: Wallstein, 2008.

Luzzatto, Gadi. "Per uno studio sulla presenza e attività di parlamentari ebrei in Italia e in Europa." In *Saggi sull'ebraismo italiano del Novecento in onore di Luisella Mortara Ottolenghi*, edited by Liliana Picciotto, 73–92. Rome: Unione delle Comunità Ebraiche Italiane, 2003.

Luzzatto, Sergio. *The Body of Il Duce: Mussolini's Corpse and the Fortunes of Italy*. New York: Henry Holt, 2014.

Lyttleton, Adrian. "The 'Crisis of Bourgeois Society' and the Origins of Fascism." In *Fascist Italy and Nazi Germany: Comparisons and Contrasts*, edited by Richard Bessel. Cambridge: Cambridge University Press, 2000.

Mack, Arien. *Home: A Place in the World*. New York: New York University Press, 1993.

Maier, Charles S. *The Unmasterable Past: History, Holocaust, and German National Identity*. Cambridge, MA: Harvard University Press, 1988.

Maifreda, Germano. "La riaggregazione della comunità israelitica di Milano (1945–1953)." *Storia in Lombardia* 2, no. 3 (1998): 619–642.

Maiocchi, Roberto. *Scienza italiana e razzismo fascista*. Florence: La Nuova Italia, 1999.

Majer, Diemut. *"Non-Germans" under the Third Reich: The Nazi Judicial and Administrative System in Germany and Occupied Eastern Europe with Special Regard to Occupied Poland, 1939–1945*. Baltimore: Johns Hopkins University Press, 2003.

Mandel, Maud. *In the Aftermath of Genocide: Armenians and Jews in Twentieth-Century France*. Durham, NC: Duke University Press, 2003.

Mankowitz, Zeev W. *Life between Memory and Hope: The Survivors of the Holocaust in Occupied Germany*. New York: Cambridge University Press, 2002.

Mannheimer, Renato. "Gli atteggiamenti negativi verso gli ebrei. Note in margine all'indagine: Il pregiudizio nei confronti dei diversi e degli ebrei in particolare." *Rassegna Mensile di Israel* 3 (1990): 386–418.

Mantelli, Bruno. "Revisionismus durch 'Aussöhnung': Politischer Wandel und die Krise der historischen Erinnerung in Italien." In *Erinnerungskulturen: Deutschland, Italien und Japan seit 1945*, edited by Christoph Cornelissen, Lutz Klinkhammer, and Wolfgang Schwentke, 222–233. Frankfurt: Fischer Taschenbuch, 2003.

Marcus, Clare Cooper. *House as a Mirror of Self: Exploring the Deeper Meaning of Home*. Berkeley, CA: Conari, 1995.

Marcuse, Harold, Frank Schimmelfennig, and Jochen Spielmann. *Steine des Anstosses: Nationalsozialismus und Zweiter Weltkrieg in Denkmalen, 1945–1985*. [Hamburg]: Museum für Hamburgische Geschichte, 1985.

Markovitzki, Yaakov. "The Italian Government's Response to the Problem of Jewish Refugees 1945–1948." *Journal of Israeli History* 19 (1998): 23–39.

Marrus, Michael Robert. *The Holocaust at Nuremberg*. [Toronto]: Faculty of Law, University of Toronto, 1996.

———. "The Nuremberg Trial: Fifty Years After." *American Scholar* 66, 4 (1997): 563–570.

Maryks, Robert A., and Pietro Tacchi Venturi. *"Pouring Jewish Water into Fascist Wine": Untold Stories of (Catholic) Jews from the Archive of Mussolini's Jesuit Pietro Tacchi Venturi*. Leiden, Netherlands: Brill, 2012.

Marzano, Arturo. *Una terra per rinascere: Gli ebrei italiani e l'emigrazione in Palestina prima della guerra (1920–1940)*. Genoa: Marietti 1820, 2003.

Marzano, Arturo, and Guri Schwarz. *Attentato alla sinagoga: Roma, 9 ottobre 1982: Il conflitto israelo-palestinese e l'Italia*. Rome: Viella, 2013.

Massey, Doreen. *Space, Place, and Gender*. Minneapolis: University of Minnesota Press, 1994.

Mathiopoulos, Margarita. *Rendezvous mit der DDR: Politische Mythen und ihre Aufklärung*. Düsseldorf: ECON Taschenbuch, 1994.

Matt, Susan J., and Peter Stearns. *Doing Emotions History*. Urbana: University of Illinois Press, 2017.

Matta, Tristano, "Risiera di San Sabba: Il difficile cammino della memoria e della giustizia." In *I campi di concentramento in Italia*, edited by Costantino Di Sante, 300–317. Milan: Franco Angeli, 2001.

Mattioli, Aram. *Experimentierfeld der Gewalt: Der Abessinienkrieg und seine internationale Bedeutung 1935–1941*. Zurich: Orell Fossli, 2005.

———. *"Viva Mussolini!": Die Aufwertung des Faschismus in Italien Berlusconis*. Zurich: Neue Zürcher Zeitung, 2010.

Mazzini, Elena. "Aspetti dell'antisemitismo cattolico dopo l'Olocausto." In *Storia della Shoah in Italia: Vicende, memorie, rappresentazioni*, edited by Marcello Flores, Simon Levis Sullam, Marie-Anne Matard-Bonucci, and Enzo Traverso, 321–335. Turin: UTET, 2010.

———. "Memory of the Shoah in the Italian Jewish Press (1945–1965)." In *Justice, Politics and Memory in Europe after the Second World War: Landscapes after Battle*, edited by

Suzanne Bardgett, David Cesarani, Jessica Reinisch, and Johannes-Dieter Steinert, 211–228. London: Vallentine Mitchell, 2011.

Mendel, Meron. "The Policy for the Past in West Germany and Israel: The Case of Jewish Remigration." *Leo Baeck Institute Year Book* 49, no. 1 (2004): 121–136.

Meng Michael. "East Germany's Jewish Question: The Return and Preservation of Jewish Sites in East Berlin and Potsdam 1945–1989." *Central European History* 38(4) (2005): 606–636.

———. *Shattered Spaces: Encountering Jewish Ruins in Postwar Germany and Poland*. Cambridge, MA: Harvard University Press, 2011.

Merritt, Anna J., and Richard L. Merritt, eds. *Public Opinion in Semisovereign Germany: The HICOG Surveys, 1949–1955*. Urbana: University of Illinois Press, 1980.

Mertens, Lothar. *Davidstern unter Hammer und Zirkel die Jüdischen Germeinden in der SBZ/DDR und ihre Behandlung durch Partei und Staat 1945–1990*. Hildesheim, Germany: G. Olms, 1997.

Mertz, Peter. *Und das wurde nicht ihr Staat: Erfahrungen emigrierter Schriftsteller mit Westdeutschland*. Munich: Beck, 1985.

Meyer, Beate. "Handlungsspielräume regionaler jüdischer Repräsentanten (1941–1945): Die Reichsvereinigung der Juden in Deutschland und die Deportationen." In *Die Deportation der Juden aus Deutschland: Pläne–Praxis–Reaktionen 1938–1945*, edited by Birthe Kundrus and Beate Meyer, 63–85. Göttingen, Germany: Wallstein, 2004.

Meyer, Michael A. *Jewish Identity in the Modern World*. Seattle: University of Washington Press, 1990.

Miccoli, Giovanni, Guido Neppi Modona, and Paolo Pombeni. *La grande cesura: La memoria della guerra e della Resistenza nella vita europea del dopoguerra*. Bologna: Il Mulino, 2001.

Michman, Dan. *Remembering the Holocaust in Germany, 1945–2000: German Strategies and Jewish Responses*. New York: P. Lang, 2002.

Miller, Judith. *One, by One, by One: Facing the Holocaust*. New York: Simon and Schuster, 1991.

Millicent, Marcus. *Italian Film in the Shadow of Auschwitz*. Toronto, University of Toronto Press, 2007.

Milton, Sybil, and Ira Nowinski, *In Fitting Memory: The Art and Politics of Holocaust Memorials*. Detroit: Wayne State University Press, 1991.

Minerbi, Sergio. *Un ebreo fra d'Annunzio e il sionismo: Raffaele Cantoni*. Rome: Bonacci, 1992.

Miron, Guy. "Emancipation and Assimilation in the German-Jewish Discourse of the 1930s." *Leo Baeck Institute Year Book* 48, 1 (2003): 165–189.

———. "The Home Experience of German Jews under the Nazi Regime." *Past & Present* 243, no. 1 (2019): 175–212.

Mitscherlich, Alexander, and Margarete Mitscherlich. *Die Unfähigkeit zu trauern: Grundlagen kollektiven Verhaltens*. Munich: Piper, 1967.

Moeller, Robert. "Germans as Victims? Thoughts on a Post Cold War History of World War II's Legacies." *History and Memory* 17, no. 1/2 (2005): 147–194.

———. *War Stories: The Search for a Usable Past in the Federal Republic of Germany*. Berkeley: University of California Press, 2001.

Momigliano Levi, Paolo, and P. Lucat. *Storia e memoria della deportazione: Modelli di ricerca e di comunicazione in Italia e in Francia*. Florence: Giuntina, 1996.

Monteath, Peter. "A Day to Remember: East Germany's Day of Remembrance for the Victims of Fascism." *German History: Journal of the German History Society* 26, no. 2 (2008): 195–218.

———. "The German Democratic Republic and the Jews." *German History* 22, no. 3 (2004) 448–468.

———. "Narratives of Fascism in the GDR: Buchenwald and the 'Myth of Antifascism.'" *European Legacy* 4 (1999): 99–112.

Moos, Carlo. "Die 'guten' Italiener und die Zeitgeschichte." *Historische Zeitschrift* 259 (1994): 617–694.

Morris, Douglas George. "The Lives of Some Jewish Germans Who Lived in Nazi Germany and Live in Germany Today: An Oral History." BA thesis. Wesleyan University 1976.

Nachama, Andreas, and Julius Schoeps. *Deutsch-jüdische Geschichte nach 1945: In memoriam Heinz Galinski*. Berlin: Argon Verlag,1992.

Naimark, Norman M. *The Russians in Germany: A History of the Soviet Zone of Occupation, 1945–1949*. Cambridge, MA: Belknap, 1995.

Neppi, Enzo. "Giorgio Bassani e Arrigo Levi: Due sguardi incrociati su 'italianità' e 'ebraicità' negli anni del fascismo e della persecuzione." In "Il tempo dello spirito: Saggi per il centenario della nascita di Giorgio Bassani," edited by Alessandro Perli. Special issue, *Sinestesie* 14 (2016): 135–154.

Nicolaysen, Rainer. *Siegfried Landshut: Die Wiederentdeckung der Politik: Eine Biographie*. Frankfurt: Jüdischer Verlag, 1997.

Niewyk, Donald L. *Fresh Wounds: Early Narratives of Holocaust Survival*. Chapel Hill: University of North Carolina Press, 1998.

Niven, Bill. "On the Use of 'Collective Memory.'" *German History* 26, no. 3 (2008): 427–436.

———. "Remembering Nazi Anti-Semitism in the GDR." In *Memorialization in Germany since 1945*, edited by Bill Niven and Chloe Paver, 205–214. Basingstoke, UK: Palgrave Macmillan, 2010.

Nolan, Mary. "Air Wars, Memory Wars." *Central European History* 38 (2005): 7–40.

———. "Antifascism under Fascism." *New German Critique* 67 (Winter 1996): 33–55.

Noll, Hans. "Früchte des Schweigens: Jüdische Selbstverleugnung und Antisemitismus in der DDR." *Deutschland Archiv* 227 (1989): 769–778.

O'Doherty, Paul. "The GDR in the Context of Stalinist Show Trials and Anti-Semitism in Eastern Europe 1948–54." *German History* 10, no. 3 (1992): 302–318.

Ofer, Dalia, Françoise Ouzan, and Judith Tydor Baumel-Schwartz. *Holocaust Survivors: Resettlement, Memories, Identities*. New York: Berghahn Books, 2012.

Offenberg, Ulrike. *Seid vorsichtig gegen die Machthaber: Die jüdischen Gemeinden in der SBZ und der DDR 1945–1990*. Berlin: Aufbau, 1998.

Olick, Jeffrey. "What Does It Mean to Normalize the Past? Official Memory in German Politics since 1989." In *States of Memory: Continuities, Conflicts and Transformations in National Retrospection*, edited by Jeffrey Olick, 259–288. Durham, NC: Duke University Press, 2003.

Oliva, Gianni. *Le tre Italie del 1943: L'alibi della Resistenza*. Milan: Mondadori, 2005.

Orvieto, Iael. "Letters to Mussolini." In *Remembering for the Future*, edited by John K. Roth, Elisabeth Maxwell, Margot Levy, and Wendy Whitworth. London: Palgrave Macmillan, 2001.

Osti Guerrazzi, Amedeo. *Caino a Roma: I complici romani della Shoah*. Rome: Cooper, 2005.

274 | Bibliography

———. "Die ideologischen Ursprünge der Judenverfolgung in Italien: Die Propaganda und ihre Wirkung am Beispiel Roms." In *Die "Achse" im Krieg: Politik, Ideologie und Kriegführung*, edited by Lutz Klinkhammer, Amedeo Osti Guerrazzi, and Thomas Schlemmer, 434–455. Paderborn, Germany: Schöningh, 2010.

———. "Italiener als Opfer und Täter: Kriegsverbrecherprozesse in Italien nach dem Zweiten Weltkrieg." In *Vom Recht Zur Geschichte: Akten aus NS-Prozessen als Quellen der Zeitgeschichte*, edited by Jürgen Finger, Sven Keller, and Andreas Wirsching, 84–94. Göttingen, Germany: Vandenhoeck & Ruprecht, 2009.

———. "Kain in Rom: Judenverfolgung und Kollaboration unter deutscher Besatzung 1943/44." *Vierteljahrshefte für Zeitgeschichte* 54 (2006): 231–268.

Ostow, Robin. *Jews in Contemporary East Germany: The Children of Moses in the Land of Marx*. New York: St. Martin's, 1989.

Ottani, Giancarlo. *Un popolo piange*. Milan: Spartaco Giovene, 1945.

Pagnini, Gian Piero. *1943–1945, la liberazione in Toscana: La storia, la memoria*. Florence: G. Pagnini, 1994.

Papcke, Sven. "Exil und Remigration als oeffentliches Aergernis: Zur Soziologie eines Tabus." *Exilforschung* 9 (1991): 9–24.

Parkin, D. J. "Mementoes as Transitional Objects in Human Displacement." *Journal of Material Culture* 4 (1999): 303–320.

Passerini, Luisa. *Women and Men in Love: European Identities in the Twentieth Century*. New York: Berghahn Books, 2012.

Passmore, Kevin, "'A and Not A': What Is Fascism?' Fascism: A Very Short Introduction." Oxford, Oxford Academic, 2014.

Patriarca, Silvana. *Italian Vices: Nation and Character from the Risorgimento to the Republic*. Cambridge: Cambridge University Press, 2010.

Patt, Avinoam. *Finding Home and Homeland: Jewish Youth and Zionism in the Aftermath of the Holocaust*. Detroit: Wayne State University Press, 2009.

Pavan, Ilaria. "Neither Citizens nor Jews: Jewish Property Rights after the Holocaust, a Tentative Survey." *European Review of History* 28, no. 2 (2021): 301–322.

———. *Persecution, Indifference, and Amnesia: The Restoration of Jewish Rights in Postwar Italy*. Jerusalem: Yad Vashem, 2006.

———. *Tra indifferenza e oblio: Le conseguenze economiche delle leggi razziali in Italia 1938–1970*. Florence: Le Monnier, 2004.

———. "An Unexpected Betrayal? The Italian Jewish Community Facing Fascist Persecution." *Holocaust Studies* 15 (2009): 127–144.

Pavan, Ilaria, and Francesca Pelini. *La doppia epurazione: L'Università di Pisa e le leggi razziali tra guerra e dopoguerra*. Bologna: Il Mulino, 2009.

Pavan, Ilaria, and Guri Schwarz. *Gli ebrei in Italia tra persecuzione fascista e reintegrazione postbellica*. Florence: Giuntina, 2001.

Paxton, Robert. *The Anatomy of Fascism*. London: Allen Lane, 2004.

Payne, Stanley G. *A History of Fascism, 1914–1945*. Madison: University of Wisconsin Press, 1996.

Peck, Abraham J. "Jewish Survivors of the Holocaust in Germany: Revolutionary Vanguard or Remnants of a Destroyed People?" *Tel Aviver Jahrbuch für Deutsche Geschichte* 19 (1990): 33–45.

Peitsch, Helmut. "Antifaschistisches Verständnis der eigenen jüdischen Herkunft in Texten von DDR-SchriftstellerInnen." In *Das Kulturerbe deutschsprachiger Juden*, edited by Elke-Vera Kotowski, 117–142. Berlin: De Gruyter Oldenbourg, 2014.

Pelini, Francesca. "Appunti per una storia della reintegrazione dei professori universitari perseguitati per motivi razziali." In *Gli ebrei in Italia tra persecuzione fascista e reintegrazione postbellica*, edited by Ilaria Pavan and Guri Schwarz, 113–139. Florence: Giuntina, 2001.

Perra, Emiliano. "Between National and Cosmopolitan Twenty-First-Century Holocaust Television in Britain, France, and Italy." In *Holocaust Intersections: Genocide and Visual Culture at the New Millenium*, edited by Libby Saxton, Robert S. C. Gordon, and Axel Bangert. London: Modern Humanities Research Association and Maney Publishing, 2013.

———. "Legitimizing Fascism through the Holocaust? The Reception of the TV Miniseries Perlasca: un eroe italiano in Italy." *Memory Studies* 3, no. 2 (2010): 95–109.

———. "Narratives of Innocence and Victimhood: The Reception of the Miniseries Holocaust in Italy." *Holocaust and Genocide Studies* 22, no. 3 (2008): 411–440.

Person, Katarzyna. "Building a Community of Survivors in Post-War Jewish Honour Courts: The Case of Regina Kupiec." In *Shoah: Ereignis und Erinnerung*, edited by A. Bothe, M. Schärtl and S. Schüler-Springorum. Berlin: Hentrich & Hentrich, 2018.

Petersen, Jens. "Der Ort der Resistenza in Geschichte und Gegegnwart Italiens." In *Quelle aus italienischen Archiven 72* (1992): 550–571.

Petrie, Jon. "The Secular Word 'Holocaust': Scholarly Myths, History, and 20th Century Meanings." *Journal of Genocide Research* 2, no. 1 (2000): 31–63.

Pezzino, Paolo. "The Italian Resistance between History and Memory." *Journal of Modern Italian Studies* 10 (2005): 396–412.

Pezzino, Paolo, and Guri Schwarz. "From Kappler to Priebke: Holocaust Trials and the Seasons of Memory in Italy." In *Holocaust and Justice: Representation and Historiography of the Holocaust in Post-War Trials*, edited by David Bankier and Dan Michman, 299–328, Jerusalem: Yad Vashem; New York: Berghahn Books.

Phayer, Michael. *The Catholic Church and the Holocaust 1930–1965*. Bloomington: Indiana University Press, 2002.

Picciotto, Liliana. *Il libro della memoria: Gli ebrei deportati dall'Italia (1943–1945)*. Milan: Mursia, 1991.

———. "Jewish Self-Help and Italian Rescuers, 1943–1945." *Holocaust and Genocide Studies* 30, no. 1 (2016): 20–52.

———. "La ricerca del Centro di Documentazione Ebraica Contemporanea sugli ebrei deportati dall'Italia." In *Italia Judaica: Gli Ebrei Nell'Italia Unita, 1870–1945*: Atti Del 4. Convegno Internazionale: Siena, 12–16 Giugno 1989.

———. "L'attività del Comitato Ricerche Deportati Ebrei: Storia di un lavoro pioneristico (1944–1953)." In *Una storia di tutti: Prigionieri, internati, deportati italiani nella seconda guerra mondiale*, 75–96, edited by Istituto Storico della Resistenza in Piemonte. Milan: Angeli, 1989.

———. "The Persecution of Jews in Italy, 1943–1945: A Chronicle of Events." In *The Jews of Italy: Memory and Identity*, edited by Bernard D. Cooperman and Barbara Gavin, 443–454. Bethesda: University Press of Maryland, 2000.

———. "Saggi sull'ebraismo italiano del Novecento: In onore di Luisella Mortara Ottolenghi." *La Rassegna Mensile Di Israel*, vol. 69, no. 1 (2003): 21–27.

———. *Salvarsi: Gli ebrei d'Italia sfuggiti alla Shoah, 1943–1945*. Turin: Einaudi, 2017.

Piperno, Giorgio. *Ebraismo, sionismo, halutzismo*. Assisi, Italy: B. Carucci, 1976.

Plamper, Jan. *The History of Emotions: An Introduction*. Oxford: Oxford University Press, 2017.

276 | Bibliography

Poggiolini, Ilaria. "Translating Memories of War and Co-Belligerency into Politics: The Italian Post-War Experiences." In *Memory and Power in Postwar Europe: Studies in the Presence of the Past*, edited by Jan-Werner Müller, 223–243. Cambridge: Cambridge University Press, 2002.

Pollack, Craig Evan. "Intentions of Burial: Mourning, Politics and Memorials Following the Massacre at Srebenica." *Death Studies* 27 (2003): 125–142.

Pombeni, Paolo. "Il peso del passato: Storia d'Italia e strategie costituzionali all'Assemblea costituente." In *Grande Cesura: La Memoria Della Guerra E Della Resistenza Nella Vita Europea Del Dopoguerra*, edited by Di Giovanni Miccoli, Guido Neppi Modona, and Paolo Pombeni, 383–402. Bologna: Il Mulino, 2001.

Porat, Dina. *Israeli Society, the Holocaust and Its Survivors*. London: Vallentine Mitchell, 2008.

———. "One Side of a Jewish Triangle in Italy: The Encounter of Italian Jews with Holocaust Survivors and with Hebrew Soldiers and Zionist Representatives in Italy, 1944–1946." *Italia Judaica* 4 (1993): 487–513.

Poznanski, Renée. "French Apprehensions, Jewish Expectations: From a Social Imaginary to a Political Practice." In *The Jews Are Coming Back: The Return of the Jews to Their Countries of Origin after WWII*, edited by David Bankier, 25–57. New York: Berghahn Books, 2005.

Pugliese, Stanislao. "Contesting Constraints: Amelia Pincherle Rosselli, Jewish Writer in Pre-Fascist Italy." *Women in Judaism* 1, no. 2 (1998): 1–9.

Puvogel, Ulrike. *Gedenkstätten für die Opfer des Nationalsozialismus: Eine Dokumentation*. Bonn: Bundeszentrale für politische Bildung, 1987.

Rabinbach, Anson, and Jack Zipes. *Germans and Jews since the Holocaust: The Changing Situation in West Germany*. New York: Holmes & Meier, 1986.

Raim, Edith. "Der Wiederaufbau der Justiz in Westdeutschland und die Ahndung von NS-Verbrechen in der Besatzungszeit 1945–1949." In *Vom Recht zur Geschichte: Akten aus NS-Prozessen als Quellen der Zeitgeschichte*, edited by Jürgen Finger, Sven Keller, and Andreas Wirsching, 141–174. Göttingen, Germany: Vandenhoeck & Ruprecht, 2009.

Rapport, Nigel, and Andrew Dawson. *Migrants of Identity: Perceptions of Home in a World of Movement*. Oxford, UK: Berg, 1998.

Raspagliesi, Roberta. "Fascist Jews between Politics and the Economy: Five Biographical Profiles." In "Italy's Fascist Jews: Insights on an Unusual Scenario," edited by Roberta Raspagliesi. Special issue, *Quest. Issues in Contemporary Jewish History: Journal of the Fondazione CDEC* 1 (October 2017). doi:10.48248/issn.2037-741X/817.

Ravenna, Paolo. *La famiglia Ravenna 1943–1945*. Ferrara, Italy: Corbo, 2001.

Reddy, William M. *The Navigation of Feeling: A Framework for the History of Emotions*. Cambridge: Cambridge University Press, 2001.

Reichardt, Sven. "Faschistische Tatgemeinschaften: Anmerkungen zu einer praxeologischen Analyse." In *Der Faschismus in Europa: Wege der Forschung*, edited by Thomas Schlemmer and Hans Woller, 73–88. Berlin: De Gruyter Oldenbourg, 2014.

Rensmann, Lars. "Returning from Forced Exile: Some Observations on Theodor W. Adorno's and Hannah Arendt's Experience of Postwar Germany and Their Political Theories of Totalitarianism." *Leo Baeck Institute Yearbook* 49, no. 1 (2004): 171–194.

Renzo, Chiara. "'Our Hopes Are Not Lost Yet': The Jewish Displaced Persons in Italy: Relief, Rehabilitation and Self-Understanding (1943–1948)." *Quest. Issues in Contemporary Jewish History: Journal of Fondazione CDEC* 12 (December 2017). 10.48248/issn.2037-741X/822.

Reuter, Elke, and Detlef Hansel. *Das kurze Leben der VVN von 1947 bis 1953: Die Geschichte der Vereinigung der Verfolgten des Naziregimes in der sowjetischen Besatzungszone und in der DDR*. Berlin: Ost, 1997.

Richarz, Monika. "Biographie und Remigration—Die Rückkehr Julius Poseners nach Berlin." In *Integration und Ausgrenzung Studien zur deutsch-jüdischen Literatur- und Kulturgeschichte von der Frühen Neuzeit bis zur Gegenwart*, edited by Hans Otto Horch, Mark H. Gelber, Jakob Hessing, and Daniel Jütte, 335–350. Tübingen, Germany: Niemeyer, 2009.

Richarz, Monika, Stella P. Rosenfeld, and Sidney Rosenfeld, eds. *Jewish Life in Germany: Memoirs from Three Centuries*. Bloomington: Indiana University Press, 1991.

Roditi, Edouard. "The Jewish Contribution to Post-War Italian Literature." *Jewish Quarterly* 28 (1980): 20–22.

Romberg, Otto R., and Susanne Urban. *Juden in Deutschland nach 1945: Bürger oder "Mit"-Bürger?* Frankfurt: Tribüne, 1999.

Roseman, Mark. "'No, Herr Führer!' Jewish Revenge after the Holocaust: Between Fantasy and Reality." In *Revenge, Retribution, Reconciliation: Justice and Emotions between Conflict and Mediation: A Cross-Disciplinary Anthology*, edited by Laura Jockusch, Andreas Kraft, and Kim Wünschmann, 69–90. Jerusalem: Hebrew University Magnes Press.

Rosenfeld, Alvin, ed. *Thinking about the Holocaust after Half a Century*. Bloomington: Indiana University Press, 1997.

Rosenwein, Barbara H. *Emotional Communities in the Early Middle Ages*. Ithaca, NY: Cornell University Press, 2006.

———. *Generations of Feeling: A History of Emotions, 600–1700*. Cambridge: Cambridge University Press, 2016.

———. "Worrying about Emotions in History." *American Historical Review* 107 (2002): 842–845.

Rossi-Doria, Anna. "'Antisemitismo democratico' e 'mito del bravo italiano.'" *Rassegna Italiana di Sociologia* 37 (1996): 253–266.

———. *Memoria e storia: Il caso della deportazione*. Soveria Mannelli, Italy: Rubbettino, 1998.

———. *Sul ricordo della Shoah*. Turin: S. Zamorani, 2010.

Rothberg, Michael. *The Implicated Subject: Beyond Victims and Perpetrators*. Stanford, CA: Stanford University Press, 2019.

———. "Lived Multidirectionality: 'Historikerstreit 2.0' and the Politics of Holocaust Memory." *Memory Studies*, 15(6), (2022): 1316–1329.

———. *Multidirectional Memory: Remembering the Holocaust in the Age of Decolonization*. Stanford, CA: Stanford University Press, 2009.

———. *Traumatic Realism: The Demands of Holocaust Representation*. Minneapolis: University of Minnesota Press, 2000.

———. "W. E. B. DuBois in Warsaw: Holocaust Memory and the Color Line, 1949–1952." *Yale Journal of Criticism* 14, no. 1 (Spring 2001): 169–189.

Rozett, Robert. "Jewish Resistance." In *The Historiography of the Holocaust*, edited by Dan Stone, 345–347. London: Palgrave Macmillan, 2004.

Ruck, Michael. *Korpsgeist und Staatsbewusstsein: Beamte im deutschen Südwesten 1928 bis 1972*. Munich: Oldenbourg, 1996.

Rückerl, Adalbert. *NS-Verbrechen vor Gericht: Versuch einer Vergangenheitsbewältigung*. Heidelberg: C. F. Müller, 1982.

278 | Bibliography

Rusconi, Gian Enrico, and Hans Woller. *Parallele Geschichte?: Italien und Deutschland 1945-2000*. Berlin: Duncker & Humblot, 2006.

Saban, Giacomo. "Da Salonicco a Napoli." In *La comunità ebraica di Napoli, 1864/2014: Centocinquant'anni di storia: Mostra bibliografica, iconografica e documentaria, Biblioteca Nazionale di Napoli 12 novembre–12 dicembre 2014, Archivio di Stato di Napoli, 14 gennaio–26 marzo 2015*, edited by Giancarlo Lacerenza, 79–101. Naples: Giannini, 2016.

Said, Edward. *Reflections on Exile and Other Essays*. Cambridge, MA: Harvard University Press, 2004.

Salvatici, Silvia. "Between National and International Mandates: Displaced Persons and Refugees in Postwar Italy." *Journal of Contemporary History* 49, no. 3 (2014): 514–536.

Santarelli, Lidia. "Muted Violence: Italian War Crimes in Occupied Greece." *Journal of Modern Italian Studies* 9 (2004): 280–299.

Sarfatti, Michele. "Autochthoner Antisemitismus oder Übernahme des deutschen Modells? Die Judenverfolgung im faschistischen Italien." In *Die "Achse" im Krieg: Politik, Ideologie und Kriegführung*, edited by Lutz Klinkhammer, Amedeo Osti Guerrazzi, and Thomas Schlemmer, 231–43. Paderborn, Germany: Schöningh, 2010.

———. "Eine italienische Besonderheit: Faschistische Juden und faschistischer Antisemitismus." In *Judentum und Antisemitismus in modernen Italien*, edited by Gudrun Jaeger and Liana Novelli-Glaab, 131–154. Berlin: Trafo, 2007.

———. "I caratteri principali della legislazione antiebraica in Italia." In *Antisemitismo in Europa negli anni Trenta: Legislazioni a confronto*, edited by Anna Capelli and Renata Broggini. Milan: Angeli, 2001.

———, ed. *Il ritorno alla vita: Vicende e diritti degli ebrei in Italia dopo la seconda guerra mondiale*. Florence: Giuntina, 1998.

———. Introduction to "Italy's Fascist Jews: Insights on an Unusual Scenario." *Quest. Issues in Contemporary Jewish History: Journal of the Fondazione CDEC* 1 (October 2017), doi:10.48248/issn.2037-741X/36.

———. *The Jews in Mussolini's Italy: From Equality to Persecution*. Madison: University of Wisconsin Press, 2006.

———. "La 'Commissione Anselmi' (1998 -2001) sui beni degli ebrei durante la persecuzione 1938-1945." *Pagine di storia della Shoah* (2005): 51–74.

———. "Notes and Reflections on the Italian Law Instituting the Holocaust Remembrance Day." In "Miscellanea 2017." *Quest. Issues in Contemporary Jewish History: Journal of the Fondazione CDEC* 12 (December 2017), doi:10.48248/issn.2037-741X/819.

Schächter, Elizabeth. "Carlo Alberto Viterbo: A Neglected Figure of Italian Judaism." *Italianist* 33, no. 3 (2013): 505–521.

Scheer, Regina. *Im Schatten der Sterne: Eine jüdische Widerstandsgruppe*. Berlin: Aufbau, 2004.

Schlemmer, Thomas, and Alan E. Steinweis. *Holocaust and Memory in Europe*. Berlin: De Gruyter Oldenbourg, 2016.

Schlemmer, Thomas, and Hans Woller. "Der italienische Faschismus und die Juden 1922 bis 1945." *Vierteljahrshefte für Zeitgeschichte* 53, no. 2 (2005): 165–201.

Schloer, Joachim. *Im Herzen immer ein Berliner: Jüdische Emigranten im Dialog mit ihrer Heimatstadt*. Berlin: Verlag für Berlin-Brandenburg, 2021.

———. *Jüdisches Leben in Berlin 1933–1941 / Fotografien von Abraham Pisarek*. Berlin: Braus, 2012.

Schmid, Harald. *Antifaschismus und Judenverfolgung: Die "Reichskristallnacht" als politischer Gedenktag in der DDR*. Göttingen, Germany: V&R unipress, 2004.

———. "'Wiedergutmachung' und Erinnerung: Die Notgemeinschaft der durch die Nürnberger Gesetze Betroffenen." In *Opfer als Akteure: Interventionen ehemaliger NS-Verfolgter in der Nachkriegszeit*, edited by Katharina Stengel and Werner Konitzer, 27–47. Frankfurt: Campus, 2008.

Schnapp, Jeffrey T., Olivia E. Sears, and Maria G. Stampino. *A Primer of Italian Fascism*. Lincoln: University of Nebraska Press, 2000.

Schneider, Gabriele. *Mussolini in Afrika: Die Faschistische Rassenpolitik in den Italienischen Kolonien 1936–1941*. Cologne: SH-Verlag, 2000.

Schoeps, Julius H. *Aufbau nach dem Untergang: Deutsch-jüdische Geschichte nach 1945*. Berlin: Argon, 1992.

Scholz, Michael F. *Skandinavische Erfahrungen erwünscht?: Nachexil und Remigration; die ehemaligen KPD-Emigranten in Skandinavien und ihr weiteres Schicksal in der SBZ/DDR*. Stuttgart: Franz Steiner, 2000.

Schönborn, Susanne. *Im Wandel—Entwürfe jüdischer Identität in den 1980er und 1990er Jahren*. Munich: Martin Meidenbauer, 2010.

———, ed. *Zwischen Erinnerung und Neubeginn: Zur deutsch-jüdischen Geschichte nach 1945*. Munich: Meidenbauer, 2006.

Schrecker, Ellen. *Many Are the Crimes: McCarthyism in America*. Princeton, NJ: Princeton University Press, 1999.

Schwarz, Daniel R. "Why Giorgio Bassani Matters: The Elegiac Imagined World of Bassani and the Jews of Ferrara." *Shofar: An Interdisciplinary Journal of Jewish Studies* 31, no. 1 (2012): 34–51.

Schwarz, Guri. *After Mussolini: Jewish Life and Jewish Memories in Post-Fascist Italy*. Edgware, UK: Vallentine Mitchell, 2012.

———. "Appunti per una storia degli ebrei in Italia dopo le persecuzioni (1945–1956)." *Studi Storici* 41 (2000): 757–797.

———. "Identità ebraica e identità italiana nel ricordo dell'antisemitismo fascista." *L'annale IRSIFAR* 17 (1999): 27–43.

———. "On Myth Making and Nation Building: The Genesis of the 'Myth of the Good Italian' 1943–1947." *Yad Vashem Studies* 36 (2008): 111–143.

———. *Ritrovare se stessi: Gli ebrei nell'Italia postfascista*. Rome: Laterza, 2004.

———. "Un'identità da rifondare: Note sul problema dei giovani tra persecuzione e dopoguerra (1938–1956)." *Zakhor* 3 (1999): 181–208.

Schwarz, Guri, and Barbara Armani. "Premessa." *Quaderni Storici* 38, no. 3 (2003): 621–651.

Seaton, Jean. "The BBC and the Holocaust." *European Journal of Communication* 2 (1987): 53–80.

Segre, Liliana. *Le Fosse Ardeatine: Dodici storie*. Rome: Gangemi, 2020.

Sharples, Caroline. *Postwar Germany and the Holocaust*. New York: Bloomsbury Academic, 2016.

Shiloh-Dayan, Yonathan. "On the Point of Return: Heute und Morgen and the German-Speaking Left-Wing Émigrés in Palestine." In *Rückkehrerzählungen Über die (Un-)Möglichkeit nach 1945 als Jude in Deutschland zu leben*, edited by Bettina Bannasch and Michael Rupp. Göttingen, 35–57. Germany: V&R unipress, 2017.

280 | Bibliography

Shneer, David. "An Alternative World." In *Jewish Lives Under Communism* edited by Kateřina Čapková, Kamil Kijek, 153–173. New Brunswick, NJ: Rutgers University Press, 2022.

———. "Eberhard Rebling, Lin Jaldati, and Yiddish Music in East Germany, 1949–1962." *Leo Baeck Institute Yearbook* 60, no. 1 (2015): 207–234.

Silbermann, Alphons, and Herbert Sallen. *Juden in Westdeutschland: Selbstbild und Fremdbild einer Minoritaet.* Cologne: Wissenschaft und Politik, 1992.

Silverman, Lisa. "Reconsidering the Margins." *Journal of Modern Jewish Studies* 8 (2009): 103–120.

Sinn, Andrea. "Aber ich blieb trotzdem hier: Karl Marx und die Anfänge jüdischen Lebens im Nachkriegsdeutschland." *Nurinst* 5 (2010): 80–97.

———. *Jüdische Politik und Presse in der Frühen Bundesrepublik.* Göttingen, Germany: Vandenhoeck & Ruprecht, 2014.

———. "Returning to Stay? Jews in East and West Germany after the Holocaust." *Central European History* 53, no. 2 (2020): 393–413.

Smolensky, Eleonora M., and Vera Vigevani Jarach. *Tante voci, una storia: Italiani ebrei in Argentina, 1938–1948.* Bologna: Il Mulino, 1998.

Sorani, Settimio, Amedeo Tagliacozzo, and Francesco Del Canuto. *L'assistenza ai profughi ebrei in Italia (1933–1941): Contributo alla storia della Delasem, Testimonianze sull'ebraismo, 15.* Rome: Carucci, 1983.

Sòrgoni, Barbara. "'Defending the Race': The Italian Reinvention of the Hottentot Venus during Fascism." *Journal of Modern Italian Studies*, 8:3 (2003): 411–424.

Spannuth, Jan Philipp. *Rückerstattung Ost: Der Umgang der DDR mit dem "arisierten" und enteigneten Eigentum der Juden und die Gestaltung der Rückerstattung im wiedervereinigten Deutschland.* Essen: Klartext, 2007.

Spiegel, Gabrielle. Introduction to *Practicing History: New Directions in Historical Writing after the Linguistic Turn,* edited by Gabrielle Spiegel, 1–33. New York, 2005.

Steege, Paul. "Holding on in Berlin: March 1948 and SED Efforts to Control the Soviet Zone." *Central European History* 38 (2005): 417–449.

Stephan, Alexander. "Die intellektuelle, literarische und künstlerische Emigration." In *Handbuch der deutschsprachigen Emigration 1933–1945,* edited by Claus-Dieter Krohn, Patrik von zur Mühlen, Gerhard Paul, and Lutz Winckler, 30–46. Darmstadt, Germany: Primus, 1998.

Stern, Frank. "The Historic Triangle: Occupiers, Germans and Jews in Postwar Germany." In *West Germany under Construction: Politics, Society and Culture in the Adenauer Era,* edited by Robert Moeller, 199–229. Ann Arbor: University of Michigan Press, 1997.

———. *Im Anfang war Auschwitz: Antisemitismus und Philosemitismus im deutschen Nachkrieg.* Gerlingen, Germany: Bleicher, 1991.

———. "The Return to the Disowned Home: German Jews and the Other Germany." *New German Critique* 67 (1996): 57–72.

———. *The Whitewashing of the Yellow Badge: Antisemitism and Philosemitism in Postwar Germany.* Oxford: Published for the Vidal Sassoon International Center for the Study of Antisemitism (SICSA) the Hebrew University of Jerusalem by Pergamon Press, 1992.

Stille, Alexander. *Benevolence and Betrayal: Five Italian Jewish Families under Fascism.* New York: Summit Books, 1991.

Stoffregen, Matthias. *Kämpfen für ein demokratisches Deutschland: Emigranten zwischen Politik und Politikwissenschaft.* Opladen, Germany: Leske + Budrich, 2002.

Stover, Eric, and Gilles Peress. *The Graves: Srebrenica and Vukovar.* Zurich: Scalo, 1998.

Strani, Marianna. "Gli ebrei romani e la ricostruzione: Tra Stato e Comunita (1945–1948)." MA thesis, Sapienza University of Rome, 2004–2005.

Strauss, Herbert A. *Über dem Abgrund: Eine jüdische Jugend in Deutschland, 1918–1943.* Frankfurt: Campus, 1997.

Sullam, Simon Levis. *The Italian Executioners: The Genocide of the Jews of Italy.* Princeton, NJ: Princeton University Press, 2018.

Sznaider, Natan. *Gedächtnisraum Europa: Die Visionen des europäischen Kosmopolitismus. Eine jüdische Perspektive.* Bielefeld: transcript Verlag, 2015.

Tablet, Andrea. "Italy," *The American Jewish Year Book* 49 (1947): 347–54.

Tagliacozzo, Franca, and Raffaella Di Castro. *Gli ebrei romani raccontano la "propria" Shoah.* Florence: Giuntina, 2010.

Tauber, Alon. *Zwischen Kontinuitaet und Neuanfang: Die Entstehung der juedischen Nachkriegsgemeinde in Frankfurt am Main 1945–1949.* Wiesbaden, Germany: Kommission fuer die Geschichte der Juden in Hessen, 2008.

Tauchert, Stephanie. *Jüdische Identitäten in Deutschland: Das Selbstverständnis von Juden in der Bundesrepublik und der DDR 1950 bis 2000.* Berlin: Metropol, 2007.

Taylor, Stephanie. *Narratives of Identity and Place.* London: Routledge, 2010.

Terzulli, Francesco. *Una stella fra i trulli: Gli ebrei in Puglia 1933–1949.* Bari, Italy: Adda, 1995.

Timm, Angelika. "The Burdened Relationship between the GDR and the State of Israel." *Israel Studies* 2, no. 1 (1997): 22–49.

———. "Ein ambivalentes Verhältnis: Juden in der DDR und der Staat Israel." In *Zwischen Politik und Kultur: Juden in der DDR*, edited by Moshe Zuckermann, 17–33. Göttingen, Germany: Wallstein, 2003.

———. *Hammer, Zirkel, Davidstern: Das gestörte Verhältnis der DDR zu Zionismus und Staat Israel.* Bonn: Bouvier, 1997.

Torriglia, Anna Maria. *Broken Time, Fragmented Space: A Cultural Map of Postwar Italy.* Toronto: University of Toronto Press, 2002.

Toscano, Mario. "The Abrogation of Racial Laws and the Reintegration of Jews in Italian Society (1943–1948)." In *The Jews Are Coming Back: The Return of the Jews to Their Countries of Origin after WWII*, edited by David Bankier, 148–169. New York: Berghahn Books, 2005.

———. *Ebraismo e antisemitismo in Italia: Dal 1848 alla guerra dei sei giorni.* Milan: Angeli, 2003.

———. "L'antisemitismo nell'Italia contemporanea: Note, ipotesi e problemi di ricerca." *Zakhor* 6 (2003): 184–205.

———. "La politica italiana verso l'immigrazione clandestina ebraica in Palestina nel primo semestre del 1947." *Storia Contemporanea* 20 (1989): 751–802.

———. *La "porta di Sion": L'Italia e l'immigrazione clandestine ebraica in Palestine (1945–1948).* Bologna: Il Mulino, 1990.

———. "Tra identità culturale e partecipazione politica: Aspetti e momenti di vita ebraica italiana (1956–1976)." *Annuario di Studi Ebraici*, 1985–1987.

Treskow, Isabella von. *Judenverfolgung in Italien (1938–1945) in Romanen von Marta Ottolenghi Minerbi, Giorgio Bassani, Francesco Burdin und Elsa Morante : Fakten Fiktion Projektion.* Wiesbaden: Harrassowitz Verlag, 2014.

Tsuda, Takeyuki. *Diasporic Homecomings: Ethnic Return Migration in Comparative Perspective.* Stanford, CA: Stanford University Press, 2009.

282 | Bibliography

Tylim, Isaac. "Skyscrapers and Bones: Memorials to Dead Objects in the Culture of Desire." In *Living with Terror, Working with Trauma: A Clinician's Handbook*, edited by Danielle Knafo, 461–476. Lanham, MD: Jason Aronson, 2004.

Tyrolf, Alexandra. "'You Can't Go Home Again.': Erste Besuche von Gina Kaus, Victoria Wolff und Marta Feuchtwanger in Europa nach dem Ende des Zweiten Weltkrieges." In *Juden und Nichtjuden nach der Shoah: Begegnungen in Deutschland*, edited by Stefanie Fischer, Nathanael Riemer, and Stefanie Schüler-Springorum, 117–128. Berlin: De Gruyter Oldenbourg, 2019.

Uboldi, Raffaello. *25 aprile 1945: I giorni dell'odio e della libertà*. Milan: Mondadori, 2004.

United Nations War Crimes Commission. *Law Reports of Trials of War Criminals*. Vol. 7. London: HMSO, 1948.

Urso, Simona. "Due modernità a confronto: Il modernismo cattolico e il rifiuto dell'ebraismo riformato." *Nel nome della razza. Il razzismo nella storia d'Italia 1870–1945*, edited by Alberto Burgio, 293–308. Bologna: il Mulino, 1999.

Valabrega, Guido. *Ebrei, Fascismo, Sionismo: Studi Storici*. Urbino, Italy: Argalìa, 1974.

Vansant, Jacqueline. *Reclaiming Heimat: Trauma and Mourning in Memoirs by Jewish Austrian Rèmigrès*. Detroit: Wayne State University Press, 2001.

Villa, Andrea. *Dai lager alla terra promessa: La difficile reintegrazione nella "nuova Italia" e l'immigrazione verso il Medio Oriente, 1945–1948*. Milan: Guerini e associati, 2005.

Villa, Cristina. ". . . e Mnemosine, confusa e smarrita, vaga tra le rovine: Monumenti e luoghi della memoria della deportazione razziale in Italia." In *Memoria collettiva e memoria privata: Il ricordo della Shoah come politica sociale*, edited by Stefania Lucamante, Monica Jansen, Raniero Speelman, and Silvia Gaiga, 181–192. Utrecht, Netherlands: Igitur Utrecht, 2008.

Visani, Alessandro. "The Jewish Enemy: Fascism, the Vatican, and Anti-Semitism on the Seventieth Anniversary of the 1938 Race Laws." *Journal of Modern Italian Studies* 14 (2009): 168–183.

Vivanti, Corrado. *Gli Ebrei in Italia: Dall'emancipazione a Oggi*. Turin: Einaudi, 1978.

Völter, Bettina. "Die Nachkriegszeit in Biographien jüdischer Kommunisten." In *Leben im Land der Täter: Juden im Nachkriegsdeutschland (1945–1952)*, edited by Julius Schoeps, 303–315. Berlin: Jüdische Verlagsanstalt, 2001.

———. *Judentum und Kommunismus: Deutsche Familiengeschichten in drei Generationen*. Opladen, Germany: Leske + Budrich, 2003.

Von Mering, Sabine. "Grenzgang als zögernde Wieder-Annäherung: Die deutsche Staatsbürgerschaft und der jüdisch-deutsche Dialog, Deutschland und Europa: Grenzen und Grenzgänge(r)." *Eurostudia: L'Allemagne et l'Europe: Frontières et passeurs* 7, no. 1–2 (2011): 47–57.

Walston, James. "History and Memory of the Italian Concentration Camps." *Historical Journal* 40 (1997): 169–183.

Walther, Alexander. "Helmut Eschwege and Jewish Life in the German Democratic Republic." In *Rebuilding Jewish Life in Germany*, edited by Jay Howard Geller and Michael Meng, 101–117. Ithaca, NY: Rutgers University Press, 2020.

Wasserstein, Bernard. *Vanishing Diaspora*. London: Penguin Books, 1996.

Webster, Ronald. "Juedische Rueckkehrer in die BRD nach 1945: ihre Motive, ihre Erfahrungen." *Aschkenas* 5 (1995): 47–77.

Weidauer, F. J. "'Fighting for Defeat': Jewish Identity in Postwar Germany and Austria." *Seminar* (Toronto) 34 (1998): 280–299.

Weingart, Peter. *Doppel-Leben: Ludwig Ferdinand Clauss, Zwischen Rassenforschung und Widerstand.* Frankfurt: Campus, 1995.

Weisbord, Robert G., and Wallace P. Sillanpoa, *The Chief Rabbi, the Pope and the Holocaust: An Era in Vatican-Jewish Relations.* New Brunswick, NJ: Transaction, 1992.

Welzer, Harald, Sabine Moller, and Karoline Tschuggnall. *Opa war kein Nazi: Nationalsozialismus und Holocaust im Familiengedächtnis: Die Zeit des Nationalsozialismus.* Frankfurt: Fischer Taschenbuch, 2002.

Wetzel, Juliane. "Antisemitismus in Italien und Europa in der Gegenwart." In *". . . denn in Italien haben sich die Dinge anders abgespielt.": Judentum und Antisemitismus im modernen Italien,* edited by Gudrun Jäger and Liana Novelli-Glaab. Berlin: Trafo, 2007.

———. "Der Mythos des 'braven Italieners': Das faschistische Italien und der Antisemitismus." In *Vorurteil und Rassenhass: Antisemitismus in den faschistischen Bewegungen Europas,* edited by Hermann Graml, Angelika Königseder, and Juliane Wetzel. Berlin: Metropol, 2001.

Wiese, Christian. "Counter History, the 'Religion of the Future' and the Emancipation of Jewish Studies: The Conflict between the Wissenschaft des Judentums and Liberal Protestantism 1900 to 1933." *Jewish Studies Quarterly* 7 (2000): 367–398.

Wieviorka, Annette. *The Era of the Witness.* Ithaca, NY: Cornell University Press, 2006.

Wildt, Michael. *Volksgemeinschaft als Selbstermächtigung: Gewalt gegen Juden in der deutschen Provinz 1919 bis 1939.* Hamburg: Hamburger, 2007.

Wildvang, Frauke. *Der Feind von nebenan: Judenverfolgung im faschistischen Italien 1936–1944.* Cologne: SH-Verlag, 2008.

———. "The Enemy Next Door: Italian Collaboration in Deporting Jews during the German Occupation of Rome." *Modern Italy* 2 (2007): 189–204.

Williams, Allison, ed. *Therapeutic Landscapes: The Dynamic between Place and Wellness.* New York: University Press of America, 1999.

Willingham, Robert Allen. *Jews in Leipzig, Germany under Nazism, Communism, and Democracy: Politics and Identity in the 20th Century.* Lewiston, NY: Edwin Mellen, 2011.

Winkler, Andreas. *Hermann Kesten im Exil (1933–1940): Sein politisches und künstlerisches Selbstverständnis und seine Tätigkeit als Lektor in der deutschen Abteilung des Allert de Lange Verlages.* Hamburg: H. Lüdke, 1977.

Winkler, Heinrich August. *Der lange Weg nach Westen.* Munich: Beck, 2000.

Winstel, Tobias, "'Healed Biographies'? Jewish Remigration and Indemnification for National Socialist Injustice." *Leo Baeck Institute Year Book* 49 (2004): 137–152.

———. *Verhandelte Gerechtigkeit: Rückerstattung und Entschädigung für jüdische NS-Opfer in Bayern und Westdeutschland.* Munich: Oldenbourg, 2006.

Winter, Jay M. *Sites of Memory, Sites of Mourning: The Great War in European Cultural History.* Cambridge: Cambridge University Press, 1995.

Wise, J. Macgregor. "Home: Territory and Identity." *Cultural Studies* 14, no. 2 (2000): 295–310.

Wojak, Irmtrud. *Fritz Bauer 1903–1968: Eine Biographie.* Munich: Beck, 2009.

Wolffsohn, Michael. *Die Deutschland Akte: Juden und Deutsche in Ost und West.* Munich: Tatsachen und Legenden, 1995.

Woller, Hans. "'Ausgebliebene Säuberung'? Die Abrechnung mit dem Faschismus in Italien." In *Politische Säuberung in Europa,* edited by Klaus-Dietmar Henke and Hans Woller, 148–191. Munich: Deutscher Taschenbuch, 1991.

284 | Bibliography

———. *Die Abrechnung mit dem Faschismus in Italien 1943–1948.* Munich: Oldenbourg Verlag, 1996.

———. "Die Anfänge der politischen Säuberung in Italien 1943–1945: Eine Analyse des Office of Strategic Services." In *Vierteljahrshefte für Zeitgeschichte* 38 (1990): 141–190.

Wood, Denis, and Robert J. Beck. *Home Rules.* Baltimore: Johns Hopkins University Press, 1994.

Wroblewsky, Vincent von. *Zwischen Thora und Trabant: Juden in der DDR.* Berlin: Aufbau, 1993.

Yehudai, Ori. "Displaced in the National Home: Jewish Repatriation from Palestine to Europe, 1945–48." *Jewish Social Studies* 20, no. 2 (Winter 2014): 69–110.

Young, James Edward. *The Texture of Memory: Holocaust Memorials and Meaning.* New Haven, CT: Yale University Press, 1993.

Zahra, Tara. "Imagined Noncommunities: National Indifference as a Category of Analysis." *Slavic Review* 69, no. 1 (2010): 93–119.

———. *The Lost Children: Reconstructing Europe's Families after World War II.* Cambridge, MA: Harvard University Press, 2015.

Zanelli, Giuliana, and Rosa Maiolani. *Oltre il tempo della Shoah: Le carte salvate: Spigolature di cronache imolesi, ricordi e documenti, 1938–1961.* Imola, Italy: La Mandragora, 2009.

Zerubavel, Yael. *Recovered Roots: Collective Memory and the Making of Israeli National Tradition.* Chicago: University of Chicago Press, 1995.

Zieher, Jürgen. *Im Schatten von Antisemitismus und Wiedergutmachung: Kommunen und jüdische Gemeinden in Dortmund, Düsseldorf und Köln 1945–1960.* Berlin: Metropol, 2005.

Zielinski, Andrea. *Die anderen Juden: Identitätenbildung von Menschen jüdischer Herkunft im Nachkriegsdeutschland.* Munich: Lit, 2002.

Zimmerman, Joshua D. *Jews in Italy under Fascist and Nazi Rule, 1922–1945.* Cambridge: Cambridge University Press, 2005.

Zuccotti, Susan. *Under His Very Windows: The Vatican and the Holocaust in Italy.* New Haven, CT: Yale University Press, 2000.

Zuckermann, Moshe. *Zwischen Politik und Kultur: Juden in der DDR.* Göttingen, Germany: Wallstein, 2002.

Zwiep, Irene. "Goodbye to All That? Jewish Views of Europe after 1945." In *European Identity and the Second World War,* edited by Menno Spiering and Michael Wintle, 224–234. London: Palgrave Macmillan, 2011.

INDEX

Note: Page numbers in *italics* indicate images and associated captions.

Abbazia, Italy, 51
Abusch, Alexander, 39, 44, 80, 151, 170
Adenauer, Konrad, 134–35
Adorno, Theodor, 149
Allgemeine Wochenzeitung für Juden in Deutschland, 149–50
Allied powers: Allied Control Council, 106, 148; Allied courts, 106; Allied Military Government, 5; Allied military rabbis, 166; Allied occupation forces, 122; and information on death camps, 58
Almansi, Dante, 173, 211n178
Almansi, Renato, 211n178
Alternative für Deutschland (AfD), 183, 238n16
Altmann, Ferdinando, 114
American Jewish Committee (AJC), 91, 117, 132, 159
American Jewish Joint Distribution Committee, also Joint (AJDC): and good Italian narrative, 32, 91; and Italian narratives of resistance, 71; and membership in Jewish communities, 161–63; and postwar Zionist sentiment, 175; and reclamation of Jewish property, 125; and refugees' journeys home, 39; and religious discrimination in postwar Italy, 132; and scope of study, 19
American Jewish Year Book, 90
Améry, Jean, 9, 28, 189
Amsterdam, 29
Anderson, Benedict, 153
anticommunism, 21, 23–24, 77
antifascism: challenges facing postwar German Jews, 133, 135–36, 140; and collapse of East Germany, 182; and commemoration of war and Holocaust victims, 64, 66–68; and comparative

approach to study, 16–17; denazification process after war, 111; East German antifascist narrative, 77–85, 100; and gender roles and norms, 228n40; and generational political shifts, 185–87, 240n37; and German Jews' self-understanding, 57, 143, 152–53, 169–70, 179; and good Italian narrative, 88, 94; and Italian Jews' self-understanding, 146–47; and Italian narratives of resistance, 68–69; and motives of Jewish returnees, 24–27; and philosemitism, 123; and refugees' journeys home, 39
antisemitism: and antifascist East German narrative, 14, 78–80, 100; challenges facing postwar German Jews, 133–34, 136–39, 140; and comparative approach to study, 17; contemporary, 183–85, 239n21; and the Doctors' Plot, 224n228; and failures of Italian defascistization, 128–29; and German Jews' self-understanding, 151, 153, 155, 179; and good Italian narrative, 13–14, 16, 68–69, 86, 88–90, 92, 99; and motives of Jewish returnees, 20, 22, 26, 31–32, 33; and persecution under Nazism and Fascism, 2–6; postwar battle against, 22, 75, 102, 115–25; and postwar Zionist sentiments, 173; and prosecution of war criminals, 105; and religious discrimination in postwar Italy, 132; and scope of text, 18; and war's impact on Jewish identity, 159, 168–69
Antisemitismus und Rassenhetze (Kahn), 80, 151, 169
anti-Zionism, 135–138, 173, 174, 177, 226n242
Appelfeld, Aharon, 191n3
Arab-Israeli War, 177, 179

286 | Index

Ardeatine Caves, 63. *See also* Fosse Ardeatine massacre
Arendt, Hannah, 73, 104, 208n88, 228n43
Argentina, 30, 31
Arian, Enzo (Heinz), 20, 144
Assmann, Aleida, 75
Association of Jewish Communities, 105, 136
Association of Jews in Germany, 162, 163
Association of Those Persecuted by the Nazi Regime, 78
Associazione nazionale ex deportati (National Association of Ex-Deportees) (ANED), 69
Aufbau, 73, 77
Auschwitz: and commemoration of victims, 61; and contemporary Italian memory, 184–85; and German Jews' self-understanding, 152; and good Italian narrative, 86, 87, 88; and Holocaust survivor testimonies, 95–97, 99; and Italian Jews' self-understanding, 144; and Klemperer's view of Zionism, 179; and liberation, 35–36; and postwar battle against antisemitism, 121; and prosecution of war criminals, 26, 108, 113–14, 182; and reclamation of Jewish property, 127; and refugees' journeys home, 35–38, 61; and the Slansky affair, 138; and survivors' memoirs, 228n40; survivors of, 1, 12, 26, 33, 47, 53, 60, 73, 80, 82, 85, 87, 93, 102–3, 134, 170; and war's impact on Jewish self-understanding, 158, 170, 227n4
Australia, 96
Avigdor, Miranda, 53

Badoglio, Pietro, 5, 112
Baeck, Leo, 32
Bartel, Walther, 67
Barthes, Roland, 38
Bassa, Eugenia, 53
Bassani, Giorgio, 62, 98, 215n250
Bauer, Fritz, 26, 40, 108, 152, 154
Bauer, Goti, 1, 51–52, 86–87, 93
Bavaria, 152
Becher, Johannes, 152
Becker, Jurek, 124, 149
Becker, Max, 234n184
Beer, Umberto, 31

belonging, 141–80; and German Jews' self-understanding, 148–53; and Italian Jews' self-understanding, 143–48; and postwar Zionist sentiments, 171–79
Bender, Gerhard, 163–64
Benedetti, Aldo de, 93
Bergen-Belsen concentration camp, 60
Berger, Stefan, 14–15
Bergisch-Gladbach, Germany, 75
Berlin, Germany: and commemoration of war and Holocaust victims, 67, 182; fall of Berlin Wall, 182; and German surrender, 35; and hiding, 76; Holocaust monument, 240n32; Jewish cemeteries, 62; and motives of Jewish returnees, 25, 27; and refugees' decisions to return home, 23–27, 34; and refugees' journeys home, 47, 48–49, 60; returnees' memories of persecution, 50, 181; and state of returnees' homes, 54; and war's impact on Jewish self-understanding, 159, 162
Berlin Humboldt University, 139
Berlin Office for the Victims of Fascism, 80
Berlin Weissensee, 62
Berlusconi, Silvio, 184
Bernhardt, Ursula, 152
Berti, Silvia, 211n178
Biess, Frank, 93
Birkenau concentration camp, 12, 87
Bises, Andrea, 31
Bizonia, 7
Blackshirts, 91
Bolivia, 20, 29, 171
Bollettino della comunità israelitica di Milano, 147, 228n40
Bonaventura, Enzo, 231n114
Bondi, Sergio, 173–74
Bonomi, Ivanoe, 112
borders and border crossing, 15–16, 35–36, 40–45, 114–15
Boyarin, Jonathan, 61
boycotts, 3, 80, 225n240
Brandt, Heinz, 27, 137
brava gente narrative, 13, 15, 68, 85–94, 115, 187. *See also* good Italian narrative
Brazil, 29, 31, 45, 139
Brenner, Michael, 183
Breslau, 51

Britain, 7, 43. *See also* United Kingdom
British Army, 72
British occupation zone, 148
Brothers of Italy party, 185
Brüll, Rita Guetta, 126
Buchenwald concentration camp: and Holocaust survivor testimonies, 98–99; and motives of Jewish returnees, 27; and postwar revelation of atrocities, 60; and the Slansky affair, 138; and survivors' journeys home, 36; survivors of, 1, 79; and war's impact on Jewish self-understanding, 168
bureaucratic obstacles, 5, 39, 77, 120, 128, 144
Businco, Lino, 130

Camerini, Giacomo, 116
Campagnano, Shaul, 37
camp guards, 106–8
Canarutto, Emilio, 112, 113, 160
Cantoni, Raffaele, and commemoration of Holocaust victims, 61, 64–66; and failures of Italian defascistization, 129–30; and good Italian narrative, 89, 92, 158; and Italian narratives of resistance, 70–71; and postwar battle against antisemitism, 116; and postwar Zionism, 174; and religious discrimination in postwar Italy, 131
capitalism, 137–38
Caracciolo, Nicola, 184
Carlebach, Emil, 168–69
Carmi, Luigi, 85
Caspari, Adolf, 110–11
Cassuto, Nathan, 37, 61, 97
Castelbolognesi, Gustavo, 160
catechism debate, 238n14
Catholics and Catholic Church: and arrival of returnees, 44; and contemporary antisemitism, 183–84; and good Italian narrative, 69; and postwar battle against antisemitism, 116–17, 120; and religious discrimination in postwar Italy, 131–32; and war's impact on Jewish self-understanding, 157, 161–62, 168
cemeteries. *See* graves and cemeteries
censorship, 85
Central Association of those not of Jewish Faith Affected by the Nuremberg Laws, 164

Central Committee-US Zone, 32
Central Council of Jews in Germany, 238n16
Central Party Control Commission, 136, 170
Central-Verein deutscher Staatsbürger jüdischen Glaubens (Association of German Citizens of the Jewish Faith), 150
Central Welfare Board of Jews in Germany, 27
Centro di Documentazione Ebraica Contemporanea, 183
Charlottenburg (Berlin), 49
Chemnitz, Germany, 202n183
Chile, 205n37
Christian Democrats, 8, 16, 68, 69
Christianity, 75
Cimitero Monumentale, 64
citizenship status: and commemoration of war and Holocaust, 66; and failures of Italian defascistization, 128–31; and GDR constitution, 225n240; and German guilt, 74; and German Jews' self-understanding, 28, 148–50; and Italian Jews' self-understanding, 144; and Italian narratives of resistance, 71; and meanings of home, 9; and Nuremberg laws, 3; and postwar Zionist sentiments, 174, 176, 178–79; and third generation, 182
civilian tribunals (Spruchkammern), 108–9
class, 67, 82, 86, 128, 137, 145, 172
classism, 67
Clauss, Ludwig Ferdinand, 110
Cogni, Giulio, 129–30
Cohen, Daniel, 123
Cohn, Erich, 97
Cohn-Leschzer, Nelly, 73, 95
Cold War, 7–8, 17, 23, 39, 134, 184
collaborators: and contemporary Italian memory, 189; and failures of Italian defascistization, 129–30; and good Italian narrative, 70, 85, 88, 92, 99–100, 186; and Italian narratives of resistance, 70; and memory, 98; and postwar battle against antisemitism, 122; and prosecution of war criminals, 112–14; and pushback against good Italian narrative, 14, 16–17; and the Republic of Salò, 6
collective memory, 12, 15, 57, 58
colonial violence, 238n14, 240n36

288 | Index

Comitato ricerche deportati ebrei (Committee for the Search for Jewish Deportees) (CRDE), 63, 92, 113

Comitato ricerche soccorsi deportati ebrei (Committee for the Search and Rescue of Jewish Deportees) (CRSDE), 58, 63

commemorative ceremonies, 67

Commentary, 73, 103, 123, 148

Committee for the Examination of Party Members, 171

Committee for Victims of Fascism, 109

Committee of Antifascist Resistance Fighters (Komitee der Antifaschistischen Widerstandskämpfer), 136

Committee Representing the Interests of the Jewish Communities, 32

Communism and Communists: and challenges facing postwar German Jews, 120, 133, 135–39; and citizenship, 227n18; and comparative approach to study, 16; and East German antifascist narrative, 14, 77–78, 80–85, 100, 187; and failures of Italian defascistization, 129; and German Jews' self-understanding, 10, 57, 152–53, 179, 182; and Italian postwar narratives, 68–69; and memory, 15, 67; and motives of Jewish returnees, 11, 17, 20–21, 23, 25–27, 34; and postwar Zionist sentiment, 178, 237n246; and prosecution of war criminals, 106; and refugees' journeys home, 39; and restitution of property, 128; and Slansky affaire, 224n228; and war's impact on Jewish self-understanding, 160, 169–77; and Western Allies, 8

communities of experience, 57, 68–71, 100

communities of memory, 75, 100

compensation programs, 6, 19, 78, 108, 125. *See also* restitution

concentration camps, 17, 58, 80, 164, 205n48. *See also specific camp names*

conspiracy theories, 117, 224n228

Constituent Assembly, 130–32

constitutional referendums, 8, 130–32

Consultative Council of Jewish Organizations, 103

conversion, religious, 75, 141, 160–61, 166, 168, 191n10

corruption, 184, 239n21

Cramer, Sally David, 84

Cremisini, Vittorio, 113

Croce, Benedetto, 68, 118–19, 146

Cultural League for the Democratic Renewal of Germany (Kulturbund zur demokratischen Erneuerung Deutschlands), 80, 151

currency reform, 7

Czechoslovakia and Czech Republic, 6, 106, 136, 224n228

Dachau concentration camp, 26, 64, 138

Debenedetti, Giacomo, 70, 86, 122–23, 146–47

decreto legislativo luogotenenziale no. 159, article 5, 112

defascistization, 111–15, 128–129

De Felice, Renzo, 16, 211n176

Del Boca, Angelo, 68

Delegazione per l'assistenza agli emigranti ebrei (Aid Committee for Jewish Emigrants) (DELASEM), 31, 37, 71, 113

Della Pergola, Massimo, 53

Della Pergola, Sergio, 175

democracy, 23–24, 26, 225n240

denazification, 11, 106–9, 111, 134–35, 140, 156

Denmark, 26

deportations, 5, 16–17, 58, 59–60, 148

Der Irrweg einer Nation (Abusch), 80

De Rossi Castelli, Emma, 35, 145

Der Ruf (film), 133

Der Weg: on challenges facing postwar German Jews, 133–34; and German guilt, 73, 74, 76–77; on German Jews' self-understanding, 150, 167; on motives of Jewish returnees, 29; on postwar battle against antisemitism, 119–20; and postwar Zionist sentiments, 172; on prosecution of war criminals, 107–9; on the rebuilding of Jewish life in Germany, 32, 34; on refugees' journeys home, 47, 49; on vengeance, 104, 105

Detroit, Michigan, 158

Deutscher, Isaac, 234n184

Deutsches Theater, 67

Deutschkron, Inge, 26, 33, 75

Di Camerino, Roberta, 43, 44

Dichiarazione sulla razza (declaration on race), 4
Di Cori, Bruno, 29, 45–46, 94, 144
Di Cori family, 45
Diena, Leone, 172
Die Zeit, 139
Die zweite Schuld (Giordano), 74
Di Gioacchino Cassuto, Anna, 37–38, *38,* 61, 97, 199n110
Di Gioacchino Corcos, Sara, 54, 61
Di Segni Jesi, Fulvia, 29, 45, 48, 145
Di Segni Sermoneta, Fernanda, 31
displaced persons (DP): camps for, 169–70, 192n29; and cultural divisions among Jews, 6–7; and memory, 15; and postwar battle against antisemitism, 121; and postwar Zionist sentiment, 172; and prosecution of war criminals, 107; and refugees' journeys home, 40
Döblin, Alfred, 33, 120
Doctors' Plot and Trials, 107, 225n228
Donati, Max, 48
Dreifuss, Alfred, 26
Dreifuss, Julius, 110–11, 121, 177–78
Dresden, Germany, 22, 33, 35, 121, 139
Du Bois, W. E. B., 79
D'Urbino, Manfredo, 64
Düsseldorf, Germany, 110, 121, 139, 177

East Germany. *See* German Democratic Republic (GDR)
Eichmann trial, 182
Eight Jews (Debenedetti), 122–23, 146–47
Einsatzgruppen, 106–8
Eisenstaedt, Moritz, 40
Eisler, Gerhart, 23–24
Eisler, Hanns, 27, 152
Eisler, Hilde, 23–24, 84, 169, 182
Eisner, Freia, 148
Eisner, Kurt, 148
Eleventh Decree to the Law on the Citizenship, 148
Ellis Island, 23–24
Emergency Society for People Affected by the Nuremberg Racial Laws, 164
emotional communities, 10
Enciclopedia Cattolica, 117

England, 33. *See also* Britain; United Kingdom
Ente di Gestione e Liquidazione Immobiliare (Office for the Management and Liquidation of Property) (EGELI), 126, 221n152
Epstein, Israel, 64
Epstein, Kurt, 134
Erfurt, Germany, 108
Eschelbacher, Max, 104–5, 188
Eschwege, Helmut, 106, 168, 170–71, 179

Fabian, Hans Erich, 54, *54,* 76–77, 107
Fano, Vittorio, 56, 113
Farinacci, Roberto, 88
Far Right political parties, 183
Fasci Femminili, 88
Fascism and Fascists: antisemitic persecution, 4–6, 10–11, 20, 30, 53, 56, 85–86, 94, 137, 173; and commemoration of war and Holocaust victims, 67–68; and contemporary Far Right politics in Italy, 240n36; and contemporary Italian cultural memory, 184–87, 188–89; and East German antifascist narrative, 78–85; failures of Italian defascistization, 129–30; and German Jews' self-understanding, 152–53; and good Italian narrative, 13–14, 85–89, 91–94, 99–100, 206n63; and Italian Jews' self-understanding, 144, 146–47, 180; and Italian narratives of resistance, 68–69; and Italian postwar reconstruction, 8; Italy and Germany as case studies of, 16, 17, 194n60; Jewish, 4, 112, 173; and Jewish self-understanding, 141–43, 158, 161, 168; and lack of Holocaust memorials in Italy, 240n32; and *Manifesto della razza,* 4, 191n12; and origins of EGELI, 221n152; and postwar battle against antisemitism, 115–23; postwar defascistization, 111–12; and postwar Zionist sentiment, 173; and prosecution of war criminals, 105, 108–9; and reclamation of Jewish property, 126, 221n152; and refugees' journeys home, 45; and religious discrimination in postwar Italy, 130–32. *See also* antifascism; defascistization; Partito Nazionale Fascista (National Fascist Party) (PNF)

290 | *Index*

Fascist Italian Social Republic, 115. *See also* Repubblica Sociale Italiana (Italian Social Republic) (RSI); Republic of Salò

Fascist *ventennio,* 11, 112

Federal Republic of Germany (FRG) (West Germany): challenges facing postwar German Jews, 11, 103, 133–35, 139, 140; and commemoration of war and Holocaust victims, 65, 67–68; division of Germany, 7–8; and failures of German denazification, 134–35; and fall of the Berlin Wall, 182; and friendships, 154; and German Jews' self-understanding, 149, 179; and guilt, 72; and memory, 15–17, 99–100; and motives of Jewish returnees, 27, 30; and the other Germany, 75; and postwar battle against antisemitism, 120, 123; and postwar Zionist sentiment, 177–78; and prosecution of war criminals, 106, 108; and reclamation of Jewish property, 128; and scope of study, 2, 13, 19; and social memory of wartime trauma, 56–58; and war's impact on Jewish self-understanding, 165, 171

Ferramonti di Tarsia internment camp, 5, 35

Ferrara, Italy, 53, 62, 98, 185

Festa della Liberazione, 185

Feuchtwanger, Lion, 137

Fini, Gianfranco, 240n36

Fiorentini, Bruno, 130

First World War, 31, 66, 206n50

Fischer, Wolfgang, 28, 149

Fiume, Italy, 51

Florence, Italy, 54, 64, 231n114

Foa, Anna, 94

Foa, Elena, 117

Foa, Lelia, 94, 95

Foa, Vittorio, 94, 147

Focardi, Filippo, 68, 186

Forti, Carla, 13

Fosse Ardeatine massacre, 63, 65, 146, 228n31. *See also* Ardeatine Caves

France, 7, 27, 210n142

Franchetti, Luisa, 93

Frank, Kurt Israel, 121

Frankenthal, Hans: and challenges of returning Jews, 103; and failures of German denazification, 134; and friendships, 153–54; and Holocaust survivor testimonies, 95; and rebuilding Jewish life in Germany, 33; and reclamation of Jewish property, 127; and returnees' memories of persecution, 51–52

Frankfurt, Germany, 22, 40, 44, 46, 50, 124, 158

Frau in der Gemeinschaft, 167

French Fascists, 152

French occupation zone, 148

Fried, Marc, 52

friendship, 91, 137, 154, 156–57

Fulbrook, Mary, 70, 135

Funkhaus Berlin, 81

Fürth, Germany, 65–66, 67

"Future of the Jews in Germany, The" (conference), 32

Galinski, Heinz, 26, 60, 67

Gallico, Claudio, 52, 53

Ganther, Heinz, 34

Garden of the Finzi-Continis, The (Bassani), 62

Gasperi, Alcide De, 8

Gay, Peter, 231n101

gender, 21, 24, 37, 40, 55, 228n40

generational shift in attitudes, 181–82

genocide, 17, 27, 106. *See also* Holocaust

geographies of emotional life, 41

German Code of Criminal Procedures, 106

German Democratic Republic (GDR) (East Germany): and antifascist narrative, 57–58, 78–80, 84–85; and arrival, 42–43, 202n183; challenges facing postwar German Jews, 132–33, 135–39, 140; constitution, 225n240; division of Germany, 7–8; and fall of the Berlin Wall, 182; first president of, 226n252; and generational shifts in Jewish identity, 238n6; and German Jews' self-understanding, 10, 151, 153, 182; and guilt, 72; and Jewish self-understanding, 165, 166, 169–70; and memory, 15–17, 56, 99; and motives of Jewish returnees, 23–24, 26–27; and postwar battle against antisemitism, 122; and postwar Zionist sentiment, 178–79; and prosecution of war criminals, 105–6; and scope of study, 2, 13

German language, 24–25, 46–47, 150–52, 188

German Opposition to Hitler, The (Rothfels), 75

German Zionist Organization, 177

Gert, Valeska, 34, 52, 133, 152

Gestapo, 27, 138, 163

Geve, Thomas, 1, 2, 12

Geyer, Michael, 72

Ginzburg, Leone, 95, 142

Ginzburg, Natalia, 95, 141–42, 168, 171, 213n215, 237n246

Giordano, Ralph, 25, 74, 104

Giorno della memoria, 184–85

Giudaico-Romanesco, 145

Glücksstern, Georg, 172

Goethe, Johann Wolfgang von, 151

Goldschmidt, Dietrich, 133

Goldschmidt, Moritz, 75

Goldstein, Kurt, 82, 85, 152, 170

good Italian narrative, 13–14, 89–91, 115, 118, 158, 186–87, 211n170. *See also* brava gente narrative

Grand Council of Fascism, 4, 5

graves and cemeteries, 47–48, *54*, 54–55, 61–65, 121, 124, 134, 147

Greiz, Germany, 50

Grin, Mauro, 113

Grobe, Kurt, 106

Grossman, Meir, 132

Grote, Kurt, 59

Grotewohl, Otto, 169

Grundgesetz (Basic Law), 149

Grundig, Lea, 22, 33, 154

Guarnieri, Patrizia, 231n114

Guidi, Guido Buffarini, 5

Günther, Hans, 159

Gurs internment camp, 63, 82

Gützlaff, Ruth, 85

Gysi, Klaus, 151, 160

Habe, Hans, 120

Ha Kellilah, 171

Halbwachs, Maurice, 12, 57

Hamburg, Germany, 164

Hamburger, Käte, 149, 150–51, 167

Hartmann, Peter, 111

Hartogson, H., 96

Hebrew language, 47, 164, 171, 176

Heidelberg, Germany, 32–34, 123

Heimat, 9, 27–28, 42, 74

Heimberg, Siegfried, 156

Herbert Baum group, 22

Herzberg, Wolfgang, 85

Hesdörffer, Franz, 167

Heym, Stefan, 120, 202n183

Heymann, Stefan, 79

HICEM (HIAS, ICA, and Emigdirect), 39

Hildesheimer, Wolfgang, 33, 107, 149, 154–55, 178

Hilfsstelle fur rassisch verfolgte Christen (aid office for racially persecuted Christians), 163

Himmler, Heinrich, 73, 138

Hirsch, Karl Jakob, 179–80

Hirschfeld, Kurt, 76, 155, 208n87

Historikerstreit, 183

Historikerstreit 2.0, 238n14

Hitler, Adolf, 2–3, 26, 48, 62, 73, 75, 89–91, 117, 135, 141, 151

Hitler Youth (Hitlerjugend), 3, 108, 156

Hoffman, Eva, 9, 45–46, 150–51

Holocaust: and arrival, 47; and commemoration of war and Holocaust victims, 56, 62, 64, 182, 184; and comparative approach to study, 17; and East German antifascist narrative, 78; and good Italian narrative, 31, 92, 93, 186; and Italian Jews' self-understanding, 158–59, 180; and Jewish self-understanding, 18, 142, 163, 167, 169, 171; meaning of home after, 9–11; and memory, 12, 53–54, 136; and rebuilding Jewish life in Germany after, 34, 181; and state of returnees' homes, 54; and survivors' testimonies, 94–99, 214n230, 218n82

Holocaust (TV series), 184, 185

Holocaust monuments, 61, 63–67, 98, 169–70, 182, 215n242, 215n250

Holocaust: The Story of Family Weiss, 183

Holzer, Charlotte, 22, 84–85, 138

homesickness, 20, 28–29, 34, 152

Höss, Rudolf, 113

292 | Index

House of Savoy, 145
House Un-American Activities Committee, 23
housing shortages, 125–28
"How Much Home Does a Person Need?" (Amery), 9, 28
Humboldt University, 23
Hungary, 37
Huppert, Hilde, 79

Il coraggio e la pietà: Gli ebrei e l'Italia durante la guerra 1940–1945 (Caracciolo), 184
Il Manifesto di Verona (the manifesto of Verona), 5
Il Mattino d'Italia, 116
Il Razzismo (Cogni), 129
imagined communities, 153–58
Im Feuer Vergangen, 79
indemnification laws, 19
In Germany (Posener), 72
Institute for Jewish Policy Research, 183
Interlandi, Telesio, 116
international Jewish organizations, 31–32, 68
International Military Tribunal (IMT), 33, 73, 106–7
I pavidi (Cesare Merzagora), 118
I ponti di Schwerin (Millu), 87
Irgun (Zionist paramilitary group), 64
Iron Curtain, 17
Israel, 22, 33–34, 175, 176
Israel (journal), 60, 70, 88, 118–19, 129, 145–46, 166, 174–76, 206n48
Israeli-Palestinian conflict, 184
Israeli Zionist organizations, 15
Istria, Italy, 51
Italian Committee of the Association of Swiss Jewish Refugee Aid and Welfare, 112
Italian Communist Party, 8, 128, 171, 237n246. *See also* Partito Comunista Italiano (Italian Communist Party) (PCI)
Italian Constitution, 8, 130–32
Italian Ministry of Foreign Affairs, 89–90
Italian Radio Auditions Authority, 117
Italian Senate, 185

Jacobson, Hans Ludwig, 108
Jacobson, Max, 95
Jacobus, Hans, 71, 181
Jaldati, Lin, 170
Jarausch, Konrad, 72
Jaspers, Karl, 208n88
Jewish Agency, 32
Jewish Brigade, 172, 175
Jewish cemeteries. *See* graves and cemeteries
Jewish houses *(Judenhäuser)*, 3
Jewish Italian Action (Azione ebraica italiana), 173
Jewish Life, 79
Jewish National Fund, 177
Jewish Relief Unit, 32
Jews in Germany, The (Ganther), 34
Jonas, Ernst, 163
Judenfreundlichkeit (friendliness to Jews), 110
Jüdischer Anteil an der Deutschen Kultur, 151
Jüdisches Gemeindeblatt für die britische Zone, 73, 120, 134, 151
Jüdisches Gemeindeblatt für die Nord-Rheinprovinz und Westfalen, 149–50
Jungvolk, 156

Kahn, Siegbert, 80, 151, 169
Kantorowicz, Alfred: arrival, 47, 48; challenges facing postwar German Jews, 138–39; decision to return home, 20–21, 27, 41; and division of Germany, 8; and East German antifascist narrative, 77–78, 80; and German Jews' self-understanding, 151; and loyalty questions, 226n252; and the other Germany, 76; and postwar battle against antisemitism, 120
Karfunkel, Viktor, 22
Kesten, Hermann, 33, 135, 151, 187
Kindertransport, 48–49, 71, 181
Klein, Shira, 13
Klemperer, Victor: challenges facing postwar German Jews, 137–38, 139; on failures of German denazification, 135; and German Jews' self-understanding, 151; and guilt, 73, 75; and postwar battle

against antisemitism, 122; and postwar denazification efforts, 106, 109; and postwar Zionist sentiments, 179, 226n242; return to home after war, 35

Klinkhammer, Lutz, 87

Knobloch, Charlotte, 182

Komitee der Antifaschistischen Widerstandskampfer (Committee of Antifascist Resistance Fighters) (KdAW), 136

Königsberg, 51

Kortner, Fritz, 133

Kristallnacht, 3

Kruhm, August, 151

Kuczynski, Jurgen, 151

Kugelmass, Jack, 61

Landau, Ernest, 154

Landé, Margarete, 110

Landra, Guido, 191n12

Langhoff, Wolfgang, 67

La Rassegna Mensile di Israel, 118

Lasker-Walfisch, Anita, 214n230

Lateran Treaties, 131, 132

La tregua (Levi), 36

Lattes, Dante, 118

Law for the Restoration of the Professional Civil Service, 3

Law on the Revocation of Naturalizations and the Deprivation of German Citizenship, 148

Laws for the Defense of the Race, 4. *See also* racial laws

Lebanon War, 184

Lesser, Jonas, 95–96

Lettere agli uomini di Papa Celestino VI (Papini), 117

Levi, Arrigo, 30

Levi, Franco, 41

Levi, Giorgina, 20, 29, 144, 171

Levi, Guido, 200n130

Levi, Lia, 46, 58–59, 116

Levi, Primo, 36, 93–94, 97, 99, 143, 145, 227n4

Levi, Renzo, 115

Levi Coen, Clara, 41

Levinson, Nathan Peter, 162

Lewin, Ilse, 85

Lewin, Inge, 164–65

liberal Judaism, 167

Libyan Jews, 183

Lichtenberg, Germany, 76

Liebknecht, Karl, 67

Livorno, Italy, 30, 35, 145

Lodz ghetto, 181

Loewenstein, Leo, 26

Lombardi, Ricardo, 117

Lombroso, Silvia, 186

Long, Lynellyn, 28

looting of Jewish property, 6, 52–53, 54

Löwenkopf, Leo, 121, 139

Luzzati, Adriana, 48, 89

Lyttleton, Adrian, 16

Maestro, Leone, 90

Magliana, Italy, 52–53

Mainz, Germany, 111, 124

Majdanek concentration camp, 60, 80, 138

Mandate Palestine, 24

Mandel, Jean, 66

Manifesto della razza (Manifesto of race), 4, 129, 191n12

Manifesto di Verona, 144

Mann, Heinrich, 76

Mann, Thomas, 77

Marcus, Clare Cooper, 52

Marcuse, Ludwig, 42, 48

Marshall Plan, 7

Marx, Karl, 49–50, 134, 149, 160

Marxismus und Rassenfrage, (Heymann), 79

Mattarella, Sergio, 185

Matteotti, Giacomo, 185

Mauthausen concentration camp, 29, 80

May, Richard, 104, 105

Mayer, Hans, 27, 46, 47, 133

Mayer, Karl, 111

McCloy, John, 123

Meier, Wilhelm, 105, 120

Meloni, Giorgia, 185, 240n36

Memmingen, Germany, 160

Memoriale della Shoah, 185

memorials. *See* monuments and memorials

Memorial to the Murdered Jews of Europe, 182

memory: collective and individual, 11–12, 15, 57–58; and commemoration of Holocaust victims, 54, 56, 61–65, 109; and communities of experience, 68–71, 100; contemporary Italian and German, 182–86; and decisions to return home after war, 25; and East German antifascism narrative, 14, 68–69, 77–85; and German guilt, 67, 71–75; and good Italian narrative, 13, 85–94; memories of home, 45, 46; and motives of Jewish returnees, 21; and the other Germany, 75–77; and postwar information-gathering process, 58–61; returnees' memories of persecution, 49–51; and silence on Holocaust, 94–99

Mercurio, Massimo, 116

Merker, Paul, 44, 136, 138, 226n242

Merzagora, Cesare, 118

Mexico, 39, 46–47, 139

Meyer, Albert, 52

Meyer, Alfred, 72, 155

Meyer, Julius, 80, 81, *81*, 105, 136

Meyer, Max, 165

Milan, Italy, 8, 41, 50, 51, 64, 128, 147

Milano, Mariella, 143

Milano, Roberto, 176

Milano, Vitale, 117

Millu, Liana, 87, 228n40

Ministry of Finance (Italy), 218n82

"mixed" marriages, 76, 110, 156–57, 164, 167

Moeller, Robert, 72

Molo, Walter von, 77

Momigliano, Arnaldo, 118–19, 211n178

Momigliano, Eucardio, 86

Montagnana, Rita, 128, 171

Monumento al Sacrificio Ebraico, 64, *65*

monuments and memorials, 215n250; in Berlin, 182, 240n32; and commemoration of war and Holocaust victims, 61–62, 63–67, *65*; and East German antifascist narrative, 81, *81*; First World War, 206n50; and good Italian narrative, 93; and Holocaust survivor testimonies, 98; Italian Holocaust memorial day, 184–85; lack of Holocaust memorials in Italy, 240n32; literature cataloging, 206n61; and postwar Zionist sentiment, 178;

and scholarship on Holocaust memory, 56; and war's impact on Jewish self-understanding, 169. *See also* Holocaust monuments

Moravia, Alberto, 141

Morpurgo, Alma, 45–46

Morpurgo, Elena, 60, 102, 112

Morpurgo, Luciano, 89

Morpurgo, Margherita, 157

Moskowitz, Moses, 73, 103–4, 105, 123, 125, 148

mourning, 12, 17, 56, 62–64, 96–97, 115, 205n37, 206n50

Munter, Arnold, 83–84

Museo Nazionale dell'Ebraismo Italiano e della Shoah, 185

Mussolini, Benito: arrest and release of, 5; and good Italian narrative, 16, 88–91; and Italian narratives of resistance, 68, 146; and lack of Holocaust memorials in Italy, 240n32; and *Manifesto della razza,* 191n12; and modern Far Right politics in Italy, 240n36; and prosecution of war criminals, 111–12; and pushback against good Italian narrative, 17

myth of silence on the Holocaust, 12, 94–99, 193n46

Nacht-Express, 28

Nathan, Giuseppe, 92, 161, 174

Nathan, Rosi, 156

nationalist sentiment, 75, 142, 153, 172–74, 227n8, 234n184

National Museum of Italian Judaism and the Shoah, 185

Nationalsozialistische Deutsche Arbeiterpartei (National Socialist German Workers' Party) (NSDAP), 2, 77, 109, 110, 135, 139, 156

Navarro, Amalia, 37–38, *38*, 199n110

Nazi-Fascism, Nazi-Fascist, 56, 87–88, 91, 122, 126

Nazism (National Socialism): and antisemitic persecution, 2–4, 60, 124, 128; and comparative approach to study, 16; and decisions to return home after war, 20, 25; denazification process after

war, 11, 106–9, 111, 134–35, 140, 156; and
East German antifascism narrative, 13,
78–80, 82–84; and Germaness, 186; and
German guilt, 73, 75, 121; and Jewish self-
understanding, 168, 179; Nazi language,
59; Nazi propaganda, 49; and the other
Germany, 27, 76–77; and postwar battle
against antisemitism, 124; prosecution of
war criminals, 106; and racial definitions
of Jewishness, 161–62; and vengeful Jew
stereotype, 104
Neues Deutschland, 82, 136–37
Neuhaus, Leopold, 165
Neustadt camp, 199n110
New York City, 107
Nicola, Enrico de, 131
Nissim, Luciana, 96–97, 228n40
Niven, Bill, 14–15
Noack-Mosse, Eva, 43, 97
November pogroms, 3, 67, 82, 106, 122, 127
Nuremberg Laws, 3, 80, 141
Nuremberg trials, 149. *See also* International
Military Tribunal (IMT)

Oberdorfer, Sonia, 53, 64, 70
Opfer des Faschismus (Victims of Fascism)
(OdF), 120, 220n119
Orbach, Lothar (Larry), 47–48, 49, 103
Organization of Victims of the Nazi
Regime, 83
Ormond, Henry, 108
Orthodox Judaism, 166–67, 180
Ost und West, 8, 80, 139
Ottolenghi, Lea, 30, 40–41
Ottolenghi Minerbi, Marta, 61, 88
Outing of the Dead Schoolgirls, The (Seghers),
201n160
Oxfeld, Ellen, 28

Pacifici, Alfonso, 118
Pacifici, Marcello, 112
Paepcke, Lotte, 43, 71
Palazzo dell'Arte Moderna, 240n32
Palestine: and attitudes on Zionism, 135–36,
180, 188; emigration of Jews to, 7, 21, 31–32,
50, 61, 72, 82, 91, 94, 106, 155, 188, 213n200;
and Israeli-Palestinian conflict, 184,

237n246; and Jewish self-understanding
after war, 167–68; and postwar Zionist
sentiments, 171–79; return of Jews from, 7,
24, 29, 30, 33, 36, 45, 94, 106, 168, 192n30;
and transnational memory, 15; UN
partition plan, 174–75
Papini, Giovanni, 117
Paris, France, 20
Parma, Italy, 116
partisans, 64–65, 70–71, 112, 130, 147, 191n3,
228n40
Partito Comunista Italiano (Italian
Communist Party) (PCI), 171, 237n246
Partito Nazionale Fascista (National Fascist
Party) (PNF), 4, 88, 112, 191n10, 211n176,
211nn176–78
Passerini, Luisa, 186
passports, 34, 42, 149, 229n52
patriotism, 13, 16, 69, 147, 150, 176–77, 188,
200n130
Pende, Nicola, 129
Periodic Table (Levi), 145
Persian Jews, 183
Persilscheine (denazification certificates),
109, 217n50
personal geographies, 41
Pescatori, Teresa, 113
Petacci, Clara, 112
philosemitism, 122–23
photography, 27, 37–38, 53–54, 81, 169–70
Pieck, Wilhelm, 44, 169, 226n252
Piedmont region, 145
Piekatsch, Peisach, 32
pilgrimages, 63
Pincherle, Lea, 113
Pineas, Hermann, 159
Piperno, Emilia, 126–27
Pisa, Italy, 13, 59
Pisarek, Abraham, 27, 54, 81, 169, 170
Pitigliano, Italy, 50–51
Pius XII, Pope, 118
Poland, 6, 61, 66, 114
police surveillance, 115
political activism, 23–24, 39
Portugal, 32–33
Posener, Julius, 72, 73
Prague, Czech Republic, 37, 106

296 | Index

Pranzieri, David, 166
Prato, David, 159, 166, 174, 176
Pravda, 225n228
"privileged mixed-marriage," 110
Proskauer, Erna, 33
Protestant churches, Protestantism, 120, 162
purges, 106, 111–12, 128, 136–38, 140, 153, 170, 178. *See also* defascistization; denazification

Quaroni, Pietro, 36–37
Question of German Guilt, The (Jaspers), 208n88

Rabbinical College, 166
rabbis in postwar communities, 161, 165–66
racial laws: and contemporary Far Right politics in Italy, 185, 240n36; and destruction of Jews' homes, 3–4; and good Italian narrative, 88, 89, 92, 94; impact on Italian Jewish academics, 212n178; and Italian Jews' emigration to Palestine, 45; and Italian Jews' self-understanding, 145; and Jewish self-understanding, 142; and motives of Jewish returnees, 20, 31; and postwar battle against antisemitism, 118; and prosecution of war criminals, 107, 112; and refugees' journeys home, 37
racism and racial ideology: and commemoration of war and Holocaust victims, 67; and comparative approach to study, 16; and definitions of Jewishness, 162; and East German antifascist narrative, 79–80; Fascist, 11, 17, 130; and race science, 110, 129–30
Rapoport, Inge, 23
Rathé, Ellen, 62
Ravenna, Eugenio, 96–97, 114, 215n250
Ravenna, Pia Levi, 114–15
Ravensbrück concentration camp, 96
Rechtsstaat (law-based state), 105
Reckonings (Fulbrook), 70
reconstruction of postwar Europe, 26–27, 28, 30, 33, 133
reeducation, 18, 102, 120, 140
Regensburg, Germany, 34
Reiche, Peter, 48–49, 60, 125

Reichskristallnacht, 3. *See also* November pogroms
Relazione sull'opera svolta dal Ministero degli Affari Esteri per la tutela delle comunità ebraiche (1938–1943), 90
relief organizations, 15, 37
Religious News Service, 107
Repubblica Sociale Italiana (Italian Social Republic) (RSI), 5–6, 69, 87, 130, 144
Republican Party (Italy), 144
Republic of Salò, 5–6, 88, 112. *See also* Repubblica Sociale Italiana (Italian Social Republic) (RSI)
resistance movements, 6, 22, 70–71, 83, 94, 112, 147, 228n40
Resnik, Reuben, 32
restitution, 9, 62, 102, 125–28, 136, 152, 216n6, 221n152, 225n230
Riesenburger, Martin, 165
Righteous Among the Nations, 110
Risorgimento, 71, 207n81
Roccas, Fabrizio, 175
Röhm-Putsch, 106
Roman Catholic Church, 120, 165. *See also* Catholics and Catholic Church
Roman Jewish community, 85, 93, 234n166
Rome, Italy, 85; and commemoration of war and Holocaust victims, 63, 185; and good Italian narrative, 90, 92; and Italian narratives of resistance, 69; and refugees' journeys home, 35; and search for survivors, 58, 60; and size of community, 8; and state of returnees' homes, 52; terrorist attack, 184
Roosevelt, Franklin, 39
Roques, Pardo, 13, 92
Roseman, Mark, 104
Rosenholz, Enrico, 97
Rosenthal, Hans, 76
Rosenwein, Barbara, 10, 55
Rosselli, Amelia Pincherle, 143
Rosselli, Carlo, 143
Rosselli, Nello, 143
Rossi, Walter, 147
Rothfels, Hans, 75
Rothschild, Recha, 27, 39, 120, 154, 169

Sabbadini, Giorgio, 129
Sacerdoti, Giancarlo, 126
Sacerdoti, Maria Simonetta, 59
Sadun, Luigi, 129
Sahl, Hans, 42
Said, Edward, 180
San Sabba concentration camp, 113
Sarfatti, Michele, 144, 211n176
Schafranov, Sofia, 97
Scheidemann, Philipp, 67
Schiffer, Davide, 85, 86
Schlesischer Bahnhof, 49
Schmallenberg, Germany, 33, 51
Schoenmaker, Victoria, 96
Scholem, Gershom, 187–88
Schönheit, Franco, 99, 144
Schregle, Hans, 66
Schumacher, Kurt, 40
Schutzstaffel (SS), 3, 38, 63, 108, 113, 156–57
Schwarz, Guri, 13, 91
Second Vatican Council, 184
Sed, Alberto, 97
Seghers, Anna: autobiographical story, 201n160; and communism, 154; and East German antifascist narrative, 84; and German Jews' self-understanding, 151; and memories of persecution, 50; and motives of Jewish returnees, 27; rebuilding, 135; and return home, 39, 46–47, 49
Segre, Augusto, 176
Segre, Cesare, 175–76
Segre, Dan Vittorio, 87, 173
Segre, Liliana, 185–86
Segre, Sergio Camillo, 171
Selbiger, Fritz, 62, 82, 96
self-understanding: and communities of memory, 68; defined, 226n1; and German Jews' self-understanding, 10, 18, 100, 158, 178–79, 179–80; and Italian Jews' self-understanding, 10, 18, 100, 143–44, 146, 178–79; and national belonging, 227n7; and postwar Zionist sentiments, 174, 177; and scope of study, 18; and war's impact on Jewish self-understanding, 141–43, 158, 167–71
Se questo è un uomo (Levi), 93
Sereni, Paolo, 113

Sermoneta, Eugenio, 44
Servi, Eugenia, 50, 51, 93, 144, 158, 172
Shanghai, China, 26, 28, 35, 40, 149, 169–70
Shoah, 143. *See also* Holocaust
Shoah Memorial (Milan), 185
Shuster, Z., 159
Singewald, Florence, 108
Skorneck, Philip, 162
Slansky, Rudolf, 136–37, 224n228
social death of German Jews, 3–4
Social Democrats, 26, 40, 67, 154
Socialism, 26, 39, 69, 78, 152
Soliani, Alba Rabello, 200n138
Soviet Union: challenges facing postwar German Jews, 135; and fall of the Berlin Wall, 182; Soviet Army, 35, 122; Soviet Military Administration (SMAD), 27; Soviet occupation zone, 14, 15, 39, 42–43, 71, 78, 100, 106, 148, 178
Sowjetische Besatzungszone (Soviet Occupation Zone) (SBZ), 50, 78, 178
Sozialistische Einheitspartei Deutschlands (Socialist Unity Party of Germany) (SED), 39, 81–85, 128, 136–39, 168, 170, 181, 226n248
Spanish Civil War, 82, 83
Spartakusbund, 67
Spiegel, Marga, 155
Spier, Walter, 127
Spira, Camilla, 24–25
Spira, Steffie, 25, 133
Spiro, David, 66
Spizzichino, Giancarlo, 157
Spizzichino, Liliana, 116
Spruchkammern (civilian tribunals), 108–9
Stalin, Joseph, 138
Steindler, Livio, 48
Stern, Frank, 123
Sternträger, 83
Sturmabteilung (SA), 3
Stuttgart, Germany, 36
Sueddeutsche Zeitung, 183
Survival in Auschwitz (Levi), 93, 99
survivors' federations, 205n48
survivors' testimonies, 93–99, 107, 113–14
Sweden, 39–40, 49, 102, 149

298 | Index

Switzerland: emigration of Jews to, 6–7, 33, 102, 112–13, 139; and motives of Jewish returnees, 30–31; and news about death camps, 60; and refugees' journeys home, 40–41, 43, 200n138; Swiss border guides, 114–15

synagogues, 3, 5, 8, 50, 54, 64, 121, 164–66, 173, 180, 183, 184

Taché, Stefano, 184
Tagesspiegel, 122
Tagliacozzo, Emma, 125
Tagliacozzo, Mario, 124–25, 159
Tägliche Rundschau, 27
Tangentopoli, 184
Tauchert, Stephanie, 94
Tel Aviv, Israel, 33
Terracina, Piero, 30, 36–37
Terracini, Umberto, 237n246
terrorism, 184, 239n24
Theresienstadt: and East German antifascist narrative, 84; and German guilt, 76–77; and Holocaust survivor testimonies, 95, 97–98; and search for survivors, 60; and survivors' journeys home, 36, 37, 43, 46, 200n141; and theft of Jewish property, 127; and war's impact on Jewish self-understanding, 165, 167
Thiess, Frank, 77
Tito, Josip Broz, 224n228
Togliatti, Palmiro, 128, 171
To the Edge of Sorrow (Appelfeld), 191n3
trials of war criminals and collaborators, 26, 92, 103–15, 129–30, 135, 149, 182, 184
Trieste, Italy, 45–46, 48, 62
Trizonia, 7
Turin, Italy, 36, 48, 145
Tylim, Isaac, 62

Ulbricht, Walter, 81–82
Unione delle Comunita israelitiche italiane, also Unione (Union of Italian Jewish Communities) (UCII), 61, 70, 91–92, 113–15, 130–32, 161, 166, 173, 174, 206n48, 213n200.
United Kingdom, 32
United Nations (UN), 174

United States, 7, 8, 15, 20–21, 23–24, 77, 137–38, 202n183
United States' Office of Military Government, 134, 159–60
University of Rome, 212n178
US Army, 35, 48–49, 159–60
US occupation zone, 123, 148

Valobra, Lelio Vittorio, 31, 71, 89, 159, 160
vandalism, 121
Varsano, Samuele "Sami," 52
Vatican, 58, 117
Venezia, Dora, 102
vengeance, 102–5, 112, 114–15, 122, 127, 155, 166
Venice, Italy, 56
Verband der deutschen Juden (Association of German Jews), 150
Verband Schweizerischer Jüdischer Fürsorgen/Flüchtlingshilfen (Association of Swiss Jewish Welfare/Refugee Aid) (VSJF), 40
Vereinigung der Verfolgten des Naziregimes (Association of Persecutees of the Nazi Regime) (VVN), 67, 78–79, 121, 136
Victor, Walther, 39, 42–43
Victor Emanuel III, King of Italy, 5, 145
Vienna, Austria, 37
visas, 5, 21, 35, 39, 106
Vitale, Enrica, 53
Vitale, Massimo Adolfo, 92, 113–14, 116, 117, 130
Viterbo, Carlo Alberto, 70, 129, 145–46, 174
Viterbo, Giacomo, 146

Waffen SS, 156–57
Wannsee Conference, 26
war crimes and trials: Eichmann trial, 182; failures of denazification, 135–37; and failures of Italian defascistization, 129–30; and good Italian narrative, 93; and Italian Holocaust memory, 184; and postwar battle against antisemitism, 118; prosecution of war criminals, 105–15; and pushback against good Italian narrative, 17. *See also* trials of war criminals and collaborators
War Ministry (Italy), 90

Warsaw ghetto, 79, 108
Warscher, Josef, 36, 46
Wasserstein, Bernard, 175
Weil, Edgar, 29
Weil, Grete, 29, 33, 152
Weinberg, Wilhelm, 134
Weizmann, Ezer, 181
Weltanschauung, 67
Weltlinger, Siegmund, 76, 96, 150
Westemigranten, 138
West Germany. *See* Federal Republic of
    Germany (FRG) (West Germany)
Wiener Neustädt camp, 37–38, *38*
Winter, Lotte: challenges facing postwar
    German Jews, 138, 139; and East German
    antifascist narrative, 84; on Jewish self-
    understanding, 141; and memories of
    persecution, 50; return home after war,
    39, 49, 102
Winterfeldt, Hans, 1, 28–29, 38, 60
Wolff, Jeanette, 120
Wolffheim, Hans, 151
Woller, Hans, 112
work camps, 59
World Jewish Congress (WJC), 32–33, 34, 89,
    132, 148
World Zionist Organization, 177
Writing the History of Memory (Berger and
    Niven), 14–15
Wulf, Joseph, 134

Yad Vashem (Holocaust Remembrance
    Center), 110
Yiddish language, 160
Yishuv, 24
Yugoslavia, 224n228

Zaban, Luisa, 62
Zaban, Silvia, 62
Zarfati, Enrica, 37–38, *38,* 199n110
Zarfatti, Emma, 199n110
Zargani, Aldo, 93
Zentralrat der Juden in Deutschland
    (Central Council of Jews in Germany), 150
Zevi, Tullia Calabi, 30, 107
Zionism, 171–79; challenges facing
    postwar German Jews, 135–37; and
    commemoration of war and Holocaust
    victims, 64, 66; and the Doctors' Plot,
    224n228; and good Italian narrative, 91;
    Irgun paramilitary group, 64; and Italian
    Jews' self-understanding, 180; Klemperer's
    position on, 179, 226n242; and motives of
    Jewish returnees, 24; and war's impact on
    Jewish self-understanding, 143
Zolli, Israel (also Eugenio Maria Zolli), 90,
    166, 234n166
Zuckermann, Leo, 136, 138–39, 168, 170
Zweig, Arnold, 24, 27, 78, 137, 151, 179
Zweig, Beatrice, 24, 137
Zwischen den Zeiten, 151